CHARACTER ETHICS
AND THE NEW TESTAMENT

Also from Westminster John Knox Press:

Character Ethics and the Old Testament:
Moral Dimensions of Scripture

Edited by M. Daniel Carroll R. and Jacqueline E. Lapsley

CHARACTER ETHICS AND THE NEW TESTAMENT

Moral Dimensions of Scripture

EDITED BY

Robert L. Brawley

Westminster John Knox Press
LOUISVILLE • LONDON

Scripture quotations from the New Revised Standard Version of the Bible are copyright © 1989 by the Division of Christian Education of the National Council of the Churches of Christ in the U.S.A. and used by permission.

Chapter 3, "The Reorienting Potential of Biblical Narrative for Christian Ethos, with Special Reference to Luke 7:36–50," is a revised and expanded version of "The (trans)formative potential of the Bible as resource for Christian ethos and ethics," originally published in *Scriptura* 62 and is published herein with the permission of the editors and publisher of *Scriptura*.

Chapter 16, "The Beatitudes as Eschatological Peacemaking Virtues," is adapted from *Kingdom Ethics* by Glen H. Stassen and David P. Gushee. Copyright © 2003 by Glen H. Stassen and David P. Gushee. Used with permission of InterVarsity Press, P.O. Box 1400, Downers Grove, IL 60515. www.ivpress.com.

Book design by Sharon Adams
Cover design by Eric Handel, LMNOP

First edition
Published by Westminster John Knox Press
Louisville, Kentucky

This book is printed on acid-free paper that meets the American National Standards Institute Z39.48 standard. ∞

PRINTED IN THE UNITED STATES OF AMERICA

07 08 09 10 11 12 13 14 15 16 — 10 9 8 7 6 5 4 3 2 1

Library of Congress Cataloging-in-Publication Data is on file at the Library of Congress, Washington, D.C.

ISBN-13: 978-0-664-23066-1
ISBN-10: 0-664-23066-0

Contents

Preface

The history of ethics may be described as largely a history of failure. Take for instance one of the most preferred responses to what we perceive to be injustice and evil in the twenty-first century—legislation. Drug laws in the United States have not eradicated the use of drugs. Instead legislation has eventuated in a "war on drugs," which appears to be impossible to win. The shock of witnessing property damage, beatings, shootings, and even murder driven by opposition to someone else's race, religion, gender, disability, or sexual orientation has led to legislation prohibiting hate crimes. In the biblical tradition, God's gift of the law prohibited lying, stealing, and murder, but having the law did not eliminate lying, stealing, and murder in biblical communities. Similarly, legislation prohibiting hate crimes today manifests society's disdain for hate crimes. Someone who opens fire on a Jewish community center can now be charged with a hate crime. But does legislation eliminate hate crimes? The Southern Poverty Law Center counted more than 500 hate groups operating in the United States in 1998, and the Simon Wiesenthal Center monitors more than 2,100 hate Web sites on the Internet. This is something of what I mean when I write that the history of ethics is largely a history of failure.

Legislation is hardly alone in reflecting a side of ethics that can only be labeled "failure." The same is true for some of our other preferred approaches to ethics: role models, principles, and rationality. These all may seduce us into a false optimism that these sources of morality make us adequate for the task.

The bane of ethics is at least partially the problem of knowing one thing and doing another. I will venture a bit of a personal confession. I live in an advantaged neighborhood in Chicago in which I am well aware that certain privileges accrue to me that are impossible for many others who live in disadvantaged neighborhoods. But in spite of my knowing one thing, I acquiesce and profit from my privileges, which come necessarily at the expense of others. Paul, Augustine, Luther, *cf Rom? - Paul learns "ho"*

and Spinoza expressed the reality of knowing one thing and doing another under the image of slavery, bondage of the will. Spinoza held that by forming clear ideas of "affections" or "passions," reason could control the passions. When, however, we form clear ideas, the problem of knowing one thing and doing another may be even more acute. I appeal once again to my advantaged community in Chicago. There was a time when I was unaware of the structures of power and inequity from which I profit. Now I know, and I still acquiesce. I know one thing, and I do another (shades of Rom. 7:7: "If it had not been for the law, I would not have known sin. I would not have known what it is to covet if the law had not said, 'You shall not covet'").

Since Freud, however, forming clear ideas—knowing one thing—has itself been severely called into question. Western thought has been dominated by the notion of personal agency. Faced with possibilities, we human beings supposedly have the freedom to choose as if each of us can determine whether to be master over external and internal powers or slave to them, to control them or be controlled by them. But Freud challenged conscious agency as a fiction, because unconscious drives muddy all motivation. If with Freud we believe in the power of the unconscious, then forming clear ideas is forever problematic.

But the bane of knowing one thing and doing another manifests itself not only as my lack of willingness or lack of clarity but also as a sense of helplessness, as Paul Ricoeur expresses it, "The servile will . . . mediates itself by passing through all the figures of our helplessness."[1] In spite of my acquiescence to social privilege, I am deeply and sincerely opposed to the social stratification in Chicago that enables me to profit at the expense of others, and although I have engaged in some social activism, my opposition is virtually matched by feeling helpless against structural systems in society.

Along with legislation, role models, principles, and rationality, character ethics is also constrained to occupy a place in the history of ethics as largely a history of failure. It too participates in knowing one thing and doing another, in a lack of clarity, and in a sense of helplessness. But each of these approaches may have something to contribute to the overall project of living an accomplished life. So, in spite of the history of failure, readers of this volume will also recognize that the authors who are represented here are hopeful—full of hope. They are full of hope because they write with the prospect and proposal that the New Testament has a place in human formation which will bear fruit in an accomplished life.

I intentionally couched my own ethical dilemma—knowing that I profit from advantages, but nevertheless profiting from them—in personal terms, whereas most of the essays that follow begin with relationships, communal and divine, that belie the purely personal. As I have indicated, among the varieties of attempts to do ethics in the face of injustice and evil, which I have characterized as inevitably failures, character ethics likewise is inevitably a part of the history of ethics as a history of failure. On the other hand, character ethics begins not with ethics as such but with what shapes human identity. The starting point is not an argument for a correct stance on controversial issues such as abortion, capital

(handwritten marginalia) he · he · re l'une cleave avec power free/no 1 well · me too · gu ?) · Too personale · "Ch"? · The · Deu · final · chd

(handwritten note at bottom) ? Look at what B. Thaton has done thru indiv'e Conversion — & the many indiv'ue (doctor, lawyer who as missand etc) "chapers"

punishment, and war and peace, even though character ethics most assuredly expects to eventuate in just responses to such issues. But there is a prior concern. Before considering what ethical life looks like in actual existence, character ethics has to do with formation as the presupposition and source of that life.

The chapters in this volume are concerned with the role the New Testament plays in the formation of Christians so that when they act, their formation bears fruit in concrete behavior. It is as if essence does precede existence, or at least that essence and existence are intimate companions. The wager is that what we do is a matter of living out who we are.

Formation itself, however, is also problematic, in that our environment inevitably also makes "customs" the presupposition and source of life. In this sense, Nietzsche could go so far as to define morality as customs, customs that may get in the way of what is truly beneficial. The struggle for civil rights in the United States bears agonizing witness to the power of customs to impede justice. Not only can customs impede justice; even worse, they can be grounds for perpetrating violence, as in the case of Paul, who claims that zeal for the traditions of his ancestors motivated him to persecute the church of God violently (Gal. 1:13–14). Because formation according to customs is thus problematic, readers can witness in this volume a feedback loop in which there is hope for the New Testament to form the community even as the community forms believers. What the Christian community is cannot be defined apart from the interpretation of the biblical text that lies in its heart.

One stream of character ethics with points of reference in the Stoic tradition interprets suffering as having educational value: suffering builds (good) character. In his contribution to this volume, Clifton Black asks if the Gospel of Mark represents such a view. By focusing on Markan narratives in which God restores suffering bodies (including social bodies), Jesus' own torment, and a loving God who ultimately restores beyond the terrifying reality of suffering, Black determines that in Mark suffering does not form moral character as such. Rather, by way of Jesus' crucifixion disciples learn how to learn. The cross is epistemological. In contrast to the Stoic tradition, in Mark suffering is not educational but epistemic, a way of knowing how to discern reality.

Another vein of character ethics out of the Hellenistic tradition is inherited from Aristotle. According to him, formation takes place by cultivating the virtues. From this point of view, cultivating virtues enables humans to act virtuously in a given situation. Glen Stassen begins his chapter by asking, "Which virtues should Christians nurture?" But virtues can also be problematic in that they may be ideals that protect self-interest. The heroic ideal of bravery and sacrifice in a soldier, for example, may be in the service of imperial domination. Further, virtue also may seduce us into a partnership with the false optimism that it is a source of morality which makes us adequate for the task. But what distinguishes Stassen's work from Aristotle is that, in his investigation of the Beatitudes, the virtues are those of the eschatological reign of God rather than the traditional Aristotelian virtues. Something of this Aristotelian tradition survives also in Drew

Smith's chapter when he describes "character traits," but they are character traits of a community, or communal norms, which are also the norms of Jesus and which construct a social identity for disciples of Jesus. This social identity is specifically set against the social identity shaped by the norms of the Roman Empire and the imperial cult, which Smith translates into the political context of the twenty-first century. Willard Swartley also emphasizes the practice of virtue, with emphasis on peacemaking, but he does so in the broad scope of five paradigms for formation of the moral self: individualism, communitarianism, institutionalism, pluralism, and multiculturalism. Further, his article is one of the places readers will encounter communal aspects, not only with respect to how the community forms the individual, but also with respect to the formation of the community itself. How does the use of the New Testament form the church?

All three of these chapters focus on political formation; Smith is more explicit, whereas Stassen and Swartley expect the political factors of formation to be self-evident. Another set of contributions very purposefully raises political dimensions of character ethics. Jens Herzer, Sylvia Keesmaat, and Clinton McCann all address the issue of forgiveness and reconciliation. First, Keesmaat reverses the conventional interpretation of Romans 13 in terms of "the divine right of kings" by suggesting a Pauline subversion of Roman imperial politics. Second, by reading the imprecatory psalms from the perspective of oppressed victims in the context of the cross and the gospel, McCann makes an appealing case for the establishment of God's justice and a nonretaliatory lifestyle, with specific reference to the quest for human rights in Guatemala. Third, as a Christian and a citizen of the former German Democratic Republic (East Germany), Herzer invests personal involvement in correlating reconciliation in Titus 3 with German reunification and his own attempts at reconciliation in his family with a brother-in-law who was a member of the Stasi, the secret police of the Communist regime. Jinseong Woo invests personal involvement even more intensely as he responds to the contributions by Keesmaat, McCann, and Herzer with his gripping account of four years of political imprisonment in South Korea because of his involvement in demonstrations for reunification of North Korea and South Korea. He bears strong testimony to reading the Bible from one's social location.

Further, Drew Smith, Neil Elliott, and Jae Won Lee resolutely correlate interpretations of the New Testament with political formation. As already indicated, Smith reads formation for discipleship in Mark as a countercultural dissent from Roman imperial politics and the imperial cult. Neil Elliott reacts against the conventional reading of conflict in Romans as a problem between Jews and Gentiles. In fact, he rejects "Gentile" as an ethnic designation over against Jews as an ethnic designation, and argues instead that the cultural context is the alleged superiority of Roman imperial ideology, which expected the Jewish people to submit to the Pax Romana as inferiors to superiors. At first glance his nonethnic reading appears to contradict Jae Won Lee's reading of the Antioch incident in Galatians. She contends that in this particular instance Paul takes the side of Gentile Christians who were under pressure from Jewish Christians to adopt a Jewish lifestyle.

But in contrast to Elliott's critique of ethnic interpretations of Paul, when she interprets Paul as an advocate of "equality with difference," she is not concerned with Gentile ethnicity as such, nor with Jewish-Gentile relationships on a universal scale, but with a very local situation in Antioch where "circumcision" and "foreskin" are the marks of group identity. She underscores the local nature of Paul's argument by showing that Paul reverses his support of groups in Romans 14–15, where Jews are not required to sacrifice their Jewish lifestyle under pressure from Gentile Christians. In addition, Lee relates her reading of "equality with difference" to the question of the reunification of North and South Korea.

The chapters in this volume originated in discussions in the Character Ethics and Biblical Interpretation Group of the Society of Biblical Literature. One of the presuppositions of the Character Ethics and Biblical Interpretation Group is that ethics is interdisciplinary, and our programs at the annual meeting of the Society of Biblical Literature have always entertained discussions among biblical scholars, ethicists, and theologians. Several contributions to this book tackle questions of method, including interdisciplinary issues. How is the New Testament used in ethical formation, and even how is ethics possible in the first place?

To a certain extent every contribution in this book deals with methodological issues, but five are particularly focused on method. Allen Verhey inquires about the relationship between the interpretation of the New Testament as scripted (as written literature) and as script to be performed, while insisting that ethicists and biblical interpreters need to hear the minds of others, including the communal voice of canonical readings in synagogue or church. Briefly put, his is an essay on how the Bible is to be read and "performed." Although Ann Jervis writes at the level of academic exegesis, she takes issue with the presumption of objectivity in traditional scholarly exegesis and proposes instead to search the Scriptures with subjective concerns. Her particular subjective concern is suffering—her own and her empathy for the suffering of others. Although Elna Mouton also writes at the level of scholarly exegesis, she underscores the use of the New Testament in Christian liturgy as fundamental to the formation that eventuates in Christian ethics. Further, rather than suppose that the use of the New Testament in liturgy gives us final answers, she maintains that it constantly disorients our orientation in order to reorient us. Moreover, she too is subjectively engaged with new realities in her native South Africa, rejoicing over a new democratic society but lamenting divisions that still exist.

A second contribution from Jens Herzer tackles the theological and philosophical problem of theodicy by relating interpretations of Job to Paul's understanding of God's justice and human righteousness. He addresses the question of how attention to specific texts shapes the way we do theology and ethics, or inversely how attention to theology and ethics influences the way we interpret the New Testament. He demonstrates how the two "crises of wisdom" represented by Job and Paul provide a new pattern for theological thinking and ethical arguments. My own chapter on "Identity and Metaethics" attempts to integrate some philosophical and feminist understandings of identity with social identity theory

under the assumption that identity is a source for ethics. It then interprets justification in Galatians 2:16 as a relationship with God at a metaethical level, that
is, as the presupposition and source for ethics at a convictional level. From this,
Paul develops a social identity of the Galatians as God's children and heirs of
Abraham, and this identity based on a relationship with God, which Paul calls
justification, eventuates in concrete ethical behavior.

In a second contribution, I emphasize similarly a relationship with God as the
source for ethics in a reading of Mark. I especially utilize literary theory of characterization, which I supplement with Charles Peirce's abductive reasoning, in
order to read Mark for the characterization of God. Accordingly, I discover that
in Mark, Jesus mediates an experience of God, especially in terms of fictive kinship, in which disciples are children of a divine parent and siblings of Jesus and
one another. Ethics in Mark is primarily the fruit of such a relationship with God
and with a community of disciples.

To return to where I began, readers of this volume will constantly encounter
the problem of ethics—the inevitable failure. But they will also constantly encounter
the hope of ethics. Here it is especially the hope that interpretations of the New
Testament form both communities and persons for living accomplished lives. In
addition, more than occasionally readers may perceive touches upon their souls
that may contribute to their own formation. God is not finished with us yet.

Note

1. *Freud and Philosophy: An Essay in Interpretation* (New Haven, CT: Yale University Press, 1970), 547.

Contributors

C. Clifton Black, Otto A. Piper Professor of Biblical Theology, Princeton Theological Seminary, Princeton, New Jersey

Robert L. Brawley, Albert G. McGaw Professor of New Testament, McCormick Theological Seminary, Chicago, Illinois

Neil Elliott, Acquisitions Editor, Augsburg Fortress Press, Minneapolis, Minnesota

Jens Herzer, Professor of New Testament and Director of the Institut für die Neutestamentliche Wissenschaft, University of Leipzig, Leipzig, Germany

L. Ann Jervis, Professor of New Testament, Wycliffe College, Toronto, Canada

Sylvia C. Keesmaat, Adjunct Faculty Member, Institute for Christian Studies, Toronto, Canada

Jae Won Lee, Assistant Professor of New Testament, McCormick Theological Seminary, Chicago, Illinois

J. Clinton McCann Jr., Evangelical Professor of Biblical Interpretation, Eden Theological Seminary, St. Louis, Missouri

Elna Mouton, Professor of New Testament, University of Stellenbosch, Stellenbosch, South Africa

C. Drew Smith, Visiting Assistant Professor of History, Henderson State University, Arkadelphia, Arkansas

Glen Stassen, Lewis B. Smedes Professor of Christian Ethics, Fuller Theological Seminary, Pasadena, California

Willard M. Swartley, Professor Emeritus of New Testament, Associated Mennonite Biblical Seminary, Elkhart, Indiana

Allen Verhey, Professor of Christian Ethics, Duke Divinity School, Durham, North Carolina

Jinseong Woo, Candidate for the Ph.D. Degree in New Testament, Claremont Graduate School of Religion, Claremont, California

Abbreviations

AAR	American Academy of Religion
AB	Anchor Bible
ANRW	*Aufstieg und Niedergang der römischen Welt: Geschichte und Kultur Roms im Spiegel der neueren Forschung.* Edited by H. Temporini and W. Haase. Berlin, 1972–
BDAG	Bauer, W., F. W. Danker, W. F. Arndt, and F. W. Gingrich. *Greek-English Lexicon of the New Testament and Other Early Christian Literature.* 3rd ed. Chicago, 1999.
BETL	Bibliotheca ephemeridum theologicarum lovaniensium
BHT	Beiträge zur historischen Theologie
Bib	*Biblica*
BJRL	*Bulletin of the John Rylands University Library of Manchester*
BNTC	Black's New Testament Commentaries
BTB	*Biblical Theology Bulletin*
CBQ	*Catholic Biblical Quarterly*
CSEL	Corpus scriptorium ecclesiasticorum latinorum
EdF	Erträge der Forschung
EHS	Europäische Hochschulschriften
EKK	Evangelish-katholischer Kommentar zum Neuen Testament
HBT	*Horizons in Biblical Theology*
HNT	Handbuch zum Neuen Testament
HSRC	Human Sciences Research Council
HTK	Herders theologischer Kommentar zum Neuen Testament
HTR	*Harvard Theological Review*
HvTSt	*Hervormde teologiese studies*
IDB	*The Interpreter's Dictionary of the Bible.* Edited by G. A. Buttrick. 4 vols. Nashville, 1962
Int	*Interpretation*

JAC	Jahrbuch für Antike und Christentum
JBL	*Journal of Biblical Literature*
JR	*Journal of Religion*
JRE	*Journal of Religious Ethics*
JSHRZ	*Jüdische Schriften aus hellenistisch-römischer Zeit*
JSNTSup	Journal for the Study of the New Testament: Supplement Series
JSOT	*Journal for the Study of the Old Testament*
JSOTSup	Journal for the Study of the Old Testament: Supplement Series
JTS	*Journal of Theological Studies*
JTSA	*Journal of Theology for Southern Africa*
KEK	Kritisch-exegetischer Kommentar über das Neue Testament (Meyer-Kommentar)
KNT	Kommentar zum Neuen Testament
Neot	*Neotestamentica*
NICNT	New International Commentary on the New Testament
NIGTC	New International Greek Testament Commentary
NovT	*Novum Testamentum*
NovTSup	Novum Testamentum Supplements
NTL	New Testament Library
NTS	*New Testament Studies*
ÖBS	Österreichische biblische Studien
OBT	Overtures to Biblical Theology
OTL	Old Testament Library
Per	*Perspectives*
PSB	*Princeton Seminary Bulletin*
RevExp	*Review and Expositor*
RHPR	*Revue d'histoire et de philosophie religieuses*
SBL	Society of Biblical Literature
SBLDS	Society of Biblical Literature Dissertation Series
SBLSS	Society of Biblical Literature Semeia Studies
SNTSMS	Society for New Testament Studies Monograph Series
SNTSU	Studien zum Neuen Testament und seiner Umwelt
ST	*Studia theologica*
TDNT	*Theological Dictionary of the New Testament.* Edited by G. Kittel and G. Friedrich. Translated by G. W. Bromiley. 10 vols. Grand Rapids, 1964–1976
TJT	*Toronto Journal of Theology*
TLZ	*Theologische Literaturzeitung*
UNISA	University of South Africa
WBC	Word Biblical Commentary
WCC	World Council of Churches
ZNT	*Zeitschrift für Neues Testament*
ZNW	*Zeitschrift für die neutestamentliche Wissenschaft und die Kunde der älteren Kirche*
ZTK	*Zeitschrift für Theologie und Kirche*

PART I
ETHICS AND
THE GOSPELS

Chapter 1

Does Suffering Possess Educational Value in Mark's Gospel?*

C. CLIFTON BLACK

As the old saying goes, "Suffering builds character": in all likelihood, a conflated paraphrase of Romans 5:3–4. Affliction is a topic so pervasive in Mark that one popular introduction to the New Testament typifies it as "The Gospel of Suffering."[1] The question before us in this essay is whether Mark either explicitly or tacitly agrees with Paul on this point. That question may be modestly framed: Does the Second Gospel suggest that suffering carries educational value?

o edijvcatéonal.

Bearing in Recent Research

In a slender yet useful monograph, *Learning through Suffering: The Educational Value of Suffering in the New Testament and in Its Milieu,*[2] Charles Talbert has surveyed the New Testament's literary environment for ancient expressions of the pedagogical value of suffering. In the Old Testament the phenomenon of suffering is explained in various ways, such as the consequence of sin (e.g., Neh. 9:26–27; Ps. 73:12–20) and as a vicarious boon for others (Isa. 53:2–12; 2 Macc.

u

*An earlier version of this study was originally published in *Perspectives in Religious Studies* 28 (2001): 85–98. It is reprinted here by kind permission of that journal's editors.

7:37–38). Talbert's study focuses on a particular biblical view of suffering: namely, "a divine education by which moral and spiritual development are facilitated."[3] Ancient Judaism likened God's merciful discipline of his people to a parent's loving punishment of a child: "Son, do not despise the Lord's discipline [*paideias*] nor relax his reproof; for the one whom the Lord loves, he disciplines"[4] (Prov. 3:11–12a LXX; see also Deut. 8:5; Jdt. 8:27; *Pss. Sol.* 10:1–23; 13:7–11; 1QH[a] 8; 4QDibHam[a] 3; Philo, *Congr.* 175, 177). A similar view was later attributed to rabbis like Akiba: "Chastisements are precious" (*b. Sanh.* 101a; *b. Ber.* 5a–b). Greek authors regarded suffering as a test of character (Plato, *Republic* 413D–E; 503A), a struggle that increases the sufferer's stamina (Aeschylus, *Agamemnon* 176–77; Sophocles, *Oedipus at Colonus* 7). That idea was popularized by first-century Stoics, who compared suffering to parental discipline (Seneca, *On Providence* 1.5; 2.5–6) and athletic training (Epictetus, *Discourses* 1.29.33; 3.10.7–8). "Hardships, my friend, are a kind of preparatory astringent to the children with a view to the virtue that will come with full maturity" (Pseudo-Theano, *Letter to Eubule*).[5] "Consequently," observes Epictetus, "when a difficulty befalls you, remember that God, like a trainer of wrestlers, has matched you with a rough young man . . . so that you may become an Olympic champion" (*Discourses* 1.24.1–3).

Such Jewish and Greco-Roman views are blended in 4 Maccabees, wherein martyrs for Torah undergo hideous deaths at pagan hands with the noblest equanimity:

> And immediately they led [a Jewish martyr] to the wheel, and while his vertebrae were being dismembered upon it he saw his own flesh ripped around and drops of blood flowing from his entrails. When he was about to die he said, "We, you most abominable tyrant, suffer these things for our godly training and virtue [*paideian kai aretēn theou*]; but you, for your impiety and bloodthirstiness, will endure unceasing tortures." (4 Macc 10:8–11; see also 11:9–12, 20–27; 16:25; 17:11–22)

Talbert identifies Romans 5:3–4 as a conceptual bridge to earliest Christianity from its Mediterranean milieu: "We boast in our afflictions, knowing that affliction produces endurance; and endurance, character; and character, hope. And hope does not disappoint, for God's love has been poured into our hearts through Holy Spirit given to us" (see also 1 Cor. 11:32; Rev. 3:19; *1 Clem.* 56:16).

New Testament documents as various as the Epistle of James, 1 Peter, the Epistle to the Hebrews, and Luke–Acts describe human suffering in a manner analogous with this topos in Mediterranean antiquity. Adversity corrects misdeeds (Heb. 12:5–11; Jas. 5:13–20), strengthens endurance (Heb. 10:32–34; 11:1–12:4, 12–13; Jas. 1:2–18), and purifies Christians' faith (1 Pet. 1:6–7; 4:1–6, 12–19). Those who temporarily suffer receive God's compensatory blessing now (1 Pet. 3:13–14a) and ultimately will be vindicated (5:7–10). While his self-sacrifice was a priestly atonement for sin (Heb. 13:11–12), Christ's own obedience was perfected through suffering (Heb. 2:9–10, 18; 5:8–9; 12:1–4). In Luke–Acts Jesus' spiritual development, through suffering unto death, is normative for his followers, like Paul. Sharing in Christ's experience may catalyze the conversion of pagans (1 Pet. 2:18–25; 3:14b–22). Rejecting a reductionist exegesis that would force all New Testament reflection on suffering into a single category, Talbert identifies a cluster of pervasive images: "Suffering is the arena in which the Christian can be (1) disciplined, in the sense of training that develops strength; (2) refined, in the sense of the smelting process's use of fire to purify precious metals; and (3) educated, in the sense of learning the right way to live."[6]

Whereas Talbert's investigation does not treat in detail suffering in Mark's Gospel, other recent studies have done so. In a composition-critical dissertation (Emory, 1986), Sharyn Echols Dowd considers the theological function of prayer in the Second Gospel, a book she construes as "a didactic biographical narrative whose purpose is to shape the community that takes its identity from the central figure," Jesus Christ.[7] Dowd notes that Mark's longest, most strategically positioned instruction on prayer is 11:22–25 (the withered fig tree as an occasion for faith in God, who can do the impossible); Mark's longest, most strategically positioned modeling of prayer is 14:32–42 (Jesus' petitions for deliverance from the cross, if it be God's will). In Dowd's reading, these texts are sharply contrastive, generating a tension between divine power and human suffering that Mark never resolves, but to which prayer is closely related. "What makes discipleship in the Markan community so difficult is not that it involves suffering, but that it involves suffering by those who participate in God's power to do the impossible."[8] Jesus' stress on faith is an implied exhortation, directed to Mark's audience, to persist in believing that for God everything is possible, despite unanswered prayer and relentless challenges to that worldview. Because he entertains no limitation on divine power, the evangelist can provide no rational defense of God, "a solution to the problem of theodicy." What Mark offers his readers, instead, is encouragement in their relation to God, "a way of coping with the tension that pervades their existence as empowered sufferers."[9]

Susan Garrett has explored the trials both of affliction and of seduction that beset Jesus and his disciples (thus, Mark 4:19; 13:33–37).[10] She regards the Second Gospel as a complex precipitate of traditions about testing (*peirasmos*) in antiquity, which variously portray God (Deut. 8:2–5; Jdt. 8:25–27; Sir. 4:17; 4 Macc. 17:20–22; *Pss. Sol.* 13:7–11) and Satan (Job 1–2; *T. Job* 37:5–7; 2 Cor. 12:7; 2 Thess. 2:9–11; Rev. 2:9–29) as agents of *peirasmoi*. In Garrett's treatment of Mark, Jesus epitomizes "one who in every respect has been tested as we are, yet without sin" (Heb. 4:16).[11] The entire course of Jesus' ministry is subjected to temptation, not merely by Satan in the wilderness (Mark 1:12–13), but by religious adversaries (8:11–13; 12:13–17; 14:43–15:15; see Wis. 2:12–14) and even his own disciples (Mark 8:17–21, 31–33; 9:34; 10:35–37), all of whom blindly collude to "make a straight path crooked" for God's Messiah (see Mark 1:2–3; Acts 13:10).[12] Jesus' life under trial reaches its climax at Golgotha, where for a brief time God stands aside to test his Son (Mark 15:23–34; see *T. Jos.* 2:4–7). Because he was "tried and [proven] true," Jesus' perfectly obedient endurance resulted in God's acceptance of his death as an acceptable sacrifice, ransoming others from sin (Mark 10:45; 14:24) and empowering his followers to see clearly, to think the things of God, to persevere during their own times of trial (see Heb. 5:7–10; 10:20). "Only after Easter would the disciples be given full sight and brought to singleminded faith" (see Mark 10:39; 14:27–28; 16:5–7).[13]

At important points the investigations by Talbert, Dowd, and Garrett intersect and, just as significantly, diverge from one another. All three recognize the seriousness with which biblical authors reckon with suffering, whether of Jesus or of his followers. All three acknowledge the Bible's multiple explanations for suffering; all resist any forcing of the evidence into a uniform pattern. All discern in the New Testament clear echoes of older or contemporaneous Jewish and Greco-Roman thought, while underlining the distinctive adaptation of those beliefs by early Christians.

The differences among these treatments arise from their distinctive aims and from their authors' exegetical intuitions. These three studies are focused on three theologically distinguishable issues: early Christians' adoption of their culture's view of suffering as divine education (Talbert); Mark's emphasis on the endurance of trials to prove purity of faith that is acceptable to God (Garrett); Mark's exhortation to prayer in response to a paradox produced by unswerving belief in God's omnipotence and the incontestable reality of suffering (Dowd). While prayer amid suffering is regarded by Dowd as a practice that shapes the ethos of Mark's community, she does not clearly characterize it as a form of Christian *paideia*; Talbert points up the *paideia* in suffering itself, saying comparatively less about the role of prayer. Although Garrett and Dowd concentrate their energies on Mark—occasionally, with differences of nuance, on prayer in Mark[14]—in a way that Talbert does not, in some respects Garrett's approach and conclusions are closer to Talbert's than to Dowd's. Thus, Garrett's description of Jesus in Gethsemane as momentarily double-minded, experiencing "a conflicted state of being" that is overcome by his vow of obedience to God, no matter what, chimes with Talbert's comments about Jesus' own "spiritual growth": "The Lukan Jesus, through prayer, has come to see that he is about to enter a new phase of God's plan for him . . . [in which] he will learn obedience through what he suffers."[15] For Dowd, by contrast, the terror in Gethsemane lies, not as something *within Jesus* that might cause him to flee the cup of suffering, but in the fact that a God powerful enough to intervene and to prevent that suffering wills otherwise.[16]

As the pieces fall, so emerge the overall patterns. Dowd's reading of Mark leaves unresolved the tension between a mercifully omnipotent God and the suffering unto death of his beloved Son and of those who follow him. In its prayers the community is "forced to entertain conflicting propositions simultaneously."[17] Whether that conflict would be moderated by Jesus' transfiguration (9:2–8), resurrection (8:31; 9:31; 10:34; 9:9; 16:6), and promise of reunion with his disciples (14:28; 16:7) remains moot in Dowd's study. Garrett's interpretation of Mark is less equivocal and more reassuring: "Jesus [has] made the perfect and once-for-all sacrifice, accepted by God as atonement for the sins of the people."[18] While Mark's readers continue to be genuinely tested, "The Good News is that by his own endurance Christ has empowered followers to persevere in the straight and narrow way of the Lord."[19] One leaves Garrett's book wondering why Mark's priestly Christology and view of discipleship are considerably more muted than that of Hebrews (9:11–10:14) and of Matthew (16:17–23; 28:16–20). Of Luke–Acts Talbert says: "Master and disciple learn obedience through what they suffer. In this sense their suffering is part of their divine education."[20] If applied to Mark, it is as hard for me to imagine Garrett's disagreement with that conclusion as to expect Dowd's acceptance of it.

A Triptych of Suffering in Mark

There are many means of approaching the question of suffering's disciplinary import in Mark. One of the least promising paths is that of simple word study. *Paideia*, the term we have witnessed in other Hellenistic documents, never appears in the Second Gospel, though it occurs a half-dozen times elsewhere in the New Testament (Eph. 6:4; 2 Tim. 3:16; Heb. 12:5, 7, 8, 11).[21] *Paschein* ("to suffer") is found forty-two times throughout the New Testament,[22] but only thrice in Mark (5:26; 8:31; 9:12). Although "teaching" is probably the activity of Jesus most frequently mentioned in Mark,[23] the content of that teaching is sparse in comparison with the other Gospels and by no means limited to the topic of suffering. If we want to probe the question of educational suffering in the Second Gospel, we shall have to find a better way than word study.

I propose to examine three Markan pericopae in which suffering is conspicuous: the restoration of Jairus's daughter (5:21–24 + 5:35–43), the healing of a woman with vaginal bleeding (5:25–34), and Jesus' prayer in Gethsemane (14:32–42). These episodes are instructive as much for their representative differences as for their compatibility. The first two are among the lengthiest of those tales of Jesus' healings that occupy so much of the Second Gospel's first half. The account of Gethsemane, some nine chapters later, may be second only to the crucifixion in capturing the anguish of Jesus himself in Mark's second half, dominated by the passion narrative. If asked why I have selected for investigation three *narratives*, I would reply, first, that narrative is the evangelist's favored mode of presenting "the beginning of the gospel of Jesus Christ" (1:1). Second, by his intercalation (or "sandwiching") of the stories of Jairus and the woman who touched Jesus' garment, Mark could send us no clearer signal that he intends for the stories in his Gospel to interpret one another.[24] Third, while we would be blind to ignore instruction that takes up suffering (such as the cycle of passion predictions in 8:31; 9:31; and 10:33–34), it seems to me equally myopic to disregard the pedagogical dimension of Mark's tales and legends.[25] Again the evangelist tips his hand by such wording as we find in 1:27; 4:34; and 7:17: Mighty works blend indissolubly into "new teaching" in this Gospel, even as Jesus' speech is irreducibly parabolic.

Here, then, is a brief, "trifocal" exegesis of three illustrative excerpts from Mark. Convenience and clarity will be better served if I reproduce these pericopae at this point.

The Synagogue Leader's Daughter

[5:21] And when Jesus had crossed again in the boat to the other side, a great crowd gathered about him, and he was beside the sea. [22] Then came one of the archisynagogues, Jairus by name; and seeing him, he fell at his feet [23] and begged him saying, "My little daughter is at the point of death. Come, lay your hands on her, so that she may be made well, and live." [24] And he went with him. And a great crowd followed him and pressed around him. . . . [35] While he was still speaking [to the woman: 5:34], some came from the archisynagogue's house who said, "Your daughter is dead. Why are you still troubling the teacher?" [36] But overhearing what they said, Jesus said to the archisynagogue, "Don't be afraid, just keep having faith." [37] And he let no one accompany him but Peter and James and John, James's brother. [38] And they came to the house of the archisynagogue, and beheld an uproar, with great weeping and wailing. [39] And when he had entered, he said to them, "Why all the uproar and wailing? The child is not dead but sleeping." [40] And they laughed at him. But he threw them all out, and took the child's father and mother and those with him, and went in where the child was. [41] And taking the child's hand he said to her, "*Talitha koum*," which means, "Little girl, I tell you, get up." [42] And immediately the girl got up and walked around, for she was twelve years old. And immediately they were stunned with amazement. [43] And he strictly ordered them that no one should know this, and told them to give her something to eat.

The Woman with Chronic Hemorrhaging

[5:25] And there was a woman who had a flow of blood for twelve years, [26] and who had suffered much under many physicians, and had spent all that she had, and had been in no way helped but rather had grown worse. [27] She had heard about Jesus, and came up behind him in the crowd and touched his coat. [28] For she had said, "If I touch even his clothes, I shall be made well." [29] And immediately the font of her hemorrhage dried up; and she knew in her bones that she had been healed of her affliction. [30] And immediately Jesus, inwardly knowing that power had gone out of him, turned around in the crowd, and said, "Who touched my clothes?" [31] And his disciples said to him, "You see the crowd pressing around you, and you say, 'Who touched me?'" [32] And he looked around to see who had done it. [33] But the woman, in fear and trembling, knowing what had happened to her, came and fell at his feet, and told him the whole truth. [34] And he said to her, "Daughter, your faith has made you well. Go in peace, and be healed of your affliction."

Jesus in Gethsemane

[14:32] And they came to a spot by the name of Gethsemane, and he said to his disciples, "Sit here while I pray." [33] And he took Peter and James and John with him, and he began to be utterly despondent and anguished; [34] and he said to them, "My soul is crushed, even to the point of death. Stay here, and stay awake." [35] And going a little farther, he fell on the ground and prayed that, if possible, the hour might pass from him. [36] And he said, "Abba, Father, all things are possible for you. Divert this cup from me—yet not what I want, but what you want." [37] And he came and found them sleeping, and he said to Peter, "Simon, are you sleeping? Weren't you able to stay awake for one hour? [38] Stay awake and pray that you may not enter into temptation: The spirit is indeed eager but the flesh, weak." [39] And again he went away and prayed, saying the same thing. [40] And again he came and found them sleeping, for their eyes were weighed down, and they did not know what to answer him. [41] And he came the third time and said to them, "Still sleeping? Still at ease? Enough! The hour has come. See! The Son of man is betrayed into the hands of sinners. [42] Get up, let's go. Look—here comes my betrayer."

The threads interlacing the stories of the woman and Jairus's daughter are many:

a. Those healed are both women (5:25, 41), referred to as "daughters" (vv. 23, 34, 35) who have experienced something (infirmity or life) for twelve years (vv. 25, 42).

b. The petitioners for healing prostrate themselves at Jesus' feet ([pros]piptō): vv. 22, 33).

c. Both sufferers undergo hopeless circumstances: incurable illness (v. 26) or death (v. 35).

d. Both women suffer conditions rendering them unclean—a bloody discharge (vv. 25, 29), death (v. 35)—which would restrict or exclude their movements within cult, home, and society (see Lev. 12:1–8; 15:19–30; Num. 19:1–22).[26]

e. People oscillate between fear (Mark 5:33, 36) and faith (5:34, 36).

f. In both stories Jesus demonstrates uncommon insight through a statement that is seemingly absurd (vv. 30, 39) and instantly rebuffed (vv. 31, 40a; see v. 35).

g. Effected in both cases by touch (vv. 23, 27–28, 41), Jesus' healing contravenes the prior activity of professionals: physicians (v. 26) and mourners (vv. 38, 40b; see b. Ketub. 4.4).

h. Both women are restored (sōzō: Mark 5:23b, 28, 34a),

i. a reality immediately confirmed (5:29a, 42a) and recognized (vv. 29b–30a, 42b).

Most commentators detect in Mark 5:21–43 echoes of two ancient tales of prophetic restoration: Elijah's raising of the Sidonian widow's son (1 Kgs. 17:17–24) and Elisha's resuscitation of the Shunammite's son (2 Kgs. 4:18–37). While neither of these Old Testament stories should be shrunk to fit a Markan mold, both share many features I have just itemized: (a) the involvement of women (d) beyond Israel's conventional boundaries (1 Kgs. 17:9; 2 Kgs. 4:8); (h) revival of their dead children (g) by extraordinary means (1 Kgs. 17:17, 21–23; 2 Kgs. 4:20–21, 32–35); (f) incomprehension (1 Kgs. 17:18; 2 Kgs. 4:28) (i) that yields to acclamation (1 Kgs. 17:24; 2 Kgs. 4:47). Other reverberations seem particularly strong between 2 Kings 4 and Mark 5: the social standing of the parents (the wealthy Shunammite, 2 Kgs. 4:8, 22, 24; Jairus the archisynagogue, Mark 5:22, 35–38); the uncertain condition of two children (whether dead or comatose: 2 Kgs. 4:23, 26, 32; Mark 5:39); and prostration before the healer (2 Kgs. 4:37; Mark 5:22, 33).[27]

In 1 and 2 Kings, as in Mark, the religious dimensions of these tales quickly bubble to the surface. There are differences, however. Throughout, God or God's agent is acknowledged as source or conduit of health and life (1 Kgs. 17:24; 2 Kgs. 4:37; Mark 5:23, 28). Only the tale of Elijah and the widow of Zarephath contemplates a connection between a child's death and a parent's sin (1 Kgs. 17:18, 20);[28] none of these stories suggests that the suffering of parent or child is invoked by God for disciplinary purposes. Mark reiterates a point that rides on the surface of the Shunammite's assurance to her husband and Elisha's assistant, Gehazi (*Shalom*, "It's all right": 2 Kgs. 4:23, 26): namely, that faith—a persistent reaching out toward God or God's Messiah—is *antecedent* to health and structures the context within which infirmity and its relief by God may be properly understood as a sign of divine grace.[29]

The importance of faith for Mark is indicated by the term's almost immediate juxtaposition in Jesus' assurances to the woman and to the archisynagogue (*pistis*, 5:34; *pisteuein*, 5:36). Furthermore, faith is underscored by many aspects of the evangelist's account. To a degree greater than Luke (8:40–56) and far more than Matthew (9:18–26), Mark recounts in excruciating detail the woman's desperate straits and Jesus' time-consuming endeavor to find her amid the throng, before she steps forward to tell the whole truth (5:25–33). The time expended in that narration effectively simulates (1) how long she has suffered and (2) the heightening plight of Jairus, whose daughter is dying as precious minutes dwindle away (see 5:35).[30] The greater the sense of hopelessness, the more critical the need for faith. By contrast, nowhere in 5:21–43 does Mark invest such care in describing either the healer's technique or the crowd's acclaim for wondrous works (see 7:32–37).[31] Nor should we disregard the narrative context in which Mark has placed these interlaminated tales: immediately following an exorcism (5:1–20) whose terrified witnesses push Jesus away (5:15–17), amid a sequence of mighty works that begins with the stilling of a storm and the disciples' craven lack of faith (4:35–41) and ends with Jesus' own astonishment at the faithlessness (*apistia*) among those, back home, whom he cannot heal (6:1–6a; see 5:42). The hemorrhaging woman and (at least by implication) the distraught father are enabled to do what eludes so many in Mark: to penetrate their fear with faith, thus allowing wholeness to happen.[32]

Although the terms *pistis* and *pisteuein* do not appear in Mark 14:32–42, Gethsemane dramatizes Jesus' own crisis of faith in the Second Gospel. The similarities between this episode and the very different, sandwiched tales in 5:21–43 seem to me more than purely coincidental. They are, in any case, worth pondering.

- All three stories describe a change in location (5:21, 24, 37–38a; 14:32) and attendant shifts in mood (5:23, 30, 38b–40; 14:33). Curiously, different "children" in Mark 5 (v. 39b) and 14 (vv. 37, 40, 41; see 10:24 [*tekna*]) are mysteriously asleep.
- Present in all three pericopae are the disciples, notably the inner circle of Simon Peter, James, and John (5:37; 14:32–33). Characteristically, they misapprehend or disobey their teacher (5:31; 14:34, 37–38, 40).[33]
- Hopelessness suffuses all these tableaux. The archisynagogue's little daughter is at death's door (*eschatōs echei*, 5:23a); the woman's chronic

bleeding has worsened (5:25–26);[34] Jesus in Gethsemane is tormented, even to death (*heōs thanatou*, 14:34a).

- The protagonists' initial responses to crisis is fear (5:33, 36; 14:33), whose source Jesus alludes to as human frailty, "weakness of the flesh" (14:38; see Isa. 40:6).
- In every case someone falls to the ground in distress (Mark 5:22, 33; 14:35).
- A bond of familial affection is articulated by an interlocutor, who in two of three cases is the petitioner: "my little daughter" (5:23a), "Abba, Father" (14:36).[35] In the third instance, the one who tenderly refers to the woman as "Daughter" (5:34) is himself God's "beloved Son" by heavenly acclamation (1:11; 9:7).
- A forthright plea for relief from distress is offered (5:23b; 5:27–28), with Jesus thus beseeching God three times (14:36, 39, 41). None of the principals expresses nobility in suffering. All are in pain; all want it to stop.
- A peculiar tension is manifest in the will of each protagonist, particularly that of the woman and of Jesus. Like her (5:28, 33a), Jesus knows the way ahead (8:31; 9:31; 10:33–34, 45; 12:1–11). In the critical moment he, like her, temporarily resists discovery (5:32; 14:36ab). Ultimately, both the Son and the daughter come forward, not only to face the truth about themselves, but to tell it (5:33b; 14:36c, 41–42, 61–62).
- All of these stories are cast in a muted apocalypticism that is intensified toward their endings: Jesus' declaration that the woman depart in peace (5:34); his raising of the little girl (*egeirō, anistēmi*, 5:41–42; see also 6:14, 16; 8:31; 9:9–10, 31; 10:34; 12:25–26; 14:28; 16:6); later, his references to "the cup" (14:36; see also 10:38–39; Isa. 51:17, 22) and to "temptation" (Mark 14:38; see also 1:13) and his repeated rousings (*grēgoreō*, 14:34, 37–38; 41ab) of disciples who sleep (*katheudō*, 14:37, 40, 41), which culminate in announcement that the hour (*hē hōra*) has come (14:41c; see also 14:35, 37). These tones acquire greater sonority from the eschatological contexts in which the evangelist has positioned them: the inbreaking of God's kingdom and its concomitant rout of demonic forces in the first half of Mark (1:14–15; 3:22–27; 4:35–41); the kingdom's consummation and its preliminary persecution of believers, predicted on the Mount of Olives in chapter 13 (n.b., *hē hōra*, vv. 11, 32; *katheudō*, v. 36; *grēgoreō*, vv. 34, 35, 37).

If these observations be accepted, some corollaries follow. First, Mark appears to have blended the genres of tale and legend in such a manner that stories of healing highlight the need for faith, and a crisis in Jesus' faith exposes his own affliction and need of healing.[36] In Mark's apocalyptic view God may be trusted to restore ruptured wombs, crushed souls, breathless bodies—the collapse of social bodies, as well (10:28)—though that restoration take years (5:25), though death be unavoidable (5:35), betrayal inevitable (14:41b–42), and afflictions inescapable this side of the age to come (10:29–30).

Second, Mark seems to align the sufferings of those whom Jesus heals with Jesus' own torment, which can be redeemed only by God (10:45; 14:24). Such a conclusion appears counterintuitive, since the evangelist accents the vindication of martyrs, those who suffer voluntarily and specifically for the sake of Jesus and his gospel (8:34–9:1; 10:28–31, 39b–45; 13:9–13, 24–27). It is unwise, however, to draw too sharp a distinction between "human misery" and "Christian suffering," lest we dismiss Mark's many healing narratives—which account for slightly less than one-third of the Gospel—or distort his presentation of "the good news." Nowhere in Mark does Jesus leave demoniacs in thrall to Satan, or refuse to heal the afflicted, on the grounds that their suffering was not provoked "for the gospel's sake." To the contrary: God is God not of the dead but of the living (12:27). "The glad tidings of God's sovereignty" (1:14–15) carry no provisos. By drawing together Jairus and Jesus, menorrhagic woman and dead child and crucified Messiah, Mark suggests that physical torment and spiritual anguish are different dimensions of an interconnected whole, which humans can alleviate but only "Abba, Father," a loving God, can ultimately restore.[37]

Third, in Gethsemane—and later, at Golgotha—Jesus evinces what for Mark is the sufferer's appropriate response: faith manifested by prayer. This ought not surprise us: throughout Mark, Jesus is portrayed as a prayerful person (1:35; 6:46; 11:24, 25; 13:18) who encourages and honors faith in God (1:15; 2:5; 4:40; 5:34, 36; 9:23, 42; 10:52; 11:22–24, 31). Still it confounds us, whenever we smuggle into the Second Gospel images of Jesus foreign to it: whether that of the tragic hero, abused child, or deluded fanatic.[38] The Markan Jesus is none of these things. Finally, he is God's Son, as obedient as he is beloved, a little child able to enter the kingdom (10:13–16), the servant and disciple of divine sovereignty that none of his own disciples proves to be (9:33–37). As in his mighty works, so also in his plaintive cries: Jesus faithfully enacts Scripture. If the prophet is transparent through Jesus the healer, the psalmist's lament bleeds through Jesus the sufferer: "My soul is heavy within me" (Pss. 42:5, 11; 43:5 LXX; Mark 14:34), "My God, my God, why have you forsaken me?" (Ps. 22:1; Mark 15:34).[39]

A Summing Up

We opened this essay by reviewing recent, book-length considerations of biblical suffering by other New Testament investigators. A comparison of my outcomes with theirs is a fitting note on which to conclude.

1. This study has found little to support Susan Garrett's suggestion of a peculiar theological affinity between Mark and the Epistle to the Hebrews. In Hebrews 5:5–10 I hear an echo of the Synoptic portrayal of Jesus in Gethsemane; in Mark 10:45 and 14:24 I can imagine that theological acorn from which a mighty oak like Hebrews might have grown.[40] It is harder for me to perceive that development having already occurred in the Second Gospel. In Mark, Jesus sends someone to a priest (1:44) and announces the obliteration of the temple (13:1–2; see also 11:15–19; 15:38). The replacement of that temple by another, heavenly

or otherwise, is a matter of perjured testimony (14:58) or ridicule (15:29b–30); Jesus himself is no superior priest by virtue of what he suffered (see Heb. 5:5–10; 8:1–10:39).[41] On the other hand, like Garrett's study, this essay has identified in Mark's Gospel a christologically articulated view of suffering that is a complex precipitate of particular ancient, especially scriptural, conceptions.

2. Does Mark ever reconcile the paradox, described by Sharyn Dowd, between an omnipotent God and relentless suffering? This study suggests an affirmative response that is neither, to be sure, a philosophical formulation nor, *pace* Dowd, a means by which Christians cope with affliction. The resolution, I think, is revealed at Gethsemane and Golgotha, where, in unimaginable anguish, Jesus steadfastly prays to "Abba, Father," "my God," whose will is done at that moment when his mercy is invisible. It is one thing to ask whether God can make a mountain unmovable by divine hands.[42] The more interesting question is why Jesus *refuses to ask* God to move that mountain which must remain fixed (see 11:22–24).[43] By the time Mark's readers have reached the climax of the passion narrative, they can intuit an answer: Through prayer Jesus has been formed into a child who can lose his life for the gospel, if God's will demands—for only by doing so can his life be made whole (8:35–37).[44] The evangelist emphasizes that conclusion with another, sharply etched intercalation: at precisely the moment Jesus acknowledges who he is (14:53–65), Peter lies, not merely about his master, but about his own identity (14:66–72). Nowhere in Mark is there a more transparent case of one who, by seeking to save his own life, loses himself utterly. But then, nowhere in Mark has Peter or any of the Twelve ever demonstrated faith or besought God in prayer (see 9:28–29).

3. Does suffering possess educational value in Mark's Gospel? In the terms used by Charles Talbert to characterize that view within and beyond the New Testament, I do not think so. Nowhere does the Second Evangelist suggest that God afflicts mortals for the purposes of training their obedience, refining their faith, or teaching them endurance (see 1 Pet. 1:6–9; 2:19–25; 4:12–19). Contrary to Akiba, chastisements in Mark are not precious; God is no punishing agent, and affliction is terrifying. No one in Mark ever faces death with heroic dignity; between the last words of elderly Eleazar (4 Macc. 5:1–6:35) and Jesus of Nazareth (Mark 15:34–37) lies a world of theological difference.[45] In another sense, however, the sympathetic reader of Mark does learn something through the pain of its protagonists, particularly Jesus. What is learned is subtler than didacticism, less utilitarian. In the Second Gospel God does not employ suffering to enhance human virtue. Rather, only at the cross can one recognize God's Son (15:39) or construe adherence to the Messiah (8:34) or understand what prayer is and why faith saves. Our moral or spiritual faculties are not expanded or disciplined by affliction. Instead, from the cross what disciples learn is *how to learn*: how to discern reality as it truly is, how to distinguish Holy Spirit from Beelzebul (3:22–29), how to discriminate things of *theos* from things of *anthropos* (8:33). Of the Second Evangelist, I believe, one can justly say what J. Louis Martyn has helped us to understand about Paul, and for the same apocalyptic reasons: "The cross is *the* epistemological crisis for

the simple reason that while it is in one sense followed by the resurrection, it is not replaced by the resurrection."[46] If that be so, then in Mark's Gospel suffering is fundamentally, not educational, but *epistemic*—in much the way that another parent who surrendered a child to death has eloquently expressed:

> So suffering is down at the center of things, deep down where the meaning is. Suffering is the meaning of our world. For Love is the meaning. And Love suffers. The tears of God are the meaning of history. . . . When God's cup of suffering is full, our world's redemption is fulfilled. Until justice and peace embrace, God's dance of joy is delayed. The bells for the feast of the divine joy are the bells for the shalom of the world.[47]

Notes

1. Robert A. Spivey, D. Moody Smith, and C. Clifton Black, *Anatomy of the New Testament: A Guide to Its Structure and Meaning*, 6th ed. (Upper Saddle River, NJ: Pearson Prentice Hall, 2007), 53–87.
2. Collegeville, MN: Liturgical Press, 1991.
3. Talbert, *Learning through Suffering*, 10; see also 9–13.
4. Here and throughout, all translations are my own unless otherwise indicated.
5. Trans. Abraham J. Malherbe; cited in Talbert, *Learning through Suffering*, 19.
6. Talbert, *Learning through Suffering*, 92.
7. Dowd, *Prayer, Power, and the Problem of Suffering: Mark 11:22–25 in the Context of Markan Theology*, SBLDS 105 (Atlanta: Scholars, 1988), 16.
8. Ibid., 158.
9. Ibid., 158–65 (quotations, 162).
10. Garrett, *The Temptations of Jesus in Mark's Gospel* (Grand Rapids: Eerdmans, 1998).
11. Garrett (*Temptations of Jesus*, 106–10) discusses theological parallels between Mark and Hebrews.
12. Jesus' ongoing temptation throughout Mark's narrative distinguishes Garrett's exegesis from that of Ernest Best, *The Temptation and the Passion: The Markan Soteriology*, 2nd ed., SNTSMS 2 (Cambridge: Cambridge University Press, 1990).
13. Garrett, *Temptations of Jesus*, 142 (italics in original).
14. For Garrett, prayer tends to be an activity of the faithful: "Prayer is the means by which persons put doublemindedness behind them, as Jesus demonstrates in his move from distress and grief (14:33–34) to confident obedience (vv. 35–36)" (*The Temptations of Jesus*, 98). For Dowd, prayer tends to be an instrument of God, "the vehicle [in Mark 11:22–25] by means of which the God who can do the impossible meets the needs of the Christian community" (*Prayer, Power, and the Problem of Suffering*, 129).
15. Garrett, *Temptations of Jesus*, 98; Talbert, *Learning through Suffering*, 85–86.
16. Dowd, *Prayer, Power, and the Problem of Suffering*, 151–62.
17. Ibid., 162.
18. Garrett, *Temptations of Jesus*, 121.
19. Ibid., 18; see also 159–63.
20. Talbert, *Learning through Suffering*, 89–90.
21. The cognate verb *paideuein* is more frequently attested but, again, never in Mark (see Luke 23:16, 22; Acts 7:22; 22:3; 1 Cor. 11:27; 2 Cor. 6:9; 1 Tim. 1:20; 2 Tim. 2:25; Tit. 2:12; Heb. 12:6, 7, 10; Rev. 3:19).

22. Twelve occurrences are in 1 Peter (2:19, 20, 21, 23; 3:14, 17, 18; 4:1 [twice], 15, 19; 5:10), which makes of that letter a principal canonical basis for Talbert's *Learning through Suffering* (42–57).

23. Jesus as "teacher" (*didaskalos*): 4:38; 5:35; 9:17, 38; 10:17, 20, 35; 12:14, 19, 32; 13:1; 14:14; "to teach" (*didaskein*): 1:21, 22; 2:13; 4:1, 2; 6:2, 6, 30, 34; 7:7; 8:31; 9:31; 10:1; 11:17; 12:14, 35; 14:49; "teaching" (*didachē*): 1:22, 27; 4:2; 11:18; 12:38.

24. See James R. Edwards, "Markan Sandwiches: The Significance of Interpolations in Markan Narratives," *NovT* 31 (1989): 193–216.

25. I use these terms in their classic, form-critical senses. See Martin Dibelius, *From Tradition to Gospel* (New York: Charles Scribner's Sons, 1934), 70–132; Rudolf Bultmann, *History of the Synoptic Tradition*, rev. ed. (New York: Harper & Row, 1963), 214–15, 267–68.

26. See Marla J. Selvidge, "Mark 5:25–34 and Leviticus 15:19–20: A Reaction to Restrictive Purity Legislations," *JBL* 103 (1984): 619–23. Judging Selvidge's assessment overstated, Sharyn Dowd summarizes a wealth of ancient religious and medical evidence for gynecologic disorders (*Reading Mark: A Literary and Theological Commentary on the Second Gospel* [Macon, GA: Smyth & Helwys, 2000], 57–58).

27. In "Jesus and Elisha," *Per* 12 (1971): 85–104, Raymond E. Brown finds a closer analogue for the Gospel accounts in the Elisha catena of miracles than in either the Elijah cycle or Greco-Roman "aretalogies" (so-called).

28. Citing 2 Sam. 6:6–7, Amos 6:10, Mark 1:24, and Luke 5:8, John Gray refers to "the incompatibility of the Holy and other than holy" (*I & II Kings: A Commentary*, 2nd rev. ed.; OTL [Philadelphia: Westminster, 1970], 382). While the Gospels do not deny sin and its consequences for judgment, in Luke (13:1–5) and John (9:1–5) Jesus repudiates the assumption that victims of calamity have been specially punished by God.

29. As Joel Marcus notes (*Mark 1–8: A New Translation with Introduction and Commentary*, AB 27 [New York: Doubleday, 2000], 360–61), it is especially at this point that Jesus' mighty works in Mark diverge from other tales of healing, in which miracles stimulate faith (see also 1 Kgs. 17:23–24)—not the other way around.

30. In a classic study Heinz Joachim Held commented, "Matthew preserves the essential elements of the Markan narrative. What he omits are the descriptive nonessentials" (Günther Bornkamm, Gerhard Barth, and Heinz Joachim Held, *Tradition and Interpretation in Matthew*, NTL [Philadelphia: Westminster, 1963], 173). To the contrary: the plethora of detail, which Matthew (or Held) may have regarded as nonessential, Mark has apparently elaborated to strengthen his theological objectives.

31. The command of secrecy in 5:43 subverts any ploy to compel faith by miracle; "[t]he signs of the kingdom have become signs for faith in Jesus" (M. E. Glasswell, "The Use of Miracles in the Markan Gospel," in *Miracles: Cambridge Studies in Their Philosophy and History*, ed. C. F. D. Moule [London: Mowbray, 1965], 149–62 [quotation, 161]).

32. For a sensitive reading of Mark 5:21–43, among other Markan tales of "Faith and the Powerless," consult Christopher D, Marshall, *Faith as a Theme in Mark's Narrative*, SNTSMS 64 (Cambridge: Cambridge University Press, 1989), 75–133.

33. Here, another echo with 2 Kgs. 4:27–31: Gehazi first rebuffs the Shunammite, then later proves incapable of reviving her child. See above, n. 27.

34. Since blood was identified with life in Hebrew thought, incessant menstruation could be reckoned as a literal wasting away of the woman's life. See Hans Walter

Wolff, *Anthropology of the Old Testament* (Philadelphia: Fortress, 1974), 19, 60–62.

35. Some of Joachim Jeremias's conclusions regarding Jesus' address to God as "Abba"—in particular, that such address was utterly unique, implying Jesus' self-consciousness as the singular "Son of God"—have been roundly criticized in recent scholarship: see James Barr, "'Abba' Isn't 'Daddy,'" *JTS* 39 (1988): 28–47; Mary Rose D'Angelo, "*Abba* and 'Father': Imperial Theology and the Jesus Traditions," *JBL* 111 [1992]: 611–30). Nevertheless, there remains in Jeremias's study much of value for the interpreter of Paul (Rom. 8:15; Gal. 4:6) and Mark (14:36): thus, as Father, "God is the *one who helps in time of need* . . . , when no-one else can help" (*The Prayers of Jesus* [Philadelphia: Fortress, 1967], 11–65 [quotation, 19]).

36. So also William C. Placher: "Mark uses every strategy to say two things at once: yes, this is the Messiah, the greatest of miracle workers, the Son of God, but, no, that does not mean at all what you thought it meant" ("Narratives of a Vulnerable God," *PSB* 14 [1993]: 134–51 [here, 146]).

37. See also C. Clifton Black, "The Persistence of the Wounds," in *Lament: Reclaiming Practices in Pulpit, Pew, and Public Square*, ed. Sally A. Brown and Patrick D. Miller (Louisville, KY: Westminster John Knox, 2005), 47–58. On the broader scriptural background in which God is said to suffer with and for the people, see Terence E. Fretheim, *The Suffering of God: An Old Testament Perspective*, OBT (Philadelphia: Fortress, 1984), esp. 127–48.

38. The perceptive, zesty account by Charlotte Allen, *The Human Christ: The Search for the Historical Jesus* (New York: Free Press, 1998), traces these and other misconceptions.

39. Commentators frequently observe that, contrary to customary expectation, Jesus' contact with perpetual menstruation (Mark 5:27–29) and a corpse (5:41–42) does not defile him (see, 7:15a, 18b) but, rather, purifies both women (see, e.g., Marcus, *Mark 1–8*, 367–68). Less often noted is that, by his own prayers at Gethsemane (14:36, 39) and Golgotha (15:34), Jesus utters the rest of his revisionist definition of *kashrut*: that "clean" and "unclean" are *from within* and come *out of* a person (7:15b, 20).

40. While the point is much debated, I can further imagine that underlying both Mark and Hebrews is a tradition of a human's metaphorical self-sacrifice as a sin offering, which may go back as far as Isa. 53:12. On the evolution of that tradition, consult George Foot Moore, *Judaism in the First Centuries of the Christian Era* (New York: Schocken, 1971), 1.546–52.

41. I concede the possibility that Mark intimates its original community's supplanting Jerusalem's temple, which the evangelist knew to have been destroyed: thus, Francis J. Moloney, *The Gospel of Mark: A Commentary* (Peabody, MA: Hendrickson, 2002), 226, 302–3, following Donald H. Juel, *Messiah and Temple: The Trial of Jesus in the Gospel of Mark*, SBLDS 31 (Missoula, MT: Scholars Press, 1977). At most, however, that is only an intimation; Mark's Gospel is never so explicit in this matter as, say, Paul's metaphor in 1 Cor. 6:19.

42. On the Hellenistic debate over divine omnipotence and intervention, see Dowd, *Prayer, Power, and the Problem of Suffering*, 78–94.

43. *Pace* Dowd: "Now, however, God's will is different from the will of the petitioner" (*Reading Mark*, 151). In the light of Mark 14:36c, to say nothing of the resurrection's fulfillment (16:1–8) of Jesus' repeated predictions (8:31; 9:31; 9:9; 10:33–34), is it *finally* so?

44. With the benefit of other canonical and liturgical resources, later Christian theology, pondering the interwoven mysteries of God's humanity and Christ's divinity, could develop Mark's abbreviated implications: God was in Christ,

allowing the death of his beloved Son for the world's redemption; Christ was of God, cooperating with his dear Father in the same of work of healing love. For a somewhat Pauline interpretation of the thorny relationship in Mark between Jesus' death and God's will, see Donald H. Juel, *The Gospel of Mark*, Interpreting Biblical Texts (Nashville: Abingdon, 1999), 157–65.

45. See Adela Yarbro Collins, "From Noble Death to Crucified Messiah," *NTS* 40 (1994): 481–503, who correctly points out that, like Eleazar, Jesus does offer his own life for the benefit of many.

46. J. Louis Martyn, "Epistemology at the Turn of the Ages: 2 Corinthians 5.16," in *Christian History and Interpretation: Studies Presented to John Knox*, ed. W . R. Farmer, C. F. D. Moule, and R. R. Niebuhr (Cambridge: Cambridge University Press, 1967), 269–87 (quotation, 286).

47. Nicholas Wolterstorff, *Lament for a Son* (Grand Rapids: Eerdmans, 1987), 90–91.

Chapter 2

Scripture as Script and as Scripted

The Beatitudes

ALLEN VERHEY

Scripture is both scripted and script. It is scripted—that is to say, it was written. The various texts of Scripture were written once upon a particular time by authors who did certain things with the words they had available to them. And it is script—that is to say, it is to be performed.[1] It is performed again and again in the rhetoric and practices of the churches, in their theology and in their worship, in their ethics and in their politics. Scripture as scripted is an object to us, a given, the product of the activity of others. Scripture as script is an instrument for us[2] and a vocation to activity of our own.

Because Scripture is both scripted and script, it is open to at least two different kinds of interpretation. "At least two different kinds of interpretation"—that may win the prize as the most understated remark of this volume. I mean, of course, simply to distinguish the interpretation of Scripture *as scripted* from the interpretation of Scripture *as script*. And I distinguish them in order to ask about their relationship.

We might begin with the conventional assignment of the interpretation of Scripture as scripted (or exegetical interpretation) to biblical scholarship and the interpretation of Scripture as script (or performance interpretation) to moral theologians. It is a convenient division of labor and surely correlates with the way many biblical scholars and at least some moral theologians construe their tasks. The burden of my remarks, however, is that it is a bit more complicated than that. Attention to Scripture as scripted finally requires attention to Scripture as a text appropriately read when it is used to do certain other things, when it is, if you will, performed. And attention to Scripture as script to be performed is surely enriched by attention to Scripture as scripted. After making a case for each of those claims, I will illustrate the claims by attending to the Beatitudes as scripted and as script.

The general point I want to make was captured by a very pious but slightly senile old pastor. Given to the use of clichés in his prayers, he frequently included the familiar petition that God would make us "ever mindful of the needs of others." One morning, however, that cliché came out a little differently. He asked instead that God would make us "ever needful of the minds of others."[3] I intend to echo that petition. Biblical scholars and moral theologians need each other, and both need the church as an interpretative community. It is important, therefore, not only to sustain the conversation between biblical scholars and moral theologians, not only to nurture some colleagues who are at least minimally competent in both exegesis and the assessment of performance, but also to nurture communities of faith as communities of interpretative and moral discernment.

Scripture as Scripted

Consider, first, Scripture as scripted. Surely biblical scholarship has properly focused on Scripture as scripted, as written.[4] Textual critics have worked to figure out what words were in fact written. Philologists have worked on what those particular words or expressions or figures meant in their own cultural and social and literary contexts. And still other biblical scholars have worked on figuring out who wrote these texts and to whom, at what particular time and in response to what specific conditions they wrote them, what sources and genres the authors had available to them, and whether and how they used and modified these sources and genres. That is only a partial list of the contributions of biblical scholarship to the effort to interpret Scripture as scripted. The whole list stands in the service of the vocation to make some sense of the Scripture *as scripted*, to understand it as written, to interpret it. We owe a great debt to these scholars, and we ought to be reminded that we are "needful of the minds of others" each time we pull down, for example, an edition of Aland's Greek Text of the New Testament or one of the great lexicons or a good commentary. My claim, however, is that the vocation to interpret Scripture as scripted also and finally requires attention to Scripture as script.

Scripture as scripted is an object to us, a given, the product of the activity of others. Look upon this object. It looks like a book. To be sure, some books—and some Bibles—are only for display; but page through it. What you see, of course, are words on a page. Well, perhaps that is too generous. Some of us look upon the *Biblia Hebraica* and see not words but marks on a page. But let's be generous.

Suppose we recognize that the marks make words and, more than this, that the words make sentences, and the sentences make paragraphs. If we are interested enough, we may try to read a page, to make sense of it. The interest, of course, may be idle curiosity. We may simply be curious about what sort of writing this is. Such curiosity, however, may be more than idle, for to make some sense of a text, to interpret it, we have to make a decision about *what sort of writing* this is.

If we had opened *Biblia Hebraica* to *Tehillim* we might identify the sort of writing it is as "praises" from the title, or as "lament" if we read a particular psalm. If we had opened it to Leviticus, we might identify the sort of writing it is as a law code. Such judgments, of course, would be important to the effort to make sense of what we had read. But as a word makes sense in a sentence and a sentence in a paragraph, so presumably we would want to interpret the lament or the law in the context of the larger whole within which each is found. To make sense of a text, we will also have to make decisions about whether it is a part of a larger whole and, if so, about how to identify and characterize the whole of which it is a part. What is the whole? And what sort of writing is it?

Different sorts of texts, of course, require different sorts of readings, different sorts of interpretation. One does not read a phone book the same way one reads a screenplay. Different sorts of writing are associated, in other words, with different sorts of interests and with different sorts of uses. To be sure, we can put the same text to different uses. We can read a phone book to find the telephone number of an acquaintance or, while we wait for an answer, to entertain ourselves. (Does this city have a Herman Utics?) In the case of the phone book, of course, it is fairly clear what set of interests and uses are appropriate to it. But to make a decision about what sort of writing we have before us is also to make a decision about what would count as an appropriate interest, an appropriate use, of this writing. Because writing, like speaking, is an intentional activity,[5] the text is not only an object, not only a product, but also an instrument.

Consider the piece of writing known generously as the instruction manual for the assembly of my grandson's wagon. It looked to me like marks on a page, but when I knew what kind of text it was, I knew that I was interested in it, since I wanted to put his wagon together. I also knew what would count as the appropriate use of this text and what would count as the primary form of its interpretation. Marks on a page—but appropriately used in the effort to put a wagon together. Since one instruction was to read the text through before beginning to assemble the wagon, I had done that. Indeed, I had looked for other sheets, a larger whole, that would help me interpret this complicated text. Not finding any, I read and reread the text I had as I attempted to perform the text by assembling a wagon. I was grateful for the help received in reading the text and in performing it. Interpreting the text as written and performing it were intimately related, but I did not fully (or even adequately) understand the text as scripted, as written, until I had (with the help of others) performed it.

I am not suggesting that the Bible is an instruction manual. But I am suggesting that the vocation to interpret any part of it requires the interpreter to make judgments about the sort of text it is, about the whole of which it is a part (identifying the whole and characterizing the whole), about the interest appropriate to it, and about the appropriate use of this object as instrument, the performance of this text. There is, I think, no escape from the personal responsibility to make such judgments.

Suppose, for example, that the particular psalm we read in *Biblia Hebraica* was Psalm 22. We might judge that psalm to be lament, set it in the context of ancient Near Eastern religious literature of complaint, and be interested in it—and use it—for its confirmation or challenge to certain scholarly generalizations about that literature. Given another set of judgments, we might take the psalm to be lament, to be sure, but set it in the context of the history of Israel, and be interested in it—and use it—as a source of information for the reconstruction of a history of Israel's "religion." Or, given yet another set of judgments, we might set the lament in the context of the whole of the *Tehillim*, characterized as the songbook of the second temple, and be interested in it not only as a product of one pious Jewish sufferer but also as an instrument by which a community gave voice to the sufferers in their midst. Or, again, we might set it—and the *Tehillim* and the *Biblia Hebraica*—in the context of the whole that Christians call "canon," and be interested in it as the complaint of both pious Jews and of one particular pious Jew named Jesus, who made the human cry of lament his own cry.

Psalm 22, of course, may be regarded and read in any of these ways, but the judgments about what sort of text this is and about the whole to which it belongs will make a difference to the ways it is read and used. Shall we use the text as a source of information about that ancient culture and history or as somehow normative for the faith and life of those who own it as canon? Shall we "perform" the text by an act of historical reconstruction or by acts of community formation, by making a place in the community (as in the canon) for the voice of those who suffer? Shall we read the text simply as an artifact or as a vocation to share in the suffering of Jesus and, because we share in his suffering, to give voice to our own, confident that God does "not despise or abhor the affliction of the afflicted" (Ps. 22:24 NRSV), and to show compassion to other sufferers? Decisions about what sort of writing this is and about the whole of which it is a part are clearly related to the appropriate use of this object as instrument. The vocation to interpret Scripture as scripted requires such decisions.

To say that these are personal decisions, however, does not mean that they are arbitrary. Even if it is the *reading* of the text (and not just the text itself as scripted) that embodies decisions about what sort of readings of this text are appropriate, the text itself will rule out some judgments about the sort of text it is and about uses appropriate to it. Moreover, the reading of any text is not a purely private matter. Reading is always conditioned by the interpretive community to which the individual reader belongs.[6] The personal responsibility of the interpreter will take place in the context of a community of readers, and the interpreter will be both equipped by and answerable to the community. So another and fundamental judgment is necessary, a judgment about the interpretative community with which one identifies when one would read and interpret Scripture. Should one identify with a community of scholars who value their (presumed) transcendence over particular communities and their traditions? Or should the interpreter identify with a community of Christians who value this canon and the story it tells as constitutive of their identity and as determinative for their discernment? Again, one might give either reply, I suppose; but if "Scripture" and "church" are correlative concepts,[7] then it can hardly be arbitrary to say that the community that should equip the interpreter and to whom the interpreter should be responsible is the church.

Without the church the writings called "Scripture" would not exist. It was the church that gathered these documents into a collection, a whole, because (and for the sake of the fact that) in them she found the story of her life. Without the church, these writings are at best simply a little library of ancient Near Eastern religious literature. Apart from the synagogue and the church, moreover, the canons of the synagogue and the church fall into fragments, and we find ourselves back at the place where we were interested in an artifact of Israel's history. But if there is no "Scripture" without church, neither is there any church without Scripture. Without Scripture the church loses her identity and her way, her character in the drama of the script. Within the churches, however, these writings are "canon," and to read Scripture within Christian community means, therefore, that we read any part of it as a part of that whole and recognize that the appropriate use is somehow to perform it.

The interpreter, we said, will be both equipped by and answerable to the community. The community and its performances of the text equip the interpreter. The interpreter does not (and cannot) simply transcend the tradition and community that link him or her to the text. The interpreter can begin to understand the text only by being part of the tradition and community that is already part of the effect of the text, shaped by past interpretative performances of the text.[8]

The interpreter is also answerable to the community. She is answerable to the community that owns these texts as canon and that refuses to substitute its too frequently inept performances for the script it still loves to read and longs to perform. That community, it must be observed, includes not just biblical scholars but saints and strangers, little ones who are still too often neglected, those on the margins who are still too often oppressed.

I have been arguing that interpretation of the Scripture as scripted finally requires judgments about the sort of writing a text is, about the whole of which a text is a part, about the interests—and uses—appropriate to a text, and about the interpretative community by which the interpreter is empowered and to which she is responsible. It may appear that some of the judgments I have identified (and would recommend) abandon attention to Scripture *as scripted*. Against that inference, I note that attention to the text as part of a whole and to a particular community of readers need not—and should not—dispense with attention to the text as scripted, as written by particular authors who did things with the words available to them.

First, the canon itself is quite candid about the fact that the works collected have a history, that they did not simply fall from heaven, that they are "products." Moreover, the works are evidently part of a tradition, even if their canonical status renders them (as a whole) the normative part of the tradition. The Chronicler revised the work of the Deuteronomic Historian; it does not substitute for it in the canon. Matthew and Luke revised Mark, but the church collected four Gospels, not just one nor a harmony or synthesis. Those Gospels each revisit Psalm 22 in telling the story of Jesus, but they do not make the old laments, including Psalm 22, superfluous. Indeed, most obviously and significantly, the Old Testament is reread and interpreted in the New Testament, but the New Testament does not substitute for the Old or make it superfluous. The canon invites the church to read each part both as scripted, as an author responded to a particular crisis or context in ways that were faithful to and creative with the tradition, and as a part of the whole. To read any text as canon, therefore, is not to dismiss attention to the text as scripted.

Second, the Christian community with whom an interpreter may read Scripture includes those who were the authors of Scripture. When postmodernism insists that meaning is not simply in the text but created by the reader of the text, the obvious risk is the loss of criteria to tell what readings are good readings or even fair readings. The danger is that the text can mean anything at all (and then it means nothing at all). The danger is that Scripture will no longer be able to function "over against" the reader or the community. We have noted that one protection against the risk of arbitrariness is to insist that reading is not simply an isolated or private experience. Reading is influenced by the interpretative community with which the reader identifies. But if the communal context is the church, then it includes not only our contemporaries and not even only Barth and Schleiermacher and Calvin and Aquinas but also the authors of Scripture themselves. In this community a "fair" reading will require that justice be done to the text and to Paul and to Mark and to Amos and to a host of anonymous authors.

If the communal context is the church, with its recognition of the Scripture as canon, then another point may be insisted upon. The canon as canon will not permit the substitution of a particular community's particular reading of the writings for the writings themselves. It is the text as scripted, as object, that exists prior to our reading it (and prior even to the church's collecting it) and provides constraints upon interpretation. A "fair" reading will require that justice be done to the text as scripted.

There is a feedback loop here, sometimes called a hermeneutical circle, between the parts and the whole. The parts can finally be understood only in the light of a whole, but the whole can be understood only in the light of the parts. The understanding of each is always provisional, always challenged and corrected as the parts are illumined by the whole and the whole by the parts. This is one reason we keep reading Scripture in the church.

In all of this the tools of the historical-critical method can make a genuine contribution,[9] but interpretation finally requires judgments about the sort of writing a text is, about the whole of which a text is a part, about the interests—and uses—appropriate to a text, and about the interpretative community by which the interpreter is empowered and to which she is responsible. Attention to Scripture as scripted is (at least) enriched by attention to Scripture as script. That is my first claim.

Scripture as Script

My second claim is that attention to Scripture as script is surely assisted by attention to Scripture as scripted. If the biblical scholar is conventionally charged with the task of considering Scripture as scripted, the moral theologian is charged with (part of) the task of attending to performances. Moral theologians review and assess performances, attending to the character and conduct of the believing community and its members, her ethics and politics. The assessment may—and finally must—evaluate the performances as performances of Scripture as script. And if the biblical scholar can hardly undertake his task without indebtedness to and attention to the interpretative performances of the text in community, the moral theologian can hardly undertake her task without attention to the Scripture as scripted. The moral theologian is "needful of the minds of others," indebted both to the biblical scholars and to the community.

The life of the church, its practices and politics, its conduct and character, is a performance of Scripture, and such performance is, of course, an interpretation of Scripture. Indeed, as Nicholas Lash has observed, the life of the believing community is "the fundamental form of the *Christian* interpretation of scripture."[10] Moral theologians may—and must—construe the life of the believing community as a performance of Scripture, and they may—and must—assess the truthfulness or the integrity of performances (in part, at least) by attending to Scripture as script. The review and assessment of performance requires (at least) some interpretation of the script as scripted.

A performance of any script is an interpretation. A performance can be improved if someone in the acting troupe attends carefully to what the author did once with the words at his or her disposal. To be sure, such study is hardly a guarantee of a good performance. Lacking other gifts, a troupe will give a wooden and spiritless performance of a carefully studied text. Moreover, careful study of the script is not even strictly necessary for an excellent performance. A troupe may have seen (or heard) enough fine performances in the past to perform not just adequately but splendidly. Even so, even though careful study of the original script as scripted is neither sufficient nor strictly necessary, it remains important. It is important both for those who would check the "integrity" of a performance (or review and reform a tradition of performance) and for the troupe, for those who have the responsibility to perform. Moreover, because there are different performances (and traditions of performance), and because no performance definitively captures the meaning of the script, study of the script as scripted, as written, remains critically important as a test for and guide to performance.[11]

This is true, I suppose, of any performance of any script, of a performance of Shakespeare's *Romeo and Juliet*, for example; but it is surely true of the performance of Scripture as script. Let it be admitted that Scripture is not simply an "object" waiting to be used, that it is always already used and "performed" in the life of particular churches. But Scripture may also not be reduced simply to the set of performative interpretations of any particular church. We may not substitute any church's performative interpretation of Scripture for Scripture itself. Such a substitution would vitiate the possibilities of reform and renewal of a church and its common life by reading Scripture together, for such a reading would simply be to look at an image of ourselves and to authorize it as biblical. Scripture is not *simply* "object," but it is "object," independent of the churches' interpretation.

I hope it is clear that I am making a case for careful exegesis, for consideration also by moral theologians of what the authors of Scripture did with the words at their disposal. To read Scripture as script to be performed, some in the community must read it carefully as scripted, as written once upon a particular time by authors who did certain things with words. The rule that we must read Scripture in Christian community is not a license to neglect exegesis, as though we could simply substitute some particular tradition of performance/interpretation for the script. On the contrary, to read Scripture in Christian community requires that the community nurture and sustain biblical scholarship as an important contribution to the communal effort to understand and perform Scripture.

I hope it is also clear, however, that I have not abandoned the point made in the first part of this essay. The interpretation of Scripture as scripted finally requires judgments about the kind of writing a particular text is, about the whole of which it is a part (both identifying it and characterizing it as a whole), about the appropriate interest in and use of a text, and about the interpretative community to which it and the interpreter belong. We observed in the first part that an interpreter might answer these questions in a variety of ways, even if some of the answers were more appropriate to these texts than others. Some of the possible judgments warrant using the text as an instrument of historical reconstruction but hardly warrant attention to Scripture as a script to be performed. Indeed, some critical readings of Scripture refuse to warrant such attention to Scripture as script, given Lessing's "ugly ditch" (the contingent facts of history can never be the basis for absolute truth). But some other possible judgments, judgments that seem to me to be more appropriate to these texts, virtually require attention to Scripture as script.

If "Scripture" and "church" are correlative concepts, then the appropriate interpretative community is the church with its faith and practices. To read Scripture in Christian community has a number of implications,[12] but chief among them is that Scripture is read as canon, as a rule for the church's faith and practice. "Canon" serves both to identify the whole within which any part must be understood and to characterize the whole as somehow normative for the church's thought and conduct. The Christian canon, moreover, may be further characterized as an extended narrative. The wholeness of this whole is a narrative wholeness.[13]

The story begins with creation, with God making all things and making all things good. The story continues—and the plot thickens—with human pride and sloth, with the human refusal to honor God as God or to give thanks to God. Human sin might have smashed the cosmos back to chaos, but God would not let sin or death or the flood be the end of the story. God comes again to covenant and to bless. God calls Abraham and begins a project that promises blessing not only to Abraham's children but to all the nations. When the church rejected Marcion and formed its canon, it said that Israel's story is our story too. At the center of the Christian story—and of the Christian canon—is Jesus of Nazareth. He came announcing the good future of God, and he made that future present, its power felt, in his works and in his words. He was put to death on a Roman cross, but God raised him up from the dead and vindicated him as Lord and Christ. Because Jesus was raised, the Spirit was poured out, and because the Spirit was poured out, a community was formed in memory of Jesus, in confidence of the presence of the living Christ, and in hope for God's good future. At the end of the story, all things will be made new.

To read any part of Scripture in the light of the whole is to read it in the light of that whole, as a part of the story. The story has hermeneutical priority. The community reads with discernment when it reads any part (and every part) in the light of the story. The lament will be read in the light of that whole. Wisdom will be read not as free-floating counsel but as part of the whole. That law in Leviticus will be read as statute to be sure, but it will have authority as part of the story, not simply or fundamentally as statute. It is the story we love to tell—and long to live. That's the key. It is *our* story. It is the church's canon, and it is the church's story.

The story is also, of course, as both the beginning and the ending witness, a universal story, the story of all things. It is the story that gathers in and transforms all our other stories into the light of the God's work and project. It is not—or at least it ought not be—that our identity is provided by some other story so that we salvage something from Scripture and leave the rest for Waste Management. No, it is this story in which we find ourselves, this story that gives us an identity and makes us a community, this story that is determinative for what we salvage and redeem from the other stories of our lives, taking every thought captive, discerning together what is fitting to the story, what is worthy of the gospel.

Moreover, it is a continuing story. We claim to know something about the end of the story by the resurrection of this Jesus from the dead, but we do not claim that the story has ended. Scripture is script, but the curtain has not yet fallen. We are not only readers but performers, and as performers we find ourselves a part of the drama. Scripture as script does not invite us to pretend we live in David's Jerusalem or in Jeremiah's. It does not demand that we pretend to live in the Israel of the eighth century before Christ or in the Corinth of the first century after Christ. It does demand that we live here today in a way that is worthy of the story that includes Ruth and David and Jeremiah and Amos and Mary Magdalene and Paul and that makes no sense without Jesus of Nazareth. We are actors, agents in a continuing story. Performance will require both fidelity and creativity.[14] The community performs the script with moral discernment when it tests its own actions by the story of which it too is a part. We test our character and conduct by whether they fit the story, by whether they are worthy of the gospel. Christian ethics, then, proceeds by way of reminder.

As the community exercises interpretative discernment by asking how each part of Scripture as scripted fits the whole, so the community exercises moral discernment by asking how its conduct and character fit Scripture as script. And as there is a feedback loop, a hermeneutical circle, between the part and the whole, so here too there is a feedback loop, a hermeneutical circle, between the community and the text. The interpreter and performer of the text is equipped and responsible to the community, but the interpretation and performance of a text may also challenge the reading community, requiring of it a revision of its reading, a reform of its performance. Such revision and reform may then enable a fresh reading of the text, and that fresh reading may require another revision of the life of the community. So the church—and each of its members—is called to be ever reforming as it reads Scripture and remembers its story. This is a second reason that the church keeps reading Scripture.

The Beatitudes

Permit me to attempt to illustrate what I have been saying by attending to the Beatitudes of Matthew 5:1–11. The Beatitudes are Scripture. They are scripted—that is to say, they were written. They were written once upon a particular time by an author who did certain things with words. And they are script—that is to say, they are performed. They are performed again and again by the people who set these writings aside as "holy."

If we accept the brief apology for careful exegesis above, for asking what this author has done with the words at his disposal, then we are in a position to appreciate (without overestimating) the contribution of biblical scholarship (and of so-called critical study of the Beatitudes) to the performance of this text in Christian community. If we attend to the Beatitudes as scripted, we may be in a better position to perform them more faithfully. That was the second claim. And if we attend to the performance of the Beatitudes in Christian community, we may be in a better position truly to understand them as scripted. That was the first claim.

For the sake of illustration, I need not review the debates among biblical scholars and among moral theologians concerning the Beatitudes, or report at length and in depth either the contributions of "critical" study to our understanding of these texts as scripted (or as "object") or the various traditions of performance in particular communities.

Let the following two quick points suffice to illustrate the contributions of biblical scholarship with its attention to Scripture as scripted, one attentive to form criticism and the other to source criticism. Attention to the form of the Beatitudes enables the observation that this form was not invented by Jesus or by the author who scripted this text. The form was familiar to the sage and used regularly in Wisdom literature. The beatitude was one of the ways wisdom teachers expressed the principles learned from experience (or from observation of the natural world), the principles at work in the world willy-nilly, the principles to which it is both moral and prudent to conform.

But attention to the form also enables the observation that the conventional form has been modified. Jesus—or the early tradition—has done things with the form at their disposal. The modified form speaks to the present in view of the coming good future of God; in the modified form, the present tense confronts the future, and the future breaks through into the present.[15]

This juxtaposition of present and future tenses, of present and future, is not only present in these Beatitudes, of course. Indeed, it is typical of Jesus' preaching. It is present, to give just one example, in Matthew 23:12: "Whoever exalts himself shall be humbled and whoever humbles himself shall be exalted." The context for this eschatological wisdom form is the proclamation of the coming cosmic sovereignty of God, first by Jesus and then by the early church.

Jesus came announcing the good future of God and already making its power felt in his works of healing and in his words of blessing. And the early church proclaimed that in Jesus—in his words and works, in his cross and character, and in his resurrection!—the good future of God was made known and made present.

The Beatitudes are wisdom, but an eschatological wisdom. These words, like miracles, make the future present. They give voice already to God's eschatological blessing. They still express principles, principles to which it is still both prudent and moral to conform, principles operative in God's cosmic sovereignty, whether we like it or not, but principles that are known, not in the distillation of commonplace experiences, but in the experience and memory of Jesus as the agent of God's good future.

Attention to the sources used by the one who scripted these words allows the reader to observe what the author did with the words at his disposal. The sources for Matthew included Mark and Q. It would be useful here, of course, to compare Luke's version of the Beatitudes with Matthew's to see what each did with the words available to them from their source, but I will leave such comparisons aside.[16]

I do want to call attention to the way Matthew orders his sources. It is clear that Matthew self-consciously orders his Gospel to include five discourses and that the Sermon on the Mount is the first discourse. It is also clear that Matthew utilizes Mark (1:14–19) to establish the narrative context for the Sermon on the Mount and for the collection of miracles that follows it. Before the first discourse, Matthew has announced to the reader that Jesus came proclaiming the kingdom and calling those who hear him to repentance (4:17); already the reader has heard the call to discipleship (4:18–22); and already the reader has been given a (Matthean) summary of the way God's future made its power felt in Jesus' ministry, in his teaching and healing (4:23–25), a summary repeated (9:35) after the account of Jesus' teaching in the first discourse and the account of Jesus' miracles in the next narrative.

What Matthew did with the words at his disposal permits (and requires) one to read and perform the Beatitudes not as a calculating works righteousness, not as a set of "entrance requirements," but as an account of the ways the good future of God already makes its power felt in the formation of character. So the church is called to a "surpassing righteousness," and so the church acts as "salt" and "light" and "gives glory" to God (5:13–16).

Attention to the Scripture as script invites and requires performance, and we do not interpret Scripture well without hearing and heeding that invitation. More could be said about the Beatitudes as scripted, but the Beatitudes are also script, and I would give some brief attention to a few of the ways they are "performed" in Christian community and to the ways attention to performance might make us better readers of Scripture as script.

One "performance" of Scripture is the sermon. A sermon on the Beatitudes is a "performance of Scripture" that must be tested for its creative fidelity to Scripture as scripted. A good sermon on the Beatitudes might perform the Beatitudes by announcing the manifestation of God's good future and by inviting the congregation both to welcome the signs of it in the lives and characters of the saints and to long for and to work for its manifestation in their own lives and in their common life. And a good sermon will help the hearers to be not only better performers of the Scripture as script but better interpreters of the Scripture as scripted.

Another "performance" of Scripture—and of the Beatitudes—is prayer. In *Remembering Jesus* I asked what a "prayer-formed reading of Scripture" would look like. But it is also possible to ask what "Scripture-formed prayers" look like, and in the case of the Beatitudes there are a number of exhibits.

The Beatitudes have been used to form prayers of confession. In prayers of confession we perform the Beatitudes by hearing the announcement of the good future of God in them as "over against ourselves" and by heeding the invitation to "repent," to mourn the fact the incipient appearance of God's good future in us is so insipid. In such humility before God we learn, I think, both to read and to perform the Beatitudes better.

The Beatitudes have also been used to form prayers of thanksgiving. In prayers of thanksgiving we perform the Beatitudes by celebrating the saints among us, by thanking God that there have been and are some in the community whose character and conduct have been formed by God's grace and future. In such gratitude to God for the saints, I think, we learn both to read and to perform the Beatitudes better.

The Beatitudes have also been used to form our petitions. The practice of prayer is corrupted when we use it as a kind of magic to get what we want, whether a fortune, or four more healthy years, or a resolution to an interpretive or moral dispute. When petition is a form of attention to God, however, then we pray—and pray boldly—that God's cause will be displayed, that God's good future will be present. We pray—and pray boldly—for a taste of that future, not so much in some ecstatic spiritual experience, but in such ordinary things as everyday bread and everyday mercy, in such mundane realities as tonight's rest and tomorrow's peace, in such earthly stuff as comfort for the grieving and justice for our communities. We form and govern our petitions by this vision of God's good future and by the aching acknowledgment that it is not yet, still sadly not yet. And in such petitions we learn to read and to perform the Beatitudes better.

Worship spills over into life, of course, and we perform the Beatitudes when we form and govern not only our petitions but our deeds by this vision of God's future and by aching acknowledgment that it is not yet. We perform the Beatitudes when we interpret not only these texts but our worlds in the context of the memory and the hope of the Christian community. We perform the Beatitudes when we form and re-form our communities and their politics into something fitting "a city (πόλις) set on a hill" (5:14). We perform the Beatitudes when we form character and conduct into something fitting the way the present is met in these words by God's good future.

So we will honor the humiliated, and be humble ourselves. So we will comfort those who mourn, and weep ourselves in aching acknowledgment that it is not yet God's future. So we will meekly serve the meek. We will hunger for justice—and work for it.

We will celebrate the merciful, and be generous in our judgment and with our gifts. We will extol Christian integrity. We will seek peace, and celebrate the peacemakers. We will remember those who suffer for the sake of God's cause in the world. And we will be patient, even as we wait and watch, "on tiptoe" with the whole creation (Rom. 8:19), looking for the appearance of God's good future.

And in such performances of the Beatitudes, I dare say, we will learn to be better readers of Scripture as scripted.

Notes

1. I owe this notion—and much more in this paper—to Nicholas Lash, "Performing the Scriptures," *Theology on the Way to Emmaus* (London: SCM Press, 1968), 37–46.
2. Nicholas Wolterstorff makes this distinction between "object" and "instrument" in *Art in Action: Toward a Christian Aesthetic* (Grand Rapids: Eerdmans, 1980), 80. Scripture is both the effect of the action of writing texts and the instrument that we use to perform certain other actions.
3. This story was told to me by my friend Dr. Robert Visscher. He also traced the source of the story: Patrick Henry, *The Ironic Christian's Companion* (New York: Penguin, 1999), 153; but in Patrick Henry's telling it was his mother-in-law who, while repeating the familiar table grace asked God to make us "ever needful of the minds of others."
4. I say surely, but the observation is not to be taken lightly, nor passed over without acknowledging a debt to tradition—indeed, various debts to various particular traditions. The Renaissance insisted upon returning to the classic texts in their original languages, and the fruits of its passion were the disciplines of textual criticism and historical philology. Both of these disciplines, of course, attend to Scripture as scripted, and both insist that the text *as written* is normative for interpretation. The Renaissance also gave priority finally to "the literal sense" in the interpretation of Scripture (J. H. Bentley, *Humanists and Holy Writ: New*

Testament Scholarship in the Renaissance [Princeton, NJ: Princeton University Press, 1983]), but it was the Reformation, of course, that famously insisted on the priority of "the literal sense." Luther and Calvin wanted to reform the church and its performances by appealing to "the plain sense" of Scripture. Neither of them was a biblical "literalist"; both recognized that the "plain sense" was sometimes "plainly" symbolic. But both insisted that the Scripture as scripted was somehow normative for the performance of the churches. It must be acknowledged, of course, that the Reformers read "the plain sense" in conjunction with "the rule of faith." Indeed, from the perspective of this paper it must be not only acknowledged but celebrated, for the Reformers recognized that attention to Scripture as scripted could not finally do without attention to Scripture as script, to Scripture as the intentional Word of God and somehow normative for the thought and life of the church, for its performances. In pursuit of "the plain sense" biblical scholars of modernity have worked on figuring out who wrote these texts and to whom, at what particular time and in response to what specific conditions they wrote them, what sources and genres the authors had available to them, whether and how they used and modified these sources and genres. And, of course, they continued to work on what particular words or expressions or figures meant in their cultural and social and literary contexts. We owe a great debt to this tradition of research, and we ought to be reminded that we are needful of the minds of others each time we pull one of the great introductions from our shelves. But a fateful shift occurred when the context shifted from the church to the university, or perhaps I should say when the university became "enlightened" and sought to transcend the particularity of particular traditions and communities, sought an "objective" reading and interpretation of Scripture, sought to read Scripture without understanding it as script for a particular community. In Romanticism the "plain meaning" became "the intended meaning," and the effort to discern the author's intention required an effort to get behind the text into the mind, the psyche, of the author. It has been widely observed that the effort to get inside the mind of the author is neither possible nor necessary to reading a text. Nevertheless, as long as speaking and writing are intentional activities, as long as people do things with the words they use, it seems impossible to do without some concept of intended meaning. It is not, however, some subjective state of affairs behind the text that must be attended to, but the text itself as a communicative act. To attend to the text as a communicative act will be to discern the text's intelligibility as embodied in what authors did with the words and traditions available to them. Nick Wolterstorff in *Divine Discourse* (Cambridge: Cambridge University Press, 1995) acknowledges that the practice of reading for authorial discourse has been under attack for half a century, but he defends it in order to support the "interpretative practice which assumes that the Christian Bible as a whole is a medium of divine discourse and . . . seeks to discern what God was saying by way of [a] particular passage from the whole" (131). One reason, he insists, that we have for reading (at least some) texts is "to find out what the person who authored the text was saying thereby" (132), that is to say, we read (at least some) texts for authorial discourse. Wolterstorff defends the legitimacy of the practice of authorial-discourse interpretation against Derrida's rejection of it, and he defends attention to the author's intention against Riceour's focus on textual sense interpretation. The salvageable and indeed necessary task is not to attempt to uncover some psychological state of affairs but to attend to the text as a "speech act," as intentional. In fact, against Riceour and the New Criticism, Wolterstorff claims that "textual sense" interpretation is not a coherent alternative to authorial-discourse interpretation because, whether "surreptitiously or openly," we will use authorial-discourse interpretation to determine the "sense of the text." We use it, for example, to determine that Locke's "reason is the candle of the Lord" is a metaphor (172–73).

6. See Stanley Fish, *Is There a Text in This Class? The Authority of Interpretive Communities* (Cambridge, MA: Harvard University Press, 1980), and Stanley Hauerwas, *Unleashing the Scriptures: Freeing the Bible from Captivity to America* (Nashville: Abingdon, 1993). I cite them for their emphasis on the community of readers, but a caveat must be mentioned. Both authors turn from the text (and from the author behind the text) to the reader in front of the text. Meaning for them is not in the text; it is created by the reader of the text. So interpretation is not simply conditioned by the interpretative community but determined by it.

7. David Kelsey, *The Uses of Scripture in Recent Theology* (Philadelphia: Fortress, 1957), 89–119. "Part of what it means to call a community of persons 'church' . . . is that use of 'scriptures' is essential to the preservation and shaping of their self-identity [and] part of what it means to call certain writings 'scripture' is that . . . they ought to be used in the common life of the church to nourish and reform it" (98).

8. See Hans-Georg Gadamer, *Truth and Method* (New York: Crossroad, 1989), 300–307, and his notion of *wirkungsgeschichliches Bewusstsein* ("historically effected consciousness").

9. The point was forcibly made by Clayton Libolt at the meeting of the AAR/SBL where this paper was first read that the Bible is not *either* "canon" *or* a little library of ancient Near Eastern religious literature, but *both*. A faithful reading of the text, therefore, need not dismiss the contributions of historical-critical scholarship but render them serviceable to the interpretation of the parts of the canon.

10. Lash, "Performing the Scriptures," 40.

11. Nicholas Lash observed not only that "the fundamental form of the *Christian* interpretation of scripture is the life, activity and organization of the believing community" but also that biblical scholarship and critical reflection make an "indispensable contribution" to the "performative interpretation of scripture" ("Performing the Scriptures," 42–43). For Lash there is no "performative interpretation," no set of practices in particular communities, in which the "meaning" of Scripture is definitively captured, and, because this is so, "the range of appropriate interpretations . . . is constrained by what the text 'originally meant'" (44). The performative interpretation that "*is* the life of the church" must also always, therefore, be open to reform and renewal by the effort to understand Scripture as scripted and by reflection about the relation of such interpretation to performative interpretation.

12. See further Stephen E. Fowl and L. Gregory Jones, *Reading in Communion: Scripture and Ethics in Christian Life* (Grand Rapids: Eerdmans, 1991), and Allen Verhey, *Remembering Jesus: Christian Community, Scripture, and the Moral Life* (Grand Rapids: Eerdmans, 2002), 57–76.

13. There are other ways to characterize the wholeness of Scripture, of course. See further Kelsey, *Uses of Scripture.*

14. Fidelity to the narrative requires a process of continual change, of creativity. Without it performance of the script is rendered anachronistic eccentricity. Nicholas Lash makes the point quite nicely with respect to the traditions of ecclesiastical dress among the Franciscans. "If, in thirteenth-century Italy, you wandered around in a coarse brown gown," he said, ". . . your dress said you were one of the poor. If, in twentieth-century Cambridge, you wander around in a coarse brown gown, . . . your dress now says, not that you are one of the poor, but that you are some kind of oddity in the business of 'religion'" ("Performing the Scriptures," 54). Samuel Wells, *Improvisation: The Drama of Christian Ethics* (Grand Rapids: Brazos Press, 2004), 62–63, objects to the notion of the performance of

a script as insufficiently creative. The notion of performance, he says, fails "to make some allowance for the new circumstances," "gives the impression that the Bible encompasses the whole of the church's narrative," "suggests the recreation of a golden era," and "can militate against genuine engagement with the world" (63). If these charges were accurate, the notion of performance of Scripture as script would indeed have to be given up, but I think the notion of performance not only has room for creativity but requires it, and I worry that the notion of "improvisation" does not sufficiently emphasize fidelity. Even so, with its emphasis on an interpretative and performative community and its attention to the "drama" of Scripture and of Christian ethics, Wells's book makes a wonderful contribution to the relation of Scripture and Christian ethics.

15. See James M. Robinson, "The Formal Structure of Jesus' Message," in *Current Issues in New Testament Interpretation: Essays in Honor of Otto Piper*, ed. William Klassen and Graydon Synder (New York: Harper & Row, 1962), 91–110.

16. In Luke the Beatitudes display Jesus as the one anointed to preach good news to the poor (see Luke 4:17–19).

Chapter 3

The Reorienting Potential of Biblical Narrative for Christian Ethos, with Special Reference to Luke 7:36–50

ELNA MOUTON

> *The task of hermeneutical appropriation requires an integrative act of imagination. . . . [W]henever we appeal to the authority of the [Bible], we are . . . placing our community's life imaginatively within the world articulated by the texts.*
>
> (Hays 1990, 45–46)

Through the ages—at least until the Enlightenment—Christian believers listened to, interpreted, and appropriated the Bible in a great variety of ways with a view to understanding *their everyday lives.* They were not so much interested in the Bible itself or in the *academic* or *intellectual* study of the Bible, but in the Bible as canon, as norm—a guiding lamp, a light for their path. Without appropriating the Bible into their needs, challenges, suffering, fears, and hopes, reading would for many be incomplete and pointless. For them the Bible would be useful only insofar as it helped them to live *coram Deo* (see Smit 1998a, 275–91).

Since the Enlightenment, however, the Bible has been approached differently, by means of different sets of questions. Paradoxically, people often became more interested in the ancient canon as an object for study—as distinguished from understanding life by means of it. The questions asked of the Bible were increasingly scientific, theoretical, 'objective,' instead of being personal, existential, and related to the life situations of its recipients (Smit 1998a, 291–96).

This is a revised and expanded version of "The (trans)formative potential of the Bible as resource for Christian ethos and ethics," *Scriptura* 62 (1997): 45–57. I gladly acknowledge the research assistance of, and stimulating discussions with Christelle Bekker during its preparation.

At the moment—broadly speaking, since World War I—Christianity is going through a phase during which many believers worldwide are rediscovering the (trans)formative potential of the Bible for their daily lives. The cumulative debate regarding the use of Scripture in Christian ethos and ethics needs to be appreciated within this context.[1] It forms part of a much broader discussion among literary critics on "the ethics of interpretation" (Fiorenza 1988; Smit 1990a, 1990b, 1991a, 1998b; Botha 1994a, 1994b), which emphasizes that people take responsibility for their acts of reading—both with regard to the nature of the literature involved and the sociohistorical contexts within which it is being read. An ethics of biblical interpretation is concerned with the multidimensional, relational nature of the Bible (representing a wide variety of witnesses to a relationship between a living God and historical human beings in their sociocultural realities), and its appropriation in terms of contemporary experiences and needs.[2]

Faith communities explicitly appeal to, or implicitly presuppose, the continuing authority of biblical writings when using them to explain and justify moral arguments and behavior. The question is not whether the Bible is authoritative for Christians, but how authority is defined, and how its continuing relevance across times and cultures is understood. That this is by no means a straightforward issue is evident from the variety of ways in which the Bible has been interpreted and appropriated during the course of history.[3] The wonder and complexity of the matter are *inter alia* due to the dynamic, yet intricate nature of the biblical documents themselves (Lategan 1982), as well as the vast temporal, sociohistorical, and philosophical differences between the worlds of the Bible and of contemporary audiences. These factors account for differences between biblical and Christian ethos and ethics.[4] This is confirmed by the hermeneutical approach of "contextual" (e.g., feminist) interpreters who view with suspicion the Bible as a resource for the Christian life, because it is embedded in the patriarchal value system of the ancient Near Eastern world, and because of its silence on, for example, slavery as an institution. In light of the differences between biblical and Christian ethos, the ethics of interpretation holds contemporary readers responsible for their understanding of the authority of Scripture, and particularly for the consistent appropriation of the implied rhetorical effects of those writings.

This essay views biblical authority with the acknowledgment of the dynamic, complex linguistic, literary, sociocultural, and theological-rhetorical nature of these texts. In accordance with their implied moral effects, readings have to be legitimized by corresponding publicly accountable, trustworthy ways of living (Mouton 2001, 122–23; 2002, 176–201). Since both biblical studies and Christian ethics have developed with their own range and focus, it needs to be emphasized how they complement each other. What makes this an urgent moral issue is not only the integrity and relevance of the Bible as resource for Christian ethics, but more acutely, its influence on contemporary audiences' understanding of God, their identities, and public ethos.[5]

Consequently, a primary concern for biblical scholars and Christian ethicists is how the Bible could influence and transform the identity and ethos, the language, story, and culture of individual people and contemporary societies (Smit 1991b, 59–63; see 1990a, 1992, 1994b, 1997). Mindful that the Bible is read and lived out in diverse ways, I shall focus on its potential role in liturgy as a context for forming and nurturing the moral identity and ethos of faith communities.

Shaping a Sense of Belonging

From my early childhood the Bible inspired and intrigued me as a witness to the story of an awesome God who is involved in the everyday lives of ordinary people. It had a profound influence on my imagination and grasp of reality—as an invitation to be consoled, challenged, molded by a caring God in relation to humanity and the rest of creation. It became "the house in which I learned to live," where I belonged, where I felt secure and at home.

However, it was only as a postgraduate student in biblical and religious studies that I realized—with both disillusion and relief—that in accordance with its dynamic yet complex, relational nature, the Bible does not provide readers with neat, ready-made theological doctrines or ethical answers for all times and circumstances. The subsequent phases of disorientation and reorientation were liberating parts of my journey back to the same documents, yet with a new, more tentative understanding of their probable functions in the life of the church. I discovered that the Bible, instead of being prescriptive to all Christians in the same way, rather resembles the creative processes through which the early faith communities wrestled to understand the will of God for their particular time (see Meeks 1986; 1993, 1–17, 109–10). Characteristic of these processes of understanding were their continuous orientation to the revelation of a living God during the course of history (Mouton 2002, 189–201).

For those participants in the Judeo-Christian story—both in the Hebrew Scriptures and the New Testament—the cult, its festivals, and its liturgy provided the moral space, the frame of reference, the horizons for a reality within which they collectively expressed and cultivated their vision of and trust in an omnipotent God. Through rituals of public worship (sacrifices, hymns, confessions of faith and guilt, prayers, blessings, listening to the covenant stories and the Torah, and later the participation in baptism and the Eucharist) they were reminded of, empowered, and encouraged by who God is and by what God had done in the past. By retelling and reactualizing their stories from within the covenant relation, their moral identity and ethos as God's alternative family, as "a community of character" (Hauerwas 1981; see Richardson 1994), was shaped and constituted.[6] Collective memory thus played a crucial role in the formation of their self-understanding—not only the memory of times of harmony and peace, but also the deliberate recalling and uncovering of past sins and negligence. Through repentance and reconciliation, remembering became a hopeful act, a confession of faith in the living God of history, which opened up new perspectives on the present and future (see Mouton 1997n8). Closely related to cultic practices, the process of moral formation found its focus in the context of family life (see Deut. 6:6–25; 1 Pet. 3:1–7; Eph. 5:21–6:9 and other domestic codes in the NT).

Similarly, the biblical documents have stimulated and facilitated an ongoing process of interpretation (see Verhey 1984, 179–87). The imperative of such an ongoing process is in fact implied in the very nature of these texts (Lategan 1982, 48–50; Fowl and Jones 1991, 36–44). Ethical interpretations of the Bible by subsequent audiences therefore calls for continuous imaginative, Spirit-filled, critical, and faithful reflection on the active presence of God in ever-changing times and circumstances. In this sense biblical scholars and Christian ethicists share the moral obligation to engage in the creative tension between the dynamics of biblical texts and their 'moral worlds,' and the 'socio-cultural worlds' of present-day readers (Fiorenza 1988, 13)—between history and eschatology, between remembrance and hope. It is the creativity of in-between, liminal stages that provided the biblical authors with the stimulus, values, and virtues to redefine their humanity and moral existence in different times and places, under diverse circumstances (see Mouton 2003; McFague 1982, 154).

The experience of God on the threshold between (past) memory and (future) hope (Russell 1985, 139) is epitomized in the ministry, death, resurrection, and ascension of Jesus Christ. The Christ event challenged and reshaped previous experiences and interpretations of the God of the Hebrew Scriptures (see Johnson 1999, 93–153). In Jesus, God is found in places where God would otherwise not be perceived. In Jesus, God is dramatically present at the margins of human existence. This is not to say that God is not at the center of life, but in Jesus the center shifts to marginal people and places. Jesus is born in a place where no child was meant to be born, and Jesus dies at a place where criminals were executed. Through the trauma of his death, humiliation, and shame, a shocking vision of God is presented. The ultimate site where God would not be perceived, paradoxically becomes the site of God's presence. As such, the cross not only reveals human sin, but concretizes the presence of God in the midst of human sin.

This radical reversal reveals not only who God is, but also what it means to be human, with radical implications for all forms of life. In showing compassion to children, tax collectors, Samaritans, women (particularly prostitutes and the demon-possessed), Jesus subverts the values of power in the moral world of first-century Palestine. In shifting the center to the margins and the margins to the center, God's concrete presence in Jesus becomes a radical shock, inviting people to see things differently, to adopt new roles, to reorient their understanding of God and traditions in light of God's liberating presence in Christ (2 Cor. 5:17; see Mouton 2001, 121–22).

The identity and ethos of the Jesus followers and early Christian communities was thus determined by their *reorientation* to this alien, yet for them *truthful* story of Jesus Christ—a story that was characterized particularly by the shameful symbol of a *cross*. This symbol was reinterpreted and became an honorable symbol for those who adhere to Christ by faith (Meeks 1993, 14–15, 131–35; Olyan 1996). The dramatic consequences of his death and exaltation for both Jews and Gentiles are described in transitional terms: Those who were dead have been made alive; those who were far away, excluded from citizenship in Israel, have been brought near; and those who formerly had been without power and status, foreigners and aliens, have been made fellow citizens with God's people and members of God's household (Eph. 2). In this way Christ gave birth to a new creation, a new humanity with a new identity and lifestyle.

In general terms one may summarize the implied moral effect of the biblical writings as the radical revisioning of life from within a faith relationship with a living God. Christian life is about living in relation to the mystery of the Triune God (Smit 1997, with reference to L. Gregory Jones).[7] Within such processes of continuous reorientation the transformative potential of these texts is experienced by later audiences. How could such processes work?

The Referential Power of Biblical Narrative as a Key to Its Transformative Potential

With respect to the transformative aspects of the biblical documents, I shall focus on the (re)orientating potential of metaphor and story.[8] My interest in metaphor and story lies particularly in their referential and relational nature (Lategan 1985, 1994, 1996, 223–29; Van Huyssteen 1987). Lategan (1994, 134) rightly claims that a "better understanding of the function of reference in all its forms holds the key to unlock the transformative potential of (biblical) texts in contemporary situations." According to Ricoeur (1975; 1976, 89–95; 1977, 216–56), the referential or transformative power of a text lies in its ability to suggest, to open up, to facilitate, to mediate, to make possible, to produce (glimpses or fragments of) a "world in front of it," a "proposed world" that readers may adopt or inhabit, an alternative point of view with which they can identify. In this way a text discloses a possible new way of looking at things (see Thiselton 1992, 351–72; Lategan 1992, 154; 1994, 131–33).

Since the development of reader response theories, Iser's concept of the 'implied reader' became a powerful tool in describing the role of readers in the process of understanding. The implied or textually defined reader refers to "the anticipated role a potential reader is expected to play in order to actualize the text . . . (It) is a device to engage the real reader by offering a role to be played or an attitude to be assumed" (Lategan 1989, 5, 10). In this sense metaphor, tradition (as extended metaphor), and parable (story) are important lenses, clues, signals or shifting devices by means of which an author can instruct or guide an audience toward adopting a preferred position or inhabiting a new moral world. In helping them to *see* differently, these lenses may help readers to integrate and redescribe their experiences—insofar as they are willing to accept their alternative perspectives. As creative acts of remembrance and dismembrance, metaphor and story then become crucial instruments for moral formation.

Metaphors and stories function on two important levels. First, they are used to identify different dispensations and preferred or nonpreferred positions, attitudes, and actions. Second, they are used "*to effect the shifting of position*" (Lategan 1993, 402). Indicating preferred and nonpreferred positions is one thing. To achieve a shift in the right direction is quite another. How do the biblical authors ensure the desired result? How do they influence readers to accept their new position and lifestyle *coram Deo*? And how is the change of attitude and behavior on the side of the audience supposed to take place?

For the biblical authors the key to moral formation and change of viewpoint is provided by the interrelated communication processes of *orientation, disorientation,* and *reorientation* (Ricoeur 1976, 46–53; 1977, 65–100; McFague 1982, 46–48), or *association* and *disassociation* (Lategan 1993, 402). These processes essentially reveal the reorientating or transformative potential of metaphorical language, which forms the heart of biblical hermeneutics.[9] I briefly show how the memory of Jesus can function metaphorically in liturgy.

With reference to McFague (1982, 31–66, 90–194), Jesus' role in the early Christian writings and in ongoing moral formation may be described as that of an extended "metaphor or parable for God," and a "model for Christian behavior."[10] These notions provide important insight into the processes through which the Christian story may impact on biblical readers by continuously reorienting their self-understanding and ethos as disciples of Jesus Christ:

> If we say . . . that Jesus of Nazareth is par excellence the metaphor of God, we mean that his familiar, mundane story is the *way*, the indirect but necessary way, from here to there. . . . (M)etaphoric meaning is a *process*, not a momentary, static insight; it operates like a story, moving from here to there, from "what is" to "what might be." (McFague 1975, 32–33)

Like metaphor, the essence of parable or narrative is that it works through the ordinary, mundane, and secular—by indirection—to bring about new insight. This means that we start with the (more familiar) work of Jesus from "below," and move to the invisible (unfamiliar) God whom Jesus represents. The whole network of Jesus' life thus provides a grid through which the understanding of God may be redefined or *reoriented* (see McFague 1982, 49–54; Hays 1990, 45–50; Ricoeur 1975, 122–28; 1976, 89–95; 1977, 216–56). As a true and novel parable, Jesus reorders, shocks, and upsets familiar, conventional preconceptions and understandings of God. In this sense liturgy should distance (alienate) its participants from the obvious values and virtues of their life and traditions by offering them alternative perspectives and lifestyles. I have chosen Jesus' anointing by a woman in Luke 7:36–50 to suggest how such a reading process works.

To summarize, the starting point of persuasive strategies is the delicate tension between identification, alienation, and reorientation. For later readers these processes hold the key to the transformative potential of the biblical documents. To inhabit their strange, alternative world is as much a gift of God's grace as a faithful hermeneutical choice: "In a cooperative shared work, the Spirit, the text, and the reader engage in *a transforming process*, which enlarges horizons and creates *new horizons*" (Thiselton 1992, 619).

(Re)imagining God through Jesus' Response
to a "Woman in the City" (Luke 7:36–50)

Unlike the other Gospel writers,[11] Luke places the account of a woman anointing Jesus outside the passion narrative, in the context of Jesus' ministry in Galilee (Luke 4:14–9:50).[12] The narrator reconfigures the story of Jesus in a sociopolitical context probably after the Jewish-Roman war of 66–70 CE. Of all the Jewish religious groups, only the Pharisees seem to have been able to regroup after the destruction of the temple, evidently with greater emphasis on the observance of their interpretation of Torah than before. By 85 CE the Pharisees accepted a clause in which the Jesus followers were cursed and banned from their synagogues (Bosch 1993, 2–10).

Against this background the question may be raised as to how Luke's audience was supposed to (re)imagine God through Jesus' response to the unnamed woman in Luke 7. I start with a brief look at the immediate literary context within which the anointing story is situated. In the Lukan narrative, 7:36–50 occurs after Jesus' authority as a teacher and healer has been revealed—*inter alia* through his Sermon on the Plain (6:17–49), the healing of a centurion's servant (7:1–10), and the raising of a widow's son from Nain (7:11–17). The story unfolds according to the program that Jesus announced in Nazareth (4:16–21), whereby his earthly ministry would focus on ἄφεσις (4:18), his encompassing power (δύναμις, 4:14; 5:17) to heal, and his authority ἐξουσία, 5:24) to forgive sins and to release all kinds of captives (such as poor and socially disowned people, the sick and demon-possessed, strangers and outsiders).[13]

Beginning in 5:17, the narrator shows special interest in Jesus as the proclaimer of the release of sins by artfully connecting a diverse group of stories related to this theme. As each new episode is sounded, the audience is able to recall and compare related episodes with enriching harmonies (Tannehill 1986, 103–9). The story of the healing of the paralytic in 5:17–26 is Jesus' first encounter with the scribes and Pharisees and the beginning of a series of controversies with them (see 5:27–32; 7:18–50). It is also the first reference in Luke to Jesus' forgiving sins, and it is presented in such a way that the audience may know that Jesus' authority is epitomized by his divine power to release sinners (5:24).

Luke 7:36–50 is the final unit of the section 7:1–50, in which the relationship between the ministries of John the Baptist and Jesus has been the leitmotif. Luke 7:18–50 has a number of points of contact with previous material. The question of John in 7:19 (σὺ εἶ ὁ ἐρχόμενος ἢ ἄλλον προσδοκῶμεν;—"Are you the one who is to come, or are we to wait for another?") allows Jesus to summarize his previous activity. In 7:29–30 the narrator remarks that all the people except the Pharisees and lawyers acknowledged God's purpose and were baptized by John.[14] In 7:31–35 Jesus responds to criticism of his association with tax collectors and sinners. This leads into the story of anointing in vv. 36–50, which illustrates by way of an extreme example the narrator's observation in vv. 29–30. Jesus' response is concluded by an idiomatic expression in 7:35 (καὶ ἐδικαιώθη ἡ σοφία ἀπὸ πάντων τῶν τέκνων αὐτῆς, "Nevertheless, wisdom is vindicated by all her children"). This is probably a revised version of a saying from Q (see Matt. 11:19; Sir. 26:29) and suggests that Luke understands Jesus to say that "wisdom shows her true potential when a broad range of humanity is enclosed in her family" (Danker 1988, 168)—including tax collectors, sinners, and (other) outsiders. In the context, divine wisdom is justified over against/despite her children who have rejected her (Marshall 1978, 303). It would also imply that wise persons "prove their social abilities by the outcomes of their behavior" (Malina and Rohrbaugh 2003, 254–55). The story of 7:36–50 exemplifies this saying.

The passage occurs directly before references to (other) women who served Jesus (8:1–3) and various parables, which are all about listening, perceiving, and understanding (see 8:4–21). This is followed by Jesus' calming of a storm, to which his disciples respond with fear and amazement, asking: "Who then is this, that he commands even the winds and the water, and they obey him?" (8:22–25). Further healings are reported (8:26–56; 9:37–43), Jesus sends out the twelve (9:1–9), feeds five thousand people (9:10–17), and subsequently confronts his disciples with: "Who do you say that I am?" (9:18–21). Jesus announces his death for the first time (9:22–27), thereafter his identity is affirmed by a voice from the cloud ("This is my Son, my Chosen," 9:28–36). He refers to his betrayal and death a second time, but the disciples still do not understand the meaning of his words (9:44–45). Jesus then uses a little child to explain what it means to be the greatest in God's kingdom (9:46–50). This is followed by the beginning of Jesus' journey to Jerusalem (9:51), where he will be executed by religious leaders who "rejected God's purpose for themselves" (7:30).

Luke 7:36–50 thus occurs in a literary context of utterances on the radical nature of Jesus' divine power and authority (ultimately to forgive sins), on God's alternative kingdom, on prophetic wisdom, the Pharisees' (and even disciples') lack of understanding, and the crowds' responses of amazement and awe.

With respect to the contents of the pericope, John Nolland (1989, 353) makes the following broad structural observations:

> The material of the pericope is structured around three instances of report and accompanying evaluation (vv. 36–38/39; vv. 40–42/43; vv. 44–46/47) with vv. 48–50 as an epilogue. The unit vv. 36–39 is bracketed by the mention of the Pharisee in the opening and closing verses. In vv. 40–43 the extremities are marked by bracketing in a chiastic form: in v. 40 Jesus asks for an audience and Simon agrees; in v. 43 Simon produces his judgment and Jesus agrees. In v. 39 and v. 43 the evaluations are those of Simon. Failing to recognize the equivalence between the situation of vv. 37–38 and that of the story in vv. 40–42, he passes opposite judgments in the two situations. Vv. 44–46 function to uncover the equivalence by retelling vv. 37–38 in light of vv. 40–42. Then in this third sequence of report and evaluation, the Pharisee who has passed judgment in the first two sequences becomes

now the one whose judgment is itself judged. The epilogue vv. 48–50 brings the story to its completion by allowing Jesus to address the woman whose behavior has been the subject of his interchange with Simon.

An Impure Woman Near a Pharisee's Table?

The literary link to the previous passage is established at once by the introduction of the first (as yet unnamed) character, "one of the Pharisees" (7:36), and the fourfold repetition of "Pharisee" in verses 36–39. Jesus is invited by a Pharisee (later referred to as Simon) to have dinner at his house.[15] Jesus "took his place at the table" (v. 36) / "reclined at the table" (NIV) (κατεκλίθη), which indicates that the Pharisee was hosting a significant meal, probably a luxury meal (Robbins 1996, 90)—a formal banquet or Sabbath meal. "It was quite common to invite a visiting rabbi or teacher to the Sabbath meal after he had taught in the synagogue. If it was a banquet meal, Jesus may have been invited because of his reputation as a prophet" (Stein 1992, 235–36; see Fitzmyer 1981, 688). They were dining "in the Hellenistic manner which was to lounge on one's side, with the feet pointing away from the table" (Johnson 1991, 127; see Malina and Rohrbaugh 2003, 256; Taylor 2004, 30–31, 42–45). The reclining posture (which the Jews had adopted for festive banquets) would make Jesus' feet most accessible, and probably accounts for the later attention to the feet. Charles Talbert (1984, 86) notes that in the ancient Near East "the door of the dining room was left open so the uninvited could pass in and out during the festivities. They were allowed to take seats by the wall, listening to the conversation between the host and guests" (see Bock 1994, 694).

In continuation with the theme of 7:34 (Jesus being called "a friend of sinners"), a second character is introduced, an unnamed "woman in the city who was a sinner" (γυνὴ ἥτις ἦν ἐν τῇ πόλει ἁμαρτωλός, v. 37). By introducing the woman at the beginning of what appears to be the Pharisee's story, the narrator emphasizes her role from the outset. Of particular importance is the introductory καὶ ἰδού ("behold") in verse 37 (see 7:34), alerting the audience to an unusual development and important point to be made (Danker 1988, 169), often associated with a prophetic utterance. According to Nolland (1989, 353) it is best to connect ἐν τῇ πόλει with ἁμαρτωλός, and to give it in accord with Semitic idiom a sense like "publicly known." He continues by saying that "(t)he dramatic impact of the woman's actions appears most strikingly if 'sinner' is understood as a euphemism for 'prostitute' or 'courtesan'" (1989, 353; see 360).[16] As a member of the (silent) spectator-audience, she takes initiative and boldly steps forward, bringing with her a precious alabaster jar of perfumed oil. It seems that her intention to anoint Jesus is "the single aspect of the woman's behavior which is indicated as clearly premeditated. The alabaster jar here is a flask carved from the expensive soft alabaster which was believed to help preserve ointments and perfumes" (Nolland 1989, 354; see 355, 361; Mark 14:3). She comes prepared in a way fit for anointing a king. Crossing sociocultural boundaries, she steps into a public space where a ritually impure woman would not be expected—least of all in a Pharisee's house![17] She stands behind Jesus at his feet, weeping, and begins to bathe his feet with her tears and to dry them with her hair.[18] The story intensifies as the narrator reports: "Then she *continued kissing* his feet (κατεφίλει—imperfect) and anointing them with the ointment" (v. 38).[19]

Jesus' passivity in the face of this behavior is extremely eloquent (v. 39). That he allows the woman to act in this way evokes a negative response from his host. In a "moral world" where collective honor was a pivotal value, associating with or accepting actions of a shameless person would bring shame to oneself. In fact, to take a shameless person seriously and to show courtesy to her/him would make one a fool (Malina 1993, 39, 45, 53–54; Malina & Rohrbaugh 2003, 255; see York 1991, 123n4). When the Pharisee *saw* (ἰδών) what the woman did he said to himself, "If this man were a prophet ("the" prophet—Nolland 1989, 350–51), he would have known who and what kind of woman this is who is touching him—that she is a sinner" (οὗτος εἰ ἦν προφήτης, ἐγίνωσκεν ἂν τίς καὶ ποταπὴ ἡ γυνὴ ἥτις ἅπτεται αὐτοῦ, ὅτι ἁμαρτωλός ἐστιν—v. 39).[20] Apparently it is not the intrusion of a woman per se that was such a shock and a scandal to Simon's Pharisaic sensibilities, but that it was this particular woman:

> *Yet worse* . . . was the failure of his guest, Jesus, to repulse her attentions. . . . Jesus accepts it all and Simon is confirmed in his skepticism about the popular view that Jesus might be a prophet (see 7:16; 9:19). *Ironically*, Jesus, aware both of the woman's condition and of Simon's state of mind, fulfills precisely Simon's conception of prophetic awareness. (Nolland 1989, 361; emphasis mine)[21]

The Pharisee's question in verse 39 puts the central issue of the narrative, namely Jesus' authority and identity—and thus his honor—on the table (see v. 49). "By accepting the actions of a shameless person, Jesus was bringing shame to himself. He therefore could not possibly be God's prophet. However, the story makes clear that . . . rather than losing his own honor, Jesus restores the honor of the woman" (York 1991, 123). At the same time two ironic references to "seeing" in verses 39 and 44—ὁράω and βλέπω respectively—emphasize the Pharisee's inability to see, to observe, to perceive, to recognize, to be aware, to understand, to discern prophetically (by implication, like Jesus and like the woman; see Taylor 2004, 72–76).

Jesus is the first character to speak. Aware of the Pharisee's thinking, he takes initiative—addressing the Pharisee by his name[22]—and tells him a brief story of a creditor who had two debtors. One owed 500 and the other 50 denarii (a denarius being about a day's wage for an agricultural laborer [Johnson 1991, 127; Nolland 1989, 355]). When neither could pay him back, he canceled the debts for both. The spare reporting of the parable may suggest that the focus is on what is to come in Jesus' follow-up question. Jesus interrogates Simon in the so-called Socratic style (Danker 1988, 170–71; Talbert 1984, 86) by asking, "Now which of them will love him more," that is, will be more grateful? (Johnson 1991, 127; Nolland 1989, 356). The Pharisee responds rather halfheartedly by saying

"I suppose the one for whom he canceled the greater debt." In spite of possible reservations on the Pharisee's side, Jesus commends his answer.[23]

Turning toward the woman, Jesus then says to Simon: "Do you see this woman?" (v. 44), that is, "Do you not recognize in this woman's behavior the love of one who has been forgiven much?" (Nolland 1989, 356, 361). Jesus now inter- prets her courageous actions toward him by contrasting it with the Pharisee's omission of hospitality rituals—water for cleansing his feet, a kiss of greeting, and oil for anointing his head (vv. 44–46).[24] Jesus uses the parable ironically to show why the woman has performed special acts of hospitality, thereby implicitly unmasking Simon's failure to accept God's forgiveness and love.[25] In these verses the "imagery of being a good host(ess) in receiving Jesus takes the place of what was earlier viewed as a display of affectionate gratitude by a forgiven debtor" (Nolland 1989, 357). Since Simon does not recognize the relationship between the woman's actions (vv. 37–38) and the parable (vv. 41–42), Jesus uses the para- ble artistically "to uncover the equivalence, by *retelling* verses 37–38 in light of verses 40–42" (Nolland 1989, 357; emphasis mine). In the reiteration,

> Jesus describes not only Simon, but also the woman, as performing the role of the host. As a host Simon has not been impolite or rude. Throughout, his behavior has been correct, but *only* correct. By contrast the woman has shown those marks of thoughtfulness and honor which would mark the hos- pitality of a host who owed a debt of affectionate gratitude to his [*sic*] guest. It is precisely in that which goes beyond the immediate polite demands of respectability that this woman's true attitude comes to expression. (Nolland 1989, 361; see 357)

Jesus then concludes their dialogue: "Therefore, I tell you, her sins, which were many, have been forgiven (ἀφέωνται, perfect passive); hence she has shown great love."[26] The point is clear: Because her "many sins" had been forgiven, she hon- ored Jesus lavishly in a moment of sacred affection and gratitude (see v. 42). She welcomed God into her life—literally and ironically to "host" God's love and for- giveness. "But the one to whom little is forgiven, loves little" (v. 47).

At this moment Jesus turns to the woman and says: "Your sins are forgiven" (v. 48). . . . "Your faith has saved you; go in peace" (v. 50).[27] Up to this point Jesus has quietly allowed the woman's display of affection without directing his attention to her. However, by deliberately turning toward her, he now draws together the threads from verses 37–39 and 40–43. As a result the other guests are amazed and ask: "Who is this who even forgives sins?" (v. 49). Could this amazement reflect their recognition of God's wisdom behind the actions of both Jesus and John—wisdom that here found yet another of her children (v. 35)?

The story of the unconventional anointing of Jesus by this woman in Simon's house conveys an ironical reversal of the roles of both characters initially pre- sented in the narrative:

> In the beginning the Pharisee is the host, the woman is a sinner. He is inside; she is outside. He has honor; she is shameless. As the story develops, she acts

hospitably; he fails to show any special kindness towards Jesus. She understands him to be a prophet; he rejects Jesus' prophetic character. She is forgiven much and loves much; he is forgiven little and loves little. . . . She now has honor; Simon is shamed. The outsider has become an insider; Simon, the supposed insider, has become an outsider. (York 1991, 125–26)

Luke 7:36–50 portrays Jesus as one who has compassion on sinners, liberates and heals them, and allows them to serve him, even lavishly. This is how Christian communities toward the end of the first century remembered Jesus (see Moltmann-Wendel 1982; Dunn 2003, 543–611). Yet what would be the rhetorical effect of the passage? What was it supposed to *do* to its audience?

It seems that Luke was creating a particular frame of reference, a moral horizon, glimpses of an alternative world with its own distinctive atmosphere and language, images, values, dispositions, habits, which was meant to be inhabited by Jesus' followers (see Meeks 1986; Smit 1991b, 59, with reference to Lindbeck). How was this supposed to happen? The narrator uses the story of a most unlikely character from within that moral world as a parable, a metaphorical lens through which the radical nature of Jesus' identity and ministry could be recognized. Jesus' prophetic wisdom—his reversal of the expected order—challenges the usual assumptions about what would be regarded as honorable in a fundamental way. Although the anointing woman is mute throughout the story (see Dewey 1996, 1997), she is "open to God's mercy" and reveals "a more basic orientation to God" than does the Pharisee (Fitzmyer 1981, 687). Through her actions she acknowledges Jesus' liberating, healing authority. Her great love and gratitude toward him allow her to act freely and creatively, to risk and be vulnerable, to imagine new possibilities of serving God amid sterile sociocultural and religious conventions.[28]

The story is open ended. Later audiences fill gaps such as where the woman would find a safe moral environment after Jesus sent her away in peace (7:50), and where the Pharisee would find creative space to engage his position in light of his encounter with the "friend of sinners."

Continuing Encounters with the Living God

The transformative potential of this story, and biblical narrative in general, lies in its referential power, its ability to point beyond itself to an awesome reality that it could describe only in limited human language: the rich and full story of God's engagement with creation. Its authority—its liberating and healing power for subsequent audiences—resides in encounters with the living God mediated by it (see Lategan 1992, 154; 1994, 131–33; Mouton 2002, 192–94). Such encounters do not necessarily allow for final answers, decisions, and certainties. They rather encourage and challenge us to live patiently and humbly with glimpses of God's presence in the world and with the creative tension of risk, paradox, pain, and even ridicule.

In continuation with the dynamics of the anointment story, a further question (after the how question) would be a where question. Where could such attitudes and virtues develop? Where could encounters with a living God and members of this God's household be embodied?

Of all the contexts that may be conducive to shaping our moral worlds, I focus briefly on the reorienting role of liturgy—probably the primary context where this text functioned in the early church (Mouton 2001, 123–25). The worship service as the central point of all ecclesial activities and experiences is essentially transformative and rhetorical in nature.[29] It is the primary context where believers are continuously constituted and affirmed as a "community of character," as the "household of God." It is the primary location where they remember God's involvement in their and others' biographies and where they acquire a collective identity—where they learn who they are and whose they are. This is where they dream about God's eschatological future that has already become a reality in Christ, and from where they are sent out to care for one another and the world. From this *liturgy*, God's household—as a social, communicative, domestic, economic entity—moves into society to proclaim God's presence in the *liturgy* of everyday life.

In worship the Spirit shapes and refines our senses: We learn to listen to God's words, to each other and to the needs of society and the world. We learn to feel, to smell, to taste. We learn to look and see and be surprised in new ways. We learn to see God differently—with awe and reverence—and to see one another differently, as well as the vulnerable and fragile realities within and around us. Through the liturgical elements the Spirit teaches us to discern an impartial God's radical presence in this world as well as the world to come. Around the eucharistic table—the sign of the coming feast of God's restored creation—we get glimpses of God's encompassing love and hospitality. Luke's anointment story not only embodies this reality but also points toward other passages where Jesus is hosted by a Pharisee (11:37; 14:1). In the latter instance the guest list suggested by Jesus (14:12–14) derives from the announcements of the Jubilee year in ancient Israel. Indeed, the Spirit teaches us passionately to yearn for God's will to be done on earth, and to groan with creation in labor pains for the fulfilment of God's promises.

In Luke the heart of the drama of Jesus' life and death is the tension that it manifests between *accepted ways of relating to God and others*, and *new ways of living in the world* (see McFague 1982, 51–54). In concert with the story in Luke 7, Jesus' life continuously calls into question the comfortable and secure homes that our interpretations of God have built for us. Like Jesus, faith communities are called to live in criticism of the status quo. By inviting them to assume their honorable status as a new humanity in Christ, this passage offers its recipients a new self-understanding, leading to a new ethos, new attitudes, and new actions. This means that specific virtues and values associated with Jesus (such as love, compassion, forgiveness, humility, holiness, righteousness, and hope) are generated toward those who identify with him. Therefore, to respect the transformative potential of this text is to dedicate ourselves to accomplishing the full potential of the body of believers and to grow beyond limited and stereotypical views of creation. Anything less would be contradictory to the theological nature of this text.

South Africa celebrated its first decade of democracy in 2004. We looked back with gratitude for many meaningful societal shifts that have taken place, but also with deep lament for divisions that still distort the rich humanity and community in and among the people of our country, particularly in the churches (see Ackermann 1991, 1992, 1994). No one is unaffected by it—we all carry personal scars and the collective scars of our country's history (Mouton 2001, 111–19).

South African Christians—people sharing the biblical perspective of forgiveness and reconciliation—have much to celebrate and to lament. Liturgy provides space for both. As a crucial starting point for change—the metaphorical bridge from where we are to where God intends us to be—liturgy provides room to lament our losses. It allows both perpetrators and victims—both self-righteous Pharisees and "sinful people of the city"—the opportunity to lament the loss of their full humanity. In liturgy the Spirit teaches us to name our sins and to grow from remembering our inherited traditions of alienation to dismembering them in the light of God's mercy. We learn to see our past, our personal and collective scars of sins committed and omitted for what it is, but also boldly to revisit our own and others' stories through the lens of Christ's forgiving and healing love and God's great deeds in history. Liturgy thus provides hermeneutical space where disowned people's experiences may be subverted and radically reinterpreted, and where they—*in memory of Luke's "woman in the city"*—can move from shame to worthiness. In this way the Spirit teaches us to think, speak, and act from a new collective identity, and to accept the life stories of others—all "others"—as if they were our own. From there we learn to see the future differently and are challenged to live with courage and hope in the present.

I believe that any form of art begins with a moment of awe—also the art of understanding, of seeing, of remembering, of living. Likewise, the key to the transformative potential of biblical narrative lies in the ongoing encounter with an awesome God. While Jesus—explicitly and implicitly—recast both the woman and the Pharisee in Luke's narrative in the honorary role of "hosting God's love and forgiveness," later readers are invited to do likewise.

Notes

1. The debate distinguishes Christian ethics as a critical, scientific discipline from Christian ethos (morality) as "the habitual character and disposition of a group . . . how people behave themselves, what they think and believe, like and dislike, what they hope and fear, what they regard as shameful or as praiseworthy . . . in short, the factors influencing (their) 'moral world'" (Smit 1991b, 52; see 1992, 303–17; see Birch & Rasmussen 1989, 39; Meeks 1986; 1993, 4). Ethos is more influential, often determing ethics, whereas ethics seldom influences ethos (Smit 1991b).
2. Ethical reading basically refers to choices readers have to make: "(T)he ethics of interpretation asks (i) who (. . . which individual or group) reads (ii) which Bible (. . . what view of the text does the interpretive community hold, what authority does it grant the text) (iii) how (. . . methods) and (iv) why (. . . whose inter-

ests are at stake, what does the interpretive community want to achieve with their acts of interpretation")? (Botha 1994b, 4–5; see Mouton 2002, 10–13).

3. See Smit 1994a for a typology of historical paradigms in Christian ethics, with dominant questions asked in different phases. A major implication of this overview is that historically the Bible has been used in many different ways with regard to Christian ethos—depending on the question(s) being put to it. This confirms the relational nature of human knowledge, including interpretations of the Bible (see Botha 1994a, 40–42; Hartin 1991, 2–4; Mouton 2002, 201–19).

4. Christian ethos and ethics (the dynamic and creative reinterpretation of biblical perspectives by readers in different sociohistorical circumstances) are distinguished from biblical ethics, that is, the implied ethos of each biblical document in its particular context (Verhey 1984, 159–60, 169–97; Gustafson 1984, 151–54; Birch and Rasmussen 1989, 11–14; Botha 1994a, 36–42).

5. "The difference between ethics and ethos often has something to do with the difference between (moral) decisions and acts and (moral) human beings, between acts and agents" (Smit 1991b, 52; see Richardson 1994, 89–96), or the difference between an ethics of Doing (*Sollen*) and an ethics of Being (*Sein*; see Birch and Rasmussen 1989, 39–62). Hauerwas (1981, 1985a, 1985b) and others have argued for a shift toward the latter. His interest is in the formation of "communities of character" and the role the Bible plays in it. Hauerwas "challenges the popular inclination to link ethics with difficult decisions and argues instead for the importance of creating contexts more conducive to deciding one way or another. Contexts like these are found in communities, like the church: social institutions seeking to embody a specific configuration of virtues in its members. These virtues are formed by the language, the 'grammar,' the collective stories of the group. . . . Much more important, according to Hauerwas, than looking at the role of the Bible in particular difficult decisions and acts, is therefore to look at the role of the Bible within the social institutions where the people's ethos is being formed" (Smit 1991b, 53; see 1994b). What we do depends on who we are (see Heinz Tödt's processes of ethical decision making, and particularly the role of identity and "seeing" in each phase; Tödt 1977; Mouton 2002, 243–51).

6. Biblical communities did not so much have a social ethic as be a social ethic, a koinonia ethic in process. "The community's task was to socialize its members into forms of life which displayed the kind of conduct befitting the experience of God in community. To be a Jew was to learn the story of Israel and the rabbinic traditions well enough to experience the world from within these stories, and to act in accord with that experience as a member of an ongoing faith community. Similarly, to be a Christian was to learn the story of Israel and of Jesus and the ongoing church traditions well enough to experience the world from within those stories, and to act in keeping with that experience, as a member of that community" (Birch and Rasmussen 1989, 21, see 66–84; Hauerwas 1985a, 181–84; Meeks 1993, 172–73, 189–210). Liturgy nurtures communal identity and the corresponding ethos (see Olyan 1996; Smit 1997; Mouton 2001).

7. Gustafson's *Ethics from a Theocentric Perspective* (1981, 1984) emphasizes the essence of Christian ethics as faith in a sovereign God. He argues for relationality as primary for Christian ethics. With God at the center of moral activity, he focuses on the Christian's response to what God does in history. His approach is closely related to that of H. Richard Niebuhr (1941) who underlined the responsibility to listen carefully, to be open and responsive to the work of God (see Botha 1994a, 41–42; Stassen 1996; Mouton 2002, 227–43). Because of the

awesome yet mysterious ways in which God is revealed, metaphorical language about God (as the only way to speak about God) is a humble, preliminary, tentative effort to interpret God.

8. In the metaphorical theology of Sallie McFague (1982) "metaphor" and "parable" are central for the formation of moral people—similar to "story" in Hauerwas. These have the potential to continuously reorient and redefine Christian self-understanding and ethos as disciples of Christ.

9. Biblical metaphors *inter alia* serve as windows through which identification, estrangement, and reorientation, typical of the image-making capacity of the human mind can be viewed. Creative acts of interpretation, discovery, decision making, transition, or transformation can be recognized as the imaginative combination and synthesis of the familiar into new wholes (McFague 1982, 35–36), which is a *redescription* of reality (Ricoeur 1975, 122–28; 1976, 45–69).

10. For McFague (1982, 31–54), basic characteristics of metaphorical language (indirection, extravagance, mundanity) apply to Jesus as parable. In general parables play on two different orientations to reality. Different perspectives are in tension with each other, and their interaction produces disorientation. Drawing on Ricoeur, McFague (1982, 46–47) suggests that parables work on a pattern of orientation, disorientation, and reorientation. Parables reverse listeners' expectations and shift their vision and behavior in radical ways (see Lategan 1992, 154).

11. Biblical references are from the NRSV except where indicated otherwise.

12. The resemblances and differences among Mark 14:3–9; Matt. 26:6–13; Luke 7:36–50; and John 12:1–8 and whether they refer to the same tradition have been much debated. For discussion see Malone 2000, 48–49; Pesonen 2000; Schaberg 1998, 373–75; Bock 1994, 689–93; Johnson 1991, 128–29; York 1991, 118–19.

13. The verb ἀφίημι ("to cancel a debt") often has a financial connotation (see Luke 11:4; 16:5, 7). The noun ἄφεσις refers to the remittance of trespasses or juridical acquittal. This is the word group that Luke commonly uses for forgiveness (ἄφεσις as "freeing, releasing" and ἀφίημι—"to free, release"). He uses the same metaphors with regard to uplifting the weak and healing illness, making use of images of release from debt or from prison (see Bosch 1993).

14. The structure of 7:18–50 suggests that the woman's acquaintance with forgiveness (v. 47) may have come from John's ministry, and that her coming to Jesus was to express gratitude for the forgiveness proleptically bestowed on her by John (3:3; Nolland 1989, 351, 354, 360).

15. This is the first of three occasions, found only in Luke, where Jesus eats with Pharisees (see 11:33–54; 14:1–24). On each occasion Jesus is put to the test, and his behavior scandalizes the host (see York 1991, 122; Nolland 1989, 353). These encounters emphasize that the Pharisees' interpretation of Torah resulted in a "harsh look" at socially disowned people (note "seeing," "watching," "the eye" in 7:39, 44; 11:33–38). That Jesus dined with Pharisees hardly means they endorsed him but rather indicates his standing as a well-known teacher (Nolland 1989, 360).

16. Luke introduces the woman as "a sinner" even though the context suggests that her sins had been forgiven (note the repetition of the perfect ἀφέωνται in vv. 47–48). By identifying the woman as a sinner Luke emphasizes her shameless status in the cultural context. Feminist critics such as Jane Schaberg and Mary Malone, assuming that the four Gospel accounts refer to the same event, point out that Luke changes the context and purpose of the woman's act in Mark 14:3–9. For Schaberg (1998, 375), Luke erases a female prophet by reducing the original story "to a display of unusual affection on the part of an intruding woman." Malone (2000, 49) describes Luke's version as "a remarkable gesture

of sorrow by a repentant woman [that] has been beloved by countless numbers of artists in the Christian tradition. This is the conventional image of woman, the daughter of Eve, who knows her place because of her sinful nature." Schaberg (1998, 375) concludes: "Given the emphatic nature of Mark 14:9, Luke's editing displays real arrogance. Politically, prophetically, what she has done will *not* be told in memory of her." From the probable redaction and history of interpretation, the point holds. I deal with the incident, however, as a distinct event in Luke's literary context, with an implied rhetorical purpose.

17. Her behavior might have been acceptable to a Greek audience but would conflict with Jewish purity. According to Malina (1993, 39, 51), an honorable person in the first-century Mediterranean world would be "one who knows how to and can maintain his or her social boundaries in the intersection of power, gender, and social respect, including God. The shameless person is one who does not observe social boundaries . . . any physical boundary-crossing on the part of another presumes and implies the intention to dishonor. In honor societies, actions are more important than words, and how one speaks is more important than what one says" (Malina 1993, 41). On honor and shame see Malina 1993, 28–55.

18. According to Nolland (1989, 354), "(w)eeping in Luke normally connotes a sharp distress (often in bereavement) which does not fit here with the woman's other gestures." Difficult as it may be to interpret her emotions, the context suggests tears of gratitude (or remorse) rather than anguish, since she has found peace (v. 47).

19. Nolland (1989, 354–55).

20. As with table fellowship, the separation between the pure and impure had much to do with what/whom could be touched and what/whom could not (Johnson 1991, 127; see Lev. 5:2–3; 6:18, 27; 7:20; 22:4–9). For the touching of an unclean woman, see Lev. 13; 15:19–32; Num. 12:10–15. According to Malina and Rohrbaugh (2003, 251), judging people is a common feature of gossip in honor-shame societies. Gossip functions "as an informal means of social control. 'Judging' . . . is largely a matter of stereotyping, usually entailing negative judgment or condemnation. Labels for people (sinner, tax collector, woman of the city, artisan's son) are shorthand designations that pigeonhole them and thereby both describe and determine honor status. They also provide others with a guide and control for social interaction." The main quality of such relationships is favoritism (see Mouton 2002, 72n21; Malina 1996, 145).

21. Whether the idea of Jesus as a prophet "was one to which Simon had himself been inclined, or whether he repeats popular sentiment (see 7:16; 9:19)" is unclear. "Behind Simon's thought lies the unexpressed assumption that a prophet would maintain the same respectable distance as Simon himself would from a notorious sinner. The underlying scandal of Jesus' behavior is here once again that he is friend to tax collectors and sinners (v. 34)" (Nolland 1989, 355).

22. This is unique to this passage—elsewhere in Luke, Pharisees are not introduced by name.

23. See Malina 1996, 143–75 on patron-client relationships as analogous to the theologies of the Synoptic Gospels. As usually happens in the Gospel accounts, Jesus (and finally God) also in this story ironically becomes the ultimate patron who shows compassion to socially disowned people. Such a shift necessarily would generate social dynamite in Luke's day.

24. To provide water for guests to wash their feet after travel is well attested, but not indicated as compulsory for guests (Nolland 1989, 357; see Marshall 1978, 312). Likewise, it was customary to anoint the head with oil at formal meals as a sign of honor (Malina and Rohrbaugh 2003, 255; Taylor 2004, 45–50). However, it

was not necessarily expected for a host to extend this courtesy. The kiss of greeting also was not mandatory hospitality, even though it was an accepted form of
greeting (see Luke 22:48; Nolland 1989, 357). Jesus allows the woman's kisses
to be part of his welcome, thereby casting her in the honorary role of host (see
Nolland 1989, 357).

25. The point seems to be that when the woman anointed Jesus' feet, her actions
went beyond the normal courtesy of washing a guest's feet with water (see
Fitzmyer 1981, 691; Nolland 1989, 357). The narrator powerfully expresses this
dramatic contrast and irony through word order. See the threefold repetition of
αὕτη δέ in vv. 44–46.

26. The ὅτι may be logical here: "The woman's profound display of grateful affection is a clear indication that she has been freed from the great burden of her
moral debt" (Nolland 1989, 358).

27. Whereas the connection between forgiveness and Jesus' authority has been
implied in the context, it now becomes explicit (in 5:20 for the first time, and
here as confirmation and deepening of the restored relationship with God). Jesus'
word of peace to the woman (v. 50) is the pronouncement of God's encompassing righteousness and conciliation (wholeness, salvation, holiness, *shalom*) to her
(see Bosch 1993, 33).

28. Passivity and unwillingness to risk would be typical characteristics of (positive)
"female shame" in an honor-shame society (Malina 1993, 50–53).

29. Through various elements Christians are touched and moved in numerous ways.
As we learn to receive and share God's grace and love, we are radically renewed
by the life-giving Spirit of God. While we learn to accept Christ's forgiveness,
we also learn to resist our own tendency to sin and any other forces of suffering and evil that go against God's will, and that seek to destroy ourselves and
others.

Works Cited

Ackermann, Denise 1991. "Being Woman, Being Human." In *Women Hold Up Half the
Sky: Women in the Church in Southern Africa*, D. Ackermann, J. A. Draper, and
E. Mashinini, eds., 93–105. Pietermaritzburg: Cluster Publications.

———— 1992. "Defining Our Humanity: Thoughts on a Feminist Anthropology." *JTSA*
79: 13–23.

———— 1994. "Faith and Feminism: Women Doing Theology." In Villa-Vicencio and
DeGruchy, eds., *Doing Theology in Context*, 197–211.

Birch, Bruce C., and Larry L. Rasmussen 1989. *Bible and Ethics in the Christian Life*. Minneapolis: Augsburg.

Bock, Darrell L. 1994. *Luke, Vol. 1: 1:1–9:50*. Baker Exegetical Commentary on the New
Testament. Grand Rapids: Baker Books.

Bosch, David J. 1993. *Good News for the Poor . . . and the Rich*. Pretoria: CB Powell Bible
Centre (UNISA).

Botha, Jan 1994a. "The Bible and Ethics." In Villa-Vicencio and De Gruchy, eds., *Doing
Ethics in Context*, 36–45.

———— 1994b. *Subject to Whose Authority? Multiple Readings of Romans 13*. Atlanta: Scholars Press.

Brown, William P, ed. 2002. *Character and Scripture: Moral Formation, Community, and
Biblical Interpretation*. Grand Rapids: Eerdmans.

Curran, Charles E., and Richard A. McCormick, eds. 1984. *The Use of Scripture in Moral
Theology*. New York: Paulist.

Danker, Frederick W. 1988. *Jesus and the New Age: A Commentary on St. Luke's Gospel*. Rev.
and expanded ed. Philadelphia: Fortress.

Dewey, Joanna 1996. "From Storytelling to Written Text: The Loss of Early Christian Women's Voices." *BTB* 26/2: 71–78.

——— 1997. "Women in the Synoptic Gospels: Seen but Not Heard?" *BTB* 27/2: 53–60.

Dunn, James D. G. 2003. *Jesus Remembered. Vol. 1 of Christianity in the Making.* Grand Rapids: Eerdmans.

Fiorenza, Elisabeth S. 1988. "The Ethics of Biblical Interpretation: Decentering Biblical Scholarship." *JBL* 107/1: 3–17.

——— 1999. *Rhetoric and Ethic: The Politics of Biblical Studies.* Minneapolis: Fortress.

——— 2001. *Wisdom Ways: Introducing Feminist Biblical Interpretation.* Maryknoll, NY: Orbis.

Fitzmyer, Joseph A., SJ 1981. *The Gospel according to Luke (I–IX): Introduction, Translation, and Notes.* AB 28. New York: Doubleday.

Fowl, Stanley E., and L. Gregory Jones 1991. *Reading in Communion: Scripture and Ethics in Christian Life.* London: SPCK.

Gustafson, James M. 1981, 1984. *Ethics from a Theocentric Perspective.* 2 vols. Chicago: University of Chicago Press.

——— 1984. "The Place of Scripture in Christian Ethics: A Methodological Study." In Curran and McCormick, eds., *The Use of Scripture in Moral Theology,* 151–77.

Hartin, Patrick J. 1991. "Methodological Principles in Interpreting the Relevance of the New Testament for a New South Africa." *Scriptura* 37:1–16.

Hauerwas, Stanley 1981. *A Community of Character: Toward a Constructive Social Ethic.* Notre Dame, IN: University of Notre Dame.

——— 1985a. "The Gesture of a Truthful Story." *TToday* 42/2: 181–89.

——— 1985b. *Character and the Christian Life: A Study in Theological Ethics.* San Antonio: Trinity University.

Hays, Richard B. 1990. "Scripture-Shaped Community: The Problem of Method in New Testament Ethics." *Int* 44/1: 42–55.

Johnson, Luke T. 1991. *The Gospel of Luke.* Sacra Pagina 3. Collegeville, MN: Liturgical Press.

——— 1999. *The Writings of the New Testament: An Interpretation.* Rev. ed. Minneapolis: Fortress.

Lancaster, Sarah H. 2002. *Women and the Authority of Scripture: A Narrative Approach.* Harrisburg, PA: Trinity Press International.

Lategan, Bernard C. 1982. "Inleiding tot de Uitlegging van het Nieuwe Testament." In A.F.J. Klijn, ed., *Inleiding tot de studie van het Nieuwe Testament,* 47–70. Kampen: J.H. Kok.

——— 1985. "Reference: Reception, Redescription and Reality." In B.C. Lategan and W.S. Vorster, *Text and Reality: Aspects of Reference in Biblical Texts,* 67–93. Philadelphia: Fortress.

——— 1989. "Introduction: Coming to Grips with the Reader." *Semeia* 48: 3–17.

——— 1992. "Hermeneutics." In David N. Freedman, ed., *The Anchor Bible Dictionary* 3: 149–54. New York: Doubleday.

——— 1993. "Textual Space as Rhetorical Device." In S.E. Porter and T.H. Olbricht, eds., *Rhetoric and the New Testament: Essays from the 1992 Heidelberg Conference,* 397–408. Sheffield: JSOT.

——— 1994. "Revisiting Text and Reality." *Neot* 28/3: 121–35.

——— 1996. "Imagination and Transformation: Ricoeur and the Role of Imagination." *Scriptura* 58/3: 213–32.

Malina, Bruce J. 1993. *The New Testament World: Insights from Cultural Anthropology.* Louisville, KY: Westminster/John Knox.

——— 1996. *The Social World of Jesus and the Gospels.* London: Routledge.

Malina, Bruce J., and Richard L. Rohrbaugh 2003. *Social-Science Commentary on the Gospels.* 2nd ed. Minneapolis: Fortress.

Malone, Mary T. 2000. *Women and Christianity*. Vol. 1, *The First Thousand Years*. Maryknoll, NY: Orbis.

Marshall, I. Howard 1978. *The Gospel of Luke: A Commentary on the Greek Text*. NIGTC. Exeter: Paternoster.

McFague, Sallie 1975. *Speaking in Parables: A Study in Metaphor and Theology*. Philadelphia: Fortress.

——— 1982. *Metaphorical Theology: Models of God in Religious Language*. London: Fortress.

Meeks, Wayne A. 1986. *The Moral World of the First Christians*. Philadelphia: Westminster.

——— 1993. *The Origins of Christian Morality: The First Two Centuries*. New Haven, CT: Yale University.

Moltmann-Wendel, Elisabeth 1982. *The Women around Jesus: Reflections on Authentic Personhood*. London: SCM.

Mouton, Elna 1997. "The (Trans)formative Potential of the Bible as Resource for Christian Ethos and Ethics." *Scriptura* 62: 245–57.

——— 2001. "A Rhetoric of Theological Vision? On Scripture's Reorienting Power in the Liturgy of (Social) Life." *Neot* 35(1–2): 111–27.

——— 2002. *Reading a New Testament Document Ethically*. Atlanta: SBL / Leiden: Brill.

——— 2003. "(Re)Describing Reality? The Transformative Potential of Ephesians across Times and Cultures." In A.J. Levine, and M. Blickenstaff, eds., *A Feminist Companion to the Deutero-Pauline Epistles*, 59–87. Cleveland: Pilgrim Press.

Mouton, Johann, and Bernard Lategan, eds. 1994. *The Relevance of Theology for the 1990s*. Pretoria: HSRC.

Niebuhr, H. Richard 1941. *The Meaning of Revelation*. New York: Macmillan.

Nolland, John 1989. *Luke 1–9:20*. WBC 35A. Dallas: Word Books.

Olyan, Saul M. 1996. "Honor, Shame, and Covenant Relations in Ancient Israel and Its Environment." *JBL* 115/2: 201–18.

Ogletree, Thomas W. 1983. *The Use of the Bible in Christian Ethics*. Philadelphia: Fortress.

Pesonen, Anni 2000. "The Weeping Sinner: A Short Story by Luke?" *Neot* 34(1): 87–102.

Richardson, Neville 1994. "Ethics of Character and Community." In Villa-Vicencio and De Gruchy, eds., *Doing Ethics in Context*, 89–101.

Ricoeur, Paul 1975. "Biblical Hermeneutics." *Semeia* 4: 29–148.

——— 1976. *Interpretation Theory: Discourse and the Surplus of Meaning*. Fort Worth: Texas Christian University.

——— 1977. *The Rule of Metaphor: Multi-disciplinary Studies of the Creation of Meaning in Language*. Trans. by R. Czerny, K. McLaughlin, and J. Costello. Toronto: University of Toronto.

Robbins, Vernon K. 1996. *Exploring the Texture of Texts: A Guide to Socio-Rhetorical Interpretation*. Valley Forge, PA: Trinity Press International.

Russell, Letty M. 1985. "Authority and the Challenge of Feminist Interpretation." In L.M. Russell, ed., *Feminist Interpretation of the Bible*, 137–46. Philadelphia: Westminster.

Schaberg, Jane 1998. "Luke." In Carol Newsom and Sharon Ringe, eds. *Women's Bible Commentary*, expanded ed. with Apocrypha, 363–80. Louisville, KY: Westminster John Knox.

Smit, Dirk J. 1990a. "The Ethics of Interpretation—New Voices from the USA." *Scriptura* 33: 16–28.

——— 1990b. "The Ethics of Interpretation—and South Africa." *Scriptura* 33: 29–43.

——— 1991a. "Wat beteken 'die Bybel sê'? 'n Tipologie van leserkonstrukte." *HvTSt* 47/1: 167–85.

——— 1991b. "The Bible and Ethos in a New South Africa." *Scriptura* 37: 51–67.

———— 1992. "Oor 'Nuwe-Testamentiese etiek', die Christelike lewe en Suid-Afrika vandag." In C. Breytenbach and B. Lategan, eds., "Geloof en Opdrag: Perspektiewe op die etiek van die Nuwe Testament." *Scriptura* S9a: 303–25.

———— 1994a. "Morality and Individual Responsibility." *JTSA* 89: 19–30.

———— 1994b. "A Story of Contextual Hermeneutics and the Integrity of New Testament Interpretation in South Africa." *Neot* 28/2: 265–89.

———— 1996. "Saints, Disciples, Friends? Recent South African Perspectives on Christian Ethics and the New Testament." *Neot* 30/2: 451–64.

———— 1997. "Liturgy and Life? On the Importance of Worship for Christian Ethics." *Scriptura* 62: 259–80.

———— 1998a. "Biblical Hermeneutics: The First 19 Centuries." In S. Maimela and A. König, eds., *Initiation into Theology: The Rich Variety of Theology and Hermeneutics*, 275–96. Pretoria: J.L. Van Schaik.

———— 1998b. "Biblical Hermeneutics: The 20th Century." In Maimela and König, *Initiation into Theology*, 297–317.

———— 2002. "'Seeing Things Differently': On Prayer and Politics." In L. Holness and R.K. Wüstenberg, eds., *Theology in Dialogue*, 271–84. Grand Rapids: Eerdmans.

Spohn, William C. 1995. *What Are They Saying about Scripture and Ethics?* Fully rev. and expanded ed. New York: Paulist.

Stassen, Glen H. 1996. "A New Vision." In G.H. Stassen, D.M. Yeager, and J.H. Yoder, *Authentic Transformation: A New Vision of Christ and Culture*, 191–268. Nashville: Abingdon.

Stein, Robert H. 1992. *Luke*. New American Commentary 24. Nashville: Broadman.

Talbert, Charles H. 1984. *Reading Luke: A Literary and Theological Commentary on the Third Gospel*. New York: Crossroad.

Taylor, Birgit 2004. "Outrageous Women: A Comparison of Five Passages within the Canonical and Empty Tomb Narratives Emphasizing the Role of Women." MA diss., University of Cape Town.

Tannehill, Robert C. 1986. *The Narrative Unity of Luke–Acts: A Literary Interpretation*. Vol. 1, *The Gospel according to Luke*. Philadelphia: Fortress.

Thiselton, Anthony C. 1992. *New Horizons in Hermeneutics: The Theory and Practice of Transforming Biblical Reading*. Grand Rapids: Zondervan.

Tödt, Heinz E. 1977. "Versuch zu einer Theorie ethischer Urteilsfindung." *Zeitschrift für Evangelische Ethik* 21: 81–93.

Van Huyssteen, Wentzel 1987. *The Realism of the Text: A Perspective on Biblical Authority*. Pretoria: UNISA.

Van Staden, Piet J. 1991. "Compassion—the Essence of Life: A Social-scientific Study of the Religious Symbolic Universe Reflected in the Ideology/Theology of Luke." *HvTSt* Supplementum 4.

Verhey, Allen 1984. *The Great Reversal: Ethics and the New Testament*. Grand Rapids: Eerdmans.

Villa-Vicencio, Charles, and John De Gruchy, eds. 1994. *Doing Ethics in Context: South African Perspectives*. Cape Town: David Philip.

York, John O. 1991. *The Last Shall Be First: The Rhetoric of Reversal in Luke*. JSNTSup 46. Sheffield: JSOT.

Chapter 4

[handwritten annotations: As to Christology, Brawley sees Jesus as 'son to ...Father' but it ... divinity]

Generating Ethics
from God's Character in Mark

ROBERT L. BRAWLEY *[handwritten: a real problem # OT text of ... a fine contextual study ie making sense of all its interrelationship, lasts]*

Against the Western myth of self-sufficient autonomy, anthrax-laced letters, and smart bombs that fail their final exams bring to the surface a vulnerability that perturbs us and draws us toward dependence upon one another. Mark's first hint of anthropology expresses the vulnerability that perturbs us as sin and dependence upon one another as repentance and forgiveness. John the Baptist and Jesus play out a script of interdependence when Jesus is baptized by John, who in turn prophesies about a superior baptism that is to come from Jesus (Mark 1:2–9). Alasdair MacIntyre has recently reconsidered vulnerability and dependence as qualifications on human ability to develop ethical character.[1] Although I find MacIntyre persuasive, the qualification of ethical character on the basis of vulnerability and interdependence among human beings is premature without an account first of God's character. God's character, however, is in turn penultimate to an encounter with God. My thesis is that in Mark human behavior is relational and derivative, and when behavior is ethical it derives from a relationship with God. This chapter, therefore, is an account of Mark's characterization of God as a locus for an encounter with God. Characterization is sequential and cumulative, though sequential development requires constant correction, redirection, and extension of readers' anticipations. What follows is essentially a sequential

57

reading of Mark for the character of God, though I occasionally violate sequence for thematic coherence.

In technical terms God enters Mark 1:1 as an external analepsis from the cultural repertoire. In other words, the God who turns up in Mark's first verse has a prior history. As a character who inhabits Mark,[2] God immediately says: "Behold I send my messenger before your face" (1:2). Because Mark 1:2–3 folds echoes of Exodus 23:20 and Malachi 3:1 with Isaiah 40:3, Mark's God is imbedded in biblical history.[3]

In 1998, I did a research project at University of Tübingen in Germany. I had a German tutor, a university graduate working at the Max Planck Institute, who was educated under the communist system in Dresden in the former East Germany. When he asked me what I was doing in Germany, I told him that I was studying Abrahamic covenant traditions. He then said, "I think I have heard of Abraham. Who was he?" Mark anticipates no such biblical illiteracy. So when characters from the biblical world, such as David, Moses, and Elijah, make appearances, Mark expects readers already to know who they are. In discussing divorce, Jesus drives God's history back to creation (10:6; see 13:19). God's history also extends into the future. Retrospectively, God's future gives a special meaning to "the beginning" in 1:1. If Mark's story is but the beginning of the proclamation of the gospel, the proclamation continues into a future beyond the ending in 16:8.[4] God's history spans a time from before creation into an indeterminate future.

Though Mark presumes God from the cultural repertoire, a relationship with a son begins to revise God's character straightaway (1:1).[5] God is thus the first character to act in the story by sending John the Baptist, who is to prepare God's way, which is also the way of Jesus. Hence the God of the cultural repertoire acts in a new way. Some manuscripts omit "son of God" in 1:1. But even if this textual variant takes away the parent-child relationship, the voice from heaven in 1:11 gives it back.[6] "Son of God" also rings with echoes of Israel's king (e.g., Ps. 2).[7] It is otherwise inexplicable that Bartimaeus suddenly addresses Jesus as "son of David" (Mark 10:47). Though God retreats to the background, from 1:11 on, God is implicated in what God's son says, does, and is, and in what happens to him.[8] Reiterations of the parent-child relationship in 9:7; 14:61–62; and 15:39 reinforce God's characterization by close association with Jesus.

God is also characterized by association with John the Baptist and the "way of the Lord." John's baptism of repentance presumes an ethical God. Baptism and the way of the Lord are parts of Mark's emphasis on God's will (3:25; 10:19). But Joel Marcus shows that the way of the Lord is not only the way humans should walk, but the path that none other than God takes.[9] Thus events in Jesus' story, including his crucifixion and resurrection, are parts of God's way.

Though the spirit also enters Mark from the cultural repertoire, the spirit's relationship with God is somewhat nebulous.[10] (1) John's words in 1:8 identify the spirit as the *holy* spirit. (2) The voice from heaven is associated with the descent of the spirit and interprets this descent in terms of a parent-child relationship (1:10–11). (3) Evocations of biblical anointings give the descent of the spirit messianic overtones.[11] (4) In the thematic development of what drives Jesus' activity, the roles of God and the holy spirit can be interchanged (see 3:29; 12:36; 13:11). (5) Further, in Mark's cultural repertoire the spirit is a way of speaking of God's power.[12] In 8:11 some stereotyped Pharisees ask Jesus for a sign from heaven. Jesus refuses, but *readers* have already observed the spirit descending from heaven like a dove.[13]

The correlation of Jesus with God makes the satanic opponent in Jesus' temptation also God's opponent. God is thus strongly characterized by the opposition to Satan. Such opposition surfaces explicitly in exorcisms (3:23), in the parable of the sower (4:15), and in Peter's confession (8:33), but is also presupposed from 1:13 henceforth.[14]

God's commonwealth also characterizes God in Mark. God's commonwealth is God's activity to rule over a community and the cosmos against the powers of evil.[15] Interpreters who recognize God as a character tend to characterize God by values, such as justice. But God is primarily a God who acts. Jesus reinforces this at his trial by directly characterizing God by the epithet "power" (14:62). The way God's commonwealth impacts human life characterizes God as a power that gives life, in contrast to a God who remains separate from "unclean" tragedies of health and social marginalization.[16] But if God *rules*, ethical correlates are predicated of humans who live under this rule. God's rule entails changing the way one lives and believing in the good news (1:15). Belief includes the confidence that Jesus stands in a relationship with God as a child to a parent (1:1, 11).[17] God is therefore characterized by relationships with human beings in which in repentance they also act. Such relationships make it superfluous to ask whether ethical action depends on God or human beings. When God rules human beings, they act ethically.

The restoration of marginalized people to the social order dramatizes God's rule. As a focal instance, the predicament of the man with the unclean spirit in Mark 1:23–27 is that a demonic invasion of the human realm has separated him from God's rule.[18] The setting on the Sabbath in the synagogue elevates expectations of divine activity. There Jesus' rebuke restores the boundary between the unclean spirit and the man. In Jesus' exorcisms the demons know that he is God's son, who derives power from God and manifests God's rule (e.g., 3:11; 5:7).[19]

Jesus' opponents, who have a different view of God, set Mark's characterization of God in relief. The healing of the paralytic reiterates the nature of Jesus' power as deriving from God by juxtaposing it to a different view (2:1–12).[20] This event hangs on relationships. Jesus establishes fictive kinship with the paralytic by calling him "child" (τέκνον), which in the light of 3:31–35 implies a sibling relationship with Jesus and a parent-child relationship with God. Further, the debate with stereotyped scribes over who has power to forgive exposes a relationship between Jesus and God. Although Jesus' announcement of forgiveness can be a divine passive, the scribes take it as Jesus' claim to forgive as his prerogative. The evaluative point of view in the narrative agrees with the scribes that only God can forgive. Their logic (enthymeme) is deductive on the pattern of rule + case = result. The rule is only God can forgive. The case is Jesus' announce-ment of forgiveness. The result is blasphemy. By contrast, Jesus' reasons abduc-tively. Abduction typically leaves a step in the enthymeme unexpressed, which readers supply. Further, abduction associates elements whose relationship with each other has hitherto not been observed, and hence it occasions surprise. In the interchange with the scribes the healing itself is the surprise. Abduction follows the pattern: rule + result = case. The rule is only God can forgive. The result is Jesus heals and forgives. The unexpressed case that readers supply is that Jesus stands in a derivative relationship with God—the only one who can forgive.[21]

Jesus intends the healing to be a way for the scribes to know (2:10). Presum-ably they do gain knowledge and are among "all" those who glorify God. As prominent secondary actors, they join the crowd and the people who brought the paralyzed man to Jesus and who recognize God's rule in the healing.[22]

In Mark 2:16 stereotyped scribes misunderstand Jesus' violation of norms of table fellowship. Only one proposition in their enthymeme is expressed, but the cultural repertoire enables readers to determine the other two. The scribes ques-tion Jesus' association with tax collectors and sinners. Their logic is deductive: rule + case = result. Rule: Eating with tax collectors and sinners defiles. Case: Jesus eats with tax collectors and sinners. Result: Jesus is defiled. Their interpretation neglects the repentance that the context has established as part of Jesus' procla-mation. Jesus leaves one step unexpressed in his abductive enthymeme: rule + result = case. The rule is that physicians heal the sick. The unexpressed result that readers supply is that Jesus heals sinners. The case is that Jesus calls sinners and eats with them.

A literary reiteration at the end of the healing of the Gerasene demoniac indi-cates the derivative nature of Jesus' exorcisms. Jesus refuses to allow the healed man to accompany him but tells him to proclaim what great things the *Lord* had done for him. In the repetition in the narrator's summary, the man proclaims what great things *Jesus* had done for him. In the act of Jesus, readers behold what God has done.[23]

The characterization of God as the source of Jesus' redemptive activity is strengthened by stereotyped scribes, who accuse Jesus of being socially deviant by claiming that his exorcisms derive from the ruler of demons (Mark 3:22). Their characterization stands in a context that presents competing identities of Jesus and in which Jesus' family stunningly identifies him as insane (3:21). Jesus responds in two ways. First, in an attempt at indirect persuasion, Jesus gives metaphors of a divided kingdom, a divided house, and binding a strong man. Second, in a direct riposte, Jesus labels the scribes' charge as blasphemy against the holy spirit. His reasoning is again abductive. Jesus states a rule categorically ("all things will be forgiven"—a divine passive as in 2:5) with an exception (except blasphemy against the holy spirit).[24] The result is that by naming the source of Jesus' exorcisms demonic, the scribes call the holy spirit a demon—an unforgiv-able blasphemy. The case which readers supply is that Jesus stands in a derivative relationship with God. In competition with the dominant point of view, the scribes' evaluation proves false and so strengthens the characterization of God as the origin of Jesus' exorcisms.

The epithet "son of humanity" broadens Jesus' characterization precisely where Mark indicates that Jesus' power to heal and forgive originates from God (2:10). In the first half of Mark, the epithet occurs in controversies only here and in 2:28.[25] After Jesus' announcement of his passion and resurrection (8:31), "son of humanity" occurs with greater frequency but always in connection with the passion, resurrection, and Parousia.

Because Jesus fulfills the social role of teacher, Vernon Robbins repeatedly refers to Jesus' attempts to persuade disciples to adopt his system of thought and action. This raises two questions. First, from 1:3 Mark's story is the way of the Lord rather than Jesus' system. Second, Mark gives readers samples of Jesus' thoughts and actions, hardly his system.[26] Thus, rather than repeat Jesus' teachings, recipients and witnesses of exorcisms and healings bear testimony to activity that derives from God. A leper who is healed preaches (1:45). So does the Gerasene demoniac (5:20). After the healing of a deaf man who could hardly speak, he and others preach (7:36). The witnesses of the healing of the paralytic glorify God (2:12).

Jesus' position as an intermediary in God's activity is reiterated in his call of followers. The pattern of calling emphasizes Jesus' initiative, and the calling depends on Jesus' perception of those whom he calls (1:16, 19), rather than on their perception of him.[27] "Following" in distinction from "imitation" involves spatial proximity (even if metaphorical) and solidarity. To be sure, this spatial proximity is different for Mark's readers than for the actors in the narrative, and in fact, following is seldom found in expressions of relationships with Jesus in the post-Easter Christian community. But 14:28 and 16:7 indicate that following continues as a relationship with the risen Jesus.[28] The failure of other characters in Mark to imitate Jesus speaks against confidence in readers to accomplish what the characters do not.[29] This makes it inappropriate to take characters as role models. They are too deficient for readers to imitate.

Jesus' sending of disciples makes their mission derivative. For Mark, the purpose of the call of the Twelve is that they might be sent out to preach (3:14). The actual sending of the Twelve in 6:7 reiterates and reinforces this thematically. So when the Twelve go out, their power derives from Jesus (6:7–12). The reference to the apostles' teaching in 6:30 is the only place in Mark where anyone other than Jesus teaches. They teach because Jesus gives them "power."

The violation of social norms recurs in the episode of eating grain on the Sabbath (Mark 2:23–28). Interpreters often overlook a theocentric focus in this incident in their efforts to draw parallels between human characters—between David and his cohorts, and Jesus and his. Beyond correlations among human characters, God's house parallels the grainfields. The case is not merely David's violation of temple regulations. Rather, the God, whose house David enters, provides for and vindicates Jesus' disciples, just as God provides for and vindicates David. Mark's Jesus is a bucolic romantic who makes grainfields comparable to God's dwelling place, where humanitarian need overrides social norms. Because Jesus is the lord of the Sabbath, the prerogatives of his disciples derive from him.

Violations of norms persist in the healing of a man with a withered hand on the Sabbath (Mark 3:1–6). Not only does the incident reinforce the notion that humanitarian need overrides social norms; it also reinterprets Sabbath laws. When Jesus poses the question of whether it is lawful to do good or harm on the Sabbath, Sabbath legality no longer proscribes but prescribes activity, namely, redemptive activity.

Jesus' claim to fictive kinship in Mark 3:32–35 reinforces the derivative nature of ethics. It is conventional to portray God as father under patron-client codes.[30] But parent-child more appropriately reflects kinship codes. A part of Mark's portrayal of God as father is that when family members evaluate Jesus as insane (3:21), Jesus supplants blood kinship with fictive kinship. Incidentally, fictive kinship is real. That is, when Jesus speaks of sisters, mothers, and brothers, he is naming genuine relationships with metaphors. His criterion for kinship is doing God's will. Through following Jesus, disciples develop a kinship that derives ultimately from God. The relationship between kinship and doing God's will supports both the objective genitive in "the will of God" (a wish that resides in God) and the subjective genitive (the act of willing that comes from God).[31] None other than God ties people together in kinship.

The parable of the Sower also reflects action that derives from a relationship with God (Mark 4:1–9).[32] In the parable (1) the dominant images are sowing seed and bearing fruit. (2) The imagery of the seed shifts in meaning. The seed is the word (4:14). But the seed is also those who receive the word (4:15–20). (3) Some interpreters call the parable a "seed" parable, others a "soil" parable, but the issue is the *relationship* of seed to mother earth. (4) Jesus names Satan the malevolent source that prevents some seed from bearing fruit, whereas the source of productivity remains unstated. (5) But Jesus interprets his words explicitly as a parable of God's commonwealth (4:11). This places emphasis on the destiny of the word in God's commonwealth.

This word undoubtedly includes Jesus' programmatic proclamation: "The time is fulfilled and God's commonwealth is at hand. Repent and believe in the good news" (1:15). But 1:1, 11 establishes that this good news includes the parent-child relationship between God and Jesus. In the face of failure of the word, God produces a striking harvest. Irony demonstrates how precarious it is to be insiders and how important a constant relationship with the ground is for bearing fruit. Startlingly the insiders in 4:11 do not understand the parable. They hear but do not understand, according to Isaiah 6:9.[33] Thus they shift their identity to outsiders. Ultimately God is the ground of being from which the word produces a harvest.

Whereas Jesus often transgresses cultural boundaries in order to benefit others, in Mark 5:25–34 the woman with the flow of blood is the one who violates norms. The embedding of her story in the raising of Jairus's daughter invites comparison of the woman's social marginalization with that of someone who is dead.[34] Jesus interprets her touching him, a violation of social norms, as faith. In spite of her marginalization, she is confident that she is of enough value in God's commonwealth to violate social barriers in order to derive the healing from Jesus that he derives from God. Against the expectation that the woman transfers uncleanness to Jesus, he transfers healing to her.[35] After the healing the woman comes fearing and trembling. Inasmuch as fear and trembling are formulaic for experiencing the divine, Timothy Dwyer appropriately interprets what happened in her as an encounter with God.[36] Mary Ann Tolbert suggests that although calling the woman "daughter" makes the woman a part of Jesus' kinship group, she is subordinated to him as a new father.[37] But in the fictive kinship based on doing God's will (3:31–35), the woman is God's daughter rather than Jesus'.

Like the woman with the flow of blood, Jairus's daughter is of enough value in God's commonwealth for social norms associated with death to be violated. Jesus' exhortation to Jairus to have faith is juxtaposed to the faith of the woman with the flow of blood, and thus it means for him to be confident that Jesus stands in a derivative relationship with God. "Faith" is also nuanced by antithesis to fear (5:36). Jairus already manifests some such faith. His plea for Jesus to come and touch his daughter implies a derivative power that is passed on by touching. Out of a relationship with God, Jesus is able to raise the girl (5:23). When he seizes her hand, he violates norms. Though touching a corpse rendered a person unclean (Num. 5:2), it was a cultural expectation that family members would contract uncleanness in preparing a body for burial and then go through purification. Thus Jesus acts in accord with the fictive kinship of Mark 3:31–35.

Some people in Nazareth explicitly raise the question of the derivative nature of Jesus' power. "From where do these things come to this man? What is the wisdom that has been given to him? From where do such deeds of power that happen through his hands come?" (6:2, my trans.). Their question presumes that Jesus fulfills the social role of a teacher.[38] Some of the Nazarenes attempt to resolve their questions by a deductive enthymeme: rule + case = result. Rule: Status is derived from lineage (unconventionally from Jesus' mother). Case: Jesus fulfills the role of a teacher. Result: Jesus acts beyond his status. Their resolution of their questions results in a scandal in which they shame Jesus. Jesus' enthymeme is abductive: rule + result = case. Rule: Prophets are honored except among their own. Result: Jesus is a prophet. Case: Some of the Nazarenes dishonor Jesus. Jesus' status from his parentage does not account for his wisdom and power, because these Nazarenes presume the wrong parent-child relationship.

The feeding of the five thousand is a concrete case of derivative benevolence (Mark 6:35–44). The narrative need is to provide for hunger. Jesus obligates his disciples to be channels of benevolence, but they fail the competence phase. They are either unwilling or unable to reverse the need. Jesus, however, is obliged, willing, and able. Readers may gloss over Jesus' look into heaven as a perfunctory mealtime blessing. But aside from a reference to the "birds of heaven" in the parable of the Mustard Seed (4:32), "heaven" has not appeared in Mark since the voice from heaven that acclaimed Jesus God's son (1:11). Jesus' act of looking at the place from which he heard the acclamation evokes memory of his relationship with God, and the feeding is benevolence derived from this relationship. For astute readers, this feeding also qualifies as a "sign from heaven," which stereo- typed Pharisees request in Mark 8:11. Whereas the disciples originally failed the competence phase, Jesus makes them competent by giving them food so that they might give it derivatively to the people (6:41).[39]

The word "again" in Mark 8:1 invites readers to take the feeding of the four thousand as a reiteration of the feeding of the five thousand. As in the first feed- ing, the mealtime prayer is indicative of God's gift (8:6). As a literary reiteration, however, the second feeding redirects attention from the divine source to Jesus' compassion (8:2). Nevertheless, this comes shortly after Jesus makes behavior a matter of a heart that is in a proper relationship with God (7:6, see below), and compassion is synonymous with the heart.

In the question of eating with unwashed hands, violation of norms comes under direct consideration (Mark 7:1–23). One's place in the social order is at stake, because stereotyped Pharisees and scribes attempt to exclude those who violate norms from normal society. The taxonomy of challenge-riposte antici- pates social regulators who expect their challenge to result in social degradation for the loser. The stereotyped Pharisees and scribes are social regulators (from Jerusalem!). Mark makes it clear that some of the disciples of Jesus are viola- ting Pharisaic and Jewish customs *that are tantamount to morality* (7:3–4). The enthymeme of the Pharisees and scribes expresses only one proposition: "Why do your disciples . . . eat with unwashed hands?" (7:5, my trans.). Their logic is deductive: rule + case = result. Rule: Eating with unwashed hands defiles. Case: Some disciples eat with unwashed hands. Result: The disciples are defiled. Jesus first issues a riposte, which essentially is that the heart of his interlocutors is dis- tanced from God (7:6), and this produces immorality (7:23). Evil is thus also derivative. But then Jesus uses abductive reasoning to redefine the issue not as a relationship to norms but with God: rule + result = case. Rule: The relationship between the heart and God determines behavior. Result: Nothing outside can defile. Case: Eating with unwashed hands does not defile. The inverse holds as well. Rule: The relationship between the heart and God determines behavior. Result: What comes from the inside can defile. Case: Evil motivations defile.

If the relationship between the heart and God determines behavior, how sur- prising that in the next episode Jesus dishonors a Syrophoenician woman and her daughter! In his culture the woman and her daughter are triply cursed—ethni- cally, religiously, and genderwise. Moreover, demon possession devalues the daugh- ter additionally. Still, Jesus' metaphor of giving bread to children expresses the derivative nature of the power to reestablish proper boundaries between the demonic and the human and to restore human beings to the social order. But his image of children excludes the woman and her daughter. The woman, however, trumps Jesus. Her metaphor is dogs under the table who eat the children's crumbs. As a result, Jesus affirms that this woman lifts the derivative nature of the power to cast out demons and to restore people to the social order to a higher level.

The notion of the heart that is distanced from God is reiterated in Peter's confession of Jesus as messiah. The criterion for understanding what it means for Jesus to be messiah is expressed in the verb φρονέω (8:33), which means to have the mind set on a purpose. Jesus contrasts his mind-set with Peter's as a clash between human things, which are also satanic, and God's things. The human things mean the human sphere separated from God and invaded by the satanic, whereas God's things reiterate the relationship of a heart that is not distanced from God.

In Mark 9:17–29 Jesus directly interprets both the disciples' inability to cast out a malevolent spirit and his own ability to do so. Though he had earlier conferred power on the Twelve (3:15; 6:7), they cannot cast out the spirit. Jesus interprets their inability as the product of their parentage. They are faithless "offspring" (γενεά). The father of the child with the malevolent spirit raises the question of power: "If you are able . . ." In response Jesus states a rule: "All things are possible to the one who has faith" (9:22–23 [my trans.], reiterated in 10:27; 14:36). Having faith means commitment to Jesus who stands in a relationship with God to the extent that one partakes of God's power as God's own offspring (in contrast to faithless offspring). But who is "the one who has faith"? The father has a measure of faith. But his plea for help in unbelief qualifies it (9:24). Jesus explains further that the exorcism occurred through prayer (9:29). Mark does not propose that the disciples imitate Jesus as an example but rather suggests a relationship with God in prayer.[40] Jesus' explanation of the healing of the man's son is also abductive reasoning: rule + result = case. The rule is that all things are possible to the one who has faith. The result is the healing, and the case is Jesus' own faith.[41]

The disciples' dispute about greatness implies their autonomy (Mark 9:34). By contrast, Jesus derives a nexus of relationships from God by grounding the reception of a child in his name in God (9:37). From the perspective of readers, this nexus of relationships means that an encounter with Jesus in the narrative implies an encounter with God.[42] The reception of the children in 10:13–16 is a literary reiteration of 9:37. The desire of parents for Jesus to touch their children suggests passing on a blessing that emanates from God.[43] Conventionally "as a child" is interpreted adverbially—one receives *as a child*. But in parallel with 9:37 it is likely that "child" is accusative in relation to "kingdom"—one receives the kingdom *when one receives a child*.[44]

In discussing divorce Jesus explicitly does ethical reflection (10:2–12). An unexpressed major premise that Jesus and his interlocutors share lies behind the discussion: Understanding divorce depends on interpreting Scripture. On the basis of this premise, Jesus makes an abductive combination of Moses (Gen. 2) with the question of divorce. The association of God's intention at creation with opposition to divorce shocks the interlocutors who associate Moses (Deut. 24:1) only with the stipulation that divorce requires a man to produce a certificate of divorce. The shock enables readers to discover a new relationship between Genesis 2 and divorce. Jesus uses abductive reasoning: rule + result = case. Rule: God made male and female. Result: God joins the two. The case is no separation. This abduction then becomes a rule for two deductive enthymemes (rule + case = result). Rule: God joins male and female. Moses' allowance for divorce is, therefore, not the rule but the case. The result is hardness of heart against God's intention. The other enthymeme is grounded in the same rule: God joins male and female. The case is divorce and remarriage, and the result is adultery. Jesus' ethical reflection here depends not on God's command but on God's character reflected in creation.

In Mark 10:17–22 the rich man directly characterizes Jesus as "good teacher." Jesus deflects this characterization to God alone. Is the rich man wrong in so characterizing Jesus? Is Jesus also derivatively good? Jesus' deflection clearly distinguishes between God and himself. Then, Jesus' reference to the commandments (1) develops the characterization of God and (2) partially answers the rich man. (1) From Mark's cultural repertoire God is a God of commandments. Readers can then conclude that the good God wishes for humans to honor father and mother and does not wish for humans to murder, commit adultery, steal, or bear false witness. (2) The reference to the commandments only partially answers the rich man, because something more is needed, that is, following Jesus. Following Jesus, however, is to live under a rule of God that leads beyond what commandments stipulate.

Jesus' affirmation of leaving everything for his sake in 10:29–31 concludes with an enthymeme of reversal. This too is abductive reasoning: rule + result = case. The rule is the inversion of first and last. The result is Jesus's passion and resurrection (10:32–34). The case is the reversal of Jesus' degradation into his exaltation. In addition, James and John seek to be first in Jesus' glory and thereby become the objects of anger from the other ten. The way for all of them is derivative—Jesus' purpose is to serve and give his life for many (10:45). The apostles' service on behalf of others derives not from Jesus' example but from his ransom for them. God's commonwealth transforms their self-interest into service.

Jesus' explanation of his claim on the temple draws on the cultural repertoire in which God is related to the temple ("my house," Isa. 56:7; see Mark 2:26) but also to all nations. Conventionally, the intercalation of the fig tree and the temple incident supposedly implies a curse on the temple/Israel. But the fig tree is actually correlated with temple *functionaries* (11:15) who correspond to the violent tenants in the parable in 12:1–12.[45] Werner Kelber shows that Mark does not say faith can move mountains. Rather faith addresses "this mountain," that is, the temple mount. This saying and Jesus' declaration that the temple is to be a house of prayer for all nations (11:17) mean that faith and prayer replace the temple. Later the splitting of the temple curtain in Mark 15 symbolizes the physical destruction of the temple (13:2).[46] But Kelber fails to note that the intercalation of the temple incident and the withered fig tree also shows that the issue is the failure to bear fruit. Further, Jesus links bearing fruit to prayer. Faith and prayer are relationships with God that produce fruit. True, in 11:25 one forgives in order that God may forgive. Derivation is reversed like water flowing uphill. But not too fast! Under the expression "when you pray" (11:25), those who forgive already stand in a relationship of prayer with God as children to a parent ("your Father"). The water flows both ways.

In Mark 11:27–33 the high priestly coterie explicitly raises the question of the derivative nature of Jesus' power, which incidentally they presuppose. The issue is its origin: human beings or God? "Authority" inadequately translates ἐξουσία, if this means legitimated power, because in Mark ἐξουσία is the power to speak, to forgive, to cast out demons, to restore marginalized people to the social order, and to make claims on the temple outside legitimated channels. Burton Mack takes Jesus' ἐξουσία to be authoritarianism. But David Rhoads, Joanna Dewey, and Donald Mitchie show that Jesus' ἐξουσία is limited.[47] Jesus does not compel but employs the power of persuasion. In one sense, the question of Jesus' ἐξουσία goes unresolved. The challenge from the high-priestly coterie receives a counterchallenge, and both sides refuse to continue the contest. In another sense, however, the resolution is startlingly clear. Jesus presents the issue as analogous to John's baptism. The question is clearly its derivation: divine or human origin? Challenge-riposte drives toward a social evaluation, and the social evaluation is on the side of divine origin. "All held John to be truly a prophet" (11:32). Ironically the dialogue among the high-priestly party shows that their response is from human origin—they fear the people (11:32). Because the high-priestly party derives its opinion from human origin, whatever Jesus says will be taken as from another human opinion. Irony runs deep.

In the parable of the Violent Tenants, the owner expects the tenants to act out honor/shame codes and respect his son. The son plays a double role as the owner's broker and his beloved child (Mark 12:6). This parable is a *mise en abyme*, that is, a literary device that reflects in miniature the narrative that contains it.[48] The parable also echoes Isaiah 5. In Isaiah 5, the vineyard is destroyed, whereas in Mark it passes to other tenants with the expectation that it will bear fruit. Thus parable is not a judgment on Israel, as commonly claimed, but on the high-priestly party.[49] Nevertheless, Mark underscores the derivative nature of the son's mission and death: "This happened from the Lord" (12:11).

The question of the first commandment expands the notion, expressed in Mark 7, that ethics derives from a heart that is in a proper relationship with God. A scribe inquires about ethics in the abstract: "Which commandment is the first of all?" (12:28). Grounding himself in God's monotheistic character, Jesus repeats Deuteronomy 6:5 with some echoes of Joshua 22:5, enjoining love of God. Via correctly discerns that ethics in Mark means giving up knowing in advance what one is to do. But Via makes the love command an exception.[50] Love is, however, not an exception. One cannot know in advance the shape love of neighbor will take, because it takes shape in a specific context. Further, love of neighbor is derivative in that it is the *second* command. Given the thematic development of hearts that are distanced from God in Mark 7:6, Jesus' abduction that the scribe is not far from God's commonwealth indicates a heart that is not distanced from God. Is it possible for Jesus to persuade even a scribe?

In close proximity, the scribes who devour widows' houses can hardly be loving neighbor or God (Mark 12:38–40). By contrast, the poor widow is a concrete case of a heart that is not distanced from God (12:41–44). But she is also a problem in that Jesus has just agreed with the scribe that loving God and neighbor is greater than temple institutions (12:33–34), and the widow casts her all (ὅλον τὸν βίον) into the temple. Moreover, by announcing its destruction Jesus makes the temple penultimate. This announcement is hardly anti-temple polemic. Rather, the widow's commitment is viewed from a retrospective reflection on the destruction of the temple.

Mark 13 links the destruction of the temple to opposition to the Jesus movement and responds confidently that God works beyond both the destruction and the opposition. Wilhelm Vorster notes the parenetic character of Mark 13 (21 imperatives, 27 futures). He deduces that here Mark's Jesus exhorts ethical behavior that is attached to eschatology. The promises of the future evoke a certain kind of behavior. The parenesis, however, is more about Christology than ethics. The imperatives are not associated so much with behavior as with fidelity in the face of false messiahs. But then Vorster shows that the future has to do with how God is at work, or as Joachim Gnilka puts it, Mark affirms that God remains Lord in a world that can turn into chaos.[51]

The clearest case of the derivation of Jesus' behavior from God is the Abba prayer (Mark 14:36). Jesus' address to God as ἀββὰ ὁ πατήρ in two languages doubles the characterization of God as parent. It also reiterates 1:1, 11; 3:11; 5:7; 8:38; 9:7 (cf. 12:6; 14:61; 15:39), and it is woven into the characterization of God as the one for whom all things are possible. The characterization of Jesus as a child whose behavior depends on the parent is equally strong. If Jesus is the master example of how to face trials in prayer,[52] then his disciples who fall asleep show how *ineffective* the example is. Rather than function in the narrative as an example for others, Jesus is a concrete case of a child whose behavior derives from his parent. Although the possibility of avoiding "this cup" stands in tension with Jesus' passion predictions, the prayer anticipates an outcome that depends on deriving his behavior from his divine parent.

Is Jesus' Abba prayer related to the cry of dereliction? He prayed that the cup might pass from him. But when he drinks the cup, he cries: "My God, my God, why have you forsaken me?" (15:34). Does this break the parent-child relationship of prayer to Abba? The form of the cry as a prayer to God already deconstructs God forsakenness.[53] Further, it is virtually impossible to miss that the allusions to Psalm 21 LXX evoke its context. The crucifixion and the actions of opponents repeat the plot of the psalm. The Abba prayer is a cry to God by night, but the one who prays finds absurdity (21:3). On the cross Jesus is scorned by others, and despised by the people (21:7). Those who mock him shake their heads (21:8). Jesus' crucifiers divide his clothes, as do the opponents in 21:19. With the abundance of allusions to Psalm 21 LXX beyond the cry of dereliction, readers who know the psalm may also hear: "He hoped in the Lord, let him rescue him, let him save him, because he loves[54] him" (21:9 LXX, my trans.).

The cry of dereliction is hardly sufficient for readers to revise their understanding of the character of Jesus as God's son. Rather, the cry of dereliction and the entire crucifixion are reasons for readers to revise their understanding of the character of the God whose son Jesus is. This God has a son whose destiny is crucifixion. Does God then abandon the son in suffering? The reality of Jesus' suffering cannot be diminished. But it is also not isolated from the announcement at the tomb that Jesus has been raised (16:6, divine passive). In keeping with Psalm 21 LXX, the Lord does rescue him, because he loves him.

In trying to make sense of Mark's ending, Don Juel resists betting on the women or the readers to rescue the story. I personalize this a bit. Don was my dissertation advisor, and I write this shortly after his untimely death at the age of sixty-one gave his own life an ending that, like Mark's, begs for an interpretation to make sense of it. In *A Master of Surprise*[55] Juel responds to Frank Kermode's *The Sense of an Ending* and *Genesis of Secrecy*.[56] Kermode presupposes that reality is chaotic and that human stories superimpose order onto this chaos in a delusive attempt to render reality coherent and purposeful. Kermode appropriates Franz Kafka's parable of a man seeking admittance to the Law as the controlling image for the ending of Mark and argues that with the ending of Mark "the door of disappointment is finally shut on us" (*Genesis of Secrecy*, 145). Juel finds, however, an open door at the end of Mark. It is the open door of five foreshadowings in Mark of Jesus' resurrection and of Jesus' promise to go before his disciples into Galilee. Though readers see Jesus in a way characters in the narrative cannot, the story provides little basis for expecting readers to prove faithful where the disciples and the women fail.[57] But Juel finds hope in Jesus' words that are present by allusion in the message at the tomb: "He leads you to Galilee. There you will see him, as he told you."[58] This prolepsis pushes Mark's ending beyond the women's silence. Disciples are still to follow Jesus on the way in a "massive investment in the reliability of Jesus' words." Readers' hopes at the end of Mark depend, however, not on the fidelity of these disciples but on the fidelity of Jesus who makes a promise. Nevertheless, hope comes not only from what Jesus says but also from the God whose son he is, the God for whom all things are possible (Mark 10:27; 14:36). This God remains related to God's child in the divine passive in Mark 16:6—ἠγέρθη ("he has been raised"). Mark begins with God as an analepsis from the cultural repertoire and ends with God as a prolepsis in the form of a relationship between parent and child that stretches out into an unformulated future.[59]

Notes

1. *Dependent Rational Animals: Why Human Beings Need the Virtues* (Chicago: Open Court, 1999).
2. B. van Iersel omits God from Mark's characters and elements of greatest importance, though God is behind the scenes (*Reading Mark* [Edinburgh: T.&T. Clark, 1989], 5, 34, see 158). On God as a character, see D. Rhoads, J. Dewey, and D. Michie, *Mark as Story: An Introduction to the Narrative of a Gospel* (Minneapolis: Fortress, 1999), 78–82.

3. For W. Marxsen, Mark's good news of Jesus begins in Old Testament prophecy (*Mark the Evangelist: Studies on the Redaction History of the Gospel* [Nashville: Abingdon, 1969], 42). J. Marcus finds extensive echoes from Isaiah in Mark 1:1–15 that indicate an Isaianic context (*Mark 1–8: A New Translation with Introduction and Commentary*, AB 27 [New York: Doubleday, 2000], 139, 147, 165).

4. E. Lohmeyer, *Das Evangelium des Markus: Übersetzt und erklärt*, Kritisch-exegetischer Kommentar über das Neue Testament, 1.2 (Göttingen: Vandenhoeck & Ruprecht, 1967), 10. εὐαγγέλιον is characteristically a dynamic proclamation in Mark. Mark 1:1 claims to be the beginning of such a proclamation and so also looks forward to an anticipated proclamation that follows the reading of Mark. Thus "the beginning of the gospel" is also proleptic. See Marxsen, *Mark*, 117–38; G. Strecker, "Literarkritische Überlegungen zum εὐαγγέλιον Begriff im Markusevangelium," in *Eschaton und Historie: Aufsätze* (Göttingen: Vandenhoeck & Ruprecht, 1979), 76–89.

5. John Donahue suggests that bracketing the relationship of Jesus to God is necessary for determining Mark's view of God, though he later returns to that relationship ("A Neglected Factor in the Theology of Mark," *JBL* 101 [1982]: 563–94, 564–65). Leander Keck emphasizes the relationship of Jesus to God as necessary for Christology ("Toward the Renewal of a New Testament Christology," *NTS* 32 [1986]: 362–77). Jesus derives status as God's *son* (P. Danove, "The Narrative Function of Mark's Characterization of God," *NovT* 43 [2001]: 19–30). The character of God is likewise dependent on the relationship with Jesus, as well as other characters.

6. Marcus considers the reading secondary (*Mark*, 141). For its authenticity, see J. Gnilka, *Das Evangelium nach Markus*, 2 vols., EKK 2.1 (Zurich: Benziger and Neukirchen-Vluyn: Neukirchener Verlag, 1978), 1.43.

7. On echoes of Psalm 2 in Mark 1:9–11, see E. Haenchen, *Der Weg Jesu: Eine Erklärung des Markus-Evangeliums und der kanonischen Parallelen* (Berlin: de Gruyter, 1968), 54; J. Marcus, *The Way of the Lord: Christological Exegesis of the Old Testament in the Gospel of Mark* (Louisville, KY: Westminster/John Knox, 1992), 48–79; C.-A. Steiner, "Le lien entre le prologue et le corps de l'Évangile de Marc," in *Intertextualités: La Bible en échos*, ed. D. Marguerat and A. Curtis (Geneva: Labor et Fides, 2000): 166–71. Against Jesus as Davidic in Mark, see W. Kelber, *The Kingdom in Mark: A New Place and a New Time* (Philadelphia: Fortress, 1974), 94–97; P. Achtemeier, "'And He Followed Him': Miracles and Discipleship in Mark 10:46–52," *Semeia* 11 (1978): 125–32.

8. ". . . every statement about Christ implicates God" (Keck, "Toward the Renewal," 363); Danove, "Narrative Function," 26–27; Marcus, *Mark*, 146–48; E. Schweizer, "Mark's Theological Achievement," in *The Interpretation of Mark*, ed. W. Telford, Studies in NT Interpretation (Edinburgh: T.&T. Clark, 1995), 65–69. A. Hultgren calls Mark's Christology "theopractic" (*Christ and His Benefits: Christology and Redemption in the New Testament* [Philadelphia: Fortress, 1987], 61–63). V. Robbins suggests that Jesus acts as an autonomous teacher (*Jesus the Teacher: A Socio-Rhetorical Interpretation of Mark* [Philadelphia: Fortress, 1984], 57–68, 118–19, 200), but the parent-child relationship means Jesus is never autonomous. See R. Fowler, *Let the Reader Understand: Reader-Response Criticism and the Gospel of Mark* (Minneapolis: Fortress, 1991), 20–21.

9. That is, "the way of the Lord" can be a subjective genitive (Marcus, *Way of the Lord*, 29–31). See Tolbert, *Sowing*, 240–44.

10. The absolute use of "the spirit" is an earmark of Christian texts (see R. Bultmann, *History of the Synoptic Tradition* [New York: Harper & Row, 1963], 251). It appears, however, in 1 QS 4.6. In Jewish tradition God's spirit is an agency of God (*Sim. Enoch* 49:3, *T. Levi* 18:7, *T. Judah* 24:2). Holy spirit appears in 1 QS 4.21.

11. C. Grabbe, "Baptême de Jésus et baptême des premiers chrétiens," *RHPhR* 73 (1993/4): 377–93, 381.
12. F. Baumgärtel and E. Schweizer, "πνεῦμα," *TDNT* 6.362–65, 397–98.
13. See Fowler, *Let the Reader*, 15–16. Mark stereotypes Jewish groups but also differentiates them. B. Mack therefore incorrectly claims: "Mark, or course, lumps all forms of Judaism together" (*A Myth of Innocence: Mark and Christian Origins* [Philadelphia: Fortress, 1988], 13, see 34–52, 65–66). With the exceptions of Essenes and Sicarii, Mark names every faction that Mack does. Further, Mark distinguishes between Jerusalem and Galilee. See Kelber, *Kingdom*; E. Malbon, *Narrative Space and Mythic Meaning in Mark*, New Voices in Biblical Studies (San Francisco: Harper & Row, 1986).
14. See J. Robinson, *The Problem of History in Mark*, Studies in Biblical Theology (Naperville, IL: Allenson, 1957), 27, 33–38, 59; Gnilka, *Markus*, 1.59.
15. H. Kee, *Community of the New Age: Studies in Mark's Gospel* (Macon, GA: Mercer University Press, 1983), 107–16, 121, 133. M. Tolbert suggests that Mark develops spatial notions of God's commonwealth (*Sowing the Gospel: Mark's World in Literary-Historical Perspective* [Minneapolis: Fortress, 1989], 172). Van Iersel proposes that God's kingdom is parabolic with no unambiguous referent (*Reading*, 42). God's commonwealth is realized in the present by anticipation and therefore is fulfilled in the future (D. Via, *The Ethics of Mark's Gospel? In the Middle of Time* [Philadelphia: Fortress, 1985], 60, 63). See Gnilka, *Markus*, 1.66–67.
16. D. Rhoads, "Social Criticism: Crossing Boundaries," in *Mark and Method: New Approaches in Biblical Studies*, ed. J. Anderson and S. Moore (Minneapolis: Fortress, 1992), 154–55.
17. Jesus' proclamation in 1:15 is programmatic, but in connection with 1:1, it also means that Jesus is the good news. That is, the genitive εὐαγγέλιον τοῦ Ἰησοῦ Χριστοῦ is both objective and subjective. See Marxsen, *Mark*, 66, 117–50; van Iersel, *Reading*, 21.
18. G. Theissen, *The Miracle Stories of the Early Christian Tradition* (Philadelphia: Fortress, 1983), 4–5, 43–45, and passim. On the dramatization of God's commonwealth, see Kelber, *Kingdom*, 17 and passim. On restoration to the social order, see Haenchen, *Weg*, 113–15; W. Kelber, *The Oral and Written Gospel: The Hermeneutics of Speaking and Writing in the Synoptic Tradition, Mark, Paul, and Q* (Philadelphia: Fortress, 1983), 26.
19. Violence in the demonic sphere is reversed in the divine sphere (Robinson, *Problem*, 39). I judge H. Waetjen's association of the unclean spirit in 1:23 with the synagogue as an oppressive institution to be without merit. Further, Jesus' restoration of marginalized people to normal society indicates that he exaggerates a reordering of society (*A Reordering of Power: A Sociopolitical Reading of Mark's Gospel* [Minneapolis: Fortress, 1989], 81–82, 86–100).
20. Reiteration with variation is significant for thematization in Mark. Variation, however, also induces readers to revise their anticipations of what is true in the narrative world. M. Bakhtin, *Problems of Dostoevsky's Poetics*, Theory and History of Literature 8 (Manchester: Manchester University Press, 1984), 106; J. Kristeva, *Desire in Language: A Semiotic Approach to Literature and Art* (New York: Columbia University Press, 1980), 36–37, 66, 69; W. Iser, *The Implied Reader: Patterns of Communication in Prose Fiction from Bunyan to Beckett* (Baltimore: Johns Hopkins University Press, 1974), 278.
21. On abductive reasoning, see R. Lanigan, "From Enthymeme to Abduction: The Classical Law of Logic and the Postmodern Rule of Rhetoric," in *Recovering Pragmatism's Voice: The Classical Tradition, Rorty, and the Philosophy of Communication*, ed. L. Langsdorf and A. Smith (Albany: SUNY Press, 1995), 49–70;

G. Bateson and M. Bateson, *Angels Fear: Toward an Epistemology of the Sacred* (New York: Macmillan, 1987), 26, 174–75, 192. Abduction is tropic or metaphoric.

22. Fowler takes 2:10 as a narrator's indirection to readers and claims that no characters in the story take up "so that you may know" (*Let the Reader*, 103). But the "all" who praise God in 2:12 take it up.

23. Marcus, *Mark*, 354. Thus the roles of Jesus and God intersect.

24. On categorical statements and exceptions as established Jewish rhetoric, see Marcus, *Mark*, 284.

25. On the title in contexts of conflict and vindication, see Kelber, *Kingdom*, 83.

26. Robbins agrees (*Jesus*, 58).

27. E. Best, *Following Jesus: Discipleship in the Gospel of Mark*, JSNTSup 5 (Sheffield: JSOT, 1981), 171. Jesus' call of disciples differs from biblical and rabbinic patterns where disciples seek a teacher, and corresponds to Greco-Roman patterns of teacher-disciple relationships (Robbins, *Jesus*, 87–119). Nevertheless, similarities to rabbinic patterns are not to be overlooked. See A. Schulz, *Nachfolgen und Nachahmen: Studien über das Verhältnis der neutestamentlichen Jüngerschaft zur urchristlichen Vorbildethik* (Munich: Kössel, 1962), 63.

28. Best finds "following" too complex to be described as imitation but also sees the beginnings of a cruciform imitation of Christ in Mark (*Following Jesus*, 35–36, 39, 40–41, 58, 80, 127, 248). Best neglects deriving action from a relationship with Jesus. H. Betz takes Jesus' call of followers in Mark already as implying a relationship with the exalted one (*Nachfolge und Nachahmung Jesu Christi im Neuen Testament*, BHT 37 [Tübingen: Mohr, 1967], 32). Similarly, Haenchen, *Weg*, 36.

29. The presentation of the disciples, first favorably, then with deficiencies, evokes readers' identification and then confronts them with a revision of norms (R. Tannehill, "The Disciples in Mark: The Function of a Narrative Role," *JR* 57 [1977]: 393–405). See Best, *Following*, 12–13. Best inexplicably omits relationships between disciples and God from his consideration of "following."

30. B. Malina and R. Rohrbaugh, *Social Science Commentary on the Synoptic Gospels* (Minneapolis: Fortress, 1992), 236–37. For them, God's commonwealth is patronage (243).

31. Marcus, *Mark*, 277.

32. Tolbert takes the parable as a plot summary that also discloses characters (*Sowing*, 127–230). Literary theory on *mise en abyme*, a microcosmic reiteration of the larger story embedded in the story, would strengthen her case. See L. Dällenbach, *The Mirror in the Text* (Chicago: University of Chicago Press, 1989).

33. S. Moore, "Deconstructive Criticism: The Gospel of Mark," in *Mark and Method: New Approaches in Biblical Studies*, ed. J. Anderson and S. Moore (Minneapolis: Fortress, 1992), 87–89, 92–93; Robbins, *Jesus*, 138; R. Fowler, "Reader-Response Criticism: Figuring Mark's Reader," in *Mark and Method: New Approaches in Biblical Studies*, ed. J. Anderson and S. Moore (Minneapolis: Fortress, 1992), 72–73; *Let the Reader*, 102, 115, 168–70.

34. E. Malbon, "Narrative Criticism: How Does the Story Mean?" in *Mark and Method: New Approaches in Biblical Studies*, 39.

35. See Gnilka, *Markus*, 1.93.

36. T. Dwyer, *The Motif of Wonder in the Gospel of Mark*, JSNTSup 128 (Sheffield: Sheffield Academic Press, 1996), 117–18.

37. M. Tolbert, "Mark," *The Women's Bible Commentary*, ed. C. Newsome and S. Ringe (Louisville, KY: Westminster/John Knox, 1992), 268. See Malina and Rohrbaugh, *Social*, 210.

38. Robbins, *Jesus*, 75–119, 163, and passim.

39. See Marcus, *Mark*, 420; van Iersel, *Reading*, 98–99.

40. Best, *Following*, 69. Against Lohmeyer's portrayal of Jesus as an example for the crowd, the man, and the disciples (*Markus*, 191).

41. See Lohmeyer, *Markus*, 186.

42. Smith, "Theology," 77–78.

43. Gnilka, *Markus*, 2.80.

44. See Lohmeyer, *Markus*, 204; Fowler, *Let the Reader*, 173; Via interprets 10:15 both ways: accepting like a child, accepting a child (*Ethics*, 83, 88, 128–33).

45. Kelber, *Kingdom*, 99–102. Though Kelber notices the temple functionaries, he understands the withered fig tree as a parable of the temple's demise (*Mark*, 61–62). Gnilka takes the incident as a negative characterization of the temple and the rejection of Israel (*Markus*, 1.28; 2.125, 129–31). Rhoads et al. show the focus on leaders (*Mark*, 52, 84). So also van Iersel (*Reading*, 145–48, 153). Robinson helpfully sees a positive claim on Israel's heritage (*Problem*, 48).

46. Kelber, *Kingdom*, 103–4. For Lohmeyer, "this mountain" is the Mount of Olives (*Markus*, 239n2). In Jewish sacred geography the temple precincts include the Mount of Olives.

47. Mack, *Myth*; Rhoads et al., *Mark*.

48. See R. Brawley, *Text to Text Pours Forth Speech: Voices of Scripture in Luke–Acts*, Indiana Studies in Biblical Literature (Bloomington: Indiana University Press, 1995), 27–41. Cf. Tolbert, *Sowing*, 231–70; van Iersel, *Reading*, 148–51.

49. A. Milavec, "The Identity of 'the Son' and 'the Others': Mark's Parable of the Wicked Husbandmen Reconsidered," *BTB* 20 (1990): 30–37.

50. Via, *Ethics*, 135. For Kee, Jesus is a paradigm for the disciples, and the disciples paradigms for the community, though in failures they are models to be avoided (*Community*, 110, 153). Kee takes the discussion of the first commandment as a shift from prescriptive to affective levels, but still emphasizes "moral obligation" (deontology) and "guidelines" (158). How is it possible for guidelines to supersede the "first" command?

51. W. Vorster, "Literary Reflections on Mark 13:5–37: A Narrated Speech of Jesus," in *The Interpretation of Mark*, ed. W. Telford, Studies in NT Interpretation (Edinburgh: T.&T. Clark, 1995), 283–85; Gnilka, *Markus*, 2.199.

52. So Gnilka, *Markus*, 2.256.

53. Robinson suggests that Jesus in Gethsemane is separated from the power of the spirit like the disciples (*Problem*, 70). But the form of the prayer deconstructs that notion. See Tolbert, *Sowing*, 283.

54. With respect to humans θέλει can mean love. See W. Bauer, 6th edition.

55. *A Master of Surprise: Mark Interpreted* (Minneapolis: Fortress, 1994), 107–21.

56. *The Sense of an Ending: Studies in the Theory of Fiction* (Oxford: Oxford University Press, 1966) and *Genesis of Secrecy* (Cambridge, MA: Harvard University Press, 1979).

57. This perspective modifies Tolbert's claim that Mark uses women as role models ("Mark," 263, 266–67, but see 274). On readers as the ones who are to be faithful, see T. Boomershine, "Mark 16:8 and the Apostolic Commission," *JBL* 100 (1981): 225–39; J. Magness, *Sense and Absence: Structure and Suspension in the Ending of Mark's Gospel*, SBLSS (Atlanta: Scholars Press, 1986); Fowler, *Let the Reader*, 79, 154.

58. Juel, *Master*, 107–21. A. Lincoln also emphasizes expectation of fulfillment of promises despite failure of human actors ("The Promise and the Failure: Mark 15:7, 8," *JBL* 108 [1989]: 291–96). The analepsis in 16:7 is not to the coming son of humanity in 13:26 and 14:62 but to the Jesus who goes to Galilee in 14:28. See C. Evans, "I Will Go before You into Galilee," *JTS* 5 (1954): 3–18; R. Stein, "A Short Note on Mark XIV.28 and XVI.7," *NTS* 20 (1973–74): 445–52; Magness, *Sense and Absence*, 120–21.

59. Juel sent his essay on the ending of Mark to Kermode, and part of a letter Kermode wrote in response follows: "It is a pleasure to be criticized so seriously. I remember at the time of writing that I found part of my mind rebelling against my own arguments, and in a sense it is a relief that you have been able to dismiss all the more obvious excuses, stick to the text that ends at 16:8, and still find the door open. And so I find myself trapped by my own Kafkaesque evasions—or by your knight's move, the introduction of all those other open doors. However, I daresay you wouldn't deny that the finding of that answer was motivated by what I. A. Richards used to call 'doctrinal adhesion'—you couldn't accept that aspect of others' work and found a different answer, prompted by your faith" (quoted from T. Gillespie, "A Case of 'Doctrinal Adhesion,'" *PSB* 24 [2003]: 184–89).

PART II
ETHICS AND PAUL

Chapter 5

Paul, Job, and the New Quest for Justice

JENS HERZER   *Leipzig*

Job within the New Testament

In both Job and Paul, the quest for justice is the major issue. Despite this undisputed coincidence, one might raise the question: What has Job to do with Paul, what has Job to do with the New Testament at all? In fact, this is one of those questions one has to think about twice in order to get at least some clue of what kind of answer could be given.[1] Of course, one may first of all think of James 5:11, where the *patience* of Job is praised as a virtue worth being taken seriously for Christians too.[2] This is the only clear reference to the character of Job and his story in the entire New Testament. Without any particular quote, in James 5:11 the wealthy reversal of Job's miserable fate serves as a paradigm for the value of Christian patience in hard times. The author claims that trusting in God's mercy will finally overcome evil, even in a situation of contest when a believer cannot easily be faithful at all. David Clines called such a one-sided reading of Job "palpably untrue to the book as a whole."[3]

There is, however, a discussion whether James 5:11 has the book of Job in mind at all. Although the Letter of James and Job are both part of the Jewish wisdom tradition, according to Berndt Schaller, James 5:11 rather refers to the Jewish Job

Aggadah, represented mainly by writings such as the *Testament of Job*.[4] Besides, however, the traditional way of asking for the relationship between the Old Testament and the New Testament is to look for quotations and allusions. As James 5:11 already shows, this perspective is not sufficient, in particular with regard to the book of Job. We find fairly *clear* quotations of Job in the New Testament only in Paul's letters, namely in 1 Corinthians 3:19 (Job 5:13), Romans 11:35 (Job 41:3), and Philippians 1:19 (Job 13:16). These rare references to Job in Paul are nevertheless of particular interest and meaning for Paul's most important issue of justice or justification and the ethical consequences of his new understanding. As I will show, on the basis of given wisdom traditions Paul refers at certain points of his argument to Job because the apostle's new quest for justice builds on the rebellious questioning of the traditional thinking represented in the book of Job.

At this point I may hint at the enormous impact the figure of Job had on Western philosophy, culture, and literature over the centuries,[6] in particular on the works of Jewish authors in the twentieth century, who impressively reflect on the fate of the Jewish people in the Holocaust in the light of Job's suffering.[7] Job has been a paradigm for many of the older Greek and Latin interpreters of the New Testament and also for the patristic, medieval, and modern commentators of the book that bears his name.[8] Although the so-called Job question of innocent suffering was already present in ancient Near Eastern religions,[9] for the Western Jewish and Christian culture the biblical version of the story has definitely become a cultural phenomenon. The name Job became a synonym, an identification figure for all times, for expressing the experience and spirituality of individuals and groups who face hard times of suffering, distress, poverty, and deadly sickness.[10] Although the book of Job is rarely quoted and hardly alluded to in New Testament writings, in the commentaries of its Christian interpreters in late antiquity and medieval times the biblical personage himself served not only as a model of a Christian life, but even as a type for Christ himself in his suffering as the righteous one.[11] Such a typological reading of Job has not become a mainstream characterization and has gained—as far as I see—no further place in the history of interpretation. In more recent times, the Swiss theologian Karl Barth called Job a "witness of the truth," a "witness of Jesus Christ."[12] In his commentary on Romans, Barth could even say that there is no other relationship to God than the one that develops in the book of Job.[13] In contrast, the French theologian René Girard sees the passion narratives of the Gospels as the key to the understanding of the book of Job.[14]

Remarkably, in the Latin Church of the West the first major commentaries *on Paul* by Jerome, Victorinus, and Augustine appeared only in the fourth century, at the time when the interest *in Job* increased and major commentaries were written, such as those of Ambrose, Hilary, Gregory the Great (a very influential allegorical commentary), and again Augustine.[15] Assuming that this coincidence is not accidental, Wilhelm Geerlings explored the link between the problem of theodicy in Job and the new interest in Paul in the Latin Church of the fourth century. Apart from the intention of an allegorical and christianizing exegesis of Job, Geerlings suggests that the circumstances in religion, politics, and economy had deteriorated in the fourth century. He calls this a crisis of the ancient idea of *paideia* (education) as the common Christian concept of salvation.[16] In this situation, Geerlings argues, the question of theodicy became relevant again, and Paul's concept of righteousness functioned as an important element for an appropriate theological answer. The former focus on Job as *exemplum patientiae* (example of patience), once integrated into the concept of salvation as education, now shifts to a focus on Job as *exemplum iustitiae* (example of righteousness) and the question for theodicy.[17] A new interpretation of Paul's concept of righteousness provided a helpful solution beyond the older concepts of Marcion and the Manicheans.[18] However, Geerlings fails to provide a reasonable answer *why* Paul could be read as solution of the Job problem.

Paul, Job, and Intertextuality— Some Methodological Presuppositions

For most scholars, Job primarily raises the classical question of justice and righteousness in the relationship between God and humans. The book of Job witnesses to the crisis of wisdom by raising the issue of so-called theodicy—a term that implies the question if God is just/δίκαιος, what has God to do with evil, and the quest for God's justification in view of the suffering and evil in the world[19]—thus questioning the traditional *Tun-Ergehens-Zusammenhang* (built-in-consequence—the idea that human deeds have consequences). Job's questioning of God's justice refers to a crisis of the just and reliable world order, and it represents a major turning point in the history of thought in Judaism of the Persian period.[20]

As already mentioned, looking for certain quotations and allusions of the Old Testament in the New was—and still is—the standard scholarly approach to evaluate the relationship between the two testaments,[21] although it has been differentiated particularly in some major contributions of North American research.[22] A purely literal approach, however, is not sufficient for evaluating the influence of Old Testament traditions in writings of New Testament authors.[23] I would rather argue that *explicit* quotations do not *necessarily* indicate that an author finds a certain passage of Scripture particularly important; vice versa, the *lack* of explicit quotations does not necessarily mean that a certain Scripture passage or a religious idea is *not* relevant for a New Testament author like Paul. As a trained Pharisee, Paul knows Scripture much better—and deeper—than we can possibly explore by our electronic allies. To quote Richard Hays: "We will have great difficulty understanding Paul, the pious first-century Jew, unless we seek to situate his discourse appropriately within what Hollander calls the 'cave of resonant signification' that enveloped him: Scripture."[24] Therefore, quotations or allusions alone do not adequately indicate the influence of ideas. For Paul, Scripture is much more than a source of references suitable to underline certain arguments. Basically, Scripture forms the background of Paul's thinking, and thus one has to be aware that in lining out his arguments, Paul has much more of the tradition in mind than what appears in quotations and allusions on the surface of his writings. The problem is to identify and to describe this complexity appropriately.

Two examples underline what I mean by this presupposition. The first is the reference to Isaiah 52–53, verses of which are explicitly quoted within christological arguments only twice within the entire New Testament.[25] Nevertheless, Isaiah 52–53 became one of the most influential texts for the traditional understanding of Christ's death. Given the fact that Paul certainly knew this prophetic text, did its pattern also influence Paul's theological thinking? The second example refers to an intertextual relation within Paul's writings. No one would deny that according to the mighty first two chapters of 1 Corinthians the term "cross" is of utmost importance to describe and summarize Paul's theology. Some would even go so far as to call Paul's theology a "theology of the cross." On the other hand, no one would deny either that the Letter to the Romans is the apostle's most impressive attempt to summarize and clarify his theology. And yet, in the entire letter the noun "cross" does not occur a single time. There must be a certain reason for Paul not to mention it there, although one could hardly draw the conclusion that it is no longer important to him. What Paul had in mind extends beyond his explicit words and influences their meaning.

Therefore in our case of the relationship of Paul to the book of Job, I would like to draw attention to the conceptual issues of how wisdom concepts have changed and how those changes have shaped sapiential thinking. Methodologically, this is the question of intertextuality, of an intertextual reading of Paul in the light of Job and his approach to wisdom. Taking the explicit quotations of Job as hints at a deeper meaning, I am asking primarily for structural parallels in the understanding of wisdom, which Paul and Job may have in common, rather than *only* interpreting certain *literal* parallels. To put it into a question: What does Job's wisdom contribute to a better understanding of what Paul meant to be God's wisdom and the essence of God's justice? This is, in fact, a question of intertextuality or, as Richard Hays puts it more vividly, a question of "*sounding echoes of Scripture.*"[26]

The discussion over the last decades has shown that the understanding of intertextuality within scholarship is very diverse.[27] Moreover, the concepts of intertextuality depend to a high degree on the presuppositions of the individual interpreter. Some understand it just as another expression of the classic method of tradition history, looking for certain references or parallels of expressions and words in earlier writings in order to explain a certain passage. The approach of intertextuality in semiotic research, however, intends to explore the meaning and significance of a text in relation to other texts or, rather, to other textual *universes*—whether or not there is a *direct* reference or word parallel to encounter. Semiotics seeks to explore the interrelations in the discursive universes of the author and reader when producing or reading texts, not primarily in the texts itself. "Discursive universe" means the intelligible world that is constituted by certain knowledge, traditions, social class, ethical values, and thus influences the capability and the ability of someone to understand, interpret, and communicate with others. Taking up a definition of Wesley Kort, intertextuality is primarily a phenomenon of cultural or religious discourses, not simply a method of analyzing texts.[28] Texts, in this regard, are witnesses of interacting discourses, and to ask for their interactions is to ask for intertextuality.

Accordingly, dealing with Paul and Job in terms of justice and ethics, I would like to expand the perspective from a tradition historical approach to the question of how Paul's discursive universe is affected by wisdom thought and especially by Job's problem of theodicy that—in its time—marked an important turning point of wisdom. Both Job and Paul share the quest for justice and righteousness as a quest for God's wisdom. From an intertextual perspective, I suggest that Paul's take on this issue is, indeed, a solution to the classic problem of Job.

Paul's References to Job and the Understanding of Justice

Applying the theory of intertextuality to Job and Paul, one might learn how Paul's new discursive universe is affected when taking into account the importance Job has had in wisdom tradition. Richard P. C. Hanson even called the book of Job "the Epistle to the Romans of the Old Testament."[29]

Paul's place within Judaism, as well as his understanding of justice and justification, is closely related to Jewish wisdom tradition,[30] but explored from a new christological or rather messianological point of view. Given this "new perspective of Paul," which he gained by what he describes as a revelation from God (Gal. 1:16), and given the intertextual relations to Job's challenge to wisdom, I would argue that Paul's messianic perspective witnesses to a new crisis of wisdom. As the law has been the ultimate expression of wisdom in Pharisaic Judaism,[31] the new crisis of wisdom for Paul is mainly a crisis of the law. This is why in Paul's understanding of Judaism the law plays such an important role in his theology. Thus Paul's messianic perspective on wisdom and the law attests to a crisis that was as dramatic as the crisis of the *Tun-Ergehens-Zusammenhang* in Job's wisdom. As the book of Job witnesses to a crisis of Israel's wisdom, so does Paul witness to a crisis of contemporary wisdom, which—in his view—has ruled both the Jewish world with focus on the law and also the pagan world of his time with focus on philosophy (1 Cor. 1–2). From Paul's messianic point of view, there is no difference between these two discursive universes of wisdom or philosophy.

The central point of Paul is a new quest for justice and righteousness, which is no longer focused only on Israel, but also on the nations. For Paul, the link between Israel and the nations is still God's universal wisdom, which is constituted by a new understanding of the law from the perspective of the messianic promises, and which now is represented by the crucified Messiah Jesus, as Paul points out in 1 Corinthians 1:30 (my trans.): "From God you received your life which is based on Christ Jesus, who [i.e., according to the context, as the crucified!] became for us wisdom from God, that is righteousness and sanctification and redemption." It is therefore not accidental that we find one of Paul's rare explicit quotations of Job in 1 Corinthians 3:19—in the résumé of his long argument on God's wisdom and the world's foolishness: "For the wisdom of this world is foolishness with God. For it is written, 'He catches the wise in their craftiness'" (NRSV; a quotation from Job 5:13, by which Paul refers back to 1 Cor. 1:19).[32] Paul does not explicitly mention Job himself. But even so, this verse shows how much Paul's idea of God's wisdom carries the same critical potential as Job's questioning of the traditional patterns of wisdom.

For both Job and Paul, God's wisdom is at stake. Both plead for an understanding of God's wisdom beyond the contemporary human perception. Like Job, Paul gets also an impression of God's wisdom by a divine revelation (Gal. 1:16). In 2 Corinthians 4:6, he describes this outstanding experience in creation terminology as a process of understanding and enlightenment: "For it is the God who said, 'Let light shine out of darkness,' who has shone [enlightened] in our hearts to give the light of the knowledge of the glory of God in the face of Jesus Christ" (NRSV).[33]

Thus the question arises, What is "new" with respect to the wisdom about God's justice and righteousness that is represented by the crucified Christ, revealed in terms of enlightenment, and thus proclaimed as the λόγος ὁ τοῦ σταυροῦ, the "word of the cross" (1 Cor. 1:18)?[34] Here we turn to Romans 11. As mentioned above, in his Letter to the Romans Paul does not necessarily need the term "cross" in order to express his understanding of this new wisdom. He does not even need the term "wisdom" (σοφία) to do so. In Romans 1:14, 22, Paul uses the term σοφοί in the same sense as in 1 Corinthians 3:19, yet the noun σοφία we find *only once*, in Romans 11:33, just before Paul's reference to Job 41:3 in Romans 11:35:

> 33 O the depth of the riches and wisdom and knowledge of God! How unsearchable are his judgments and how inscrutable his ways! 34 'For who has known the mind of the Lord? Or who has been his counselor?' 35 '*Or who has given a gift to him, to receive a gift in return?*' 36 For from him and through him and to him are all things. To him be the glory forever. Amen. (NRSV, my emphasis)

Here again, as in 1 Corinthians 3:19, the quotation from Job is part of the résumé of a larger argument, that not only includes Romans 9–11, but spans from Romans 1:16–11:32. The center of this main corpus of Romans—ending up in chapter 11 with a quotation of Job (!)—is, of course, Romans 3:21–26.[35]

It is in this passage that Paul gives a new answer to Job's classical question, whether God is righteous. The term δικαιοσύνη θεοῦ (God's righteousness) appears four times in six verses, two times within the phrase εἰς ἔνδειξιν τῆς δικαιοσύνης αὐτοῦ (in order to prove his righteousness). Romans 3:26 leaves no doubt that *God's* righteousness is Paul's main concern, because this verse is loaded with the claim that God is just. Only if God proves to be just, can humans become righteous before God. For Paul, however, the *proof* of God's justice is the way God acted on Jesus of Nazareth, the Jewish prophet, who was crucified because of challenging the traditional wisdom of his time. From this perspective,

Paul realizes that in the way this prophet challenged wisdom, was crucified, but in the end was justified by God himself, God revealed *God's own* justice and wis- dom *against* traditional human understanding.

What, then, is the function of Romans 11:33–35? After talking about justice and justification and the way God's wisdom and righteousness appeared anew in the Messiah Jesus, Paul needed to explain what that means to *Israel* and its rela- tionship to God, because this question arises necessarily from his argument (see already Rom. 3:5). Paul experienced that his teaching of God's new wisdom in Christ was mostly rejected by his fellow Jews. Consequently he asks: "Has God rejected his people?" (Rom. 11:1) The only possible answer is: Of course not, because this would *disprove* God to be just, for it would question the promises God granted Israel. In the end, Paul argues in a way similar to the book of Job: It is only temporarily that God has rejected his people—as he dealt also with Job. Yet, this does not mean that God is unjust but that God's aim was also to include the nations in the promises. Especially in Romans 11 Paul points out that this is exactly what could already be found in the Scriptures. In terms of Israel's lasting relationship with God, Paul—at this very last point of his argument in Romans 11:33–35—offers no other solution than the book of Job:[36] God's wisdom and knowledge of salvation for all humans is based on the confidence that God is the creator of all things: "For from him and through him and to him are all things" (Rom. 11:36). In Paul as in Job, it is the wide horizon of creation that makes one believe in God's wisdom.

Concluding Remarks: The Impact on Ethics

In 1 Corinthians 3:19 as well as in Romans 11:35, Paul refers to Job at the very end of his theological argument. In Romans 11 it is even the very last quotation of Scripture before the ethical part of the letter. Earlier on, I mentioned Karl Barth calling Job the witness to the true witness Jesus Christ. On the basis of my intertextual reading, the conclusion seems likely that Paul would probably *never* have said this. He would rather call Job the witness to the way God's wisdom is being newly revealed, namely, by challenging the ways humans think about God, God's wisdom, and God's justice. Like the book of Job, Paul has impressively shown what deep impact this new perspective on God's own justice has on ethi- cal values. Therefore the most intriguing result of Paul's theological argument is the challenge of new ethical standards for Gentiles and the new foundation of the old ethical values for the Jews. Living a new life with new values and a new perspective is possible only because God himself challenged the way humans were getting used to thinking of God and God's justice. Again, we find the same pat- tern of argument as in the book of Job: God challenges human wisdom that makes people think about God and God's relationship to humans in a certain way, and the challenge consists of giving a new perspective. Thus it becomes clear that only God's own justice is the sufficient and efficient basis of human right- eousness and the ability to meet and to realize ethical standards.[37]

Notes

1. Berndt Schaller, "Zum Textcharakter der Hiobzitate im paulinischen Schrifttum," *ZNW* 71 (1980): 20–26, 20 states: "Die biblische Hiobdichtung hat—soweit das literarisch faßbar ist—in der urchristlichen Frömmigkeit und Theologie keine besondere Rolle gespielt. Unter den neutestamentlichen Schriftstellern ist Paulus der einzige, der Kenntnis des Hiobbuches selbst verrät."

2. See Theresia Hainthaler, *'Von der Ausdauer Ijobs habt ihr gehört' (Jak 5,11): Zur Bedeutung des Buches Ijob im Neuen Testament*, EHS XXIII/337 (Frankfurt/Main et al.: Peter Lang, 1988), 315–24.

3. David J. A. Clines, "Why Is There a Book of Job, and What Does It Do to You If You Read It?" in *Interested Parties: The Ideology of Writers and Readers of the Hebrew Bible*, ed. David J. A. Clines, JSOTSup 205 (Sheffield: Sheffield Academic Press, 1995), 122–44, 137.

4. Schaller, "Textcharakter," 20n1. See also Gabrielle Oberhänsli-Widmer, "Hiobtraditionen im Judentum," in *Das Buch Hiob und seine Interpretationen: Internationales Symposium auf dem Monte Verità, Ascona (Schweiz) 14.-19. August 2005*, ed. Konrad Schmid (forthcoming). The same volume will include an extended and different version of this paper, in which the issue of James and Job as well as the problem of James and the Testament of Job will be explained in more detail under the title "Jakobus, Paulus und Hiob—Die Intertextualität der Weisheit."

5. The list in the 27th edition of Nestle-Aland provides eighty-two references, of which four are highlighted as quotations: 1 Cor. 3:19 = Job 5:13; Rom. 11:35 = Job 41:3, and Matt. 21:9//Mark 11:10 = Job 16:19, though the last one is not convincing at all, because only the phrase ἐν ὑψίστοις appears, which is much too common and here, if anything, intentionally more closely related to Ps. 148:1 (see Hainthaler, *Bedeutung* [see n. 2], 58–59). Remarkably, in contrast to the 25th edition of Nestle-Aland, Phil. 1:19 is not any longer regarded as a quotation of Job 13:16, but see Schaller, "Textcharakter," passim; Hainthaler, *Bedeutung*, 221–26.

6. See recently Gabrielle Oberhänsli-Widmer, *Hiob in jüdischer Antike und Moderne: Die Wirkungsgeschichte Hiobs in der jüdischen Literatur* (Neukirchen-Vluyn: Neukirchner Verlag, 2003).

7. Cf. Georg Langenhorst, "Ijob—Vorbild in Demut und Rebellion," in *Die Bibel in der deutschsprachigen Literatur des 20. Jahrhunderts*, Bd. 2: *Personen und Figuren*, ed. Heinrich Schmidinger (Mainz: Matthias-Grünewald-Verlag, 1999), 259–80.

8. Cf. Hainthaler *Bedeutung*, 13–20; David Clines, "Job and the Spirituality of the Reformation," in idem, *Interested Parties*, 145–71.

9. See Ronald J. Williams, "Theodicy in the Ancient Near East," in *Theodicy in the Old Testament*, ed. James L. Crenshaw, Issues in Religion and Theology 4 (Philadelphia: Fortress/London: SPCK, 1983), 42–56. Hans-Peter Müller, *Das Hiobproblem: Seine Stellung und Entstehung im Alten Orient und im Alten Testament*, EdF 84, 2nd ed. (Darmstadt: Wissenschaftliche Buchgesellschaft, 1982); Dorothea Sitzler, *Vorwurf gegen Gott: Ein religiöses Motiv im Alten Orient (Ägypten und Mesopotamien)* (Wiesbaden: Harrassowitz, 1995).

10. See radically and exemplary David J. A. Clines, "Job and the Spirituality of the Reformation," 156: "Luther's Job is a Luther clone, a model of the Reformer's own self-image."

11. See for example Hesychius, *Homilies on Job 22*, PO 42,2, 532–553; see Hainthaler, *Bedeutung*, 18.

12. Karl Barth, *Kirchliche Dogmatik* IV/3 (Zurich: Theologischer Verlag, 1989), 443–44 (with reference to Wilhelm Vischer, *Hiob: Ein Zeuge Jesu Christi* [1933, 6th ed. 1947]) and 448: "Immerhin steht dem Ungleichen in allen diesen Punkten so viel Gleiches gegenüber, daß man gerade im Blick auf diesen ersten und für das Ganze entscheidenden Aspekt seiner Existenz im Verhältnis zu der Jesu Christi wohl von einer Analogie und also von Hiob, bei aller gebotenen Zurückhaltung, als von einem Typus Jesu Christi, einem Zeugen des wahrhaftigen Zeugen reden darf."

13. Karl Barth, *Der Römerbrief*, 2nd ed. 1922 (Zurich: Theologischer Verlag, 1999), 3.

14. René Girard, *La route antique des hommes pervers* (Paris: Grasset, 1985), 237.

15. Wilhelm Geerlings, "Hiob und Paulus: Theodizee und Paulinismus in der lateinischen Theologie am Ausgang des vierten Jahrhunderts," *JAC* 24 (1981): 56–66, 57–58.

16. Geerlings, "Hiob und Paulus," 59.

17. Geerlings, "Hiob und Paulus," 61; see Ambrosiast. *Quaest.* 118,2 (CSEL 50:355).

18. Geerlings, "Hiob und Paulus," 62–66; Geerlings closes with the thesis: "Pointiert dürfte man aufgrund der vorangegangenen Überlegungen nun vielleicht formulieren, daß Hiob und Paulus auf dem Hintergrund der Situation des vierten Jahrhunderts sich wie Frage und Antwort zueinander verhalten, daß in den Hiobkommentaren und Traktaten zum Hiobbuch sich die Krisenstimmung der ausgehenden Antike artikuliert, daß mit Hilfe der paulinischen Kategorien, vornehmlich denen des Römerbriefs, eine Antwort auf diese Anfragen gegeben wird. Die Pauluskommentare versuchen, einer veränderten anthropologischen Situation und einem neuen Nachdenken über Ohnmacht und Möglichkeiten des Menschen gerecht zu werden" (66).

19. On theodicy in the Hebrew Bible, see for example the collection of essays (positions of research in the twentieth century) in James L. Crenshaw, *Theodicy*.

20. See Müller, *Hiobproblem*.

21. This is true of some strands in German and Anglo-American scholarship, for example (to name only a few), Dietrich-Alex Koch, *Die Schrift als Zeuge des Evangeliums: Untersuchungen zur Verwendung und zum Verständnis der Schrift bei Paulus*, BHT 69 (Tübingen: Mohr Siebeck, 1986); Hans Hübner, *Vetus Testamentum in Novo*, 2 vols. (Göttingen: Vandenhoeck & Ruprecht, 1997 and 2003); E. Earl Ellis, *Paul's Use of the Old Testament* (Edinburgh/London: Oliver & Boyd, 1957); especially on Job and the New Testament, see Hainthaler, *Bedeutung*.

22. Donald Hagner, *The Use of the Old and New Testament in Clements of Rome*, NovTSup 34 (Leiden: Brill, 1973); Richard B. Hays, *Echoes of Scripture in the Letters of Paul* (New Haven, CT: Yale University Press, 1989); Robert Brawley, *Text to Text Pours Forth Speech: Voices of Scripture in Luke–Acts*, Indiana Studies in Biblical Literature (Bloomington: Indiana University Press, 1995).

23. See, for this approach, in particular Hainthaler, *Bedeutung*.

24. Hays, *Echoes*, 21, with reference to John Hollander, *The Figure of Echo: A Mode of Allusion in Milton and After* (Berkeley: University of California Press, 1981), 65.

25. 1 Pet. 2:21–25; Acts 8:32–33.

26. Hays, *Echoes*, esp. 14–21 (emphasis mine). Hays also uses the expressions "intertextual relations with Scripture" (xi), "intertextual echo" (xii and passim).

27. As an overview, see, for example, Stefan Alkier, "Intertextualität—Annäherungen an ein texttheoretisches Paradigma," in *Heiligkeit und Herrschaft: Intertextuelle Studien zu Heiligkeitsvorstellungen und zu Psalm 110*, ed. Dieter Sänger,

Biblisch-Theologische Studien 55 (Neukirchen-Vluyn: Neukirchner Verlag, 2003), 1–26. Particularly on Paul: Richard B. Hays, "Schriftverständnis und Intertextualität bei Paulus," *ZNT* 14 (2004): 55–64.

28. See Wesley A. Kort, *"Take, Read"—Scripture, Textuality, and Cultural Practice* (University Park: Pennsylvania State University Press, 1996). I can touch on this matter only briefly here, and I only mention the important issue of defining the relationship of an intertextual approach to critical-historical approaches. Richard Hays has convincingly shown that the theological and hermeneutical profits are not against but *beyond* classical solutions of textual and historical criticism. On this, see for example Hays, *Echoes*, xi–xii, 5–10, 15. Hays, however, proposes an application of intertextuality in "a more limited sense, focusing on his actual citations of and allusions to specific texts" (15). In this regard, his careful exploration of the echo of Job 13:16 in Phil. 1:19 is unsurpassed; see Hays, *Echoes*, 21–24, 25–31.

29. Richard P. C. Hanson, "St Paul's Quotations of the Book of Job," *Theology* 31 (1950): 250–53, 253.

30. See Ed P. Sanders, *Paul and Palestinian Judaism* (London: SCM / Philadelphia: Fortress, 1977); James D. G. Dunn, *The Theology of Paul the Apostle* (Edinburgh: Clark, 1998).

31. See *Odes Sol.*; *Pss. Sol.*, Apocalyptic Literature.

32. For the form of the Greek text of the quotation from Job 5:13, see Schaller, "Textcharakter," 23–25; further Hainthaler, *Bedeutung*, 258–63. Schaller argues for all three quotations of Job in 1 Cor. 3:19, Rom. 11:35, and Phil. 1:19 that they all rely on the Septuagint; for a different view on 1 Cor. 3:19 and Rom. 11:35, see Ellis, *Use*, 144 (with note 3) and 14–20. Ellis, p. 154, counts Phil. 1:19 not as quotation but as allusion, yet to the Septuagint version of Job 13:16.

33. Some regard this verse as a reference to Job 37:15. See Hainthaler, *Bedeutung*, 263–66.

34. NRSV interprets: "the message *about* the cross"; RSV: "the word of the cross"; KJV: "the preaching of the cross."

35. For this, see for example Douglas A. Campbell, *The Rhetoric of Righteousness in Rom 3:21–26*, JSNTSup 65 (Sheffield: Sheffield Academic Press, 1992).

36. See also Hanson, "Quotations," 251.

37. Paul's approach, of course, is one way of taking up the classical question of Job. In the introductory remarks I mentioned the letter of James as another example, focusing more explicitly on the martyrological side of Job's patience and its relevance for Christian ethics. In order to argue this way, James had to answer the question of the origin of evil within his argument on wisdom in the very first chapter: The temptation of evil is not from God (Jas. 1:13)! And therefore it's not God but the diabolos, the great confuser, the addressees should resist (4:7). In this regard, James represents a different strand of the perception of Job in early Christianity, which might be connected to some aggadic Job traditions such as the *Testament of Job*. See also Herzer, "Jakobus." Further Berndt Schaller, *Das Testament Hiobs*, JSHRZ III/3 (Gütersloh: Gütersloher Verlagshaus, 1979), 308–9.

Chapter 6

Freeing Exegesis

L. ANN JERVIS

The typical motivation for those who undertake graduate training in biblical studies is the upward call of being able to do "exegesis," which signifies to such intrepid souls becoming competent to read the text rightly, in distinction from "amateur," "pious" readings. We biblical scholars often see ourselves as especially skilled at taking from the text only what the text wants to and should give. The special "status" accorded exegetical reading in certain circles validates a biblical scholar's paychecks. Most people can find meaning in the Bible if they so choose,[1] but the biblical scholar as an exegetical reader can read best.

While this paradigm for the role of biblical scholars has had its benefits, one of its disadvantages is that it tends to distance the work of the biblical scholar from much of life. In particular, it has either resulted in or required a separation of the work of exegesis from the life of the scholar herself and the life of the community of faith in which she lives. I would suggest that this is a large part of the reason for the tragic and problematic divide between biblical scholars and their colleagues who work in theology and ethics.

This is an abbreviated and altered version of a chapter in *At the Heart of the Gospel: Suffering in the Earliest Christian Message* (Grand Rapids: Eerdmans, forthcoming). Used by permission.

In what follows, I as a biblical scholar attempt a description and demonstra-
tion of a type of Bible reading that is more comfortably, unapologetically, and
self-consciously connected to the living of my life and our lives. I begin by setting the stage for the type of exegesis I propose.

Setting the Stage

On the stage is a backdrop that depicts a critical acceptance of postmodernism's
exposure of the flaws in the Enlightenment project, in particular the Enlightenment conviction that humans are capable of separating reason from belief and
experience. This "fictitious objectivity"[2] as it relates to biblical scholarship manifests itself in a misguided confidence in biblical scholarship's ability, based
on historical-critical methods, to interpret the Bible from an objective stance.
Postmodernism has opened our eyes to the fact, among other things,[3] that the
quest for one true meaning is fruitless and illusory,[4] and that the reader/hearer/
interpreter can never escape her own horizons. Postmodernism contends that
what one of modernity's preeminent spokepersons in biblical studies describes as
a two-stage interpretative process—exegetes are to ask what a text meant and
preachers what a text means[5]—is neither possible nor perhaps desirable. K. Stendahl considered it crucial to keep the two tenses apart and so to divide the job of
interpretation between the exegete (who asks what a text meant) and the preacher
(who is responsible for translating the original past sense of the text into the tense
of the present day).[6] Modernity's exegete, in other words, is to stay within the
limits of the past, asking what the text meant.

Without engaging with specific postmodern thinkers, or with a type of postmodern reading, I simply here credit postmodern thinking with drawing our
attention to the fact that our present experiences, and reflections upon them, necessarily inform and shape our understandings.

The backdrop on our stage is rather more complex than simply a representa-
tion of this postmodern epistemological claim. It stands on stage to create a space
shaped by, as mentioned above, a *critical* acceptance of what postmodernism recognizes about our capacities to know. This backdrop is three dimensional; its
depth comes from bas-relief figures depicting intense and energetic conversation.
The effect of these figures is to draw the eye to the struggle, the possibility, and
the ethical imperative of communication between others. The figures demonstrate the importance of respectful communication—seeking to hear an other,
while seeking at the same time to be heard; being willing to question the privilege of one's self, while honoring and being honest about one's self and at the same
time recognizing and respecting the otherness of the other.

These figures are, as mentioned, carved onto the surface of postmodernism.
The dominant features of these figures are shaped by postmodernism's critics, in
particular their portrayal of enthusiastic engagement in communication reflects
the hand of these critics.[7] The figures, each of which is extravagantly individual,
are listening and speaking to each other and reading intently a book. The effect

is to convey the idea that communication of this sort is possible. At the same time, on the backdrop's framework we see painted depictions of modernity's biblical scholars, with blank, expressionless faces, looking uniformly similar, seriously pickaxing away at the biblical text—reminding us of traditional biblical critics' attempt to ignore or hide the interpreter's own personality. *or preachers*

The effect of the juxtaposition of the bas-relief figures with the framework of the backdrop is to create a sort of rapprochement between these representations of the significance of the interpreter. It is clear that neither one is adequate on its own: the figures, standing alone, could easily be understood to be creating their own world of ideas, unchecked by sober second thought, reason, and the hard work of scholarship, while the blank, serious faces on the frame, seen alone, would provoke the question of how their work relates to anything other than the text, especially whether it relates to and reflects the concerns of the scholars themselves. However, the dynamic created by the two apparently conflicting aspects of the backdrop is to draw the eye from one to the other and so to create the understanding that there is a "circle of reader and text."[8] The effect is to convey the idea that the reader's self-understanding and life situation, the reader's prior encounter with the text, and the reader's conversation about her engagement with the text, inform and shape her interpretation of it,[9] but that this neither precludes nor obviates the need for critical thinking and research.

In front of this backdrop we see a biblical scholar in intimate conversation with the biblical text, walking between various venues on stage—a study, a bedroom, a kitchen, a park, and a church sanctuary. These stage sets are meant to convey the quotidian, the daily round—life's moments. In each of these venues are other people. While in almost all of the stage settings the people are very much alive, in the study the people have a rather shadowy cast.

The biblical scholar moves from one venue to another, book in hand, engaging with where she is. The dramatic effect is that she and the book are in continual conversation even as she lives her life. She and the Bible together live her life. She performs a "trialogue"—she, the Bible, and the moments and people in her life.

The energy motivating this trialogue stems from a conviction on the part of the exegete both that the biblical text has something to offer to her and that legitimately and unavoidably her life with its concerns should shape the work of interpretation. The drama on stage is propelled by two dynamics—the biblical scholar's belief that the biblical text might illuminate present experience, and her contented embrace of postmodernism's insight that an interpreter's concerns are always present in the act of interpretation. Her stance effectively casts a shadow on the backdrop's framework, which represents the "modern" biblical scholar's quest for the interpreter's invisibility, while not obliterating from view their stern, hardworking faces.

As the biblical scholar moves about the stage, spending time in one venue and then another, we come to understand her to be building a bridge across the "ugly, broad ditch"[10] that has divided traditional biblical criticism from the life of faith. Her trialogue is energized by her scholar's conviction that the Bible is germane

If postmodernism is saying that we each read thru the lenses of our own experience, etc. – of course. That is so. Deus

to the present life of faith. Her actions demonstrate the premodern (and now contemporary)[11] understanding that the Bible may be heard well with the ears of faith.[12]

On stage there is one venue, her study, where the biblical scholar spends a disproportionate amount of time, more than anywhere else. Here we see her in conversation with various scholars struggling to hear the otherness of the text. The discipline of this form of conversation is motivated by the long and sound arm of modernity, which guides her to believe in the possibility of rational communication, provided one seeks to understand the language and the historical context and particularity out of which the text's words come. This arm, however, is more flexible than expected—it is capable of absorbing also the impulses that come from the interpreter herself.

In this venue of interaction we notice what we have seen in other venues—that the exegete does not shut her life out as she listens to the voices of other scholars and strives to hear the biblical text. She is seeking to hear the Bible for the sake of her life and all that is in it; this fact is conveyed dramatically by the open door and windows of her study.

Introduction to Exegetical Demonstration

Leaving aside the metaphor of the stage, let me briefly outline the type of exegesis I am proposing. In one way it is similar to the more traditional exegesis in which many biblical scholars trade, and in two ways it is dissimilar. What is similar is that this kind of exegesis believes that the tools of our trade and the nature of texts mean that we are able to hear something in addition to ourselves when we do our work. This is not to say that we expect to encounter one true meaning, but rather that we may encounter an other.

What is dissimilar is that the entry to the exegetical task is through a specific question relating to our present life and/or the life of our faith communities and/or our world. Here the exegete approaches a biblical text not with the question, what did this text mean? but with the question, what does this text say to a particular issue? The issue that draws the interpreter to exegesis arises from the interpreter's experience of life.

The other dissimilarity is that *the exegete does not consider herself to have completed the work of exegesis until she has given her opinion on how what she has found in her research could or should be of service to those who care to use the Bible.* Her work in the study, initiated and complemented by the other moments of her life, bursts the bounds of the study into the other places where she lives. In fact, she does her work *for* the life she knows. Her biblical scholarly work is not complete until it speaks in the rest of her life.

It is now time to demonstrate this form of exegesis, one that frees the exegete to accept and address to the biblical text concerns in her context, liberating her to overstep her traditional boundaries of proposing only what the text may have meant in its original setting.

I am concerned with suffering. At present this concern is not with suffering as a philosophical or theological problem; it is not a concern with the problem of evil or with theodicy. Rather, I am concerned about suffering because I myself have known a degree of it, at one time or another people I love suffer, and I am clearly aware daily of the sufferings of people I encounter through walking the streets or being exposed to the media. I wonder about what it is to suffer as a believer in Jesus Christ. I start my exegesis by reflecting on the fact that, in my experience, being a believer in Jesus Christ does not protect one from suffering. *The beginning of this type of exegesis is not with the text but with the interpreter.*

The next task is finding an appropriate biblical text to work with—a biblical passage that might offer useful perspectives on the problem or issue about which the interpreter is exercised. This step runs the risk of choosing passages that are the least strange and foreign, the least challenging to the interpreter's expectations and assumptions about what the Bible might have to say. An aspect of this risk is that this step might dangerously encourage an interpreter's natural narcissism —finding her concern reflected in a text that might actually wish to speak to something very different. However, I can think of no reasonable and foolproof way of proceeding other than narrowing the field and making a particular choice, while being careful to notice the danger involved in that action.

For our purposes, I have chosen Philippians 3:7–11, for reasons that I trust will become obvious. The hazard involved in making this choice is that, while my concern and this text appear related—my concern is suffering as a believer in Jesus Christ, and this text, by a believer in Jesus Christ chained in prison, speaks of suffering—nevertheless I am at risk of minimizing the difference between the type of suffering Paul is speaking about and the type of suffering about which I am concerned. The danger is that, in my eagerness to bring the biblical text into conversation with my concern, I will miss the uniqueness of Paul's sufferings. Perhaps the only guard against this danger is to beware of it.

As will be clear in the following exegesis, the concern with which I the exegete enter the exegesis determines the emphasis and interests of the exegesis itself. In other words, this part of the type of exegesis here proposed is *not* comparable to Stendahl's stage one of the interpretative process—asking what the text meant. Here the exegetical task *begins* with a desire to find something useful for the present moment, albeit, as I have said, it *proceeds* by using the tools of critical biblical scholarship, and so seeks to discipline that desire with a willingness to hear the unexpected or unwanted. This type of exegesis tends more toward a hermeneutics of sympathy than of suspicion, but by maintaining the discipline of using historical-critical tools it does not allow itself to think it can readily hear the biblical text and guards against a direct appropriation of the Bible into a modern context.

Nevertheless, this type of reading accepts that the distance between past and present is already bridged on the pylons of the interpreter's articulated concern and her expectation that the Bible can be useful for the life of faith. In this regard, there are not two stages to the interpretative task, the first dealing with the past and the second with the present. To a degree, the past and the present are fused in the energy of the interpreter's concern. However, this fusion does not obliterate the entities involved. The biblical text and the contemporary interpreter remain separate; however, they are not locked in their foreign worlds but rather, because they exist in the same circle of meaning, may radiate off each other.[13] *The present tense of the interpreter commingles with the past tense of the Bible text, even during the traditional work of biblical exegesis.*

The last part of the interpretative task will be suggesting how the insights arising from the exegetical work might be useful in the present.

Philippians 3:7–11 and Suffering as a Christian

Circumstances of Writing

Paul wrote the letter that came to be known as Philippians when he was in chains. While this incarceration clearly allowed Paul enough freedom to send letters, to receive aid and news, and to continue to direct his coworkers in matters related to his mission,[14] he *is* in prison, a place designed to create enormous discomfort.[15] Paul suffers as he writes this letter. There are some who read Paul as "the Stoic sage" and hear his words as indicating that "he is anything but pained."[16] These acoustics for reading Paul's letter to Philippi are different from mine and that of many others in the long tradition of the church.[17]

What makes Philippians in general and Philippians 3:7–11 in particular pertinent to my question is that the letter as a whole provides us with a firsthand account of a believer in Jesus Christ suffering, and in the passage I have singled out Paul reflects on this situation. Paul's hardships at the time of writing Philippians are real. Paul does not describe his circumstances simply as imprisonment; he speaks rather of being in fetters.[18] That these chains were less than comfortable is indicated both by the fact that Paul makes repeated reference to them (1:7, 13, 14, 17) and by his accusation that some are trying to add pressure to them (1:17)[19]—the implication being that they already are a source of pain. Chains in imprisonment were not only a way to prevent escape. The very weight of chains was part of a prisoner's punishment. At times the weight was so great that arms and legs were permanently disfigured or disabled.[20]

Not only is Paul hurting in body; he also knows mental anguish. While Paul is bound in chains, some people are preaching Christ insincerely, probably using the fact of his imprisonment for their own advantage and to discredit Paul's message (1:15–17). The brave front Paul attempts—"What then? Only that in every way, whether in pretense, or in truth, Christ is proclaimed; and in that I rejoice" (1:18, NRSV)—barely masks his immediately preceding admission that such action has the capacity to afflict him (1:17). Moreover, Paul hints at his worry that his imprisonment has taken the wind out of the sails of some believers. When he writes that "most of the brothers have been made confident in the Lord" because of his chains (1:14), Paul implicitly acknowledges that some do find his imprisonment a threat to their faith in Christ.

Purpose in Writing

Philippians is an apology for suffering. It is primarily a defense of Paul's own suffering 'in' Christ.[21] The letter also functions as an encouragement for the Philippians to accept their sufferings 'in' Christ,[22] but space permits us to focus chiefly only on Paul's apology for his afflictions. E. Lohmeyer suggested that Paul is concerned to promote his own (or others') martyrdom.[23] I will, however, suggest that the suffering Paul discusses is, as it were, of a more pedestrian variety.[24]

Paul's eagerness to defend his difficult circumstances surfaces early in this missive. After thanking God for his addressees (1:3–11), as he does in almost every letter, Paul tells his readers that he wants them to know that what has happened to him has resulted in the advancement of the gospel (1:12). Paul's words have at least a shade of self-defensiveness. And, almost immediately, the reason for Paul's apology regarding his circumstances becomes clear; some are using his imprisonment as an opportunity to hurt his mission (1:15, 17). The letter strongly hints, then, that Paul's imprisonment is being used to discredit Paul's gospel.

Paul seeks to deal with this situation by distinguishing between those who love him and those who do not. Those who love him, Paul writes, recognize that his situation is consonant with the gospel and for the sake of the gospel (1:16). Paul's accusation is that those who do *not* love him have an incorrect interpretation of his incarceration. We may readily surmise that Paul's imprisonment was being used to claim that he and his gospel were disreputable. Calvin puts it: "those bad workmen . . . did not refrain from triumphing over the calamity of the holy man, and so making his Gospel contemptible."[25]

Whatever are the exact historical circumstances and personages motivating Paul's apology, it is clear that defending his imprisonment is a high priority for Paul. Paul opens the body of the Philippian letter with his defense, claiming that the whole praetorian guard and "all the rest" have come to see that his chains are "in Christ" (1:13). Paul's phraseology is usually interpreted to mean either that it is clear to his jailers that he is there because he is a Christian[26] or that his jailers and others (whoever "all the rest" are, we do not know) are being, perhaps successfully, evangelized by Paul.[27] What Paul says, however, is that he suffers "in Christ."[28]

The distinction is critical. Reckoning his imprisonment as being "in Christ" strongly suggests that Paul is not here pointing a finger at anyone. That is, *Paul is not interpreting his situation as one of persecution.* His imprisonment may on the surface be caused by his commitment to the gospel, but Paul chooses to interpret and present his situation from a deeper level. His suffering is shaped not by his jailers but by Christ.

In thus accepting his suffering, Paul does not accept victimization. He speaks rather as someone who has radically reversed the power dynamics of his circumstances. He is not the victim. Paul interprets the injustices he experiences in the context of being 'in' Christ; other people and circumstances may cause afflictions, but Paul does not lay blame. He rather uses his energy to draw these difficulties into the sphere he now inhabits—the sphere of being 'in' Christ. This is critical for Paul's defense of his present humiliation. For his chief point is that being 'in' Christ does not separate the believer from suffering. Paul stakes his defense on the continuing presence of the cross.

Gaining Christ Means Accepting Suffering

Christ is the lens through which Paul now views and experiences his situation. Through Christ Paul sees that all the security he had as a Hebrew of the Hebrews is actually only a liability (3:7). In fact, Christ initiated (δι' ὃν . . . ἐζημιώθην, 3:8) the loss of all Paul had.[29] Though such radical loss took place, strangely, it resulted in a gain—the gain of Christ, and of being found "in him."

The purpose clause of 3:8b–9—"in order that I might gain Christ and be found in him"—speaks of both the future and present.[30] Paul expresses here both his long-range goal and his current circumstances. When Christ effected Paul's loss of everything, Paul was not left in exile; he was embraced by Christ. Paul's resultant condition is stable, but it is not static. Paul will continue to gain Christ and to be found 'in' Christ, presumably increasing his gain and his understanding of his place. Paul clearly states that he does not already have all that the good news offers (3:12). His ongoing purpose, he says, is to know Christ and the power of his resurrection and the fellowship of his sufferings.[31]

The point should not be missed, however, that Paul understands the loss of his past as a prelude to being "found in him" (3:9). Of equal importance, Paul does not say that such loss is the same as sharing in Christ's sufferings; rather, he says that this loss is what allows him to participate in them. The stuff of Christ's sufferings, in which Paul longs to share, works with the stuff of Paul's new life 'in' Christ, not of his past. The person who shares the sufferings of Christ is not the person he was. He is a person 'in' Christ; the material on which afflictions now act is 'in' Christ material. In fact, Paul's describes himself after being found 'in' Christ as one who no longer has his own righteousness based on the law, but has the righteousness of God, which comes through the faith of Christ,[32] and is based on faith (3:9). Paul, in other words, sees his 'in' Christ self in radical distinction from what he was before. Now he is 'in' Christ; before he was apart from Christ. Now he has a righteousness that is the very righteousness of God; before he had an inferior righteousness.

At the same time, Paul is aware that he is not yet perfect. He must continue to hasten towards the prize of the upward call of God (3:14). Paul does not say that his growth in perfection requires his *suffering*. He says rather that his growth in perfection requires his *striving*. And he says that, as one who strives, he is one who has the righteousness of God and shares Christ's sufferings. It is as a person 'in' Christ, righteous with God's righteousness, suffering with Christ's suffering, that he strives. This whole human package—the righteous sufferer—is who strives for the upward call of God. Paul says that his perfection will be achieved by this striving of one who has been seized by Christ (3:12). Subsequent to this seizure, suffering is part of his makeup. Suffering is *not* an instrument of sanctification, except insofar as it is part of the condition of the whole 'in' Christ person.

It is not that Christ gives Paul and other believers an appetite for suffering. Rather, Christ shares his sufferings (3:10). And Paul considers these sufferings to be much more valuable than anything he could secure in the flesh. The fellowship of Christ's sufferings is priceless, and Paul is sure that this treasure of partnership in Christ's sufferings outweighs by far what the opponents are offering. Security in the flesh—avoidance of suffering—is an ersatz investment that in the end secures nothing. On the other hand, the suffering of believers, because it is a participation in Christ's own suffering, will, like Christ's suffering, lead to resurrection and life (3:11). What is plain to Paul, and what he wants to make plain to his converts, is that the gain Christ offers cannot be capitalized on without accepting the same loss that Christ did. Circumcision or any other action for or commitment to securing security in the flesh is woefully misguided. Paul is convinced that life and freedom from suffering will be achieved only by embracing the same afflictions as Christ—an embrace that clearly does not afford security in the flesh.

Paul defends the fittingness of his current weak and humiliated situation by extolling the necessity and value of partnership in Christ's suffering. Only such partnership, in conformity with Christ's death, will produce resurrection (3:10–11).

Suffering in Conformity with Christ's Death

Paul's use of the participle συμμορφιζόμενος ("being conformed to, taking on the same form as") in connection with Christ's death (3:10), in the same breath as speaking of his goal of knowing the power of Christ's resurrection and the fellowship of his sufferings, shows that conformity to Christ's death is the controlling factor in Paul's striving. The participle's present tense indicates an ongoing process; Paul regards the form of Christ's death as a continuing process he experiences, and this defines and shapes both his knowledge of Christ's resurrection and of the partnership of Christ's sufferings. Thus, although Christ died at a particular instant, the form of Christ's death will be experienced not in an instant but through the course of a life.

Furthermore, the fact that the participle is anarthrous indicates that Paul is describing the *circumstances* in which knowledge of Christ's resurrection and of the fellowship of his sufferings may take place. In the process of taking on the form of Christ's death, Paul can be on target for his goal of knowing both Christ's resurrection and partnership in Christ's suffering.

a. The form of Christ's death is shaped not by the pain of others but the power of life. Being governed by the form of Christ's death, the essential feature of Christlike suffering is its effect. Readers of Philippians typically regard the central feature of Christlike suffering to be its cause—it is suffering that comes from being focused on others.[33] However, nowhere in Philippians does Paul say that Christ suffered, or died, for our sakes.[34] Paul's description of Christ's suffering in Philippians is of a kind of suffering that has an astonishing result: vindication for Christ (2:9–11),[35] glory for God (2:11), and resurrection from the dead for himself and others (3:10–11). As described in Philippians, the shape of Christ's suffering and death is determined not by what causes them, but rather what they lead to—the end of suffering, defined as resurrection, vindication, and God's glory.[36] It must be, then, that those who share in Christ's suffering, being conformed to Christ's death, will also suffer in expectation of vindication, life, and glorifying God.[37] The suffering Paul describes and desires is, in other words, suffering in hope.[38]

The circumstances that require Paul to make an apology for his sufferings as actually confirming the good news (1:7b)[39] also require that he keep the glow of the resurrection in view. Paul has come to see that suffering in partnership with Christ is qualitatively different from suffering apart from Christ. He emphasizes not that he, like Christ, suffers for others. Rather, sharing the sufferings of Christ, being conformed to the death of Christ, is shaped not by the pain of others but by the power of life. The result of Christ's death is Christ's life and publicly acknowledged divinity.[40] Moreover, Christ's death ends in giving glory to God (2:11). In relating his sufferings to those of Christ (1:30), and in stating that he desires to share in Christ's sufferings (3:10), Paul interprets the pain of his fetters as being capable of transforming death into life, of revealing Christ's identity (see 1:20), and ultimately of glorifying God. Paul like Christ suffers so that life may come and so that God may be glorified.

(b.) *The form of Christ's death is the form of God's death*: The form of Christ's death is not the manner of that death.[41] Paul does not here speak of *cocrucifixion* (see Gal. 2:20). Instead, the form of Christ's death calls to mind what that death revealed and achieved. Paul emphasizes that Christ's death is a death in the context of life; he surrounds reference to Christ's death with references to resurrection, thereby underscoring that the form of Christ's death transformed his death into life (2:10–11). Paul's song about the form in which Christ accepted death—he was in the form of God but took on the form of a servant; Christ did not regard being equal to God as something to take advantage of,[42] but rather he humbly and obediently went to death on a cross—extols the form of Christ's death as the form of God's death.[43] It is as one equal to God that Christ dies. Christ's death reveals how God suffers and dies;[44] Christ's death achieved life and the capacity for all to see God's glory. The form of Christ's death, then, is anything but morbid, defeatist, or even sad. The form of Christ's death is, paradoxically, the form of life. It is God who is revealed in Christ's death.

c.) *Paul's suffering conforms to Christ's death*: Paul's desire to be conformed to this death is enacted in Paul's wish (1:19) and hope (2:23–24) to be delivered from prison. This hopeful and positive response to his imprisonment is a concrete example of sharing the sufferings of Christ while being conformed to the shape of Christ's death. Paul suffers not in despair but in hope that there is deliverance from suffering. Furthermore, his repeated references to his joy[45] and his encouragements to the Philippians to be joyful[46] reveal that Paul's suffering was shaped not by suffering itself but by his faith that life comes through such suffering. Paul's suffering is laced with joy because it is circumscribed by the form of Christ's victorious death.

In the process of making his apology for his imprisonment, Paul in essence asks his converts to interpret his current circumstances as the process of taking on the form of Christ's death. Paul's ongoing afflictions are in partnership with Christ and are shaped by the form of Christ's death, which, though gruesome—"even death on a cross" (2:8)—was the death God would have.

My exegesis of Philippians 3:7–11 in its letter context has focused on what Paul says about suffering as a believer in Christ. Many other questions could have and have been asked of this passage, questions about eschatology, Christology, and so forth. The question with which I entered the exegesis, however, determined the insights and information that emerged from my work. We now move to asking how one might use Philippians to think about, talk about, or respond to the suffering of Christians.[47] At this point I, as an exegete, bring my studied opinion to a practical and very real matter in the life of faith.

Using Philippians to Talk about Suffering

Assurance in Suffering

My reading would point to a use of this passage that first reckons with the cruciform shape of the Christian life. The good news announces the future defeat of suffering and death in the midst of the present continuance of suffering and death. The cross remains at the heart of the gospel; suffering is a given for those 'in' Christ. Acknowledging this is not a call to search out suffering. Neither should this recognition be used to validate increasing suffering for oneself or others. Nor should this understanding be used to excuse compromise or apathy in regards to injustice. Rather, the recognition that being a Christian does not separate one from suffering functions chiefly to comfort Christian sufferers. Our suffering is not a sign of our failure. Philippians encourages us to look our suffering in the face and reckon with it as part of the shape of our life 'in' Christ.

The chief use of this letter is, then, one of assurance. *The Christian sufferer is not out of step with the gospel.*

Implicit in Paul's response to his suffering in Philippians is the conviction that the horizon of reality is broader than what can be seen in the suffering moment. The horizon of God's reality is framed by life. Paul is convinced (and if we choose to appropriate his words, we may include ourselves in his conviction) that if we do so 'in' Christ, even as we suffer, we will come to see and be embraced by this reality. Suffering 'in' Christ is limited by the certainty of deliverance from suffering. Moreover, Paul is certain that the end of suffering is not just a silent black screen on which appear the words "The End." The end of suffering is rather a gloriously radiant life. This conviction does not require that we pretend that our suffering is not bitter. In fact, as mentioned, a stoic approach is quite at odds with my reading of Philippians. The acceptance of suffering does indeed recognize pain and loss.

Consequently, this letter may speak to believers' afflictions of whatever sort (imprisonment, loss, illness, and so forth, most of which in the North Atlantic context appear to have nothing directly to do with being a Christian). While persecution may be one of the types of suffering believers experience, Paul's words in Philippians may be widely applicable. Philippians addresses the reality that the gospel does not insulate believers from various kinds of troubles.

Before continuing, it is important to identify some ways in which our passage should not be used.

a. *Philippians 3:7–11 does not provide comfort for the wrongdoer.* This passage does *not* speak to the suffering that comes from wrongdoing. This letter's assurance is for the bewildered Christian sufferer—the one who asks in the face of suffering, why me, why this? The drunk driver who kills a child, the spouse who rages against or beats his or her partner, and so on, will not find in Philippians consolation regarding their subsequent suffering. Paul does not here address the issue of the guilty sufferer.

b. *Philippians 3:7–11 is not a warrant for being a victim or a victimizer.* Paul's encouragement to face, even embrace, our suffering is not an endorsement of abuse or of accepting abuse. Paul does not see himself as a victim, and his words about accepting suffering may not be used to sanction either victimization or victimhood.

Atypical Explanations for the Suffering of Believers

Paul's strange affirmation that his suffering is 'in' Christ serves to challenge the more familiar explanations for Christian suffering. Among the more typical are these: in some way we are responsible for our own suffering, and, closely related to this, our suffering is a punishment; suffering is good for us, for it makes us better people; suffering for Christians is no different from suffering for those who do not believe, since part of the nature of things in this time is that people suffer; Satan is the cause of Christian suffering; nonbelievers are the cause of Christian suffering; Christians must suffer as Christ suffers, for others and in order to help heal the world.[48] As I have read Paul here, he does not explain the suffering of himself (and, by extrapolation, of other believers) in any of these ways. (This is not to say, of course, that there are not other Pauline passages that might be used to support some of the above-mentioned explanations.)

a. *Suffering is not a punishment or a purge:* Paul exhibits no sense of guilt or responsibility for his current predicament. Philippians may, then, be used to allay Christian sufferers' fear that their suffering is the result of their having done something wrong.[49] As Paul speaks here, suffering 'in' Christ is not a punishment for past sins, nor is it an antidote to a believer's current soul sickness. Paul speaks as one who has the righteousness of God (3:9). And Paul does not say that his sufferings create more righteousness or more perfection. It is rather as a person already seized by Christ and now found in him that Paul strains toward his prize of the upward call of God. Suffering's purpose is not to purge his sin-sick soul or to punish it. As mentioned more than once, for Paul suffering as one 'in' Christ is shaped by the form of Christ's death. Such suffering does not serve the purpose of either purifying or punishing the individual. Its purpose is, rather, to produce life.

The distinction may be hard to grasp. For Paul's statement that the purpose of sharing in Christ's sufferings is so that he can achieve the resurrection can be read (and has been read) to mean that such sufferings get him ready for resurrection by cleansing him of sin.[50] However, not only does Paul *not* make the connection between sharing in Christ's sufferings and dealing with his own sin, but also, Paul *does* say that it is as one who has the righteousness of God that he shares in Christ's sufferings. Paul's affirmation is that he suffers 'in' Christ, and he believes these sufferings will produce wondrous life. Paul does not here see suffering itself as having an improving function.

Philippians may then be used to discredit the idea that there is a virtue to suffering because it either is legitimate punishment for past wrongs or makes us into better people. Paul does not embrace suffering for suffering's sake, but for Christ's sake. And Paul expects that this embrace will produce life. Paul's response to the sting of suffering is completely non-self-focused. Paul's suffering does not make him introspective, but Christ-focused. He sees his suffering not as the result of his failings but of his life 'in' Christ. This strange response liberates him, as it may liberate other Christian sufferers, from drawing inward in response to suffering.

'In' Christ suffering focuses on making us fit for resurrection life. This fitness requires *not the purging of sin and wickedness from our souls and bodies, but our shaping into beings dominated by life and not by death.* Perhaps this is saying the same thing from two different perspectives, but the point of perspective Paul chooses is instructive. In Philippians Paul draws attention to Christ's death—a death that Paul describes not as for sins but for life.[51] The suffering we will know as believers may, if we recognize the fact and allow ourselves to undergo the process, change us into people who radiate light and life because we actually are out of the shadow of death. Paul does not dissect this mystery; he only states it. Suffering 'in' Christ is suffering circumscribed by life. For those 'in' Christ, the controlling factor of suffering is not suffering but life. The desire for life and deliverance and the conviction that life and deliverance are imminent draw suffering into a circle of light from which it would otherwise be excluded. Such an understanding challenges believers to hope and to find the life that is there even in the midst of pain.

b. Believers do not suffer because they are targets of others or of the devil: As Paul does not blame himself for his suffering, he blames neither Satan nor other people. This observation may help redirect Christians' gaze away from their enemies, their competitors, their betrayers, and even the devil. In fact, the discovery that Paul does not lay blame for his suffering anywhere at all is pedagogically and pastorally important. Paul's words in Philippians suggest that Christian sufferers have no legitimate cause to feel victimized. There is no one to blame—not ourselves, not other people, not Satan. Such an acceptance of suffering in Paul's case, rather than flattening out emotions and deadening hopes, does the opposite. As Paul's striking use in Philippians of images from the world of the athlete shows, acceptance of suffering goes hand in hand with the thrill of pursuit of the goal.[52] As we suffer 'in' Christ, we strive toward God's radiant life.

As I read Paul's words, I do not find an ounce of defeatism or Stoicism. Paul longs for life in the midst of his pain; he longs for deliverance from prison; he believes suffering will end. He accepts suffering while striving with every ounce of his energy. He does not accept suffering because that is the wisest way to respond to the nature of things as they are. Rather, he accepts suffering because through sharing Christ's suffering the end of suffering will be accomplished. Paul suffers forward, toward a goal. His acceptance of suffering is not acquiescence. His acceptance of suffering is a sign of hope and an act of faith.

(c.) *Believers do not suffer because they are caught up in the world's pain*: Paul's conviction that he suffers 'in' Christ counters also the explanation that Christians now suffer because they like all people live in an imperfect world where there is disease, death, loss, betrayal, and so on. Paul certainly knows he is in an imperfect world and waits eagerly for the day of the Lord, when things will be set right. However, he does not in Philippians (in distinction from Rom. 8:18–25) relate his suffering to the world's strained circumstances. Paul says he shares Christ's afflictions; he does not say he shares the world's.

d. *Believers are not required to suffer for the salvation of others*: Given that Paul in our passage does not relate Christlike suffering to suffering that saves others, explaining our suffering as necessary for the sake of saving others misses the mark of Paul's words here. The importance of staying on the mark is that this can spare Christians from expending energy in the wrong directions. I am thankful that Paul's words here do not endorse messiah complexes, the sense of needing to suffer for the purpose of saving others from pain, which misinterpretation has been in part responsible for encouraging believers to accept abuse. Acceptance of suffering is a completely different thing from suffering as a result of acquiescence to unjust or abusive treatment.[53]

Summary

Paul's words in this passage may be used to help Christians reshape their understanding and experience of their particular sufferings. Whether it be the tragedies of death, the humiliations of age, or the challenges of illness or poverty, suffering as a person 'in' Christ is to suffer knowing that the power of life is greater than the power of suffering and death. This may affect the present experience of affliction, allowing the affliction to produce life both in the person who suffers and those to whom he or she is connected. *One of the manifestations of this life will be the seeking and hoping for deliverance from suffering.* Suffering 'in' Christ may shape one into a person fit for resurrection. When believers suffer, then, they suffer not in order to become better people but to become people who know the power of God's never-ending life. This suffering is not a choice; it is part of the package of being 'in' Christ. What is a matter of choice is whether or not to recognize and embrace and participate in this suffering. Presumably the fact that Paul needed to exhort the Philippians to embrace his understanding of his suffering indicates that it is entirely possible for Christians to suffer blindly, unaware of the wondrous potential and gift of sharing in the same struggle as Christ's.

Paul's identification of the critical role love plays in understanding his suffering further indicates how easy it is to misunderstand the source and significance of suffering as a believer. The paradox of joyful response to suffering is solved once love opens our eyes to whom we are suffering in, and what we are suffering for. We suffer not in lonely isolation but 'in' Christ. And we suffer for life. We suffer forward for the life of God, whose glory we will see in the day when suffering's term is ended.

Paul in chains stands before the mystery that God is not absent when Paul suffers.

The fact that biblical scholars and scholars of theology and ethics are all interested in matters that affect our lives would suggest that the above may offer a way to shorten the distances between the exegete, the theologian, and the ethicist. As we scholars of the Bible free ourselves to bring our lives in all their fullness and complexity into engagement with the biblical text, without a doubt our work will communicate with these other scholars who also care about the act of living.

Notes

1. This commonplace has been demonstrated, for instance, by J. Shea, "Theology at the Grassroots," *Church* 3 (Spring 1986): 3–7; E. Cardenal, *The Gospel of Soleniname*, 4 vols. (Maryknoll, NY: Orbis, 1976–82).
2. A. MacIntyre, *Whose Justice? Which Rationality?* (London: Duckworth, 1988), 399.
3. Postmodernism as a concept and an influence is many-faceted. For an overview of the range of meanings of the term in relation to biblical studies, see *The Postmodern Bible*, ed. E. Castelli, S. Moore, and R. Schwartz (New Haven, CT: Yale University Press, 1995), 8–15. For an outline, from a critical distance, of the postmodern paradigm for biblical interpretation, see F. Watson, *Text and Truth: Redefining Biblical Theology* (Grand Rapids: Eerdmans, 1997), 95–96; C. G. Bartholomew, "Uncharted Waters," in *Renewing Biblical Interpretation*, ed. C. Bartholomew, C. Greene, and K. Möller (Carlisle, UK: Paternoster Press, 2000), 1–39.
4. See M. Foucault, *Essential Works of Foucault, 1954–1984*, vol. 2, *Aesthetics, Method, and Epistemology*, ed. J. D. Faubion., trans. R. Hurley et al. (New York: New Press, 1994), esp. 176, 476; and comments on Derrida's problem with "hermeneutics' claim to universality" in E. Behler, *Confrontations: Derrida/Heidegger/Nietzsche*, trans. S. Taubeneck (Stanford, CA: Stanford University Press, 1991), 145.
5. K. Stendahl, "Biblical Theology, Contemporary," *IDB* 1.418–32.
6. Stendahl, "Biblical Theology," 430–31. See critique of Stendahl's model in N. Lash, *Theology on the Way to Emmaus* (London: SCM Press, 1980), 75–82.
7. Cf. J. Habermas, "Modernity—An Incomplete Project," in *The Anti-Aesthetic: Essays on Postmodern Culture*, ed. Hal Foster (Port Townsend, WA: Bay Press, 1983), 3–15. See also some biblical scholars' appropriation of critical realism, which argues that it is possible to encounter something other than ourselves when we interpret a text or an event; that interpretation is not simply self-projection (B. F. Meyer, *Critical Realism and the New Testament* [Allison Park, PA: Pickwick Publications, 1989], 17–56, 24. See also N. T. Wright, *The Climax*

of the Covenant: Christ and the Law in Pauline Theology [Minneapolis: Fortress, 1992], 32–37).

8. Meyer, *Critical Realism*, 21.
9. Cf. H.-G. Gadamer's recognition that it is possible to hear new things from a text if we "remain open to the meaning of the text" although "this does not mean that when we . . . read a book we must forget all our fore-meanings concerning the content, and all our own ideas" (*Truth and Method*, trans. J. Weinsheimer and D. G. Marshall, 2nd rev. ed. [New York: Continuum, 1994], 238). Also see P. Ricoeur, who writes: "The hermeneutic circle is 'you must understand in order to believe, but you must believe in order to understand'. This circle is not vicious; still less is it deadly. It is quite alive and stimulating . . . heremeneutics proceeds from the preunderstanding of the very matter which through interpretation it is trying to understand" (*The Conflict of Interpretations: Essays in Hermeneutics* [Evanston, IL: Northwestern University Press, 1974], 298).
10. G. E. Lessing, *Theological Writings*, ed. H. Chadwick (Stanford, CA: Stanford University Press, 1980), 55.
11. E.g., S. Fowl, *Engaging Scripture: A Model for Theological Interpretation* (Malden, MA: Blackwell Publishers, 1998); F. Watson, *Text and Truth* and *Text, Church and World: Biblical Interpretation in Theological Perspective* (Grand Rapids: Eerdmans, 1994).
12. I am not arguing that the Bible can or should be read only by people of faith, or that only people of faith can understand the Bible. I am rather arguing against the view that people of faith are necessarily imprisoned by what A. Schweitzer, referring to the church's traditional interpretation of the life of Jesus, termed the "stony rocks of ecclesiastical doctrine" (*The Quest of the Historical Jesus* [Baltimore: Johns Hopkins University Press, 1998], 399), unable to connect intelligently with the biblical text.
13. My assumption is that, while the biblical authors and the contemporary interpreter may live in different times and cultures, which necessarily affects their faith, there is enough kinship of faith that the exegete and the biblical author may be said to stand in the same "aura of meaning." See Ricoeur: "No interpreter . . . come[s] close to what his text says if he does not live in the aura of meaning that is sought" (*Conflict of Interpretations*, 298).
14. See Phil. 2:19–25, where Paul records directions involving Timothy and Epaphroditus.
15. See S. Fowl: "the manifestly gruesome conditions of imperial prisons induced despair in virtually all those subjected to them" ("Believing Forms Seeing: Formation for Martyrdom in Philippians," in *Character and Scripture: Moral Formation, Community, and Biblical Interpretation*, ed. W. Brown [Grand Rapids: Eerdmans, 2002], 317–30, 320). See B. Rapske, *The Book of Acts in Its First-Century Setting*, vol. 3, *The Book of Acts and Paul in Roman Custody*, ed. B. Winter (Grand Rapids: Eerdmans, 1994); C. S. Wansink, *Chained in Christ: The Experience and Rhetoric of Paul's Imprisonments*, JSNTSS 130 (Sheffield: Sheffield Academic Press, 1996).
16. T. Engberg-Pedersen, *Paul and the Stoics* (Edinburgh: T.&T. Clark, 2000), 98.
17. For a selective and intelligent, though brief, overview of Christian thinkers from Ignatius of Antioch to J. B. Lightfoot and J. T. Forestell who have heard suffering in Paul's Philippian words, see L. G. Bloomquist, *The Function of Suffering in Philippians*, JSNTSS 78 (Sheffield: JSOT Press, 1993), 18–34.
18. The NRSV translation "my imprisonment" (1:7) masks the actual Greek word δεσμός (chains, bonds, fetters). As G. Fee notes, while "chains" might be a metonymy for imprisonment, it is most likely that Paul was actually fettered,

perhaps to his guards (*Paul's Letter to the Philippians*, NICNT [Grand Rapids: Eerdmans, 1995], 92).

19. So, J. B. Lightfoot, who sees here a metaphorical use of θλίψις, where Paul plays with the word's literal meaning of pressure or friction (*St. Paul's Epistle to the Philippians* [Peabody: MA: Hendrickson, 1987; repr. of 1868], 90).

20. See B. Rapske, *Acts in Its First-Century Setting*, 208.

21. Throughout my text the reader will note both "in Christ" and 'in' Christ. The double quotes around both the words 'in' and 'Christ' occur when I am citing Paul's words; the single quotes around only the word 'in' occur when I am referring to Paul's 'in' Christ idea.

22. See Phil. 1:27–30, where Paul encourages the Philippians to see their suffering as allowing them to represent Christ.

23. *Die Briefe an die Philipper, an die Kolosser, und an Philemon* (Göttingen: Vandenhoeck & Ruprecht, 1953). See the critique of Lohmeyer in P. T. O'Brien, *The Epistle to the Philippians: A Commentary on the Greek Text*, NIGTC (Grand Rapids: Eerdmans, 1991), 70.

24. Contra Fowl, who sees Paul in Philippians concerned to shape his converts into people capable of understanding their potential deaths at the hands of people hostile to their faith "as willed offerings of themselves to God" ("Believing Forms Seeing," 330); also contra P. Perkins, who regards Philippians as an apology concerned with "the need to understand the social situation of the Christian community in the Greco-Roman *polis* in light of the persistent fact of persecution" ("Philippians: Theology for the Heavenly Politeuma," in *Pauline Theology*, vol. 1, ed. J. M. Bassler [Minneapolis: Fortress, 1991], 89–104, 92).

25. *Calvin's Commentaries: The Epistles of Paul the Apostle to the Galatians, Ephesians, Philippians and Colossians*, trans. T. H. L. Parker (Grand Rapids: Eerdmans, 1965), 234. See R. Jewett: Paul "was being charged with jeopardizing the mission by exhibiting a humility and suffering which were incompatible with the life of a Christian apostle" ("Conflicting Movements in the Early Church as Reflected in Philippians," *NovT* 12 [1970]: 362–90, 368).

26. So F. W. Beare, *The Epistle to the Philippians*, BNTC, 2nd ed. (London: A. & C. Black, 1969), 57.

27. So D. E. Garland, "Phil 1:1–26: The Defense and Confirmation of the Gospel," *RevExp* 77 (1980): 327–36, 331.

28. See Fee, *Paul's Letter*, 113.

29. My translation of 3:8b is: "through whom all things were forfeited"; that is, Christ's agency in this forfeiture is signaled here. We see a similar thought at 3:12, where Paul says he has been seized by Christ (κατελήμφθην ὑπὸ Χριστοῦ).

30. So Fee, *Paul's Letter*, 320; κερδήσω and εὑρεθῶ, being in the aorist subjunctive in this purpose clause, convey the idea of the future and of the present.

31. Cf. M. Bockmuehl, *The Epistle to the Philippians*, BNTC, 4th ed. (London: A. & C. Black, 1997), 208.

32. I here choose the subjective genitive rendering of πίστις Χριστοῦ. (See also Bockmuehl, *Epistle to the Philippians*, 210–11.) It is to be noted that the subjective genitive reading adds a perspective while not taking anything away. The end of the verse clearly states the critical role of the believer's faith. It is further to be noted that my choice of the subjective genitive is not critical to the point of the present interpretation. Either way, Paul is saying that he is a new person as he participates in the sufferings of Christ.

33. Fee, for instance, considers that Paul thought his sufferings reflect Christ's insofar as they, like Christ's, are focused on others—Christ's sufferings were for our

sakes and Paul's are for the sake of the gospel (*Paul's Letter*, 332–33n64); cf. G. Hawthorne, *Philippians*, WBC 43 (Waco, TX: Word, 1983), 148. F. F. Bruce goes so far as to suggest that it was Paul's hope to absorb as many of the sufferings of Christ as he could, so that he might "leave less for his fellow Christians to endure" (*Philippians* [San Francisco: Harper & Row, 1983], 91).

34. O'Brien also notices that Phil. 3:10 does not refer to Christ's redemptive death (*Epistle to the Philippians*, 405). The absence of sacrifical language is among the reasons to be cautious about E. Lohmeyer's proposal that this hymn was originally sung at the Eucharist (*Kyrios Jesus: Eine Untersuchung zur Phil. 2:5–11* [Heidelberg: Winter 1968, original 1927/28]).

35. See Bloomquist, *Function of Suffering*, 196.

36. It may be that the positive effects of Christ's suffering and death, as Paul outlines them in Philippians, are another way of saying what he says elsewhere about, for instance, Christ's death defeating sin's power (e.g., Rom. 3:23–25). The point to be noticed, however, is that Paul avoids referring in this letter to the sacrificial or vicarious aspect of Christ's death and focuses instead on the vindication and life that result from them.

37. Paul's focus in Philippians is not so much on our suffering birthing the new age (so, Bockmuehl, *Epistle to the Philippians*, 215) as it is on seeking to explain what it is to be part of this age in which it *remains* for suffering to be abolished.

38. This is a different nuance from what he says elsewhere—that our suffering *produces* that hope (Rom. 5:3–4).

39. Reading this part of the verse as "while in my chains, even (i.e., which are) in the defense and confirmation of the gospel." This reading is supported by Paul's reference to his imprisonment as an ἀπολογία ("defense," 1:16).

40. Paul writes that God bestowed on Christ "the name that is above every name," and that in the future every knee will bow at that name (2:9–10). Christ's God-bestowed name is a divine name (cf. Bockmuehl, *Epistle to the Philippians*, 142), which does not, as M. Silva notes, compromise Israel's monotheistic faith, for the name Jesus bears is the name of the one Lord, and he bears it for the glory of God the Father (*Philippians*, Wycliffe Exegetical Commentary [Chicago: Moody Press, 1988], 131); see R. P. Martin, *Carmen Christi: Philippians ii.5–11 in Recent Interpretation and in the Setting of Early Christian Worship* [Grand Rapids: Eerdmans, 1983; reprint of 1967 with new preface], 283). See also L. Hurtado, who notes that this passage's "creative use of Is. 45.23 . . . as predicting a universal acknowledgement of Jesus as *Kyrios* shows that being given this title must be the Greek equivalent to bearing the OT name of God" (*Lord Jesus Christ: Devotion to Jesus in Earliest Christianity* [Grand Rapids: Eerdmans, 2003], 112).

41. Contra R. Cassidy, *Paul in Chains: Roman Imprisonment and the Letters of St. Paul* (New York: Crossroad, 2001), 187.

42. Following N. T. Wright that ἁρπαγμός means not grasping or clinging but advantage taking *based* on equality with God. Wright translates this portion of the hymn: "Christ did not consider his equality with God as something to take advantage of" ("Jesus Christ Is Lord: Philippians 2.5–11," in *Climax of the Covenant*, 56–98, 79).

43. I am aware that this statement wades into the longstanding theopaschite controversy. See on this J. Pelikan, *The Christian Tradition: A History of the Development of Doctrine* (Chicago: University of Chicago Press, 1971), 1:270–71.

44. While not referring to this text but to Phil. 1:23, Ignatius reads something similar to Paul's words: "Allow me to be an imitator of the suffering of my God" (W. Schoedel, *Ignatius of Antioch: A Commentary on the Letters of Ignatius of Antioch*, Hermeneia [Philadelphia: Fortress, 1985], 181).

45. 1:4; 1:18; 2:2; 2:17; 4:1; 4:10.

46. 1:25; 2:17; 2:18; 2:28; 2:29; 3:1; 4:4.
47. This is not to intimate that I (or Paul) am not concerned about the suffering of those who are not Christians. The question with which I entered the exegesis is the one on which, at this point in the exegesis, I am qualified to speak.
48. See J. C. Beker for various biblical views on suffering (*Suffering and Hope: The Biblical Vision and the Human Predicament* [Grand Rapids: Eerdmans, 1987]).
49. Again, Paul's words do not address the situation of one who *does* suffer for doing wrong.
50. E.g., Hawthorne, *Philippians*, 147–48.
51. In other letters Paul does draw a connection between sin and death, and between life and freedom from sin. Those texts have a different use for the Christian believer. My point is that the usefulness of Philippians is for circumstances where the offer of comfort and hope is the most fitting response to the Christian sufferer.
52. K. Barth aptly comments: "If there is one man who knows *no* passivity, then it is the *symmorphizomenos to thanato Christou* (the man who enters into the form of Christ's death)" (*Epistle to the Philippians*, 40th anniversary ed., trans. J. W. Leitch, intro. essays by B. L. McCormack and F. B. Watson [Louisville/ London: Westminster John Knox, 2002], 106).
53. As mentioned above, acceptance of suffering 'in' Christ is *not* also acceptance of injustice for oneself or others.

Chapter 7

Identity and Metaethics

Being Justified and Ethics in Galatians

ROBERT L. BRAWLEY

Galatians conveys Paul's understanding of how his addressees stand in a relationship with God. Whereas the Synoptics often express a comparable relationship under "God's commonwealth" and John under "eternal life," Paul presents this relationship in Galatians 2:16 with the verb δικαιόω ("to justify"). An anthropocentric metaethical question is how human beings justify their ethical actions. Paul radically inverts the question: How is a human being justified? Justification is a relationship with God that does not derive "from works of law" but "through faith in/of Jesus Christ."[1]

This renowned verse stands as a basis for Paul's judgment against the withdrawal of Cephas, Barnabas, and some other Jewish messianists from table fellowship with Gentiles in 2:11–14. Paul judges their behavior reproachful on the basis of the way human beings are justified (2:11–16). The relationship of being justified then serves also as the basis for Paul's attempt to persuade Gentile messianists in Galatia not to become proselytes. "Being justified" in 2:16 pertains first to Antioch, but in 3:2, 5, it acquires a double context—Antioch and Galatia. In Bakhtin's terms 2:16 has a dialogical quality in that it has multiple addressees.[2] Galatians 2:14 implies an address to Cephas, but the Galatians are eavesdropping. In addition, Paul alludes to the interior dialogue of "those who by nature are Judeans" who have come to believe in Christ Jesus (2:15–16, my trans. throughout). The content of their interior dialogue is: "A human being is not justified by works of law but through faith in/of Jesus Christ." As in Bakhtinian dialogue, Paul is citing the interior dialogue of Judeans, and because he is a Judean, it expresses his own interior dialogue. Unavoidably Paul addresses himself as a Judean who has come to believe in Christ Jesus.

Moreover, Paul is attempting to subvert one construct of reality with another. Antioch invades Galatia, and horizons of a Gentile world merge with horizons of a Judean world. These collisions of different constructs of reality comprise Paul's world—a world that is not monotonal but multitonal. As Wayne Booth puts it, "Each of us is a 'we,' not an 'I.' Polyphony, the miracle of our 'dialogical' lives together, is thus both a fact of life and . . . a value to be pursued."[3] Threshold imagery in Galatians implies an emerging new reality out of these distinct constructs—evidence of Paul's subversion of one reality with another: redemption from slavery (3:28; 4:5), adoption (4:5), childbirth (4:19), yeast leavening dough (5:9, in a negative sense), and reaping the harvest (6:7–9).[4]

On the other hand, if the world is only multitonal, no mutuality exists for human beings to live together. For Bakhtin, centrifugal forces drive human beings toward multivocality, whereas centripetal forces rescue human beings from chaotic fragmentation.[5]

In particular, Paul's declaration of being justified in 2:16 comes in response to actions of Cephas, other Judeans, and Barnabas. In strong negative terms, Paul accuses Cephas, Barnabas, and the other Judeans of violating the truth of the gospel (2:14). In the context, this truth of the gospel has a double referent. It picks up the Jerusalem agreement in 2:7. Cephas is reneging on the agreement regarding the gospel of foreskin and the gospel of circumcision.[6] Simultaneously, it anticipates Paul's statement of being justified in 2:16 as the truth of the gospel, on the basis of which Paul rebukes Cephas and his associates. In Paul's view of reality, justification "from faith in/of Christ" holds for both the gospel of foreskin and the gospel of circumcision and is therefore the basis for egalitarian table fellowship among Jewish and Gentile believers.

Paul's claim about a relationship with God, which he calls being justified, is the metaethical basis for his rebuke of the actions at the ethical level of Cephas, Barnabas, and the other Judeans. But when the perspective changes to the addressees in 3:2–5, Paul's claim about being justified remains at a metaethical level. Paul reminds the Galatians of their original experience of a relationship with God, and the contrast between "from works of law" and "from believing [God's] message"[7] in 3:2 maintains the focus on receiving the Spirit at the metaethical level apart from any concrete action on their part. This is to say that the relationship Paul calls being justified is the presupposition, source, basis of conviction, and power for action.[8]

Further, the relationship of being justified is closely allied with identity. After Paul has stated his understanding of how human beings are justified (2:16), he moves from this convictional level to convince the Galatians of their identity as

God's offspring and heirs of Abraham. Their identity includes being empowered by a dynamic relationship with the Spirit in 3:5 and 5:16.

Charles Taylor maintains that the identity of the self is a source for ethics. This is true also for Paul, except that, in his understanding, identity is an intermediate step because it too is derivative from being in a relationship with God. In other terms, one who is justified is a child of God, an offspring of Abraham, and therefore an heir of God's promises to Abraham and to his descendants. It is clear, however, that Paul is dealing with social identity, because what is at issue is how Galatian Gentiles as a group belong to the people of God at the same time that there is a presumption that Judeans belong to the people of God as members of a different group. *Group identity for Galatian Gentiles and Judeans is different, but the relationship of being justified is the same, and this relationship is an organic part of the identity of both.*

In what follows, I focus on the relationship between being justified and action and on the dynamic relationship with God and the Spirit as the source for the actions of the Galatians. First, however, in order to gain perspective on identity, I attempt to integrate some philosophical and feminist notions of identity with social identity theory.

Identity

Identity has come into question in a least a couple of ways. (1) Postmodernism has challenged the notion of a coherent self. Because actual experiences are discrete, a unified identity exists only as a construct of the brain.[9] (2) Some feminist theories of identity have contested essentialism, whether it emanates from René Descartes or from other feminists.

Some Philosophical Notions of Identity

Paul Ricoeur deals with the problem of whether the self is a coherent whole or a conglomerate of discrete experiences by appealing to the meaning of "identity" itself as a variable. In his typical dialectical thinking, he locates one extreme under the Latin term *ispe* ("itself," "selfhood") and the alternative extreme under *idem* ("the same," "sameness"). The dominant characteristic of *idem* is permanence in time, in contrast to *ipse*, which expresses no permanence in time.[10] *Idem* and *ipse* are not themselves autonomous but stand in a dialectical relationship as dimensions of wholeness in which *ipse* echoes postmodern disintegration of the self and *idem* buttresses coherence. For Ricoeur, over against the problem of disintegration, our own narrative emplots separate experiences and integrates them into an *idem*, a unified character.[11]

Problems remain. Fallacies of human memory, such as forgetting the original context in which an event occurred and alterations in the way the brain rewires with every retelling of an experience, reinforce the postmodern contention that coherent identity is an *artificial* construct. In addition, Nietzsche contended that because human identity is determined by our will to power, Christian self-denial falsifies true human identity. What we are as driven by our will to power was for Nietzsche something worth affirmation and love. Nietzsche's proposal to invert all values is often thought of as nihilism, but for him nihilism was Christian values' falsification of our true humanity.[12]

In spite of Nietzche's inversion of identity and the postmodern distintegration of the self, Charles Taylor emphasizes what Ricoeur would call *idem*. Even if the coherence of the self must involve the fallacies of memory, human beings nevertheless make themselves a part of a narrative (as in Ricoeur) that holds past, present, and future together. Such a construct is itself an indisputable reality upon which we bet our lives.[13]

Taylor concentrates on an identity that orients human beings in the framework of their lives.[14] In keeping with Heidegger's assertion that identity is always mediated,[15] this framework of living always involves a community. For example, a community gives the language necessary for comprehending identity and engages the individual in dialogue, including dialogue with tradition.[16]

This dependence of identity on relationships resonates deeply with Ricoeur. For him, not only do *idem* and *ipse* stand in a dialogical relationship with each other, but otherness is also always implicated in identity, so that it is impossible to have "one" without the "other." It goes without saying that "one is always implicated in the other" is polysemous, depending on whether "one" and "other" function as pronouns or nouns. In addition, an interpreter's point of view may rebound back and forth between one and the other. If I occupy the subject position, I stand in relation to otherness. But when an other is the subject, I become the other.

Like Taylor and Ricoeur, Emmanuel Levinas is concerned with the interface between identity (being) and acting. The views of all three fit under Levinas's assertion that "ontology is resolved in ethics."[17] But whereas Taylor emphasizes being before acting, and Ricoeur makes the question of being a question of doing (being is nothing other than act and the potential to act), Levinas accentuates an encounter with the other, which he calls a phenomenology of sociality, before being or acting.[18] Because this sociality is prior to being, Levinas can avow that ethics is before ontology.[19] In fact, before moving to acting, Levinas asserts pure passivity. For example, the I is a being that did not chose to be, and this is itself witness to a lack of intentionality, which in turn puts this being into question, an accusation before there is any culpability,[20] a "responsibility . . . toward something that was never my fault, never my doing, toward something that was never in my power, not my freedom."[21] Further, this being that is called into question without intentionality on the part of the I is concretized in the demands that the face of an other facing the I makes upon the I.[22] The face is the concretization of an idea that exceeds its own conceptualization and that comes from beyond the self, that is, it concretizes the Other.[23] With reference to Levinas and alluding to Descartes's "I think, therefore I am," Derrida once wrote that solipsistic ontology (like that of Descartes), with its absorption in self is "incapable of respecting the Being and meaning of the other."[24] This is to say that, against the Cartesian

"I think, therefore I am," the I is first of all in the object position, not the subject position. Therefore, "the face of the other [is] the original locus of the meaningful,"[25] and this relationship of being put into question by the other is "irreducible."[26] Transcendence (the Other) is intimately related with human identity so that it is possible to speak of one accompanying the other.[27] For Levinas, a human being can never exist as being for itself because a human being is always called into question in the crisis of facing the other in the form of the human face.[28] This relationship is metaethical for Levinas in that the relation to the other is not ethics, whereas it is the "non-reversible circumstance of ethics."[29] Further, Levinas finds in the summons of the other upon the I nothing other than God,[30] "other than the other,"[31] a "Majesty approached as a face" that stirs up "admiration, adoration, and Joy."[32] That is, a relationship with God is lived out in social relationships with other human beings.[33]

Some Feminist Notions of Identity

Some avant-garde feminist spokespersons canonized "women's experience" as a criterion for justice but soon ran into a buzz saw from other feminists who resisted the implicit essentialism and wished to make room for difference— empirical differences in women's approach to scriptures, gender, class, race, power, culture, and wealth and poverty.[34] Not only were there womanist, mujerista, Asian, and African voices resisting the presumption of upper-middle-class Euro-American women that they could speak for them; there was also the reality of the experience of an enormous range of women outside the academy.[35]

Essentialism in some early feminism was part of a strategy to claim equality with men by asserting essential sameness. This, however, falsified women's identity by making it conform to dominant hierarchical male norms.[36] Is it possible to establish equality without sameness? According to Joan Scott, socially constructed dynamics of power have placed equality in antithesis to difference. She attempts, therefore, to expose the social construct itself as fallacious, by contending that difference does not stand in opposition to equality.[37] Further, because it overlooks power relationships, Linda Gordon labeled the mere recognition and tolerance of differences among women under conditions of class, race, sexual preference, culture, wealth, and poverty "depoliticized" and described it as "nonrelational."[38] Over against both essentialism and the nonrelational, Catherine Keller correlates identity with relationships at the same time that she disavows the notion that women are innately more relational than men.[39]

"Relationality" is a key term, because it is possible to conceive of the self and the other as binary opposites, which is susceptible to reinscribing hierarchical power relationships. This is clearly not the case for Taylor, Levinas, and Ricoeur, where the interplay between the self and the other is not oppositional but precisely relational. Once the discussion turns to relationships as the organic stuff of identity, essentialism goes out the window. In other words, identity is a variable that functions within social identity, and social identity is variable, depending on which group identity is salient.[40]

Social Identity

In contrast to the notion that personal constructs of the self are independent of, or at times in conflict with, social identity, it is now generally conceded that the two are bound together. Early social identity theory took personal and group identity as agonistic, but this has been modified to take the two dimensions of identity to be representations of the self relative to each other and to the social context.[41] "Social identity theory is the theory of the dynamic and generative interdependence of self-concept and intergroup relations."[42] Such interdependence produces a consciousness of self in both individual and collective life.[43] The outlook that individuals have toward their own potential is interdependent with the circumstances in which they live. To be sure, there is some tension between group identity and self-identity, but according to "optimal distinctiveness theory" human beings are motivated by the need to assimilate in group identity and by the need to maintain differentiation for self-identity. Driving either too far triggers the other. An appropriate balance is optimal distinctiveness.[44]

Social identity is interrelated with personal identity inasmuch as membership in groups contributes to the framework that makes sense of life. Thus, my excursus with Taylor, Ricoeur, and Levinas into the relationship between the ontology of personal identity and ethics is compatible with social identity in that personal identity occurs only within social frameworks. "Social categorization" is part of the process by which such a framework is generated. Social categorization is the classification of groups in a process of comparison with and differentiation from other groups, and this comparison and differentiation is laden with values and emotional significance. Social categorization functions "as a system of orientation which creates and defines the individual's own place in society," an orientation that is achieved mostly by comparison with other groups.[45] This is reminiscent of Taylor's framework for meaning.

Social comparison rarely occurs between groups that are radically distinct. It begins rather with a presumption of comparable status. But then it involves strange combinations of relative similarities and differences. This requires stereotyping. In social-identity theory, stereotyping is not prejudicial distortion but, rather, the characterization of a group.[46] As far as an in-group is concerned, social categorization emphasizes similarities over differences, and as far as an out-group is concerned, social categorization emphasizes differences over similarities.[47] Members of the in-group are stereotyped as similar, the in-group and out-group are stereotyped as distinct. In fact, when anyone identifies with a group, the identification will probably involve *self-stereotyping* that also leads to gains in *self-understanding*.[48]

Social Identity in Galatians

Peter Berger and Thomas Luckmann claim that individuals participate in social reality by playing roles.[49] Such a feature is clearly evident for the Galatians. In Paul's language of fictive kinship, they are siblings (ἀδελφοί) who therefore are playing a role with respect to Paul and his associates and with respect to each other and other messianists in the churches.[50] Equally significant, however, this fictive kinship expects the Galatians to play the role of children of Abraham, who are heirs of the Abrahamic covenant. In this role they are nothing less than children of God, fully God's people. Most significantly Paul presumes a role for them as οἱ ἐκ πίστεως ("those who derive from faith"), which he expects to be played out in behavior.

Galatians teems with conflict. Very early Paul claims that some unnamed movers and shakers are attempting to alter the gospel of Christ (1:7). Although he judges this alteration worthy of putting them under a curse two times (1:8, 9), the problem is not the other gospel so much as it is that the Galatian Gentiles are turning to this other gospel (1:6). A part of the quarrel has to do with the meaning and function of the law for them, and ultimately Paul directly raises the question of circumcision as the test case for the controversy (5:2, 3; 6:12, 13). Paul associates these others who are under his accusation with a group that he characterizes as deriving from works of law (οἱ ἐχ ἔργων νόμου, see also οἱ ἐκ περιτομῆς, "those from circumcision"). Their attempt to alter the gospel includes trying to persuade the Galatian Gentiles to be circumcised in order that they might become proselytes. Paul agrees that in this attempt to alter the gospel, belief in Jesus as God's messiah does not come into question. In fact, contrary to most translations and interpretations, Paul actually says that the other gospel is not another gospel (ὃ οὐκ ἔστιν ἄλλο, 1:7).[51] This other gospel, therefore, includes belief in Jesus as God's messiah. On the other hand, so much of the argument rests on the Abrahamic heritage that the issue appears to be for the Galatian Gentiles to complete their transition from a social identity as "sinners from the nations" (2:15) to the people of God and heirs of Abraham by accepting circumcision.

Even though social identity does not come without developing common bonds within the group internally, it also depends largely on differentiation from other groups. As I indicated above, social comparison rarely occurs among groups that are drastically different but, rather, among those that are closely related.[52] In contrast to the dominant history of interpretation, justification in Galatians is not the basis for disagreement between Judean and Gentile messianists but the basis for agreement.[53] Betz has analyzed the statement in 2:16 in which Paul claims that Judean and Gentile messianists alike agree that justification is not "from works of law" but "from faith in/of Jesus Christ" as part of the *propositio* that conforms to rhetorical convention.[54] For social identity theory, however, the agreement also makes the two groups closely comparable. Although we should resist making Jewish-Christian relationships today directly equivalent to the social comparison going on in Galatians, it may help to make the point that Levinas once said: "Judaism and Christianity are part of the same drama, and not different enough not to challenge one another."[55] The conflict in Galatians is not simply polemics but a part of social comparison that strengthens social identity.

A major characteristic that distinguishes one group from another is a collective name.[56] What sort of collective name does Paul employ in Galatians? Twice geographical references appear. The first is in the address to the "churches of Galatia"

(1:2). The second is the strongly worded rebuke "you foolish Galatians," which is attached to being under the evil eye—clearly a negative evaluation. Debates abound about whether Galatia refers to a region in the north of Asia Minor around Ancyra and Pessinus or to a Roman province that includes a region in the south of Asia Minor around Pisidian Antioch.[57] But a relationship to a specific territory offers little for a collective name for social identity. Paul states that his addressees were formerly enslaved to the "elemental powers" (4:9). This association is not irrelevant to identity but hardly constitutes a collective name. Further, indications of whether they were descended from the Celtic tribes who migrated into Asia Minor more than three centuries earlier are conspicuous by their absence,[58] and in spite of the derivation of Galatia from the Latin name of the Celts, no genuine naming is to be found here. Paul certainly uses the language of fictive kinship, ἀδελφοί, υἱοί, σπέρμα, κληρονόμοι, υἱοθεσία, τέκνα. But he reserves none of this language exclusively for the Galatian Gentiles. In fact, adoption as children of God in 4:5 explicitly includes those under law. The most prominent collective name that gives the Galatian Gentiles a specific identity is οἱ ἐκ πίστεως, which I construe as the equivalent of a genitive of origin, "those who derive from faith." This, however, also makes the Galatian Gentiles a part of a much larger group, which according to 2:16 includes Judean messianists. With its affirmation that for those who are in Christ there is neither Judean nor Greek, 3:28 precludes ethnic identification for this group identity. The only way for οἱ ἐκ πίστεως to give a distinctive characterization is by its antithesis, οἱ ἐκ ἔργων νόμου, "those who derive from works of law."

Further, the size of a group is important for confirmation of identity, and if the number is not large, then a substantial factor of power is needed for social identity to be confirmed. Other than the reference to churches in the plural in 1:2, little indicates the number of Galatian Gentiles. Nevertheless, the number who might undergo the proselyte process must be significant given the volume of Paul's objection. On the other hand, Paul does make the work of the Spirit a factor of power that functions as confirmation of identity. I return to this in the discussion of a dynamic view of the Divine below.

Social identity theory anticipates four basic ways of dealing with a problematic social identity. (1) If social barriers are permeable, a subdominant group may assimilate to a dominant group. (2) A group whose identity comes under a negative evaluation can redefine characteristics that have been negatively evaluated. (3) It is possible to establish a new basis for comparison. (4) It is possible to forsake membership in the group.[59]

The people whom Paul charges with attempting to change the gospel propose the first. Social identity theory anticipates that a dominant group may feel threatened by change and, if so, will predictably emphasize its distinctiveness.[60] Because belief in Jesus as God's messiah never comes into question in Galatians, the purportedly positive social identity at issue appears to be some form of Judean messianism. The barrier between messianic Judean identity and Gentile identity also appears to be quite rigid, but by means of a substantial proselyte process, including circumcision for males, it is nevertheless porous. The unnamed people whom Paul charges with trying to alter the gospel imply a negative social identity for the Galatian Gentile messianists.[61] Criteria from a dominant group are not entirely determinative for in-group identity, but the subdominant group cannot define itself independently from points of reference from the dominant group.[62] Those in the dominant group also imply that it is possible under the appropriate conditions for the Galatians to move from a group with a negative social identity to a dominant group with a positive social identity.

Paul may allude to the fourth possibility of leaving the group. In Galatians 4:9 Paul asks rhetorically how his readers can turn back to the "elemental powers." Troy Martin takes this turning back to mean that rather than face the rigors of the proselyte process, including circumcision, some of the Galatians threaten to leave the Gentile Messianists and return to paganism.[63] On the other hand, because Judeans whom Christ redeems in 4:5 were under the elemental powers, a return to the elemental powers in 4:9 does not necessarily imply a return to paganism.

In any case, Paul adopts the two middle strategies.[64] He attempts to redefine characteristics that have been negatively evaluated and to establish new grounds for comparison. Implicitly, believing God's message (3:2) has been regarded as inadequate for the Galatian Gentiles to qualify fully as God's people. Paul evaluates their belief in this message as fully adequate to make them God's people, but he does so by introducing a new basis for comparison, namely, their experience of receiving the Spirit (3:2). Paul counts on this experience being shared by all of his addressees. Closely related, the experience of the Spirit in the cry, "Abba ὁ πατήρ" is likely a liturgical acclamation that Paul assumes is a *collective* event for all those who once were enslaved to the elemental powers but now are God's children.[65] In keeping with social identity theory, this emphasis on common experiences for the in-group is part of emphasizing its unity.[66]

In all probability those whom Paul accuses of altering the gospel argued that the Galatian Gentiles did not meet the requirements to be descendants of Abraham. Jonathan Hall considers a wide range of criteria for ethnic identity in antiquity, including land, genetics, language, forms of society, and religion, but ultimately locates identity chiefly in *putative* ancestral heritage.[67] So also in Galatia putative Abrahamic ancestral heritage is crucial. In the argument that Paul opposes, the Mosaic law evidently plays a key role. In connection with the question of Abrahamic descent and the law, Paul attempts to redefine and to introduce new grounds for comparison. Abrahamic descent remains pivotal, but Paul revalues the Mosaic law as the criterion for the heritage of Abraham. Abrahamic descent is determined, rather, by justification, and precisely, as in the case of Abraham himself, justification is reckoned on the basis of faith (3:6–9).[68]

A Dynamic View of the Divine

Some might object that if the relationship with God of being justified in Paul is first of all metaethical, then a concern for actual behavior takes a back seat.

Nothing could be further from the truth. To be sure, initially being justified is not a change in ethical quality or behavior, because it means a change in the relationship of a human being with God "through faith in/of Jesus Christ."[69] But by no means does Paul neglect ethics. In fact, Galatians gives evidence that Paul's counterparts raised just this sort of issue, in that Paul is compelled to spell out how ethical behavior is possible apart from law. In short, Paul believes in the power of God that acts dynamically through the relationship of being justified to produce life among those who are in Christ. Rather than slight ethics, Paul grounds it in the power of God.

The Galatians already stand in this relationship with God, and by virtue of it they are children of God, children of Abraham, and heirs of God's promises to Abraham. The fictive kinship of being children of God is confirmed by an experience that Paul refers to as receiving the Spirit, which is also contrasted with "from works of law" (3:2). Receiving the Spirit determines their identity, and they require no further determination of it by works of law. Paul expresses this, however, in a question that focuses on the preposition ἐκ ("from") that is, the question has to do with the *source* of their experience: "*from* works of law or *from* believing [God's] message?[70] Straightaway he also describes their relationship with God as dynamic. That is, the one who supplies the Spirit for the Galatians performs δυνάμεις ("deeds of power") among them. What are these δυνάμεις? Galatians 3:5 is one of six places where the NRSV translates δυνάμεις as "miracles," and H. Dieter Betz calls the Galatians' experience of the Spirit "ecstasy" and the δυνάμεις "miracles."[71] What grounds do Betz and the translators of the NRSV have for such a construal?

Galatians itself contains three significant clues for understanding the δυνάμεις and experience of the Spirit as something quite different from miracles and ecstasy. The first is the experience of receiving the Spirit in 3:2. Paul has this experience in mind again in 3:5 when he first mentions the δυνάμεις, because he reiterates the same question of the *source* for the δυνάμεις as for receiving the Spirit: "from works of law or from believing [God's] message." Further, Paul joins receiving of the Spirit to the justification of Abraham with καθώς ("just as," 3:6). The primary expression of the δυνάμις of the Spirit is the justification of the Galatians *like* the justification of Abraham.[72]

The second clue to the nature of the δυνάμεις is the cry "Abba" in 4:6. Is this cry of the Spirit ecstasy? Because the cry is in all probability a liturgical acclamation, "Abba" is not an ecstatic utterance but an appeal to a divine parent that confirms the Galatians are God's children.

The third clue for the nature of the δυνάμεις is the fruit of the Spirit in 5:22–23: love, joy, peace, patience, kindness, generosity, faithfulness, and self-control. Ethics in Galatians is the natural fruit of the δύναμις of God in the community of those who are in Christ. In his comment on 3:5 Betz speaks of the Spirit being at work (ἐνεργῶν) among the Galatians.[73] But the neuter πνεῦμα (Spirit) cannot be the subject of the participle ἐνεργῶν (masculine). The one who is at work is God who gives the Spirit and produces the δυνάμεις in which the Galatians participate.[74] In other words, the relationship with God that Paul calls being justified is a dynamic relationship in which the Spirit of God is at work to produce fruit in the lives of the Galatians.

Moreover, the phrases "those who derive from faith" (3:9) and "those who derive from works of law" (3:10) also express dynamic relationships. Each relationship generates a certain kind of living—living "from faith" (3:11) or living "in them [works of law]" (3:12). In these cases the prepositions ἐκ and ἐν are markers indicating origin and correspond to the genitive of origin. Part of the evidence for the notion of origin in these prepositional phrases is that these verses come on the heels of 3:7, where "descendants of Abraham" is a predicate nominative corresponding to the subject "those who derive from faith," and the concept of parentage in the predicate nominative suggests a similar concept of origin in "those who derive from faith." In Paul being justified is a relationship that is expressed with the language of fictive kinship with a God who as a parent gives birth to the living of God's children. Further, the phrase "from works of law" in 2:16 is clearly not the *source* of being justified.[75] Those who are justified are children in a dynamic relationship with God in which God acts in and through them.

Inasmuch as justification is a dynamic relationship in Paul, it resists final verdicts in ethics. This relationship with God is limited only by how the community lives by the Spirit. To live by the Spirit, though not antithetical to law (5:14), means that the present is open beyond the law. When Paul says that "the whole law is summed up in a single saying, 'You shall love your neighbor as yourself,'" there is no way for the Galatians to know what love will look like in a concrete situation before they encounter it. At that point Paul's exhortation is to live by the Spirit. Being led by the Spirit means living in the present in ways that may transcend law.[76]

Works of the Flesh

Galatians sets two threshold experiences over against each other. One is the faith that comes from hearing God's message, and the other is works of law, dramatized decisively as a threshold experience by circumcision. The reference to "flesh" in 3:3 occurs in parallel with works of law in 3:2 and 3:5, and the parallelism makes flesh equivalent to works of law. Leaving aside for the moment Paul's reference to works of the flesh in 5:19, ἔργα ("works") is otherwise used in Galatians only in connection with the law.[77] Further, the opposition between the Spirit and both "from works of law" and "flesh" in 3:2–5 is reiterated in the anithesis between Spirit and flesh in 5:16–25, so that works of the flesh in the latter passage reiterate Paul's references to works of the law in the earlier passage.[78] According to Paul, for the Galatians to pass through these threshold experiences will result in either of two outcomes—blessing or curse. For Paul, receiving the Spirit makes the Galatians Abraham's offspring, which is nothing other than fulfillment of God's promise to bless all the nations of the earth in Abraham (3:2–8). On the other hand, works of law, that is, the flesh, will not make the Galatians

Abraham's offspring. Rather, for them to be "those who derive from works of law" is to be under a curse (3:10). The alternatives are astounding.

Again in 5:16–25 Paul sets flesh and Spirit over against each other again as two dynamic powers. Not only the Spirit but also the flesh can be the source of living for the Galatians. Spirit and flesh are in opposition apart from human activity (5:16–17).[79] On the other hand, the human body is a place where the battle between these two powers takes place. O. Hofius has recently shown that human beings are not the objects of simultaneous warring between these two powers. The Galatians who are "in Christ" (5:6; see 5:24) are not relentlessly subject to the battle between the flesh and the Spirit.[80] Part of the evidence for this is that when Paul exhorts his readers to walk in the Spirit, he switches from a negative of prohibition not to carry out the desires of the flesh and utilizes a subjunctive of strong denial. With the subjunctive of strong denial Paul insists that when the Galatians are led by the Spirit, they will in no way carry out the desire of the flesh.[81] Because the Galatians are under the Spirit, they are not the locus for a constant battle between the flesh and the Spirit. Still the "desire of the flesh" in 5:16 is a genitive of origin, and the verb τελέω ("carry out") entails action that derives from this power. The flesh is the source for the desire that those under its sway carry out. Correspondingly, to be led by the Spirit is to carry out action that derives from the Spirit. In short, Paul is dealing with the metaethical level of relationships in which dynamic powers—Spirit or flesh—effect the behavior of human beings.

Conclusion

In Galatians a metaethical relationship with God, which Paul calls being justified, is construed as the point of origin for social identity and understood to be a source for behavior. I appeal momentarily to my account above of Bakhtinian dialogue to underscore that Paul addresses himself as among "those who are from faith." Further, God's revelation to him in 1:15 compelled him to change his social identity. He stereotypes himself before this experience as one who was advanced and a zealot in the Judean way of life (1:14). Further, as one who is among "those who are from faith," he considers that his relationship to law has changed so that he might live out of a new relationship with God. This living out of a relationship with God in 2:19 is a parallel to being justified in 2:16. Even if the "I" in 2:19 is a paradigmatic "I" that includes Cephas or Judean messianists in general, Paul's autobiographical experience in 1:13–16 is picked up again in 2:19 and reiterated in relational terms as "dying to law and living to God."[82] Paul contrasts his new relationship of living to God on a metaethical level with a relationship with the law to which he has died. This text is a clear case that Paul's new relationship with God bore consequences in his *behavior*. He stopped destroying the church and began to proclaim the good news of God's Son.

Paul's account of his own experience of God's revelation gives some indication of what he finds problematic with works of law. In Galatians 1:13–14 Paul associates his persecution of God's church with being zealous for traditions that derive[83] from his ancestors. On the one hand, this reference to zeal for ancestral traditions is well suited for the prominence the new perspective gives to ethnic particularity. Only interethnic relationships do not come into view here. Paul was persecuting a church composed of *Judean* messianists, and he attributes his devastating activity against God's church to his zeal for ancestral traditions. It is highly probable that Paul thought he was serving God when he was trying to destroy the church, and therefore quite plausible that works of law for Paul have to do with behavior such as his own that derives from ancestral traditions.[84] This is also a reversal of subject and object positions. When Paul experienced the relationship of being justified, he stopped justifying his terror, and his ethics changed.

Notes

1. Recently Hung-Sik Choi claims to have resolved the ambiguity between the objective and subjective genitive with πίστις Χριστοῦ ("PISTIS in Galatians 5:5–6: Neglected Evidence for the Faithfulness of Christ," *JBL* 124 [2005]: 467–90). But he neglects the "faith union" implicit in "in Christ," does not recognize the function of genitives of origin (and equivalents), thus fails to consider that justification and faith are dynamic relationships (see below), and consequently makes a false dichotomy between what the Galatians do and what Christ does.

2. See M. Bakhtin, *Problems of Dostoevsky's Poetics*, Theory of History and Literature 8, ed. and trans. C. Emerson (Minneapolis: University of Minnesota Press, 1984), 6, 9, and passim. Paul is not Dostoevsky. Nevertheless, I use Bakhtin to discover features of Galatians.

3. W. Booth, "Introduction," in Bakhtin, *Problems*, xxi.

4. On ambivalent imagery, see Bakhtin, *Problems*, 126.

5. Booth, "Introduction," xxi–xxii.

6. See Jae Won Lee, "Paul and the Politics of Difference: A Contextual Study of the Jewish-Gentile Difference in Galatians and Romans" (PhD diss., New York: Union Theological Seminary = Ann Arbor: University Microfilms, 2001), 179.

7. On interpreting ἀκοή in Gal. 3:2 in the passive sense as God's message, see J. Martyn, *Galatians: A New Translation with Introduction and Commentary*, AB 33A (New York: Doubleday, 1997), 287–88.

8. P. Esler argues that when Paul turns to behavior in 5:13–6:10 "righteousness has no role whatever in that discussion" (*Galatians*, New Testament Readings [London: Routledge, 1998], 175–76. See p. 222. This ignores the larger context and the metaethical nature of being justified.

9. J. Lyotard, *La condition post-moderne* (Paris: Seuil, 1979). This was anticipated by David Hume's recognition that human beings are driven to construe diverse experiences as a cohesive identity (*A Treatise of Human Nature* [New York: Penguin Books, 1969], 251–63).

10. P. Ricoeur, *Oneself as Another* (Chicago: University of Chicago Press, 1992), 2, 115–24. D. Ford explains that Ricoeur mediates between a centered, self-positing subject and a decentered shattered subject (*Self and Salvation: Being Transformed* [Cambridge: Cambridge University Press, 1999], 8).

11. Ricoeur, *Oneself*, 140–43.

12. F. Nietzsche, "Die fröhliche Wissenschaft," in *Werke in drei Bänden*, ed. K. Schlecta (Munich: Carl Hanser, 1960), 2.210–12; "Zur Genealogie der Moral," in *Werke*, 2.788–89; F. Nietzsche, *The Will to Power: An Attempted Transvaluation of All Values* (Edinburgh: T. N. Foulis, 1909), 1.2, 5, 12, 34.

13. C. Taylor, *Sources of the Self: The Making of Modern Identity* (Cambridge: Harvard University Press, 1989), 46–52.
14. See Taylor, *Sources*, 17–18. H. Tajfel also views social identity as "a system of orientation which creates and defines the individual's own place in a society" ("Social Categorization, Social Identity and Social Comparison," in *Differentiation between Social Groups: Studies in the Social Psychology of Intergroup Relations*, ed. H. Tajfel [London: Academic Press, 1978], 66).
15. M. Heidegger, *Identity and Difference* (New York: Harper & Row, 1969), 41.
16. Taylor, *Sources*, 34–39. On language as constitutive for the construction of social reality, see P. Berger and T. Luckmann, *The Social Construction of Reality: A Treatise in the Sociology of Knowledge* (Garden City, NY: Doubleday, 1967), 26–40, 68.
17. E. Levinas, *Alterity and Transcendence*, European Perspectives (New York: Columbia University Press, 1999), 37.
18. Levinas, *Alterity*, 29.
19. Levinas, *Alterity*, 98.
20. Levinas, *Alterity*, 19–21, 28–29.
21. Levinas, *Alterity*, 32.
22. Levinas, *Alterity*, 24.
23. See Ford, *Self*, 37.
24. J. Derrida, "Violence and Metaphysics," in *Writing and Difference* (Chicago: University of Chicago Press, 1978), 141.
25. Levinas, *Alterity*, 23.
26. Levinas, *Alterity*, 25.
27. Pierre Hayat, "Philosophy between Totality and Transcendence," preface to Levinas, *Alterity*, x–xi.
28. Hayat, "Philosophy," xiii–xiv.
29. Levinas, *Alterity*, 97; quote from Hayat, "Philosophy," xxi.
30. Levinas, *Alterity*, 27.
31. E. Levinas, "God and Philosophy," in *Collected Philosophical Papers*, Phaenomenologica 100 (Dordrecht: Martinus Nijhoff, 1987), 165.
32. E. Levinas, *Totality and Infinity: An Essay on Exteriority* (Pittsburgh: Duquesne University Press, 1969), 211–12.
33. Ford, *Self*, 49.
34. See Mary McClintock Fulkerson, *Changing the Subject: Women's Discourses and Feminist Theology* (Minneapolis: Fortress, 1994), 1; Kathy Ehrensperger, *That We May Be Mutually Encouraged: Feminism and the New Perspective in Pauline Studies* (New York: Clark, 2004), 103, 192. To belong to one group does not exclude membership in other groups. See J.-C. Deschamps and W. Doise, "Crossed Category Memberships in Intergroup Relations," in Tajfel, *Differentiation*, 144.
35. See Fulkerson, *Changing*, 3–8, 17–18; Ehrensperger, *That We May Be*, 21.
36. Lee, "Paul," 52–54.
37. J. Scott, "Deconstructing Equality-versus-Difference: Or, the Uses of Poststructuralist Theory for Feminism," *Feminist Studies* 14 (1988): 38. See Lee, "Paul," 53–54.
38. L. Gordon, "The Trouble with Difference," unpublished paper. Gordon critiques the proliferation of "independent identities" as if they had no relation to one another, whereas they actually encounter each other in conflict, cooperation, and mutual influence (1, 6–7). See Lee, "Paul," 55; Ehrensperger, *That We May Be*, 22. Ehrensperger critiques feminist uses of Judaism as a negative foil for early Christianity as "anti-Judaism." See esp. 22–25.
39. C. Keller, "Seeking and Sucking: On Relation and Essence in Feminist Theology," in *Horizons in Feminist Theology: Identity, Tradition, and Norms*, ed. R. Chopp and S. Davaney (Minneapolis: Fortress, 1997), 76.

40. Manuela Kalsky calls for a Christian feminist identity-in-relation (*Christaphanien: Die Re-Vision der Christolgie aus der Sicht von Frauen in unterschiedlichen Kulturen* [Gütersloh: Kaiser, 2000], 22). See Ehrensberger, *That We May Be*, 109, 114.

41. D. Abrams, "Social Identity, Social Cognition, and the Self: The Flexibility and Stability of Self-Categorization," *Social Identity and Social Cognition*, ed. D. Abrams and M. Hogg (Oxford: Blackwell, 1999), 205–6.

42. M. Hogg and D. Abrams, "Social Identity and Social Cognition: Historical Background and Current Trends," Abrams and Hogg, eds., *Social Identity and Social Cognition*, 6.

43. J. Assmann, *Das kulturelle Gedächtnis: Schrift, Erinnerung und politische Identität in frühen Hochkulturen* (Munich: C. H. Beck, 1999), 130.

44. S. Sherman et al., "Perceived Entitativity and the Social Identity Value of Group Membership," Abrams and Hogg, eds., *Social Identity and Social Cognition*, 89–91.

45. H. Tajfel, "Social Categorization, Social Identity and Social Comparison," in Tajfel, ed., *Differentiation*, 62–66, citation 66; N. Ellemers, R. Spears, and B. Doosje, eds., "Amsterdam School," in N. Ellemers et al., eds., *Social Identity: Context, Commitment, Content* (Oxford: Blackwell, 1999), 1. See Taylor, *Sources*, 17–18.

46. J. Turner, "Some Current Issues in Research on Social Identity and Self-Categorization Theories," in Ellemers et al., eds., *Social Identity: Context, Commitment, Content*, 26.

47. Turner, "Some Current Issues," 26–28; P. Oakes et al., "Social Categorization and Social Context: Is Stereotype Change a Matter of Information or of Meaning?" in Abrams and Hogg, eds., *Social Identity and Social Cognition*, 60. Typification involving differences from other groups and similarities within a group inevitably makes social identity a bearer of ideology. I. Young critiques this as suppressing differences and argues instead for "heterogeneity rather than unity: social differentiation without exclusion" (*Justice and the Politics of Difference* [Princeton, NJ: Princeton University Press, 1990], 13).

48. Sherman, "Perceived Entitativity," 88. Stereotyping is not automatic. So L. Lepore and R. Brown, "Exploring Automatic Stereotype Activation: A Challenge to the Inevitability of Prejudice," and V. Locke and I. Walker, "Stereotyping, Processing Goals, and Social Identity: Inveterate and Fugacious Characteristics of Stereotypes," in Abrams and Hogg, eds., *Social Identity and Social Cognition*, 144–46, 173–77.

49. Berger and Luckmann, *Social Construction*, 73–75.

50. Without necessarily claiming equivalency in meaning between associations and cults on the one hand and Christianity on the other, Philip Harland has called attention to the use of fictive parental and sibling language in inscriptions and papyrus letters ("Familial Dimensions of Group Identity: 'Brothers' ['Αδελφοί] in Associations of the Greek East," *JBL* 124 [2005]: 491–513).

51. See Lee, "Paul," 149–51, and her chapter "Justification of Difference in Galatians" in this volume, p. 194. M. Nanos argues that this is irony and that the other message does not include Jesus as God's messiah, i.e., it does not have the genuine status of another *gospel* (*The Irony of Galatians: Paul's Letter in First-Century Context* [Minneapolis: Fortress, 2002], 53). Lee shows that the other gospel is the "gospel of the circumcision" assigned to Peter according to the agreement in Gal. 2:7.

52. N. Branscombe and others, "The Context and Content of Social Identity Threat," in Ellemers et al., eds., *Social Identity: Context, Commitment, Content*, 45.

53. See Lee, "Paul," 182.

54. Betz, *Galatians*, 18, 113–19.
55. Levinas, *Alterity*, 86.
56. J. Hall, *Ethnic Identity in Greek Antiquity* (Cambridge: Cambridge Univesity Press, 1997), 25.
57. Against the notion that there is no evidence of Jewish presence in the northern territory, see Nanos, *Irony*, 22n8.
58. On the Celtic conquest see S. Mitchell, *Anatolia: Land, Men, and Gods*, vol. 1, *The Celts in Anatolia and the Impact of Roman Rule* (Oxford: Clarendon Press, 1993), 42–58.
59. J. Williams and H. Giles, "The Changing Status of Women in Society: An Intergroup Perspective," in Tajfel, ed., *Differentiation*, 434–36.
60. H. Tajfel, "The Achievement of Group Differentiation," in Tajfel, ed., *Differentiation*, 86–89.
61. P. Esler, *Galatians*, 51.
62. See S. Moscovici and G. Paicheler, "Social Comparison and Social Recognition: Two Complementary Processes of Identification," in Tajfel, ed., *Differentiation*, 265; and H. Tajfel, "Interindividual Behaviour and Intergroup Behaviour," in Tajfel, ed., *Differentiation*, 31.
63. T. Martin, "Apostasy to Paganism: The Rhetorical Stasis of the Galatian Controversy," *JBL* 114 (1995): 437–61.
64. H. Tajfel points to just such a combination of reinterpretation and transformation of values, "Introduction," in Tajfel, ed., *Differentiation*, 18.
65. Similarly, J. Tyson, "'Works of Law' in Galatians," *JBL* 92 (1973): 427. T. Zahn (*Der Brief an die Galater*, KNT [Leipzig: Deichert'sche, 1905], 204–5) and H. Schlier (*Der Brief an die Galater: Übersetzt und erklärt*, KEK 7 [Göttingen: Vandenhoeck & Ruprecht, 1962], 198–99) call the cry a prayer, presumably communal prayer.
66. W. Doise, J.-C. Deschamps, and G. Meyer, "The Accentuation of Intra-Category Similarities," in Tajfel, ed., *Differentiation*, 168.
67. Hall, *Ethnic Identity*, 6–16, 25.
68. Denise Kimber Buell and Caroline Johnson Hodge claim that Paul unites Gentiles and Judeans hierarchically under Abraham, presuming a Judean identity for Abraham ("The Politics of Interpretation: The Rhetoric of Race and Ethnicity in Paul," *JBL* 123 [2004]: 235–51). They appear to be unaware that (1) Paul himself argues in Rom. 4 that Abraham is first of all ancestor of Gentiles who believe and secondly ancestor of Judeans (Rom. 4:11–12; see R. Brawley, "Multivocality in Romans 4," in *Reading Israel in Romans: Legitimacy and Plausibility of Divergent Interpretations*, ed. C. Grenholm and D. Patte [Harrisburg, PA: Trinity Press International, 2000], 86); and (2) traditions, including some that are non-Judean, envisioned Abraham as an Adamic ancestor of the human race (see R. Brawley, "Abrahamic Covenant Traditions and the Characterization of God in Luke–Acts," in *The Unity of Luke–Acts*, ed. J. Verheyden, BETL 142 [Louvain: Leuven University Press, 1999], 115–17, see n. 25).
69. Zahn, *Galater*, 126.
70. These expressions with the preposition ἐκ are equivalent to a genitive of origin. *BDAG*; See Blass-Debrunner, §162. According to H. Smyth, the genitive of origin is a particular case of the larger class of genitive of possession or belonging (*Greek Grammar* [Cambridge, MA: Harvard University Press, 1920], §1298). Smyth suggests that in the case of parentage with the verb εἶναι the genitive can be regarded as a genitive of source, though he himself prefers to regard it as possessive (§1411).
71. Betz, *Galatians*, 132, 135.
72. Zahn, *Galater*, 146–47.

73. Betz. *Galatians*, 135.
74. On the dynamic relationship of the continuous action of God in supplying the Spirit, see Martyn, *Galatians*, 285–86.
75. L. Gaston, "Works of Law as a Subjective Genitive," *SR* 13 (1984): 39–46, 42, 45. My argument for a genitive of origin or equivalent is based (1) on the context in Galatians and (2) on a dynamic notion that relationships with law, flesh, faith, or Spirit eventuate in concrete behavior. These are holistic relationships in which origin and behavior are dynamically related.
76. See R. Brawley, "Contextuality, Intertextuality, and the Hendiadic Relationship of Promise and Law in Galatians," *ZNW* 93 (2002): 99–119.
77. So D. Lührmann, *Galatians: A Continental Commentary* (Minneapolis: Fortress, 1992), 107. The singular ἔργον appears in 6:2 without reference to law.
78. In agreement that "works of law" and "works of flesh" are parallel, Esler, *Galatians*, 181.
79. See Martyn, *Galatians*, 493–94.
80. O. Hofius, "Widerstreit zwischen Fleisch und Geist? Erwägungen zu Gal 5:17," in *Der Mensch vor Gott: Forschungen zum Menschenbild in Bibel, antikem Judentum und Koran: FS Hermann Lichtenberger*, ed. U. Mittmann-Richert, F. Avemarie, and G. Oegema (Neukirchen-Vluyn: Neukirchener, 2003): 147–59.
81. On the shift from imperative to subjunctive of strong denial in Gal. 5:16, see Martyn, *Galatians*, 492, and Hofius, "Widerstreit," 156.
82. J. Lambrecht, "Transgressor by Nullifying God's Grace: A Study of Gal 2:18–21," *Bib* 72 (1991): 217–36, 221: "Although v. 18 refers back to the Antiochean incident and, because of this, the 'I' seems to include Cephas, in no way can we minimize the reference to Paul."
83. So *BDAG*, 788.
84. On law as a power to produce behavior, see Martyn, *Galatians*, 484.

PART III
FORGIVENESS AND
RECONCILIATION

Chapter 8

"These Things Are Excellent and Profitable to Everyone" (Titus 3:8)

The Kindness of God
as Paradigm for Ethics

JENS HERZER

The Situation in East Germany before and after 1989

Although many people in the former German Democratic Republic (GDR) yearned for the demolition of the wall in Berlin, hardly anyone expected it to happen the way it did. After the first days, weeks, and months of excitement about the new freedom, people in the GDR had to face a very serious problem with the former Staatssicherheitsdienst ("Stasi"), the secret service of the Communist regime and with all those fellow Germans who were tied to it in different ways.[1] Much has been written about it, and as a biblical scholar I will only give some remarks on the situation as a background of my interest in looking at a biblical text. One of the mottos of the peaceful revolution had been "Stasi in die Produktion," which means something like "instead of spying on their neighbors, those people should go back to serious and honorable work." Later on, it turned out to be much more complicated, because people did not feel comfortable working next to former Stasi employees or even officials. It was clear, just, and self-evident that at least the persons of the highest rank would be charged for what they had done. Not surprisingly, a call for reconciliation emerged in the churches, which played such an important role in the years before 1989. One of

127

the most famous examples has been the hospitality of Pastor Johannes Holmer, the dean of a Christian social welfare institution, who in his own home granted asylum to Erich Honecker, the former secretary general of the Communist Party and head of the state in the GDR. This was a highly disputed enterprise, for the understanding of reconciliation and justice was very different within various groups of the churches. Holmer's story explicitly shows to what degree both public and private concerns are at issue in the quest for reconciliation after a political breakdown of this dimension. This is what John Burgess calls "coming to terms with the past."[2] One of the main concerns in the East German churches during that time was the question of how such a process still under way could possibly be contemplated from a biblical perspective. How are we "getting along" with people who have done much harm to others, even by taking their lives, either literally in the worst case, or by imprisoning them in many cases, or figuratively in terms of destroying their personal and professional future? "Getting along" is an expression I heard many times from friends and strangers who were not Christians. It is the expression of not knowing what to do, as well as of trying to forget as time goes by.[3] This was, I suppose, their way of saying what we call theologically "reconciliation."[4] Therefore, the meaning of "sin" as a life-destroying power structure belongs definitively to this topic.[5] However, those crying for justice are themselves always in danger of wrongdoing if they do not know exactly what the person they suspect of being guilty has or has not done.[6]

In 1997, a few years after the political reunion in Germany, I taught a course with a colleague on "reconciliation and the forgiveness of sin" that combined biblical and systematic theological perspectives focusing on the reconciliation process in South Africa, that is, the work of the so-called Truth and Reconciliation Commission.[7] The reason that we did not want to deal with the situation in Germany itself was that only a relatively short time had gone by since 1989. We thought, however, that reflecting upon the experiences of others would help us to understand better our situation. We knew, of course, that the situation in South Africa had been worse than in Germany, particularly in terms of physical violence. Yet our example helped the students to understand at least that actual reconciliation between human beings is not as easy as speaking about reconciliation theologically and theoretically.[8] Therefore, I am very well aware that what I am presenting here, as the relevance of a biblical text for a certain actual context, can by no means be transferred to another situation in the same way.

Hermeneutical Considerations

"If Scripture is the foundation of Christian faith and if we are supposed to live our faith in this world, we should rely on Scripture in handling our problems." This statement of one of our students in the course mentioned above was challenging indeed. Even if one agrees with it in principle, it is difficult to consider the importance of Scripture for today's ethical arguments. The question is, how we can rely on Scripture as a basis for Christian faith and apply it to the problems we have in communicating with people, either Christians or non-Christians, who do not share the same understanding of Scripture and its ethical values?[9] This question has been my main reason for choosing a text from the so-called Pastoral Epistles, since they deal with a similar kind of ethical situation: addressing Christians who are aware of having different views of thinking and living among themselves, but who also have to live in a non-Christian world. This challenge leads to a specific tension between the foundation of Christian faith and the way of living in a non-Christian society as recognized good citizens who may be looked at not always in a friendly way, but even critically and suspiciously. The hermeneutical impact of this situation has led to the well-known characterization of the Pastorals' ethics as a civil Christianity ("bürgerliches Christentum").[10]

Secondly, I would like to raise another issue, which I have discussed many times with both Christians and non-Christians. The question is not whether reconciliation is possible, but whether we are interested in reconciliation at all. Does the "coming to terms with the past" really include what we mean theologically by reconciliation, or does it just mean getting along with the past in any way in order to cope? Although it is a decisive step in the process of reconciliation, remembering the past may be very difficult and may even hurt. For many, though, it may be easier and more important to forget or even suppress the past.[11] Being either victims or perpetrators, they may wish to "get along," especially if they think that they are now worse off than before 1989. One should also keep in mind that this "past" remains a lasting part of people's lives.[12]

Titus 3:1–8 (9–11) and Its Ethical Implications

Similar to Romans 13:1–7 and 1 Peter 2:13–17 as well-known texts on Christian attitude towards the ruling government, Titus 3:1–8 is mainly about loyalty.[13] In terms of Christian ethics under a non-Christian or even anti-Christian regime, loyalty is one of the most difficult values. In Titus 3, however, loyalty does not mean "absolute recognition" of the state's power.[14] It certainly does not have the implication of "being submissive" to the ruling government[15] as the term ὑποτάσσεσθαι could suggest, which is often translated this way, when on a very personal level the relationships between men and women (Titus 2:4, 1 Tim. 2:11; see 1 Cor. 14:34[16]) or slaves and masters (Titus 2:5) are at stake. What loyalty means becomes clear if we recognize that the first sentence of Titus 3 serves as a headline of the following general explication and the lengthy christological argument. Its structure might be described as follows:

Headline and main focus:	**3:1 Remind them to be subject to rulers and authorities, to be obedient, to be ready for every good work,**
Explication:	*2 to speak evil of no one, to avoid quarrelling, to be gentle, and to show every courtesy to everyone.*

Christological argument

[handwritten: we've been there, done that –]

1. The Past: 3 For we ourselves were once foolish, disobedient, led astray, slaves to various passions and pleasures, passing our days in malice and envy, despicable, hating one another.

2. God's doing: 4 But when *the goodness and loving kindness of God our Savior appeared,* 5 he saved us, not because of any works of righteousness that we had done, but *according to his mercy, through the water of rebirth and renewal by the Holy Spirit.* 6 This Spirit he poured out on us richly *through Jesus Christ our Savior,*

3. Consequence: 7 so that, having been justified by his grace, we might become heirs according to the hope of eternal life.

Ethical consequence: **8 The saying is sure. I desire that you insist on these things, so that those who have come to believe in God may be careful to devote themselves to good works;** these things are excellent and profitable to everyone.

Final advice: *9 But avoid stupid controversies, genealogies, dissensions, and quarrels about the law, for they are unprofitable and worthless. 10 After a first and second admonition, have nothing more to do with anyone who causes divisions, 11 since you know that such a person is perverted and sinful, being self-condemned.* (NRSV)

There is no consensus whether Titus 3:1 alludes to Romans 13 or even presupposes its readers know this text.[17] Assuming such an intertextual reference would be helpful in explaining the author's intention in terms of loyalty, for in Romans 13 the divine legitimacy of the government is decisive for the argument.[18] In Titus 3, however, this is not indicated. Being unable to give a satisfactory answer, given the various possibilities of reception,[19] we have to read Titus 3 without presupposing Romans 13 or even 1 Peter 2. This helps us to concentrate on the ethical argument.

The note about the attitude of Christians to the ruling authorities of the society is formulated as a short reminder of something "they" should already know. Who is meant by "them" is not quite clear. It could be the congregation. However, from the context of chapter 2, one might limit the reference to the groups mentioned in 2:1–9. Nevertheless, the topic of disobedience is already at stake in 1:10 and therefore seems to be one of the main concerns of the author talking about the various groups and their appropriate behavior in the congregation, as well as in the world surrounding them (2:1–14). The opening of chapter 3 takes up again the issue of disobedience and obedience from another perspective, by referring to the social authorities and the general behavior of Christians in relation to their non-Christian environment. The close connection to chapter 2 also becomes apparent from the fact that 2:15 functions as a hinge between the two passages.[20] Even the structure of each text is similar: a parenetic passage (2:1–9; cf. 3:1–3) followed by a soteriological argument (2:10–14; cf. 3:4–8).

The challenges the congregations had to face arose mainly from Jewish believers (see 1:10: "especially those of the circumcision" [NRSV]; see 1:16), who liked to dispute matters of the law (cf. 1:14; 3:9), particularly the meaning of "good works."[21] It is also unclear whether these Jewish people are disturbing the congregation from the outside or as insiders, and whether they may have been joined by Gentile Christians (see the emphasis in 1:10: "*especially* those of the circumcision"). For our topic, however, the question does not have to be decided. One should rather recognize the inside-outside perspective of a congregation's life, which is certainly important for understanding the ethical argument of Titus 3.

Given the various social statuses of the people mentioned in 2:1–9, one wonders why all members of the congregation obviously needed to be reminded that they should be obedient to the ruling powers. As mentioned above, there is also the possibility that "them" more specifically relates to the groups of people named in 2:1–9. In this case, the ruling powers would be primarily the social hierarchies and norms.[22] Thus, loyalty here means the adjustment to the structure of the society in more general terms, not specifically or exclusively the subordination under the state authorities. It seems to me that the arguments about the law have led to a certain behavior, which not only weakened the inner strength of the congregation itself, but also *started* to cause quarrels with the society around them. I deliberately emphasize "started," because there is no specific indication of state sanctions against Christian groups. What kind of disobedience the author had in mind is not even mentioned. Thus, the following admonitions in verse 2 appear to be the explication of what is meant by loyalty and obedience: "to speak evil of no one, to avoid quarrelling, to be gentle, and to show every courtesy to everyone" (NRSV). This broader formulation also strengthens the assumption that an adjustment not only to the political powers but also to the society as a whole is at stake. Since verse 1 functions as a headline, the virtues mentioned do not relate only, and perhaps not even primarily, to fellow Christians, but rather to those outside the Christian congregation.

One might assume some kind of Christian arrogance against non-Christians and even state officials, which may have emerged from a sense of being better or more privileged by God and thus may have threatened the congregation's good reputation. This assumption is based on the author's recalling of his own and his fellow Christians' past in verses 3–6. He argues that salvation has been given to the Christians not because of their own righteousness (v. 5), but exclusively because of God's mercy (see 2 Tim. 1:9).[23] He recalls baptism as the very point in life at which God's merciful acts changed not only a person's status before God but also the person's thinking and doing under the influence of the Holy Spirit (vv. 5–6). This pneumatological dimension is, in my view, crucial to the ethical argument, as it reveals the motivating force of Christian behavior toward all humans. It is in fact an argument that could have been made by Paul himself.[24]

If my outline is correct, we should now ask what the Holy Spirit stands for, which is said to be "poured out on us richly through Jesus Christ our Savior" (NRSV).

The key to an answer lies in the structure of the argument itself. God's mercy changed the life of the believers from being disobedient and ungodly people to being heirs of eternal life (3:7). God himself through Jesus Christ dramatically changed the life they once lived. This implies an unconditional forgiveness of the sins of the past, which frees the believers to gain new hope for life. This hope is based on the fact that Jesus represents the forgiving power of God.[2] Only in this relation both God *and* Jesus can be called "savior" (see 3:4, 5), because salvation is possible only through their specific relationship. Thus God's merciful and graceful acts in favor of *all humans* provide a basis on which the believers themselves should act upon every other human. Uniquely in the New Testament, Titus 3:4 expresses God's doing as χρηστότης καὶ φιλανθρωπία ("goodness and loving kindness," 3:4), which again is identified with Christ: He *in persona* is (or represents) the appearance (ἐπεφάνη) of God's χρηστότης καὶ φιλανθρωπία. Whereas verse 1 focuses on loyalty and obedience being demonstrated by an appropriate behavior, the following theological argument, formed by the key words "goodness," "kindness," "savior," and "appearing," gains a somehow subversive intention. Besides the usage in Greco-Roman literature, these terms expressing God's saving actions are often used in the language of the Roman Empire in order to describe the emperor's attitude toward his people.[26] Thus, speaking about God in this way would undermine the emperor's power, but at the same time it would strengthen the argument about loyalty, because for Christians, God's authority exceeds the power of the emperor and the powers of the society. To put it more precisely: in terms of loyalty, the emperor's authority is related to God's authority, and only by acknowledging God's authority, loyalty toward the society's demands and even state authorities can be called for. In this perspective, the "courtesy to everyone" (πραΰτητα πρὸς πάντας ἀνθρώπους, 3:2) corresponds to God's "goodness and loving kindness" (3:4).[27] God's kindness "comes to terms with the past" of the former ungodly people by granting them his mercy and by reopening new perspectives for their life. The "reborn" (3:5) shall behave to all other people likewise. Kindness therefore means a reopening of new life despite a past, which is burdened with sin and life-destroying failures.

Thus, the Holy Spirit is the force that makes Christians think of and behave toward others as God did to them. To put it according to our introductory remarks: The Holy Spirit is the power that helps us to "come to terms with the past," in order to live a new life in God's presence. And this—being the final result in verse 9—is "excellent and profitable to everyone" (NRSV). As I mentioned above, some scholars characterized this kind of ethical argument as the expression of a "civil Christianity" ("bürgerliches Christentum") in order to describe it as a further developed and rather assimilated status of Christianity.[28] Yet exactly this "civil" dimension of Christian faith within a non-Christian society lies at the heart of the ethical argument. I cannot understand it as an indication of a later state of an assimilated Christianity, since it is already present in many letters of

Paul to various congregations.[29] A Christian community always has not only to deal with its inner issues but also to be aware of its appearance to outsiders. Given these two perspectives as part of Paul's mission strategy, this complexity becomes even more relevant if one understands the Pastorals as written in a later generation of Pauline Christianity. It is an ethical perspective, theologically founded in God's mercy upon all believers, who for their part are responsible for this mercy to become known to all humans.[30]

Hermeneutical Consequences

Can this biblical perspective of Titus 3 help us in our ethical reflections on the problem East (and West) Germans had to face with the Stasi?

Again, there are two different dimensions of an answer. As to loyalty to the hierarchal structure of the society and to its official institutions expressed by obedience and good works, the first issue relates to our own conduct toward an oppressive state. Interestingly enough, unlike Romans 13, Titus 3 *does not* understand the authority of the state or the hierarchical structure of the society as given from God and therefore as theologically legitimized. Even so, however, loyalty does not mean blind or submissive obedience but has clear limits and standards. The most important one in this context seems to be the simplest one: not to speak evil against anyone. The other three characteristics given in verse 2 are intentionally related to this and are well known in Hellenistic moral philosophy.[31] Although the lists of vices and virtues in the Pastorals have their background in the Greco-Roman moral philosophy, in this particular case we are strongly reminded of the commandment not to bear false witness. Here, however, the application is much more general and thus goes beyond the commandment: one should not even utter something that could have any negative impact on others. Thus, collaboration with the Stasi clearly would *break* the limits of loyalty and not belong to the "good works."[32]

The second aspect of the answer becomes important in retrospect to 1989. It is obvious that one can speak of loyalty only in a very general way. Individually, even for Christians, many things might be much more complicated than an ethical argumentation can be aware of, due to known and unknown psychological implications. This other dimension of the question about loyalty is failure. It might truly be a difference if we are talking about Christians who have failed to meet the standards of loyalty or if we are talking about non-Christians, who have been working as Stasi employees or as "unofficial collaborators" ("inoffizielle Mitarbeiter"), having a different understanding of loyalty.[33] Even so the Scripture's ethical demand from Christians, who have been suffering in various and very different ways under this regime caused by the evil saying of others, is clearly linked to God's forgiving acts in Christ and God's saving will toward all humans. This definitely goes beyond the pure claim for justice, although it does not exclude it at all. At least Christians should be aware of the fact that juridical justice is not identical with righteousness in a theological sense or of personal forgiveness of sins.[34] That means, justice in terms of measuring and compensating for some-one's guilt has to have certain guidelines, which in a Christian perspective should be marked by God's forgiveness and salvation. The tension between the public and the personal perspective is obvious and will hardly ever be solved.

Conclusion

My "close reading" of Titus 3:1–8 does not cover every exegetical detail. How-ever, as Christians asking how to live with certain ethical standards in a world that has mostly forgotten the God we believe in,[35] we always face the challenge given by the biblical tradition. The way we take up this tradition, not only in terms of historical exegesis but also in terms of its relevance for the modern world, might remain disputed.[36] Trying to draw ethical consequences for the everyday life founded in the biblical tradition might therefore remain a very personal chal-lenge and should be considered helpful in "coming to terms with the past" within a Christian context. This assumption meets the personal dimension, which rec-onciliation between God and humans and between one person and another always has, besides any "right" theological understanding.

Therefore, I would like to conclude with a rather personal note. One of my brothers-in-law was a former Stasi major. Because of that, a split has run through our family for almost thirty years. Especially for me, studying theology and preparing for ministry, which was certainly seen as subversive, this constellation was rather difficult. In fact, I often found myself sitting between two chairs. Some members of my family who consider themselves Christians with a sound and strong belief still cannot even "get along" with the former Stasi major, though they suffered no disadvantage from his activity. Although the major was not allowed to have contact with me during the Communist regime, our relation has become better over the years. In this specific case, I would say, forgiveness or even reconciliation in a narrow theological sense does not apply to what has happened between us so far. What I tried to do was just to give him a chance to get back to a normal "civil" life within the family, and not to make permanent a situation that I already thought to be wrong before 1989. However, this is exactly what some Christian members of my family did. After 1989 and after realizing his big mistake, the former major is far from being a Christian or even a sympathizer. Yet as a Christian I should consider myself responsible for showing him an image of Christian life, which gives him at least an idea of its motivating spirit arising from God's loving-kindness to everybody—kindness in the sense of showing and granting new perspectives despite a past full of failure, knowing that even today limits of loyalty are difficult to meet. "These things are excellent and profitable to everyone" (Titus 3:8), indeed. I hope that in this process of "getting along" in different ways we may also be able to "come to terms" with our past as God, through Christ, already has dealt with the past of all human beings.

Notes

1. After 1989 it turned out that also West Germans had been working for the Stasi, a problem that today is still to be dealt with. See Marianne Birthler, the current Federal Commissioner of the Stasi Archive in *Die Zeit* 40/2000: "Ich finde es sehr erfreulich, dass allmählich die bundesdeutsche Öffentlichkeit auch zur Kenntnis nimmt, dass die Stasi ja nicht nur ein ostdeutsches Problem, sondern ein gesamtdeutsches Phänomen war. Es gab viele Opfer der Stasi im Westen, Opfer von Abhöraktionen, von Bespitzelung oder auch von Zersetzung. Uns hat die Frage zu interessieren, in welcher Weise und mit welchem Erfolg die Stasi versucht hat, westdeutsche Politik zu beeinflussen. Und wir müssen uns mit der Frage nach den IMs im Westen beschäftigen." See also the documentation *'Pfarrer, Christen und Katholiken': Das Ministerium für Staatssicherheit der ehemaligen DDR und die Kirchen*, ed. Gerhard Besier/Stefan Wolf, Historisch-Theologische Studien zum 19. und 20. Jahrhundert 1, 2nd ed. (Neukirchen-Vluyn: Neukirchner Verlag, 1992). This documentation is primarily concerned with the churches' and the clerics' various relations to the Staatssicherheit. It does also include a useful description of the structure and the methods of the Stasi's work (cf. 70–83).

2. John Burgess, "Coming to Terms with the Past: The Church, the State, and the Stasi," in *The East German Church and the End of Communism* (Oxford: Oxford University Press, 1997), 105–21, 105: "Because the East German Wende had spiritual-moral concerns at its heart, it is not surprising that questions of loyalty and integrity, both personal and corporate, came to the fore as East Germans tried to make sense of the past." "In coming to terms with the past, the church . . . had to relate its theological commitments to confession, forgiveness, and reconciliation to the practical circumstances of church life" (106). See Klaus Hartung in *Die Zeit* 40 (2000) about the former director of the Stasi Archive: "Er [sc. Joachim Gauck, JH] thematisiert und personifiziert auch den Widerspruch zwischen dem moralischen Imperativ, der in der Übernahme der Stasi-Akten liegt, mit dem rechtsstaatlichen Kompromiss, der ihre Verwendung regelt. Das Paradoxe: Gauck versöhnt dennoch—ein gesamtdeutscher Seelsorger, den oft die sentimentale Zuneigung übermannt, wenn er auf ehrliches Bemühen stößt. So gestand er 'brüderliche' Gefühle für André Brie, den PDS-Chefideologen, weil der seine Zeit als inoffizieller Mitarbeiter der Stasi selbst kritisiert . . . Ihren [sc. der Gauck-Behörde, JH] Erfolg belegt eine Zahl: Fast eine halbe Million Menschen haben ihre Akten erhalten, und dennoch ist es ist nicht ein einziges Mal zu den befürchteten Racheakten gekommen. Das ist die wirkliche Versöhnung im geeinten Deutschland."

3. See Marianne Birthler in an interview in *Die Zeit* 40 (2000): "Es waren sogar insgesamt weit mehr als eine Million Menschen, die inzwischen Einsicht in ihre Akten genommen haben oder einen Antrag gestellt haben, in ihre Akten Einsicht zu nehmen. Ich glaube, die Erfahrungen damit bestätigen die, die das Gesetz seinerzeit wollten, dass die Einsichtnahme in die Akte ja ermöglicht, dass man genauer Bescheid weiß über das, was die Stasi versucht hat, mal mit Erfolg, mal ohne im eigenen Leben anzurichten. Dieses Wissen darum gibt Menschen dann die Möglichkeit frei zu entscheiden, was sie mit diesem Wissen tun. Sie sind also wieder Herren ihrer eigenen Geschichte. Viele haben ein Gespräch gesucht. Viele haben die Dinge auf sich beruhen lassen. Es hat ihnen genügt, Bescheid zu wissen. Manche haben Anzeige erstattet aus nachvollziehbaren Gründen. Sie haben aber Recht: Mord und Totschlag wurde prophezeit; nichts davon ist passiert. Eigentlich ist die Akteneinsicht zu einem Instrument von Versöhnung geworden,

wenn man Versöhnung so begreift wie ich es tue, nämlich als einen Prozeß, der auf der Grundlage von Wahrheit und von freier Entscheidung in Gang kommen kann." The end of the term of the former Commissioner Joachim Gauck led to a serious discussion about closing the files, which was fortunately rejected by the majority of the responsible institutions.

4. Burgess thoroughly pointed out the various "ethical issues" that in the reconciliation process are to be considered and what kind of difficulties arise from a theological perspective; see "Coming to Terms," 113–16, 118–20.

5. See for example Christof Gestrich, *Die Wiederkehr des Glanzes in der Welt: Die christliche Lehre von der Sünde und ihrer Vergebung in gegenwärtiger Verantwortung* (Tübingen: Mohr, 1989), esp. 366–75, under the headline "Der Vollzug der Erneuerung:" "Der Raub von Seinsmöglichkeiten und die Zerstörung von Schöpfung durch die Sünder schafft faktische Ergebnisse, die überhaupt nicht mehr oder nicht ohne Gottes Hilfe wieder rückgängig gemacht werden können. . . . Vergebung unterbricht den Pro-zeß (Vormarsch) der Sünde" (366).

6. See Wolf Krötke, "Die wissenschaftliche Nutzung von Akten des Staatssicherheitsdienstes," in *Die Kirche im Umbruch der Gesellschaft: Theologische Orientierungen im Übergang vom 'real existierenden Sozialismus' zur demokratischen, pluralistischen Gesellschaft* (Tübingen: Mohr, 1994), 218–21: "Viele dieser Agierenden—z.B. unter den 'Inoffiziellen Mitarbeitern'—sind ja ohnehin zugleich Getriebene und Erpreßte. Der riesige Verblendungszusammenhang, der die ganze DDR prägte und das Denken des Staatssicherheitsdienstes beherrschte, läßt überdies auch die tatsächlichen Täter wie Marionetten erscheinen, die zur Würde von Personen erst wieder finden müssen. Ihnen durch das geduldige Einprägen des humanen Sinns der Aufarbeitung von Staatssicherheitsdienst-Akten dazu zu helfen, darf nicht unterlassen werden" (220–21).

7. See Joachim Zehner, *Das Forum der Vergebung in der Kirche: Studien zum Verhältnis von Sündenvergebung und Recht*, Öffentliche Theologie 10 (Gütersloh: Kaiser, 1998), 88–91 (with an extensive and differentiating bibliography on the topic). See also more theoretically Wolf Krötke, "Befreiende und tödliche Sündenerkenntnis: Die weitreichenden Konsequenzen der christlichen Sündenlehre," in *Kirche im Umbruch*, 45–57, esp. 48–51.

8. In South Africa the process of reconciliation has been understood as a different way, which could not be compared to the process in Germany after 1989; see Zehner, *Forum*, 88–89. See also Desmond Tutu, *No Future without Forgiveness* (New York: Doubleday, 1999); Joachim Braun, ed., *Versöhnung braucht Wahrheit: Der Bericht der südafrikanischen Wahrheitskommission* (Gütersloh: Gütersloher Verlagshaus, 1999); Jillian Edelstein, *Truth and Lies: Stories from the Truth and Reconciliation Commission in South Africa* (London: Granta, 2001); John W. De Gruchy, *Reconciliation: Restoring Justice* (Minneapolis: Fortress, 2002). The concept of the seminar course, however, turned out to be appropriate, and today unfortunately there are many more examples of challenges to "getting along" with experiences of betrayal, violence, and murder, in Rwanda, Sierra Leone, North Korea, China, and elsewhere in the world. See for example Christian Schüle, "Killer üben Nächstenliebe," *Die Zeit* 10 (2004).

9. See John Burgess, *Why Scripture Matters: Reading the Bible in a Time of Church Conflict* (Louisville, KY: Westminster John Knox, 1998), esp. chap. 7: "The Life of the Church as Commentary on Scripture" (120–40). Although related to a different context, Burgess's pledge for a "sacramental reading of Scripture" (125), implicating primarily the communicative aspect of the congregation's life and its ethical decisions (132–34), offers a good perspective for the question of how Scripture could matter in terms of reconciliation within a problematic ethical situation like in the postcommunist Germany.

10. Cf. Martin Dibelius and Hans Conzelmann, *Die Pastoralbriefe*, HNT 13, 4th ed. (Tübingen: Mohr, 1966), 32–33. Richard Völkl, *Christ und Welt nach dem Neuen Testament* (Würzburg: Echter Verlag, 1961), 323–41; Rudolf Pesch, *"Christliche Bürgerlichkeit" (Titus 2,11–15)*, Am Tisch des Wortes 14 (Stuttgart: Katholisches Bibelwerk, 1966), 28–33. See critically Roland Schwarz, *Bürgerliches Christentum im Neuen Testament: Eine Studie zu Ethik, Amt und Recht in den Pastoralbriefen*, ÖBS 4 (Klosterneuburg: Österreichisches Katholisches Bibelwerk, 1983); and Marius Reiser, "Bürgerliches Christentum in den Pastoralbriefen?" *Bib* 74 (1993): 27–44.

11. See Wolf Krötke, "Die fremde und die eigene Vergangenheit: DDR-Geschichte und Biographie," in *Kirche im Umbruch*, 209–17, 208, and Zehner, *Forum*, 76–88, for the complex political dimension of this issue. There has also been a large number of articles on this topic in leading news journals; see for example Christoph Dieckmann, "Das Hirn will Heimat," *Die Zeit* 44 (1996); C. Dieckmann, "Kindheitsmuster oder Das wahre Leben im Falschen," *Die Zeit* 52 (1996).

12. See Krötke, "Vergangenheit," passim.

13. Dibelius and Conzelmann, *Pastoralbriefe*, 5, understand Titus 2:1–10 as the "heart" of the letter. Therefore, after the christological note in 2:11–15, the following addition on loyalty gets a certain parenetic importance; see Hermann von Lips, "Die Haustafel als 'Topos' im Rahmen der urchristlichen Paränese: Beobachtungen anhand des 1. Petrusbriefes und des Titusbriefes," *NTS* 40 (1994): 261–80, 270.

14. As, for example, Lorenz Oberlinner, *Die Pastoralbriefe: Kommentar zum Titusbrief*, HThK 11/2.3 (Freiburg-Basel-Wien: Herder, 1996), 161, characterizes the meaning of Titus 3:1 with regard to Rom. 13:1–7 and 1 Pet. 2:13–17.

15. See the translation of the Revised Standard Version.

16. 1 Cor. 14:34 depends on the translation; see New King James Version or New Living Translation, other versions like NRSV here translate "subordinate" rather than "submissive," even though NRSV translates the same word in 1 Tim. and Titus as "submissive."

17. For this position, see Raymond F. Collins, *1&2 Timothy and Titus: A Commentary*, NTL (Louisville/London: Westminster John Knox, 2002), 357n36. Assuming fixed traditions that are taken up by the author of Titus, for example, Oberlinner, *Titusbrief*, 161; Karoline Läger, *Die Christologie der Pastoralbriefe*, Hamburger Theologische Studien 12 (Münster: LIT-Verlag, 1996), 98–102.

18. This is true under a pseudepigraphic as well as an authentic perspective. If one understands Titus as an authentic Pauline letter, as Luke T. Johnson, *The First and Second Letters to Timothy: A New Translation with Introduction and Commentary*, AB 35A (New York: Doubleday, 2001), does, it would have been written by Paul after his letter to the Romans and would therefore have a certain relation to Paul's statement in Rom. 13. But even given this, one has to take into account that this would relate only to Paul as the writer and not necessarily to Titus as the recipient as well. It is not necessary to assume that Titus would have understood Titus 3:1–11 only if he had known Rom. 13. As a matter of fact, Titus would probably have known Paul's argument on the relationship between Christians and the ruling government by personal communication rather than by written texts. A slightly different consideration applies to the pseudepigraphical perspective. In this case, it would be rather difficult to assume that both the writer and the reader did not know Rom. 13 or 1 Pet. 2 as well. One would therefore have to find here an allusion to Rom. 13, which as a strong intertextual reference would definitely change the perspective and the way of interpretation. Even so, there is one other aspect that has been often neglected, namely, the fictional character of the letter. If Titus were written pseudonymously, the writer would have

wanted his readers to receive this letter *as if* it were written by Paul. In terms of intertextual references, this makes the interpretation even more complicated, which cannot just refer to given traditions but has to explain how these traditions were meant to be recognized. This complication needs to be dealt with, but I have not found this in the commentaries so far. The only common solution is to mention that the writer developed his very "own outlook and stresses what he considers important" (I. Howard Marshall, "Faith and Works in the Pastoral Epistles," *SNTSU*, Series A 13 [1984]: 203–18, 205; see Oberlinner, *Titusbrief*, 161).

19. See note 18.

20. Ταῦτα ("these things") is clearly related to the preceding orders in 2:1–9, whereas 3:1 leads into a new direction.

21. Polemically mentioned in 1:13; 3:5, contrastingly mentioned in 1:16; 3:1, 5, 8, 19; see 2 Tim. 1:9. The relatively short letter to Titus is not—as often suggested—primarily concerned about the order of the church. This could be said only when all three of the Pastoral Epistles are seen as a compositional unit, which is certainly a misleading assumption. In the letter to Titus, only at the beginning, a few verses (1:5–9) are related to Titus's task to install elders in the congregations of Crete, supposing that Paul during his stay there had not enough time to do so. In contrast to 1 Timothy, the term ἐπίσκοπος in Titus 1:7 is apparently used, not in contrast to the term πρεσβύτερος, but rather as an explication of it in terms of the function of the elders within the congregation. Having made this clear to Titus, the author immediately turns to the major problem the congregations are facing, namely, the useless quarrels and argumentations, by which some "idle talkers and deceivers" (1:10 NRSV) confuse and disturb others. For the understanding of faith and works, see Marshall, "Faith and Works," who convincingly argues that the "Pastor" presents a genuine Pauline argument.

22. This may also be indicated by the unusual form of the expression ἀρχαῖς ἐξουσίαις ("ruling powers/authorities") without a conjunction like καί ("and").

23. See Marshall, "Faith and Works," 205–8.

24. Johnson, *Timothy*, 208: "fully Pauline in content."

25. See Johnson, *Timothy*, 205–6.

26. See Ceslaus Spicq, "La philanthropie hellénistique, vertu divine et royale: A propos de Ti 3,4," *ST* 12 (1958): 169–91, esp. 181–90, with the final note: "Cette 'épiphanie' est celle du 'Roi des Rois' (*I Tim.* VI,15), c'est-à-dire du seul vrai Dieu (*I Tim.* I,17) dont la providence eclipse celle des souveraines terrestres" (190). In the New Testament, besides Titus 3:4 the term φιλανθρωπία κτλ only appears in Acts 27:3 and 28:2 as a human quality. See also Roger le Déaut, "ΦΙΛΑΝΘΡΩΠΙΑ dans la literature Grecque jusqu'au Nouveau Testament (Tite III, 4)," in *Mélanges E. Tisserant*, vol. 1, Studi e Testi 231 (Vatican City: Biblioteca Apostolica Vaticana, 1964), 255–94.

27. Obviously, there is no specific difference between χρηστότης and φιλανθρωπία. Both should be understood as hendiadys: the kindness of God, which God grants all human beings. See, for example, Rom. 2:4; 11:22 (χρηστότης related to God, see also Eph. 2:7) and 2 Cor. 6:6; Gal. 5:22; Col. 3:12 (χρηστότης related to the believers, negatively also Rom 3:12). The addition of the term φιλανθρωπία may have been caused by the specific context dealing with loyalty and society.

28. See note 10 above.

29. Besides, of course, Rom. 13:1–7, see for example 1 Cor. 5:1; 6:1; 7:13–24; 8:10; 10:14–22; 11:2–16, among others, where always a certain kind of "civil" dimension of Christian faith and behavior is involved.

30. See 1 Tim. 2:4, 7; 2 Tim. 2:25; 4:17.
31. See Abraham J. Malherbe, "Hellenistic Moralists and the New Testament," *ANRW* II 26:1 (1992): 267–333.
32. Wolf Krötke, "Mußte die Kirche mit der Stasi reden?" in *Kirche im Umbruch*, 222–28.
33. In an "open letter" to a pastor in the GDR from 1958, Karl Barth wrote about the situation in East Germany and loyalty: "'Loyalität' dieser Ordnung gegenüber heißt (ich habe beim Folgenden die Stelle Röm. 13 vor Augen, aber durchaus auch mein eigenes Verhältnis zu der in ihrer Verfassung erklärten Ordnung der Schweizerischen Eidgenossenschaft!) ehrliche Willigkeit, ihren *Bestand* zu anerkennen und sich ihr—vielleicht unter Voraussetzung, aber unter praktischer Zurückstellung gewisser Bedenken (angesichts der ihr 'inhärierenden Gefahren')—*einzuordnen*. 'Loyalität' heißt *nicht*: Gutheißung der dieser Ordnung zugrunde liegenden Ideologie. Und 'Loyalität' heißt *nicht*: Gutheißung aller und jeder Maßnahmen der faktischen Träger und Repräsentanten dieser Ordnung. 'Loyalität' schließt den Vorbehalt der Gedankenfreiheit gegenüber der Ideologie, aber auch den Vorbehalt des Widerspruchs, eventuell des Widerstandes gegen bestimmte Explikationen und Applikationen einer vorgegebenen Staatsordnung in sich. Es gibt auch so etwas wie eine loyale Opposition. 'Loyal' gegenüber einer vorgegebenen Staatsordnung ist und verhält sich der, der deren Gültigkeit und Maßgeblichkeit auch für sich anerkennt und entschlossen ist, sich in den Grenzen des ihm innerlich und äußerlich Möglichen an sie zu halten.—Ich würde an Ihrer Stelle keine Schwierigkeit sehen, der DDR in diesem Sinne Loyalität entgegenzubringen und also die von Ihnen gewünschte Erklärung wahrheitsgemäß abzugeben" (Karl Barth, "Offene Briefe 1945–1968," in *Karl Barth Gesamtausgabe*, vol. V, ed. Diether Koch [Zurich: Theologischer Verlag, 1984], 429). The "Erklärung" refers to a declaration of loyalty that the Communist regime demanded from the church in the 1950s. See Gerhard Besier, "Karl Barths 'Brief an einen Pfarrer in der DDR' vom Oktober 1958: Kontext, Vor- und Wirkungsgeschichte," in *Die Evangelische Kirche in den Umbrüchen des 20. Jahrhunderts: Gesammelte Aufsätze*, vol. 2, Historisch-Theologische Studien zum 19. und 20. Jahrhundert 5/2 (Neukirchen-Vluyn: Neukirchner Verlag, 1994), 177–89, showing in this essay that Barth's position on loyalty was by no means undisputed. See also Wolf Krötke, "Perspektiven der Ekklesiologie Karl Barths—'Die wirkliche Kirche,'" in *Kirche im Umbruch*, 125–40, esp. 128–29.
34. See for example Krötke, "Sündenerkenntnis"; Zehner, *Forum*, esp. 334ff. and 437ff. (ethical consequences). Zehner understands interpersonal forgiveness as sacramental sign ("sakramentales Zeichen"), which also includes non-Christians as part of the process. "Zwischenmenschliches Vergeben trägt eine Verheißung, die auch *außerhalb des Raums der Kirche* gilt und wirksam wird. Wir hatten festgestellt, daß Vergeben auch eine menschliche Möglichkeit ist. Auch Menschen, die keine Christen sind, können vergeben. Freilich wissen sie nicht von der Verheißung, und sie sind nicht im Glauben getragen von Gottes vorgängiger Vergebung. Für *Christen* ist zwischenmenschliches Vergeben, wie Luther sagt, ein 'Zeichen, unser Gewissen zu stärken und fröhlich zu machen,' weil das Vergeben in der Welt an Gottes Heilshandeln erinnert. Dieses sakramentale Zeichen ist aber nicht notwendig an den Glauben gebunden" (337).
35. Wolf Krötke, "Piety in the Church—Gottesvergessenheit in Society: Observations on an Aspect of the Church's Task in Eastern Germany," *TJT* 17 (2001): 133–46, esp. 137–41, referring with the term "Gottesvergessenheit" to Friedrich D. E. Schleiermacher.

36. Biblical exegesis is only one side, and, with the Pastoral Epistles in particular, many ways of historical interpretation turned out to be on wrong tracks, not only historically but also theologically. See Johnson, *Timothy*, 20–90; Jens Herzer, "Abschied vom Konsens? Die Pseudepigraphie der Pastoralbriefe als Herausforderung an die neutestamentliche Wissenschaft," *TLZ* 129 (2004): 1267–82.

Chapter 9

If Your Enemy Is Hungry

*Love and Subversive Politics
in Romans 12–13*

SYLVIA C. KEESMAAT

Christians have struggled historically with the relationship of the Christian community to political powers. While this struggle has been more pronounced under oppressive regimes, it has also been evident when those who wield political authority are willing to be called "Christian." In fact, particularly when governments call themselves Christian while they are engaging in questionable actions, Romans 13:1–7 has played a pivotal role in discussions concerning Paul's political ethic. Under Hitler this passage was used as a reason for allegiance to the Nazi regime, with Bonhoeffer and the Barmen Declaration providing perhaps the best-known challenge to this reading. Similarly, Allan Boesak describes how Romans 13 was used under apartheid in South Africa as a stick to demand his obedience to the state.[1] In a similar way, church leaders in Rwanda justified their uncritical support of the genocidal government by appealing to Romans 13.[2] And now, of course, as the United States marches farther and farther down the path of imperial violence, these verses have become the site of struggle once again.

   This chapter will discuss Romans 13:1–7 in the larger context of Romans 12 and 13:8–14 in order to demonstrate how these surrounding verses provide a political ethic for the Roman community that undermines the political authority of Rome and the violent political ethic practiced by Rome. The current implications of this argument for Christian life in the context of the Pax Americana are, of course, not far from my sights.

A Context of Persecution by the Empire

Discussions of Romans 13 in the context of the community to which Paul addressed the letter often highlight the need for a beleaguered community to practice political quietism. Commonly the context is considered to be a possible tax revolt, and supposedly the Christian community in Rome is encouraged not to participate in such resistance to imperial rule.[3]

The larger context of Romans, however, indicates that the dominant experience of the Roman Christian community was persecution at the hands of Roman authorities. While it is not clear that *all* Jews were expelled from Rome in 49 CE, it still remains that the Jews were the subject of an edict at that time and hence the target of oppression at the hands of the imperial authorities.[4] Such persecution frames the discussion of suffering in Romans 8, with references to "oppression (*thlipsis*), distress, persecution (*diōgmos*), peril, and sword (*machaira*)" (v. 35), as well as to "death, rulers, and powers" (v. 38). This suggests that the suffering to which Paul refers had to do with rulers who had the power to wield the sword in Rome and who have already introduced oppression, distress, persecution, peril, and sword into the Jewish community there.[5]

Additional, more allusive evidence can be adduced. Like those who protest the injustice of empire in the psalms, Paul portrays Christian believers as those who cry, "Abba, Father" (Rom. 8:15). In Israel's story, the cry to God is a cry for redemption out of suffering. The Greek that Paul uses for this cry, *krazein*, is found frequently in lament psalms to describe those crying out to God in the midst of oppression. Notably, it occurs in a number of psalms explicitly quoted by Paul in Romans.[6] Further, the groans of those living in the shadow of empire are reflected in Romans 8 in the groaning of creation (v. 22), the groaning of believers (v. 23), and the groaning of God's very Spirit (v. 26). This language of groaning originated in Israel's first experience of empire, and was repeatedly used when Israel found herself suffering under imperial control during her history.[7]

In addition, the context for the intercession of the Spirit in Romans 8:26–27 is described thus by Paul: "The Spirit helps us in our *astheneia*" (v. 26). As Michael Barré has convincingly argued, based on the Septuagint and intertestamental usage, Paul uses *tē astheneia* to refer to persecutions, which are interpreted as being part of the eschatological ordeal.[8] This evidence from Romans 8 is augmented by the language of our passage, where the call to "bless those who persecute you" (12:14) also suggests that this community is facing persecution.

This imperial context heightens the question of *dikaiosynē*, the righteousness or justice of God. Is God *just* if God's people are suffering at the hands of an imperial power?[9] This was, of course, the central question of the lament psalms, many of which Paul quotes and alludes to in Romans.[10] Indeed, Paul's programmatic statement in 1:16–17 is a direct challenge to the empire: the central terms Paul uses here—the gospel (*euangelion*), salvation (*sōterion*), faithfulness (*pistis*) and righteousness, or justice (*dikaiosynē*)—are all terms weighted with symbolic and mythic import in the empire. In the face of the imperial assertion that Caesar was the one who brought "good news," the gospel of imperial victory over enemies, Paul describes his own message in terms of a different gospel.[11] At the very start of the letter, Paul seeks to redefine the terminology of the empire. This is "the gospel of *God*" (*euangelion theou*, 1:1), the gospel which describes a son of God who is not only descended from the royal lineage of Israel (1:3),[12] but who is also named son of God in power (*dynamei*, 1:3). Paul later qualifies this as "the gospel of his [God's] son" (1:9). Rather than just refer to "the gospel" in a letter to those who live in an empire, Paul is clearly and deliberately identifying the gospel he preaches as that of a messiah (1:1) who is risen from the dead and who is Lord (v. 4). Moreover, to the Romans, at the heart of an empire that lauded *fides* (the Latin equivalent of the Greek *pistis*, faith or faithfulness) as an appropriate response to the salvation of Caesar, Paul asserts in 1:16 that this gospel is the power of salvation to everyone who has faith.[13] Paul's letter begins by deliberately weaving together the central terms of the empire and replacing them with the story of salvation by a different gospel, another faithfulness and a different justice.[14]

But there is more that needs to be said about context. We need also to remember who it is that has written this passage. Mark Nanos puts it most succinctly:

> The traditional interpretations have not successfully accounted for the fact that this letter was addressed to Rome during the reign of Nero by a Jewish man whose worldview was thoroughly informed by the prophetic writings and who had, along with his whole generation, seen the continual destruction of their people and interests under the tyrannical reigns of Herod and the Roman rulers (how could one involved in declaring the Jesus crucified by Romans as King of the Jews be assumed to be so naïve as to ascribe Roman authority, ostensibly without caveat, to the ordering of God?). It is in this context that the wealth of apocalyptic literature of this period was born with many veiled references to Rome as "Babylon."[15]

This is a letter written by a Jewish man, well aware of brutality and violence at the heart of the Roman Empire. It is a letter written to those who live at the heart of this empire, to those who have experienced persecution at the hands of this empire. In this context we find chapters 12 and 13. At the end of a very detailed argument in which Paul outlines his hopes for salvation for both Jew and Gentile, we find these chapters that flesh out the shape of a new community in Christ. My argument falls into eight main points.

1. Paul Is Engaged in an Apocalyptic Challenge to the "New Age" of the Empire

The whole of this passage is framed by an apocalyptic context.[16] Paul begins by calling the community in Rome not to be conformed to this age (12:2). This language recalls the apocalyptic ordering of this world into this age, with all of its moral corruption and political oppression, and the age to come, when God's kingdom will once again ensure healing, food, justice, and peace for all God's people. Romans 13 ends with the assurance that the new age is dawning, contrasting the night that is far gone with the day that is at hand (13:12), thereby evoking the texts both of promise and judgment concerning the day of the Lord. Such texts served in times of political oppression to remind God's people that, contrary to all appearances, God ultimately reigns; God controls the story of the nations. This framing sets the passage in a context where Rome's power is already undermined. In contrast to the present age with persecution, need for the sword, evil, and enmity, the community in Rome lives in a new kingdom, where justice, peace, and joy are the rule (Rom. 14:17). As we shall see, such a subversion becomes more prominent in 13:1.

Apocalyptic language flourished particularly in times of political oppression. The highly charged language of this age and the age to come, often with vivid symbolic language, meant that those on the wrong side of history were able to live in the light of deeper realities than those that surrounded them. For the Roman community, therefore, Paul's reminder of their eschatological hope meant, as we shall see, that they are able to share a communal life that would normally be counterintuitive for those who live at the heart of an empire like Rome, but which makes perfect sense if they are truly followers of a crucified messiah.

In addition, the reference to "this age" also evokes the "new age" that Augustus inaugurated many years before and that was undergoing a revival at the time of Nero.[17] "No less than in Augustus' day, the 'gospel' of the emperor's accession proclaimed the restoration of a 'golden age,' not only for the Roman people but for all peoples fortunate enough to be brought beneath the benevolent wings of empire."[18] Paul's language here judges this new imperial age in light of the coming kingdom of God's rule, where justice (*dikaiosynē*) and peace are brought not by imperial rule but by a crucified messiah. As a result, Paul begins this section not only with a clear allusion to God's control over history, but also with a call to the community to remember who shapes their communal life and to reject the new age of the empire and all that it stands for.

2. Paul Argues for a Transformed Body Politic

This passage is also framed by the controlling metaphor of "the body." Just as *euangelion* was freighted with imperial meaning, so also *soma*, a term that referred to the body politic of the empire.[19] But Paul's language again challenges the Roman body politic. While the body over which Caesar is head (*kephalē*) functions only if all the members inhabit their correct sphere in the hierarchy of imperial order, Paul describes the Roman Christian community as the body of Christ, which functions only if its members share the gifts that God has given them.[20] These gifts have nothing to do, however, with wealth or social standing, and everything to do with prophecy, service, teaching, generosity, assistance, and acts of mercy.[21]

In a body politic, moreover, where one was to make sacrifices to the emperor and be willing to sacrifice one's body to the needs of the state, Paul calls for the

Roman Christians to present their bodies as a holy and acceptable sacrifice to God, their "reasonable worship" (logikēn latreian).[22] On the one hand, as Katherine Grieb points out, this is a "military metaphor of putting the members of one's body at the disposal of one's lord," a metaphor, moreover, which Paul uses at length in his description of the baptized in Romans 6:12–23.[23] On the other hand, this is the cultic language of sacrifice. In both instances, the political overtones are clear for the Roman community. No longer do they sacrifice to the empire, no longer do they consider themselves part of a body politic for which they would sacrifice their very selves. No, they are one body in Christ, and are to put on the Lord, Jesus the Messiah (13:14). So the passage ends by highlighting the name of the Lord they worship, not Caesar, but Jesus.[24]

3. Paul Undermines the Basis of Imperial Power: The Honor System

Paul calls this community to reject the honor/shame dynamics that drive both the patron/client system and the pattern of civic benefaction in the empire. Patron/client relationships, with the dynamic of promise of benefits from the patron in exchange for the honor and praise of clients, functioned as a powerful means of social cohesion and control in Roman society. This dynamic, which permeated personal relationships, also operated on the macro level: the emperor was the ultimate patron, bestowing benefits on those who honored him.[25] Subverting the system of relations based on status and honor that formed the building blocks for patron/client relationship, Paul counsels the members of the community not to think of themselves more highly than they ought. This is counterintuitive in a society where one was to think as highly of oneself as possible, and in such a way that others would also be moved to reinforce that status. Moreover, Paul calls the community to love one another with mutual affection and to outdo one another in showing honor (timē) (12:10). To make sure they grasp how counterimperial this showing of honor is to be, he adds, "Do not be haughty, but associate with the lowly" (12:16). The honor they are to show one another is not the honor that is due to those who already have status; this is honor that is to be shown to those who traditionally deserve no honor in Roman society.[26] "It appears that Paul's exhortation 'not to think too highly' is directed not to an individual character trait, but to a total system of relations between individuals of unequal status."[27] Throughout these verses the contrast between the empire of Rome, built upon honor and privilege, and the kingdom of the messiah, which raises up the lowly and is built upon service is unmistakable. As we shall see, this contrast permeates all of Romans 12 and 13.[28]

4. Paul Undermines the Violent Ethic of the Empire with a Call to Bless the Enemy

Paul describes the shape of this new body politic in 12:15–21 in ways that thoroughly undermine the description of the Roman state in 13:1–7. Through a series of exhortations Paul contrasts the behavior of this body of Christ not only with Roman society but also with the traditional hopes of Israel. This latter is evident in 12:14, where Paul says, "Bless those who persecute you; bless and do not curse them."

As I have recently argued elsewhere, Paul quotes and echoes many psalms of lament throughout Romans, psalms which call for the violent overthrow of God's enemies as evidence of God's justice and faithfulness to God's people.[29] Rather than reinforcing the call of these psalms, in Romans 8 Paul describes a community modeled on a different kind of messiah: Jesus, who by suffering death became more than a conqueror, and who calls the community to a similar ethic (see also 15:3). In 12:14 we see a call to be a community, therefore, that rejects a "justice" (*dikaiosynē*) achieved by the might of the sword and the defeat of enemies, and subversively seeks blessing even for those who are the perpetrators of oppression. Roman justice is turned on its head.[30]

Some argue that Paul's language a few verses later suggests that violent vengeance may in fact be due to enemies: "Beloved, never avenge yourselves, but leave room for the wrath of God; for it is written, 'Vengeance is mine, I will repay, says the Lord.'" Then Paul continues: "No, 'if your enemies are hungry, feed them; if they are thirsty, give them something to drink; for by doing this you will heap burning coals upon their heads'" (12:19–20). Let us look more closely at these verses in context.[31]

In the first instance, the Old Testament background of these verses is illuminating. Romans 12:20 follows quite closely Proverbs 25:21–22 NRSV: "If your enemies are hungry, give them bread to eat; and if they are thirsty, give them water to drink; for you will heap coals of fire on their heads, and the LORD will reward you." Interestingly enough, a few verses earlier we find: "With patience a ruler may be persuaded, and a soft tongue can break bones" (v. 15), and a few verses later we find this: "It is not good to eat much honey, or to seek honor on top of honor (*timan de chrē logous endoxous*)" (v. 27). These thematic echoes with Romans 12:10 and 21 suggest that the whole of this pericope was whispering around the edges of Paul's thought. The practice of patience with an (impatient?) ruler, who is presumably used to doing his persuading with a sword, demonstrates in an explicitly political context the same kind of nonviolent ethic that Paul is advocating in Romans 12. Similarly, Proverbs condemns precisely the kind of status seeking that was evident in Roman society and that Paul explicitly challenges.

A second possible Old Testament referent for this passage is the story of Elisha and the Aramean army in 2 Kings 6:8–23.[32] After God has struck the Aramean army blind, Elisha leads them inside Samaria. When the Lord opens their eyes the king of Israel says to Elisha, "Father, shall I kill them? Shall I kill them?" Elisha answers in this way, "'No! did you capture with your sword and your bow those whom you want to kill? Set food and water before them so that they may eat and drink; and let them go to their master.' So he prepared for them a great feast; after that they ate and drank, he sent them on their way, and they went to their master."

Several things are notable about this story. First, not only could this army be considered an enemy to Elisha personally. After all, the reason they were in Israel was to capture Elisha at the command of their king. But they were also political enemies of Israel. Elisha was eagerly sought because he kept betraying the location of the Aramean army to the Israelites so that they would not be attacked. Here food and drink are given to enemies in a decidedly political context. And the result is political as well, for "the Arameans no longer came raiding into the land of Israel" (v. 23). The result of such actions is peace—peace without the blood of the sword.

But another startling thing about this passage is Elisha's response to the king who wants to kill the soldiers. Elisha says, "Did you capture with your sword and bow those whom you want to kill?" The implied answer, of course, is, No, God captured them. The implication is that God will now kill these enemies. Contrary to expectation, however, after restoring their sight, God does not kill them. Instead the man of God prepares a great feast, sets before them food and drink, and sends them home. The implication is that while the impulse of the king is to destroy the enemy, God's way is to provide food and drink. And God's way brings peace.

If this story is read as a background to Romans 12:19–20, then the political overtones become clear. In a context of warfare, God chooses paradoxically generous means to relate to his enemies and bring peace. In addition, the vengeance of God is revealed to be deeply subversive of violent retaliation, for God's vengeance does not mirror the violence of the empire.

This is, of course, consistent with Paul's argument in Romans 5:8–10:

> But God proves his love for us that while we still were sinners Christ died for us. Much more surely then, now that we have been justified by his blood, will we be saved through him from the wrath of God. For if while we were enemies, we were reconciled to God through the death of his Son, much more surely, having been reconciled, will we be saved by his life. (NRSV)

Richard Hays comments on this passage in this way:

> How does God treat enemies? Rather than killing them, Paul declares, he gives his son to die for them. . . . It is evident, then, that those whose lives are reshaped in Christ must deal with enemies in the same way that God in Christ dealt with enemies.[33]

As the Elisha story makes clear, God's way of dealing with enemies has consistently been the unexpected path of love, from early on in Israel's story right up to the death of Jesus.[34] In Romans 12 Paul draws out the implications of Jesus' death for the sake of his enemies: The Roman community is called to be a blessing for those who persecute them.

5. Paul Rejects the Imperial Path of Peace through Conquest

Throughout Romans, Paul offers an *euangelion* of peace, not through imperial conquest but through messianic suffering. This comes to its most eloquent expression in Romans 8, where God's response to the suffering community is not revenge on their enemies but rather a relentless solidarity in their suffering in the groaning of the Spirit (8:26) and in the death of the Son (8:32). Moreover, in 8:37 this solidarity results in the community being more than conquerors.[35] The whole dynamic of this passage rejects conventional categories about who is victim and who is conquered. The messiah who died and was raised is the one in the position of authority at the right hand of God, and those who suffer are the ones who are not conquered but more than—indeed above—the conquerors. Here Paul is rejecting the imperial categories of victory, categories beloved by both Israel and Rome, and is replacing them with the category of suffering love. The way to respond to the violence of the empire is to bear it, and in that bearing to reveal that one is part of the family of Jesus (Rom. 8:17, 29) and therefore one of those who cannot be separated from God's love. It is such love, such "relentless solidarity," that enables the Roman Christians to bear the suffering that they experience at the hands of their persecutors.[36]

In this light it is not surprising that the way the Christian community in Rome is to "live peaceably with all" (12:18) by "not repay[ing] anyone evil for evil" (12:17). Then the community will "not be overcome by evil, but [will] overcome evil with good" (12:21), and peace will be the result. Again, Paul subverts the language of the conqueror by robbing it of its violent force. The resulting peace, of course, is considered the primary achievement of the Roman Empire. The Pax Romana was considered by Rome to be one of her great successes. Roman peace, however, was achieved by violent oppression of her enemies and brutal suppression of those who resisted her rule. In Romans Paul has demonstrated another route to peace; and in two places such peace is linked with suffering (5:1–5; 12:14–18). The contrast between how the body of Christ achieves peace and how the body politic of Rome achieves peace is heightened further in Romans 13:1–7.

6. Paul Denies the Divine Authority of Rome

Strikingly the vocabulary of Romans 13:1 (Let every person be subject [*hypotassesthō*] to the governing authorities) echoes Colossians 3:18 (Wives, be subject [*hypotassesthe*] to your husbands) and Ephesians 5:21 (Be subject [*hypotassomenoi*] to one another). These passages in Colossians and Ephesians can be shown to have elements that undermine the authoritarian patriarchal structures which formed the backbone of the social structure in ancient Roman society.[37] Romans 13 contains a similar dynamic. Paul's call to subjection in 13:1 first suggests the need to submit to one's place in an existing hierarchy.[38] Second, as the passage continues, it becomes clear that such subjection is very ambiguous. The very next sentence echoes a recurrent apocalyptic theme, that the governing authorities have their power only as a result of God. Even in times of oppression, such assertions are a way of insisting that although it appears that the (often evil) empire has control, it is really God who is sovereign; it is God who really has power (e.g., Dan. 2:21). As a result, "Romans 13 constitutes a severe demotion of arrogant and self-divinizing rulers. It is an undermining of totalitarianism, not a reinforcement of it."[39]

Luise Schottroff illuminatingly situates this passage in the context of loyalty tests demanded by the empire. Even though Christians would assert their loyalty to the empire, this does not mean that they were willing to worship the imperial gods, or bow the knee to Caesar.[40] She points out that:

> In the case of conflict . . . Romans 13.1–7 was insufficient in the eyes of the Roman authorities, because at that point a positive recognition of the Roman gods was demanded. If one considers the context of the Roman policy of religion, Romans 13.1–7 loses its apparently singular character and becomes a link in the long chain of declarations of loyalty of subjugated peoples toward Rome.[41]

Like the "hidden transcript" of the little people, which says what the public transcript wants to hear, Paul seems to be advocating subjection to Rome in this passage.[42] However, in rooting Rome's authority in the higher authority of God, he undermines the authority of the empire at the very outset. In Jewett's terms, "The sacred canopy of the Roman gods has been replaced."[43] Or, in the vernacular, the emperor has no clothes.

7. Paul Contrasts the Body Politic of Jesus with the Roman State Defined by Wrath and the Sword

That this passage has only the appearance of subjection is further reinforced by the way that the state is described. Here I draw on the work of Neil Elliott and Robert Jewett. Paul is writing in the midst of an empire whose boast was its ability to bring peace, especially under the rule of an emperor, Nero, who took pride in the fact that he had not won his empire by the sword. Indeed, under Nero the sword was supposed to become "a quaint relic of bygone days."[44] In the face of such imperial propaganda, Paul's words in Romans 13:1–7 "betray a sobering caution. The imperial sword is *not* idle: it continues to threaten destruction and bloodshed."[45]

Similarly, this is a rule that demands "fear" and is described as executing wrath by means of the sword (13:3–4). As Elliott points out, the imperial powers linked persuasion and force as the twin agents of consent.[46] In addition, Jews such as Philo were adept at seeming to give lip service to the honor due to rulers, but did so in a way that betrayed their real allegiance. Elliott cites a passage in which Philo describes how the Jews in the Alexandrian marketplace "quickly make way 'for the ruler, and for beasts beneath the yoke.'" Elliott continues, "Of course, Philo protests that the motive is different 'With rulers, we act out of respect [*time*]; to beasts beneath the yoke, we act on account of fear [*phobon*], so we suffer no serious injury from them.'"[47]

E. R. Goodenough describes the Philo passage in this way:

> The sarcasm at the end is clear. Philo has compared harsh rulers to savage and deadly animals throughout. When he mentions how in the marketplace the Jews have to make place for their rulers and the pack animal alike, it is part of the very caution he is counselling that he should distinguish between the two, once the rulers in Alexandria have been distinctly referred to, and

say that one gives way out of honor to the rulers, but out of fear to the beasts. . . . But his Jewish readers would quite well have understood that the reason Philo gave way to each was the same, because he knew that if he did not he would be crushed.[48]

In a similar way, while Paul appears to be paying lip service to the goodness of the Roman state, the vocabulary he uses and the context in which his discussion occurs heighten the difference between the church body that he is describing in Romans 12, and the body politic that he describes in chapter 13. One is characterized by love, hospitality to stranger, blessing of persecutors, peace, and the rejection of vengeance; the other is to be obeyed out of fear of the sword.

8. Paul Again Calls the Community of Jesus to Love, Even to Love Rome

This difference is heightened by the contrast between 13:7 and 8: "Pay to all what is owed them: taxes to whom taxes are owed, tolls to whom tolls are owed, fear to whom fear is owed, and honor to whom honor is owed. Owe no one anything, except to love one another, for the one who loves one another has fulfilled the law" (my trans.). On the one hand, Paul tells the community to fulfill their obligations; on the other, he makes it clear that the only real obligation is to love one another. In the face of a state that demanded as its right taxes, tolls, fear, and honor, Paul has been describing a community where the only law is love.

The radical character of this verse should not be lost: whether or not taxes, tolls, fear, and honor are owed to Rome (and the only one of these that is clearly owed Rome is fear, according to the previous verses), what the community owes to Rome, precisely because this community has put on a different Lord, the Lord Jesus Christ (13:14), is love. And so, even though the call to "bless your persecutors" is not preceded by the call to "love your enemies" as it is in the Gospels, that is finally where Paul ends up. Such a call has deep roots in Judaism, of course, as far back as Jeremiah's letter to the exiles to "seek the welfare of the city" in the heart of imperial Babylon (Jer. 29:7).

The question this raises, of course, is whether Paul did indeed consider taxes and tolls to be owed to the empire. Paul's language is as guarded in 13:7 as it is in the preceding verses. On the one hand, those who consider Rome worthy of honor, fear, tolls, and taxes could consider Paul to be suggesting that such things are owed to the rulers. On the other hand, those who have caught the less than enthusiastic tone of this passage might notice the rhetorical twist: although taxes, tolls, fear, and honor *may* be owed to Rome, love is the *only obligation* this community bears. Jewett suggests that rhetorically the relationship between these two verses is that of antilogical *gnōmai*. That is to say, the two verses are in tension with one another, and the second undermines the plain sense of the first. This means that the social obligations of the empire are to be replaced by a new obligation "to love one another" in a new social structure.[49]

Paul's admonition to owe no one anything except love, along with his earlier call to overcome evil with good (12:21), has caused some to read him as urging the Christian community in Rome to seek the welfare of the city by paying taxes and engaging in public acts of benefaction. While such acts of benefaction did indeed benefit the city, it is questionable whether most in the Christian community were in a position to practice such generosity.[50]

It is also not clear that the payment of taxes was of benefit to the wider community. Unlike our contemporary context, where taxes ensure access to education, a justice system, clean cities, transportation systems, and health care, in ancient Rome taxes did not necessarily benefit the communities from which they came. First and foremost, taxes supported the army. The connection between taxes and the military is made clear by Tacitus in a speech by a Roman general to a people who have attempted revolt:

> Although often provoked by you, the only use we have made of our rights as victors has been to impose on you the necessary costs of maintaining peace; for you cannot secure tranquility without armies, nor maintain armies without pay, nor provide pay without taxes; everything else we have in common. . . . Therefore love and cherish peace and the city . . . be warned by the lessons of fortune both good and bad not to prefer defiance and ruin to peace and security.[51]

However, while taxation impoverished the provinces, it did benefit those who lived in Rome. Taxes enabled the building of magnificent civic spaces in Rome, which served to visually educate the inhabitants of Rome of the supremacy of Roman arms for bringing "peace" to the world.[52] Although the lower classes benefited from such civic beauty, they also benefited through gifts designed to keep them contented with the social hierarchy of Rome. Such gifts took the form of the famous bread and circuses.[53] For the most part, however, the ruling classes were the main benficiaries of the wealth that streamed into Rome from taxes, tributes, and tolls. In such a context, I suggest, the payment of taxes is not the unambiguous good that some have suggested.

Also at issue is the question of whether those in the Christian community at Rome were in a position to owe taxes. If tax was levied on land (in the form of part of the crop) as well as on property and income, was the organization of the community in Rome one that resulted in the need to pay no tax?[54] It appears that the Christian community described in Acts 4:32–37 engaged in an economic practice that would have resulted in owing no tax to Rome. Is Paul assuming similar economic practices in the Roman community? The larger context indicates that this community is called to be generous (12:8), to contribute to each other's needs and extend hospitality to those outside the community (12:13), including enemies (12:20). These verses suggest that the community is called to practice the kind of economics described in Acts 4, in which case it is unlikely that they will owe taxes to Rome.

Perhaps Paul's challenge to this community in Romans 12 provides the exegetical clue to 13:7. Perhaps Paul is suggesting that if they indeed live an economic life which participates more in the age to come than in this present age, then they will indeed owe no taxes to Rome. It is only if they participate in the economic structures of the empire, with its emphasis on self-aggrandizement and association with those who confer honor, that they are likely to owe taxes to the empire which has made their economic wealth possible. Rather, an economics that is not conformed to this age, that practices generosity, hospitality, welcome of enemy, and association with the lowly will lack material wealth with its resultant tax obligations and give Rome only obligations that are consistent with what they are already engaged in—love.

Some might argue that an ordering of communal life which avoids paying taxes does not show respect to the governing authorities.[55] Within imperial ideology this was indeed true. Failure to pay taxes was considered treason of the highest order. Of course, this was the opinion of the empire itself. The importance of showing respect to governing authorities is often argued on the basis of an appeal to Jeremiah 29:5–7.[56] However, when Jeremiah recorded the letter to the exiles in Jeremiah 29 and called the exilic community to seek the welfare of the city, the activities he outlined that would contribute to such welfare were not what the imperial overlords necessarily demanded from the captives. Jeremiah called the exiles to build houses and live in them, plant gardens and eat what they produce, take wives and have children (Jer. 29:5–6). In short, he called them to fulfill the calling that they already had as image bearers of God—to be fruitful and multiply.[57] Then he told them to seek the welfare of the city where they were in exile and to pray on its behalf. This language is as radical as "love your enemy," and it is the culmination of the Israelites' fulfilling their creational and covenantal calling.

Paul is calling for something equally radical from the Christian community in Rome. Now, however, their calling is to bear Christ's image or "be clothed with" the Lord Jesus Christ. They are to show what it is to be the body of Christ, and this means to practice the crucified love toward enemies that Jesus enabled with his death and resurrection. This is what it means to seek the welfare of the city. This is what it means to owe no one anything but love. The paying of taxes and tolls is not what it means to be a community that bears God's love to the heart of the empire. Only a community that seeks to overcome evil with good will be able to do that.

Ironically, in the next century Christian refusal to serve in the army was considered an action of abandonment of the emperor that could lead to the dissolution of empire.[58] This was, of course, the imperial point of view, and it paralleled the imperial interpretation of a refusal to pay taxes. However, all the evidence from the first few centuries of Christian history indicates that any involvement in military activity ran expressly counter to the Christian calling to be a community refusing to engage in the sort of violence that characterized the empire. While paying taxes did not overtly contravene that calling, it is doubtful that appealing to the payment of taxes as a measure of respect for imperial authority would hold much water for a community that refused to respect the empire by fighting on its behalf.[59]

Conclusion: A New Political Ethic

This brief sketch demonstrates that Paul is calling into being a new body politic, a new people whose overt love, blessing, and care for the enemy and persecutor function as a political challenge to an empire that knows only how to rule by wrath, sword, and bloodshed. On the surface such a political ethic seems to be simplistic. In fact, to someone like myself, whose response to imperial violence has been profoundly shaped by the stories of my grandparents and their involvement in the Dutch resistance in World War II, such a political ethic seems dangerously naive. And indeed, that is how the community where I have my roots treats such discussions. But I can do no more than bear witness to what Paul calls "the foolishness of the cross." The political ethic that Paul describes here points us to a practice that could have transformative effect. As Marva Dawn pointedly puts it:

> What would happen in Third-World countries, for example, if instead of selling militants more arms or putting embargoes on their trade we worked to bring about economic justice? What would happen if we put food on their tables, taught them skills that gave them dignity, and freed them from their fears by caring about them without violence? . . . What would happen if we strengthened the economies of Third-World nations instead of threatening them militarily?[60]

These questions raised almost rhetorically find their answers in scores of organizations working to do precisely these things in the service of peace. In the face of war and genocide in Bosnia, the Fellowship of Reconciliation in the United States placed primarily Muslim students from Bosnia into Christian, Jewish, and Muslim homes in the United States so that they could continue their university studies.[61] In Hebron, Christian Peacemaker Team members walk Palestinians to work and school as a protection against Israeli violence, along with serving as intermediaries in Israeli and Palestinian disputes and riding buses that are prone to suicide attacks. In Iraq, Christian Peacemaker Teams help Iraqis find family members who have been jailed by U.S. troops and help work for their release.[62] In Mozambique, a Catholic community has been instrumental in building peace between warring parties.[63] Not only do such initiatives counter the charge that nonviolence only allows violence to proliferate; they also demonstrate that such strategies are the only way for lasting peace to be achieved.

But these questions explore only one dimension of Paul's call to be a political people who act without violence. While our obvious enemies may be those nations who appear to hate the Western world, Romans 12–13 had a more immediate referent for the Roman Christian community—the Roman Empire in which they lived. This was a question not for those at the top of political power but rather for those at the bottom. The more immediate parallel for us is the question of how we live under a state that practices the same violence as Rome, a state that as a result appears to be our enemy. What would it look like not only for us to pressure our governments to pay our debt of love to those nations that have terrorized us, but also for us to pay our debt of love to our nation, the nation that perpetuates such terror?

Perhaps the answer is found in precisely the sort of the community that Paul describes in Romans 12. Perhaps it means that the Christian community should live out the call to be an alternative community, one that does not respond to violence with violence, one that does not seek power but seeks to be found among the marginalized, one that practices an incredible generosity, even toward enemies. What would it mean to be this kind of community, which seeks to love the empire by embracing those whom the empire has abandoned and which prays for the peace and welfare of the empire by beginning to bring light and health to the very places where the darkness is deepest?[64] In the end, this is the sort of community that Paul calls the Roman Christians to be. And it is only when we realize the far-reaching implications of such a call for the community in Rome that we ourselves will begin to be transformed in the renewal of our minds, so that our imaginations will be set free to embody the crucified messiah in the middle of our imperial darkness.

Notes

1. Allan A. Boesak, "What Belongs to Caesar: Once Again Romans 13," in *When Prayer Makes News*, ed. A. Boesak and C. Villa-Vicencio (Philadelphia: Westminster, 1986), 138.
2. See Roger Bower, "Genocide in Rwanda 1994—An Anglican Perspective," in *Genocide in Rwanda: Complicity of the Churches*, ed. C. Rittner et al. (St. Paul, MN: Aegis, 2004), 41; David Gushee, "Why the Churches Were Complicit," in *Genocide in Rwanda*, 263. I owe these references to Tom Atfield.
3. See Christopher Bryan, *Render to Caesar: Jesus, the Early Church and the Roman Superpower* (Oxford: Oxford University Press, 2005), 78–82; N. T. Wright, "The Letter to the Romans," in *The New Interpreter's Bible* (Nashville: Abingdon, 2002), 10:721.
4. For recent discussions that question the historical plausibility of a wholesale expulsion of the Jews from Rome, see Mark Nanos, *The Mystery of Romans: The Jewish Context of Paul's Letter* (Minneapolis: Fortress, 1996), 372–89; Steve Mason, "'For I Am Not Ashamed of the Gospel' (Rom. 1.16): The Gospel and the First Readers of Rome," in *Gospel in Paul: Studies in Corinthians, Galatians, and Romans for Richard N. Longenecker*, ed. L. Ann Jervis and Peter Richardson (Sheffield: Sheffield Academic Press, 1994), 255–76.
5. Ernst Käsemann, *Commentary on Romans* (Grand Rapids: Eerdmans, 1980), 249, also suggests that "*machaira* perhaps means concretely execution." James Dunn, *Romans 9–16*, WBC 38b (Dallas: Word, 1988), 2:505, points out that *diōgmos* always refers to persecution for religious reasons.
6. Pss. 18:6, 41 (17:7, 42 LXX); 32:3 (31:3 LXX); 69:3 (68:4 LXX). See also Pss. 4:3; 17:6: 22:5; 28:1–2; 31:22; 55:16; 61:2 (60:3 LXX); 88:1, 9, 13.
7. See, e.g., Exod. 2:23–24; Judg. 2:18; Pss. 31:10; 38:9–10; Isa. 24:7; 30:15; Lam. 1:18, 21–22; Ezek. 21:11–12; 1 Macc. 1:26; 3 Macc. 1:18. For more on the background for the language of groaning in Israel's Scriptures, see Sylvia Keesmaat, *Paul and His Story (Re)Interpreting the Exodus Tradition* (Sheffield: Sheffield Academic Press, 1999), 107–10.
8. "Paul as 'Eschatalogic Person': A New Look at 2 Cor 11:29," *CBQ* 37 (1975): 510–12; Keesmaat, *Paul and His Story*, 120–22.

9. Within Israel's Scriptures the question of theodicy is overwhelmingly concerned with why idolatrous pagans who practice injustice appear to be triumphant. I suggest that this is true for Romans as well.

10. See Sylvia Keesmaat, "The Psalms in Romans and Galatians," in *The Psalms in the New Testament*, ed. S. Moyise and J. Maarten Menkes (Edinburgh: T.&T. Clark, 2004), 139–61.

11. On imperial overtones of the language of gospel, see: N. Elliott, "Paul and the Politics of Empire," in Richard Horsley, ed., *Paul and Politics: Ekklesia, Israel, Imperium, Interpretation: Essays in Honour of Krister Stendahl* (Harrisburg, PA: Trinity Press International, 2000), 24; Dieter Georgi, *Theocracy in Paul's Praxis and Theology* (Minneapolis: Fortress, 1991), 83; Wright, "Gospel and Theology in Galatians," 226–28.

12. This is the only reference to Jesus' royal lineage in Paul's epistles. While Paul draws extensively on the promises to Abraham in his telling of the Christian story, strikingly the promises to David are absent. This reference to David, therefore, suggests that Paul is explicitly challenging the right to the throne of the Roman ruler.

13. On *fides* as a virtue of the empire, Dieter Georgi refers to the Acts of Augustus, chaps. 31–33, in "God Turned Upside Down," in *Paul and Empire: Religion and Power in Roman Imperial Society*, ed. R. Horsley (Harrisburg, PA: Trinity Press International, 1997), 149; see also Richard Horsley, "Patronage, Priesthood and Power: Introduction," in Horsley, ed., *Paul and Empire*, 93.

14. For more detail on the imperial context of Romans, see Georgi, *Theocracy*; Michael Joseph Brown, "Paul's Use of *Doulos Christou Iēsou* in Romans 1:1," *JBL* 120 (2001): 723–37; Wright, "Letter to the Romans," esp. 404–5, 423–24, 738; Neil Elliott, *Liberating Paul: The Justice of God and the Politics of the Apostle* (Sheffield: Sheffield Academic Press, 1995); Horsley, ed., *Paul and Politics*; and, for more general background, Horsley, ed., *Paul and Empire*.

15. Mark Nanos, *The Mystery of Romans: The Jewish Context of Paul's Letter* (Minneapolis: Fortress, 1996), 290n3. Another intriguing exegesis of Rom. 13, which follows a different direction from my argument, is Nanos's suggestion that 13:1–7 concerns submission not to secular political authority but to the synagogue. The implications of his reading result in a construal of the relationship between the Christian and Jewish community in Rome that is beyond the scope of this essay. However, his argument deserves close consideration (see 289–336).

16. So also Wright, "Letter to the Romans," 701.

17. On the new age inaugurated by Augustus, see Paul Zanker, *The Power of Images in the Age of Augustus* (Ann Arbor: University of Michigan Press, 1990), chap. 5.

18. Elliott, "Paul and the Politics of Empire," 37.

19. Richard Horsley, *I Corinthians* (Nashville: Abingdon Press, 1988), 171, lists the following for the analogy between the body and the city-state: Marcus Aurelius, *Med.* 2.1; 7.13; Epictetus, *Diss.* 2.10.3–4; Seneca, *Ep.* 95.52; Livy, *Hist.* 2.32. In the last, the fable of the body was used by senators to try to make plebeians repent of plans of mutiny. It thus functioned to ensure that the ruled classes continued to fulfill civic duties. Wright, "Letter to the Romans," 710, also lists Plato, *Republic* 462c–d; Plutarch, *Arat.* 24.5; *Cor.* 6.2–4.

20. See Halvor Moxnes, "The Quest for Honor and the Unity of the Community in Romans 12 and in the Orations of Dio Chrysostom," in *Paul in His Hellenistic Context*, ed. Troels Engberg-Pedersen (Edinburgh: T.&T. Clark, 1994), 225.

21. Paul engages in a similar contrast in 1 Cor. 11:17–12.31.

22. On the contrast between the "reasonable worship," which Paul mentions here, and the debauchery and excess of the Roman worship, which Paul criticizes in Rom. 1:18–32, see Elliott, "Paul and the Politics of Empire," 39.

23. A. Katherine Grieb, *The Story of Romans: A Narrative Defense of God's Righteousness* (Louisville, KY: Westminster John Knox, 2002), 118.

24. On the political nature of *christianoi*, which was applied to followers of Jesus (e.g., in Acts 11:26), see Bruce Winter, "Roman Law and Society in Romans 12–15," in *Rome in the Bible and the Early Church*, ed. Peter Oakes (Grand Rapids: Baker, 2002), 70–74.

25. On the patronage system, see Andrew Wallace-Hadrill, ed., *Patronage in Ancient Society* (New York: Routledge, 1989); on Caesar as the highest patron, see Andrew Wallace-Hadrill, "Patronage in Roman Society," in *Patronage in Ancient Society*, 84.

26. This is, of course, exactly what Paul argues in 1 Cor. 12, a passage with extensive parallels to Rom. 12.

27. Moxnes, "Quest for Honor," 222. Moxnes thoroughly explores the context of *hybris* in Greek and Hellenistic philosophy and literature.

28. As Bruce Winter puts it, "Paul thereby overthrew centuries of Roman self-definition based on class with this countercultural self-evaluation based on God-given gifts that were meant to benefit others or contribute to their needs" ("Roman Law and Society," 79).

29. Keesmaat, "Psalms in Romans and Galatians."

30. See Sylvia Keesmaat, "Crucified Lord or Conquering Saviour: Whose Story of Salvation?" *HBT* 26, no. 2 (2004): 69–93.

31. Marva Dawn in *Truly the Community: Romans 12 and How to Be the Church* (Grand Rapids: Eerdmans, 1992), 283, appeals to the Egyptian provenance of these verses as a way of clarifying the meaning of "for by so doing you will heap burning coals on his head." Apparently bearing hot coals on one's head was a symbol of repentance; hence kindness of the enemy could be a way to bring the enemy to repentance. As we shall see below, this coheres well with a possible allusion to 2 Kgs. 6 in these verses. However, see Gordon Zerbe, "Paul's Ethic of Nonretaliation and Peace," in *The Love of Enemy and Nonretaliation in the New Testament*, ed. Willard Swartley (Louisville, KY: Westminster/John Knox, 1992), 196.

32. See Grieb, *The Story of Romans*, 122.

33. Richard B. Hays, *The Moral Vision of the New Testament: Community, Cross, New Creation: A Contemporary Introduction to New Testament Ethics* (San Francisco: HarperSanFrancisco, 1996), 330.

34. I am not arguing that this is the *only* way of dealing with enemies in Israel's Scriptures; it is, however, the thematic strand that both Jesus and Paul affirm and develop.

35. The rest of this paragraph is dependent upon my article "Psalms in Romans and Galatians," 151–52.

36. The importance of the "relentless solidarity" of God in transforming the darkness is discussed in Brueggemann, *The Message of the Psalms: A Theological Commentary* (Minneapolis: Augsburg, 1984), 12.

37. On Colossians, see Brian J. Walsh and Sylvia C. Keesmaat, *Colossian Remixed: Subverting the Empire* (Downers Grove, IL: InterVarsity Press, 2004), chap. 11. According to Philip Towner, "Romans 13:1–7 and Paul's Missiological Perspective: A Call to Political Quietism or Transformation?" in *Romans and the People of God: Essays in Honour of Gordon D. Fee*, ed. Sven Soderlund and N. T. Wright (Grand Rapids: Eerdmans, 1999), 159, this passage has all the marks of the household code tradition.

38. According to Wright, "Letter to the Romans," 720, "The word has echoes of military formation: one must take one's place in the appropriate rank."

39. Wright, "Letter to the Romans," 719.

40. Luise Schottroff, "'Give to Caesar What Belongs to Caesar and to God What Belongs to God': A Theological Response of the Early Christian Church to Its Social and Political Environment," in Swartley, ed., *The Love of Enemy and Non-retaliation in the New Testament*, 228–29.

41. Schottroff, 229.

42. On hidden and public transcripts see James C. Scott, *Domination and the Arts of Resistance* (New Haven, CT: Yale University Press, 1990).

43. Robert Jewett, "Response: Exegetical Support from Romans and Other Letters," in Horsley, ed., *Paul and Politics*, 65. He points out: "That the Roman authorities were ordained by the God and Father of Jesus Christ turns the entire Roman civic cult on its head, exposing its suppression of the truth. Its involvement in the martyrdom of Christ, crucified under Pontius Pilate, cannot have been forgotten by the readers of chapter 13 who knew from firsthand experience the hollowness of Rome's claim to have established a benign rule of law. The critique of the law in all its forms in the first eight chapters of this letter cannot have been forgotten, which explains why the proudest institution of the *Pax Romana*, the rule of law, goes unmentioned here. Nothing remains of the claim in Roman propaganda that its law enforcement system was redemptive, producing a kind of messianic peace under the rule of the gods "Justitia" and "Clementia." Christ alone is the fulfilment of the law (10:4), not the emperor or the Roman gods. . . . Submission to the governmental authorities is therefore an expression of respect not for the authorities themselves, but for the crucified deity who stands behind them" (67).

44. N. Elliott, "Romans 13:1–7 in the Context of Imperial Propaganda," in Horsley, ed., *Paul and Empire*, 203. Elliott quotes a number of sources that demonstrate this point: Calpurnius Siculus, *Eclogue* 1.45–65; Einsiedeln *Eclogues* 25–31; and Seneca, *De clementia* 1.2–4; 11.3; 13.5.

45. Elliott, "Romans 13:1–7," 203.

46. Elliott, "Romans 13:1–7," 198.

47. Elliott, "Romans 13:1–7," 200.

48. E. R. Goodenough, *An Introduction to Philo Judeaus* (Oxford: Blackwell, 1962), 57; quoted in Elliott, "Romans 13:1–7," 200–201.

49. Jewett, "Response: Exegetical Support," 67–68. David Reed drew my attention to this.

50. While this concern is raised by Towner, "Romans 13:1–7," 166, he argues that Paul expands the convention of benefaction so that it does, indeed, apply to the whole community.

51. Tacitus, *Histories* IV, 73f, quoted in Klaus Wengst, *Pax Romana and the Peace of Jesus Christ* (London: SCM, 1987), 21.

52. For example, the imagery on the *ara pacis* (Altar of Peace) combines the imagery of abundant peace with the supremacy of Roman military might. See Zanker, *Power of Images*, 172–77 and 101–66, which outlines how the mythical foundation of the new Rome was embodied in its architecture and public monuments.

53. Wengst, *Pax Romana*, 34. Zanker, 143, describes how the architecture of the city and even the import of grain into Rome were designed to remind the people of the vast empire that "they" had power over.

54. Wengst, *Pax Romana*, 59, suggests that "Jesus and his followers may not have been subject to taxes: a carpenter (Mark 6:3) who is not engaged in his craft, fishermen who have left their fishing gear by the lake (Mark 1:16–20), a publican who has left his post (Mark 2:14) have no income and therefore cannot be taxed by their ruler—nor could they be taxed by the Roman authorities. In fact, they had escaped taxation long since—at the price of a very uncertain existence.

55. This is the gist of both Bryan, *Render to Caesar*, 80–81, and Wright, "Letter to the Romans," 721–22.

56. Bryan, *Render to Caesar*, 80; Towner, "Romans 13:1–7," 163.

57. It was precisely this kind of everyday fruitfulness that was such a threat years before to the Egyptian empire.

58. *Contra Celsum* VIII.5, quoted in Jim Forest, "Soldiers of Christ," in *Transforming Violence: Linking Local and Global Peacemaking*, ed. Robert Herr and Judy Zimmerman Herr (Scottsdale, PA: Herald Press, 1998), 24.

59. For more on the Christian refusal to serve in the military, see Forest, "Soldiers of Christ," 23–33.

60. Dawn, *Truly the Community*, 269, 284.

61. Doug Hostetter, "Neighbours in the Bosnian Tragedy," in Herr, ed., *Transforming Violence*, 105–18.

62. See Tricia Gates Brown, ed., *Getting in the Way: Stories from Christian Peacemaker Teams* (Waterloo, ON: Herald Press, 2005); Kathleen Kern, "Applying Civilian Peace Teams," in Herr, ed., *Transforming Violence*, 168–76. See also the Christian Peacemaker Web site: www.cpt.org. Such actions are not without danger: in the winter of 2005–2006, four Christian peacemakers were held captive in Iraq. Three eventually were set free; the American member of the team, Tom Fox, lost his life.

63. Andrea Bartoli, "Providing Space for Change in Mozambique," in Herr, ed., *Transforming Violence*, 190–202.

64. Not only are the organizations listed on p. 153 involved in precisely these sorts of actions, but in intentional Christian communities around the world we are seeing the embodiment of Rom 12–13. In Canada and the United States, examples include the Catholic Workers Communities, the Reba Fellowship in Chicago, and the Sojourners Community in Washington, D.C. Interestingly, many of these communities practice precisely the sort of counterimperial economics that Rom 12–13 calls for.

Chapter 10

Toward a Nonretaliatory Lifestyle

The Psalms, the Cross, and the Gospel

J. CLINTON MCCANN JR.

The Psalms, especially the so-called imprecatory psalms or psalms of vengeance, are often cited as evidence for biblical religion at its worst—a vindictive God being invoked by worshipers intent upon revenge. If it were just the relatively few imprecatory psalms that conveyed this bad impression, one could perhaps dismiss these "Unpleasant and Repulsive Psalms," as Erich Zenger characterizes the general impression of them, as exceptions.[1] But this is not the case. The Psalter is full of the psalmists' requests that God destroy their enemies, as well as their frequent affirmations that God will indeed do so, or their celebrations that God has already done so. Even so, I shall attempt to demonstrate in this essay that a careful reading of the Psalms, including a reading of the psalms of vengeance in the context of the entire book of Psalms, suggests that the real issue is not vengeance or revenge but rather the establishment of God's justice, righteousness, and peace in the world. This conclusion is reinforced by Paul's use of the Psalms to support his contention that God justifies by grace, as well as by the Gospel writers' use of the prayers in the Psalter in their passion stories.

The Psalms

Already in the two psalms that serve as a paired introduction to the Psalter, "the wicked" are introduced (1:1, 4–6); and they take the form of rebellious "nations," "peoples," and "kings" in Ps. 2:1–2. In both cases, God seems to retaliate. The wicked and the rebellious will "perish" (1:6; 2:12). In Psalm 2, it is God's "anointed" (v. 2) who is the agent of destruction (vv. 8–9). Not coincidentally, it would seem, the rebellious "nations," "peoples," and "kings" reappear in Psalm 149:7–8 to form in conjunction with Psalm 2:1–2 an envelope structure for the Psalter; and here it is all God's "faithful" who will "execute on them the judgment decreed" (v. 9). From beginning to end, the Psalter seems to portray a God who is intent upon revenge, and who also authorizes God's "anointed," and indeed all God's "faithful," to participate in the exacting of revenge.

And between the beginning and the end, there are numerous other psalms that seem to suggest that God, God's "anointed," and God's people are all about retaliation. Besides Psalms 1–2 and 149, in at least fifty-eight additional psalms the psalmists either pray for, express confidence in, or celebrate divine retaliation in the form of the destruction of their enemies, including the infamous classic: "Happy shall they be who take your little ones and dash them against a rock!" (137:9).[2] It is no wonder, therefore, that at first glance the book of Psalms seems to leave little room for forgiveness and reconciliation and to offer little constructive guidance toward a nonretaliatory lifestyle.

Undoubtedly, the retaliatory tone of the book of Psalms is related to the pervasive presence of the psalmists' "foes" (3:1) and "enemies" (3:7). As Psalm 3 makes clear, the "foes" and "enemies" are synonymous with "the wicked" (3:7), who are present from the very first verse of the Psalter. Nor do they ever disappear, especially not from the prayers for help. In Books I–II of the Psalter (Psalms 1–72), where the individual prayers for help are concentrated, every psalm that is generally categorized as a prayer for help/lament/complaint contains some reference to and/or description of the work of the enemies, with the exception of Psalm 51 (in which the psalmist may be considered as his or her own worst enemy). Not surprisingly, there is a host of Hebrew words and phrases involved (besides those usually translated as "wicked," "foe," and "enemy"), variously rendered by the NRSV as "the bloodthirsty," "evildoers," "workers of evil," "pursuers," "fools," "hypocrites," "adversaries," "false witnesses," "ruffians," "wrongdoers," "those who seek my life," "the proud," "the arrogant," "assailants," "the insolent," and "the ruthless," along with metaphors like "bulls," "dogs," and "lions." In a word, the wicked/foes/enemies are virtually omnipresent in the book of Psalms, especially in the psalmic prayers.

I emphasize this fact, not as an "excuse" for the psalmists' requests for the destruction of their enemies, but rather to begin to make the point that the pervasive presence of the wicked/foes/enemies is a critical datum for interpreting the Psalms, especially when focusing upon the issue of retaliation versus reconciliation. As Fredrik Lindström helpfully points out: "The absolutely most important motif in the individual complaint psalms' interpretation of suffering is the *enemy motif*. The motif is the most important in the sense that it is found in and throughout the psalms in question."[3]

If we interpreters recognize the pervasive presence of the enemies in the Psalms, and *if* we take the psalmists' complaints and vengeful-sounding pleas as genuine, then the way is open to conclude that the praying psalmists address God without exception *as victims*. I want to emphasize the two occurrences of "if" in the previous sentence; for, in fact, many readers and interpreters of the Psalms (especially in North America perhaps) have not considered the crucial importance of the "enemy motif," and there has been and is an inclination to hear the psalmists' complaints and pleas as hyperbolic "whining" and perhaps even paranoia. The reason, I think, is this: Because *we* are not generally aware of having any enemies, we cannot imagine that the psalmists did either; or at least we do not know what to make of that persistent kind of opposition, except perhaps to conclude that it led the psalmists to say things that sound very "un-Christian." So, hymnbook and prayer book editors, along with the framers of lectionaries, have freely edited out the "unpleasant and repulsive" portions of the Psalms, while devotional readers have just skipped those parts, often writing off the psalmists as whiners.

The most extreme example of this sort of interpretive direction (of which I am aware) is found in an essay in a book entitled *Diseases in Antiquity*, in which the author concludes that the psalmist's complaint about the enemies in Psalm 35 can be attributed to "schizophrenia simplex," the psalmist's complaint about suffering in Psalm 38 evidences "hypochondriacal ideas," and the complaint about the enemies in Psalm 38:12 indicates "delusions" accompanying "a depressive psychosis."[4] In short, the psalmists did not really have problems, and they did not really have enemies. Rather, they were either insane, hypochondriacal, depressed, and/or paranoid.

My limited international experience has helped me to realize that people of faith in some other cultural settings can more readily understand the sort of pervasive opposition that the psalmists regularly articulate. For instance, José Antonio Puac, who worked throughout the 1990s for the Human Rights Office of the Archdiocese of Guatemala on the Recovery of Historical Memory Project (REMHI), lives with the realization that his life is in constant danger. His friend and mentor Bishop Juan Gerardi was murdered on April 26, 1998, on account of his leadership of REMHI. This was two days after the public presentation of the report at the national cathedral in Guatemala City, and José Antonio realizes that the same could happen to him.[5] As José Antonio and his experience help me to realize, it is not paranoia if they are really out to get you!

The same conclusion applies to the suffering psalmists. As difficult as it may be, contemporary readers and interpreters must try to hear the psalmists' complaints and their vengeful sounding pleas as evidence of real, profound, and pervasive opposition. So again, *if* we interpreters recognize the pervasive presence of the enemies in the Psalms, and *if* we take the psalmists' complaints and pleas as genuine, then the way is open to conclude that the praying psalmists address God without exception *as victims*.

More specifically, the psalmists are victims of the injustice and unrighteousness perpetrated by the wicked/foes/enemies. The psalmists, introduced in Psalm 1 as "the righteous'" (vv. 5–6), are those who constantly attend to God and God's *torah*, "instruction" (1:2). In the Psalms and elsewhere in the Original Testament, the essence of God's "instruction" or will is clear—it is "justice" and "righteousness" toward the reality of shalom, "peace" or "well-being." As cosmic sovereign, God "is coming to establish justice (on) the earth" (Pss. 96:13; 98:9, my translation). Indeed, as Psalm 82 suggests, what constitutes true divinity—what it means to be God, if you will—is the establishment of justice for "the weak" and the enactment of righteousness for "the lowly" (v. 3). Quite appropriately, Psalm 82 ends with the prayer, "Rise up, O God, establish justice (on) the earth" (v. 8, my translation). Or one might say, "Do your will," or even "Your will be done" (Matt. 6:10). Doing God's will was the responsibility of the earthly monarch, God's "anointed"; that is, the institution of monarchy was entrusted with the mission of enacting and embodying God's will in the world. So, entirely congruently with Psalms 96 and 98, the prayer for the earthly king is that God give him "your justice" and "your righteousness" (Ps. 72:1; see vv. 2, 7), so that cosmic shalom will prevail (vv. 3, 7; NRSV "prosperity" in v. 3 and "peace" in v. 7).

But in the Psalms, seldom does peace prevail. As suggested above, Psalms 1 and 2 make clear in introducing the Psalter that God, God's will, and God's "anointed" are constantly opposed by "the wicked." Indeed, if my proposal for a fresh translation of Psalm 1:5 is correct, Psalm 1 explicitly describes the typical behavior of "the wicked." Rather than NRSV's "Therefore the wicked will not stand in the judgment," I propose, "Therefore the wicked will not stand up for justice [*mishpat*]."[6] In contrast to "the righteous," who constantly attend to God's "instruction," "the wicked" neither attend to God's will nor make any attempt to live by it. Whether or not my proposed translation of Psalm 1:5 is correct, however, the book of Psalms as a whole makes it eminently clear that the wicked/foes/enemies constantly and thoroughly oppose God, God's will, God's "anointed," and God's faithful people. It is precisely this opposition—in psalmic and biblical terms, this *injustice* and *unrighteousness*—that evokes the psalmists' prayers for help. Again, it is essential to hear these prayers as the outcries of victimized persons.

Hearing the prayers for help as the outcries of victimized persons gives the psalmists' requests for the destruction of their enemies a certain "legitimacy." In situations of victimization, the absolutely worst responses are apathy and silence. The psalmists' emotionally charged, impassioned pleas for the destruction of their enemies are, from this perspective, a sign of psychological health.

But what about theological health? To be sure, it is likely that many pray-ers of the lament/complaint psalms would have welcomed a little personal revenge, just as many contemporary Christians have no qualms about asking God to retaliate on their behalf. But we have no real access to the psalmists' personal motivations and desires. What we do have access to is the book of Psalms as a literary product; and given the Psalter in its canonical form, it seems reasonable and proper to hear the psalmists' requests for the destruction of their enemies as appeals by victims of injustice that God set things right in the world. In short, the psalmists' pleas need not be heard as requests for personal revenge, but rather as prayers for justice and righteousness in the fullest sense of these terms—the creation of or restoration of conditions that make life possible for all, including, and indeed especially, the poor, weak, needy, and oppressed (see Ps. 72:12–14, a description of what God's justice and righteousness look like when put into practice by God's anointed).

The theological conviction that underlies the psalmists' prayers for justice and righteousness is stated explicitly in the concluding verse of one of the longest and most comprehensive of the psalms of vengeance—that is, God "stands at the right hand of the needy" (Ps. 109:31; see also Pss. 9:18; 12:5; 35:10; 40:17; 102:17; 103:6, where NRSV "vindication" is more literally "righteousness"; 140:12; 146:7–9; as well as the aforementioned Pss. 72:1–7, 12–14; 82:1–4). Given the very prevalence of the enemies in the Psalms, however, this apparently does not mean that God acts suddenly and unilaterally to wipe out God's foes, the enemies of God's anointed, or the opponents of God's people. But the conviction that God "stands at the right hand of the needy" does clearly locate God with the victimized.

To be sure, this conviction intends to comfort the afflicted; but beyond that, it also serves to empower the victimized in their opposition to oppression and their pursuit of God's justice, righteousness, and peace. Furthermore—and this is crucial for the topic of reconciliation—the conviction that God "stands at the right hand of the needy" invites the comfortable into solidarity with the afflicted (see Ps. 22:24). Blaming victims, and thus doubly victimizing them, is ruled out. What is commended, or commanded, is solidarity—that is, reconciliation in the fundamental sense of "re-meeting," bringing together. Because the psalmists' prayers for justice and righteousness ultimately invite persons into a solidarity founded upon the pursuit of God's justice and righteousness, Erich Zenger appropriately concludes that the psalms of vengeance "teach us to say 'no' [to violence], and beyond saying it, to be compelled to cooperate in diminishing violence and enmity."[8] In a word or two, the psalmists' prayers for justice and righteousness invite peace and reconciliation. While I am ordinarily opposed to bumper-sticker religion, there is one bumper sticker I have seen that actually captures quite well the ultimate thrust of the psalmists' prayers for the destruction of their enemies: "If you want peace, work for justice."

This same interpretive direction can be put in slightly different terms to sharpen the theological point; that is, the affirmation that God stands with suffering victims has the logical effect of obliterating the doctrine of retribution. Because it is precisely "the righteous" who suffer constantly in the Psalms, suffering simply cannot be viewed logically as divine punishment. To be sure, the psalmists sometimes speak as if God were punishing them (see Pss. 6:1; 38:1–4, 17–18); but the prayers in their final form actually undermine the doctrine of retribution as the psalmists claim God's help and favor in the midst of their suffering (see Pss. 6:8–10; 38:19–22). Again, as above, this means that victims cannot be blamed or scapegoated.

The effect of the Psalms at this point is identical to that of the book of Job, in which Job learns that his suffering is not to be understood as punishment. As René Girard in particular has recognized, the book of Job participates in "the immense biblical movement toward the refusal of victimary religion."[9] Girard recognizes as well that the Psalms, especially the prayers for help, participate in this biblical movement. As he puts it, "The psalms do much the same thing [as the Book of Job], but with much less audacity."[10] In any case, the demolition of the doctrine of retribution opens the way toward reconciliation, rather than retaliation in the form of scapegoating.

Indeed, only when the doctrine of retribution is demolished is there any logical space for grace.[11] In this regard, it is significant that the Psalms ultimately present "the righteous" not as those who deserve God's favor by their good behavior, but rather as those who live in dependence upon divine forgiveness—that is, who live by grace. Psalm 32 is particularly important, since the double beatitude with which it begins (vv. 1–2) recalls Psalm 1 and its opening beatitude. If there is any inclination on the reader's part to interpret Psalm 1 and its presentation of "the righteous" in retributive terms, Psalm 32 disallows such a conclusion. The "happy" or "the righteous" are not those who manage to "deserve it," but rather those whom God forgives and those who live in constant dependence upon God.

The Cross and the Gospel

The apostle Paul's use of Psalm 32:1–2 in Romans 4:7–8 to support his argument for justification by grace (see Rom. 3:24) is a reminder for Christian readers that the cross, along with the book of Psalms and the book of Job, is also part of "the immense biblical movement toward the refusal of victimary religion." As William Placher puts it, responding in part to Girard, "The message of the cross is more radical than Girard sees: it is not just that we should stop scapegoating the innocent, but that we should stop punishing the guilty."[12] Not punishing the guilty is almost certainly the ultimate in reconciliation or nonretaliation. While Christians may cite the cross as the fullest expression of such a nonretaliatory policy, they may also justifiably conclude that the message of the cross—grace—is to be found as well in the Psalms, which is where Paul found it!

It is certainly not coincidental that the Gospel writers could not tell the story of Jesus without frequent recourse to the book of Psalms. To be sure, they use Psalm 2 in conjunction with the claim that Jesus is the ultimate "anointed" (Hebrew *messiah*; Greek *christos*) or "son" of God (see Pss. 2:2, 7; Mark 1:1, 11; note that Mark 1:11 quotes Ps. 2:7). But the Gospel writers' use of the Psalms is most evident in their accounts of Jesus' passion; they employ especially Psalms 22, 31, 69, and 88, all prayers for help, the genre of psalms in which the "enemy motif" is pervasive. What the Gospel writers actually knew about the details of

Jesus' life and death is still being debated; but they clearly knew that Jesus endured persistent opposition to his teaching and ministry, to the point that his enemies eventually killed him or had him killed. The congruence between Jesus and the suffering psalmists is evident, and the Gospel writers' frequent use of the prayers for help suggests that they saw Jesus as the ultimate exemplar of the righteous, suffering psalmist. From the Gospel writers' presentation of Jesus and his nonretaliatory lifestyle, however, we may infer that they did not interpret the "enemy motif," along with the psalmists' requests for the destruction of their enemies (see Pss. 31:12–18, 23; 69:22–28), as a matter of personal revenge or retaliation. This seems to imply that they construed the real issue to be justice. As Paul understands it, the cross is indeed about God's establishment of justice—that is, justification—and it happens by grace, not retaliation.

One might object that the Psalms themselves do not offer an unambiguous model of a reconciliatory, nonretaliatory lifestyle; and this does seem to be the case, with the possible exception of Psalm 35:11–14. Although these verses appear to stand in some tension with the psalmist's request in 35:1–6, they articulate the psalmist's affirmation of solidarity with other sufferers, rather than any propensity to blame or scapegoat them:

> But as for me, when they were sick,
>   I wore sackcloth;
>   I afflicted myself with fasting.
> I prayed with head bowed on my bosom,
>   as though I grieved for a friend or brother;
> I went about as one who laments for a mother,
>   bowed down and in mourning.
>   (Ps. 35:13–14; NRSV)

This important "exception" captures the underlying theological dynamic of the prayers for help, replete though they may be with what appear to be unmitigated requests for personal revenge. As suggested above, in the final form of the Psalter, these requests may properly be heard essentially as prayers by the victimized for the enactment of God's justice, righteousness, and shalom in the world. More so than it may first appear, therefore, the book of Psalms invites readers and prayers toward a nonretaliatory, reconciliatory lifestyle, grounded in grace rather than revenge, in forgiving rather than finding fault. The message of the Psalms at this point is entirely congruent with the message of the cross and the gospel.

Postscript: A Contemporary Challenge for North Americans

Congruent with the above conclusion that the psalmists' prayers for the destruction of their enemies are essentially prayers for the enactment of God's justice and righteousness in the world, Roland E. Murphy and James L. Mays suggest that the enemies in the Psalms should be interpreted symbolically. As Murphy puts it, "one can see the 'enemies' as a symbol for the powers of evil arrayed against all that is good and just."[13] Mays's interpretive direction is virtually identical:

The enemies are out to deprive the afflicted of either shalom or *sedaqah* [usually translated "righteousness"—that is, the condition of things being right] or both. That is what makes them theologically important and what makes them a symbol that can be used in other and quite different social and cultural settings from the ones in which they were written. . . . We pray because we desire that God's will and mind prevail—not our own, not others'.[14]

Not only do both Murphy and Mays suggest that the enemies can be interpreted as "a symbol"; but as Mays also suggests, this opens the way for appropriating in new "social and cultural settings" what the enemies symbolize. Mays also mentions "God's will"; and both he and Murphy use terms that form an admirable summary of what God wills—good(ness), just(ice), righteousness, and shalom. As suggested above, this summary can be derived from the book of Psalms itself (see Psalms 72, 82, 96, and 98).

What about our social and cultural setting? To take the Psalms to heart will mean to stand *for* God's will—goodness, justice, righteousness, and shalom on a cosmic scale—and to stand *against* the powers and forces that oppose God's will in the world. Again, this is tantamount to saying that the psalmists' prayers for the destruction of their enemies amount to prayers for the enactment of God's justice, righteousness, and shalom. The dilemma for most North Americans is this: When we pray the psalmists' requests, we inevitably pray *from the position of victimizer rather than victim.* We do so because, as Joseph Stiglitz, winner of the 2001 Nobel Prize in Economics, points out, we are the promoters and/or beneficiaries of a global economic system—usually termed simply "globalization"—that serves "to benefit the few at the expense of the many, the well-off at the expense of the poor."[15]

From this perspective, the challenge for North American readers and pray-ers of the prayers for help is to let them *indict us,* and thereby *invite us* into solidarity with what Stiglitz describes as "the billions of people for whom it [that is, the current form of globalization] has not" worked.[16] To be so indicted and invited might be thought of in terms of practicing God's form of globalization—the world-encompassing enactment of justice, righteousness, and shalom—rather than the current form of globalization that is serving to impoverish and demoralize billions of people. In any case, the issue again involves world-encompassing reconciliation and the refusal to blame victims, two related matters to which the book of Psalms, along with the cross and the gospel, invites our faithful attention.

Notes

1. Erich Zenger, *A God of Vengeance? Understanding the Psalms of Divine Wrath,* trans. Linda M. Maloney (Louisville, KY: Westminster John Knox, 1994), 1. Zenger treats seven psalms as "psalms of cursing and vengeance" (p. 2): Psalms 12, 44, 58, 83, 109, 137, 139. For another helpful treatment of vengeance in the Psalms, see Walter Brueggemann, *Praying the Psalms* (Winona, MN: St. Mary's Press, 1982), 67–80.
2. My count includes the following (English versification): Pss. 3:7; 5:10; 6:10; 7:12–16; 9:5–6; 10:15; 11:6; 12:3–4; 17:13–14; 18:37–42; 20:8; 21:8–12; 27:2;

28:4–5; 31:17–18, 23; 34:21; 35:1–6; 37:1–2; 40:14; 41:11; 43:1; 52:5–7; 54:5; 55:9, 19, 23; 56:6–7; 57:3; 58:6–9; 59:5, 11–13; 62:12; 63:9–10; 64:7–8; 68:1–2; 69:22–28; 70:1–3; 71:13; 73:18–20; 74:22–23; 75:8, 10; 76:5–6; 79:6, 10; 82:6–7; 83:9–18; 92:9; 94:1–3, 23; 97:7; 104:35; 109:6–19, 29; 110:5–6; 125:5; 129:5–8; 137:7–9; 139:19–22; 140:10–11; 141:7, 10; 143:12; 145:20; 146:9; 147:6.

3. Fredrik Lindström, *Suffering and Sin: Interpretations of Illness in the Individual Complaint Psalms*, Coniectanea Biblica Old Testament Series 37 (Stockholm: Almqvist & Wiksell, 1994), 6; quoted in Walter Brueggemann, *An Introduction to the Old Testament: The Canon and Christian Imagination* (Louisville, KY: Westminster John Knox, 2003), 289.

4. J. V. Kinnier Wilson, "Mental Diseases of Ancient Mesopotamia," in *Diseases in Antiquity: A Survey of Diseases, Injuries, and Surgery of Early Populations*, ed. Don Brothwell and A. T. Sandison (Springfield, IL: Charles C. Thomas, 1967), 371.

5. The REMHI report in English is entitled *Guatemala, Never Again!* (Maryknoll, NY: Orbis, 1999). José Antonio Puac is listed on p. ii under the heading "Diocesan Coordinators."

6. See J. Clinton McCann Jr., "Righteousness, Justice, and Peace: A Contemporary Theology of the Psalms," *HBT* 23/2 (2001): 114.

7. Unlike the NRSV and in keeping with the Masoretic Text, I assume that the psalmist utters the prayer in vv. 6–19; the NRSV's addition of "They say" at the beginning of v. 6 attributes the prayer to the psalmist's accusers.

8. Zenger, *A God of Vengeance?* 87.

9. René Girard, "Job as Failed Scapegoat," in *The Voice from the Whirlwind: Interpreting the Book of Job*, ed. Leo G. Perdue and W. Clark Gilpin (Nashville: Abingdon, 1992), 197.

10. Girard, "Job as Failed Scapegoat," 196.

11. See Gustavo Gutiérrez, *On Job: God-Talk and the Suffering of the Innocent*, trans. Matthew J. O'Connell (Maryknoll, NY: Orbis, 1988), 88–92. Gutiérrez discusses the message of the book of Job in terms of "gratuitousness"—that is, grace.

12. William C. Placher, "Christ Takes Our Place: Rethinking Atonement," *Int* 53/1 (January 1999): 15.

13. Roland E. Murphy, *Experiencing Our Biblical Heritage* (Peabody, MA: Hendrickson, 2002), 121.

14. James L. Mays, *The Lord Reigns: A Theological Handbook to the Psalms* (Louisville, KY: Westminster John Knox, 1994), 37.

15. Joseph E. Stiglitz, *Globalization and Its Discontents* (New York: W. W. Norton, 2002), 20.

16. Stiglitz, *Globalization*, 252.

Chapter 11

Reading the Bible from a Social Location

A Response

JINSEONG WOO

My Location   *[handwritten: of Power is power]*

On September 12, 1992, I was arrested by the South Korean CIA. After being arrested, I was interrogated in one of the basement cells of the agency, a notorious space for cruel torture, under suspicion for organizing Christian groups seeking democracy and the reunification of Korea. During the eighteen days of the interrogation, I was beaten, verbally abused, and forced to stay awake for long periods of time under eight strong tungsten lights on the ceiling. Although I was not tortured to death, as sometimes happened there, I was indeed afraid that they would kill me. During that time, I was deprived of contact with members of my family and legal support from outside. In fact, I was kidnapped on the street by force, so my parents and siblings did not know what had happened to me and were filled with anxiety about me. All these things are truly dreadful to recall. I will just say that I experienced extreme fear, terror, and helplessness. All these were a part of the attempt of the Korean CIA to influence the presidential election, which was supposed to be three months later.

In short, I was sentenced to four years' imprisonment in the trial. I was imprisoned in Pusan prison, locked in a small concrete cell all day, except for thirty minutes stretching time outside. The condition of Korean prisons at that time was simply bad—no temperature control in winter or summer, no nutritious food, no freedom to write, strong censorship of books, and so forth. In prison, I experienced both loss and gain. Concerning what I lost, I do not think I need to make a list here. Readers will already know what prisoners lose. I am thankful that what I gained outweighs what I lost. Among the things I gained in prison, paramount was my experience of intense reading of the Bible. All the passages that I read in prison came to me with totally different meanings from my previous readings outside prison. The words of the Bible were not cliché anymore. They became the bread of my spirit, the source of my strength, and the ground of my life. The experience of reading the Bible in hunger, loneliness, and humbleness was the highest privilege of my imprisonment. Since then, all my biblical reading and even my biblical studies have become an extension of this experience. My responses here to Jens Herzer, Sylvia Keesmaat, and Clint McCann are based on my readings of the texts from Titus, Romans, and the Psalms that they have interpreted from my social location in light of the experience of my imprisonment. Some call this hermeneutic "reading the Bible in one's social location," borrowing the term from liberation theology.

Response to Herzer

Herzer's presentation is an attempt to address an ethical issue that has been raised after reunification of Germany, in the light of a biblical passage, and vice versa. The presentation is interesting in that it interprets a biblical passage in the light of a concrete situation, discussing its relevance to the situation. The chosen passage from Titus 3 is discussed frequently, along with the Pauline passage in Romans 13, when the relation between church and state becomes an issue. This relationship is an issue in virtually every nation and every generation, as long as Christians live in a secular state rather than in heaven. Herzer's presentation addresses specifically the German case after reunification in 1989, yet this issue is relevant to other cases, such as the United States, where the Christians need to express their attitudes on the war on Iraq and on the situation in Korea, where the progressive president MooHyun Noh leads a campaign to uncover what has been hidden under military dictatorships in the past.

In general, Herzer's exegesis is in harmony with my understanding of the context of the book of Titus. A brief discussion of my understanding of the background of theological development of the Pastoral Epistles will be helpful to understand the issues raised by Herzer. When the second-generation churches encountered an internal crisis, as their enthusiastic expectancy of Christ's imminent return turned gradually to uncertainty, they had two alternative paths in coping with the crisis. One was a more esoteric, mysterious path, which gnosticism represented; another was so-called civil Christianity, which Herzer addressed in his presentation. Whereas the former was persecuted and expelled from the "orthodox" churches as heresy, the latter managed to survive in the Greco-Roman secular society as adherents sensitively adapted themselves to the world, although they sporadically encountered persecutions by local authorities. The Pastoral Epistles are a product of this rapidly changing circumstance and an example of the church's response to the new and unanticipated challenges of the late first century and the early second century. In this understanding of the particular historical context of Titus, Herzer's statement, "Yet exactly this 'civil' dimension of Christian faith within a non-Christian society lies at the heart of the ethical argument," is right to the point. Thus, in basic understanding of the text, I am in agreement with Herzer.

But I maintain a different perspective from Herzer in some respects. First, I struggle with Herzer's interpretation of the very beginning part of the text. Herzer interprets ἀρχαῖς ἐξουσίαις ὑποτάσσεσθαι in verse 1, not as a recommendation for the "subordination under the state authorities," but as a recommendation for the "adjustment to the structure of the society." The basis for his interpretation is that there was no obvious reason that all members of the congregation needed "to be reminded that they should be obedient to the ruling powers." This contrasts with my analysis of the structure of verses 1–2. The author of the text basically makes two recommendations in infinitive form, which follow the main verb in imperative form ὑπομίμνῃσκε (to remind). The two recommending infinitives are ὑποτάσσεσθαι (to subject oneself or to obey) and ἑτοίμους εἶναι (to be ready). Each of these infinitives is followed by a word or a clause, one of which is emphatic repetition (πειθαρχεῖν: obey) and the other an elaboration (v. 2 in its entirety). The first infinitive is about "obeying the rulers," whereas the second infinitive is about "doing good works." "Obeying the government" and "doing good works" are the two most important charges for the believers to fulfill their social obligations according to the standard of the Greco-Roman society, of which they wanted to be a part. The structure of the text undeniably demonstrates this.

Thus, Herzer's interpretation of the first infinitive phrase, "obeying the rulers," as "adjustment to the structure of the society" is a tricky attempt to synchronize these two separated recommendations into one single moderate recommendation. Regretfully, I do not find extensive evidence or reason to support Herzer's interpretation. However, regardless of its validity, I am in complete sympathy with Herzer's interpretation. "Obeying the rulers" is one of the most embarrassing biblical passages for those who are struggling to achieve very basic democratic values under unjust regimes. Can we legitimate the works of secret agents in the former East Germany or brutal acts of a military regime in Korea on the basis of this passage? What should be our theological response when they excuse their behaviors based on this passage? These questions lead to a discussion of my second difference in perspective from Herzer.

For this part of the discussion, I need to return to the christological argument in Titus 3:3–8a. Comparing the argument in verses 3–8a with a similar argument in Ephesians 2:1–10 is interesting. At first glance, two differences are found in the comparison. First, the language in Titus is more akin to the contemporary emperor worship, as Herzer points out. Second, Titus reflects more institutionalized

Christianity, as seen in the Trinitarian and baptismal language in the text. However, the basic logic is the same, and this commonality outweighs the differences. Dibelius and Conzelmann describe this commonality: "Such a presentation of a person's past before becoming a Christian, followed by a description of his [sic] condition as a Christian, was one of the most common topics of early Christian preaching. The turning point was described either from the standpoint of the mission or that of the history of salvation."[1]

Titus uses exactly this common formula. Combined with the recommendations, especially with the recommendation for good works, this formula is used in the literary context of the text as the ground for doing good works for everybody. In this sense, the proposed text can be paraphrased: "Obey the rulers and do good works for everybody. You are saved not by your own deeds but by the unconditional love of God; so you should pay back God's unconditional love to others by doing good works for everybody." Interestingly, Herzer seems to decide his ethical attitude for the issue of the former Stasi on the basis of this formula. He does not directly state what his attitude toward this issue is, but a quotation from his presentation clearly shows what he is arguing: "Even so the Scripture's ethical demand from Christians, who have been suffering in various and very different ways under this regime caused by the evil saying of others, is clearly linked to God's forgiving acts in Christ and God's saving will towards all humans. This definitively goes beyond the pure claim for justice, although it does not exclude it at all."

I understand that this is Herzer's conclusive statement of the ethical questions raised, and his conclusion shows not much difference from a literal reading of Titus or my paraphrase above. This understanding of Herzer's presentation raises a significant question: Does Herzer answer the question that he asked in the beginning of his presentation? In the beginning, he asked a "how" question: "How can we apply the Christian Bible to the ethical issues in a non-Christian society?" What I expected was hermeneutical principles or criteria that we can apply to the ethical issues. Honestly, however, I do not see a clear answer to this "how" question in his presentation. If the suggestion in the quotation above is his answer to this question, can I define Henzer's ethical methodology as literal application of the Bible to the issue? My concern is not the conclusion. No one would oppose accepting the former Stasi on the basis of the love of God, since currently they are the powerless who have been the powerful in the past. My concern is how to arrive at that conclusion. If a literal understanding of the Bible is the answer to this question, this could be potentially dangerous. What alternative do we have? What implication does Henzer pose that I might not recognize?

In this regard, Polycarp's ethical attitudes toward the rulers give us significant insights. In his *Letter to Philippians*, Polycarp recommends that his readers be good citizens: "If we please him in this present world, we will receive the world to come as well, inasmuch as he promised to raise us from the dead and that if we prove to be citizens worthy of him, 'we will also reign with him'" (5:2b).

This phrase can be understood in exactly the same way as Titus's recommendations. But *The Martyrdom of Polycarp* witnesses that he refuses to swear the oath to the emperor. His disobedience results in his martyrdom by being burned alive. But his noble death as a believer brings the admiration of the crowd: "The whole crowd was amazed that there should be so great a difference between the unbelievers and the elect" (16:1). The death of Polycarp reveals an ironic aspect of the ethical attitude. By his disobedience of the ruler's command, Polycarp betrays his own recommendation of civil Christianity. But by his noble death, he achieves the aim of civil Christianity, that is, admiration of the people.

From this ironic aspect of an ethical attitude, I draw some principles. The Bible in its literal sense cannot be an absolute norm or principle for the ethical attitude even of Christians. More importance should be placed on human beings who are struggling in a particular situation to live according to the will of God. Human beings are moral agents who will decide what the will of God is in each concrete situation. Of course, the Bible is a source for that decision. However, it is not *the* source but *a* source, which should be considered with other sources such as history, tradition, reason, and values of the community. In this sense, Herzer's remark is right to the point: "Therefore, I am very well aware that what I am presenting here, as an application of a biblical text to a certain actual context, can by no means apply to any other situation in the same way." The Bible cannot tell us what is right or wrong in a situation. That should be the content of our own struggle with the Bible and with the specific context.

Response to Keesmaat

Keesmaat's presentation is a significant attempt to make a submissive text into a subversive one by reading the text against its political and social background. She reads Romans 12–13, especially 13:1–7, as Paul's subtle polemic against the Roman imperial social political system on behalf of the Roman Christians who were being persecuted. Her attempt is meaningful in that the text has been one of the most misused texts in human history, as she well summarizes in her presentation.

I like all her conclusive assertions; I even find them healing because of the political persecution that I myself have experienced. Breaking with the status quo, reversing the value system of the society that sustains the current evil structure, as according to Keesmaat Paul presumably did, is always a desire of those who put their life at stake for a better world. However, I am not yet convinced by her arguments. I do not mean that her arguments are incorrect or invalid. Rather, I mean that her arguments need to be supported by more evidence. Keesmaat packs too much in her essay. Her text covers several controversial passages that have stimulated much scholastic discussion. Considering the controversial nature of these passages, I think it would have been much better to discuss each text with more careful exegetical approaches, conversing with other scholars, including the ones with whom she disagrees. For example, Käsemann thinks that in Romans 13:1–7 Paul is dealing with local authorities rather than with the Roman emperor. Or one could say Colossians 1:15–20 is a clear example of Gnostic incorporation, arguing that the words in the text, such as "thrones or dominions or rulers or authorities," are rather reminiscent of gnostic writings. To be sure, I do not mean to argue here for or against any particular reading. I am merely suggesting that if Keesmaat had included and responded to the voices different from her position, her arguments would have been more persuasive and compelling.

Response to McCann

Not for just ordinary Christians but also for Christian scholars—especially the scholars who attempt to systematize the whole Bible with a few theological themes, and the scholars who attempt to interpret the Old Testament in light of the New Testament—the prayers for vengeance in the Psalms are problematic. The prescriptions of some interpreters to weaken the absurdity include (1) simply avoiding the problematic psalms, (2) interpreting them spiritually or allegorically, (3) disregarding them as products of ethically inferior ages, and (4) disregarding them as products of mental disorder. McCann's approach differs from these approaches. Instead of attempting any inappropriate systemization or compromise, he interprets the imprecatory psalms in context, especially in the literary context of the Psalms.

McCann's chapter is a fine example of empathetic reading of the Psalms. Although the psalms were used and are used in worship and have a spectrum of contents, the very basic nature of the psalms is poetic, and this calls for reading the poetry empathetically. If I paraphrase this idea, borrowing McCann's word "solidarity," the empathetic reading will be a reading in emotional solidarity with the victimized. I am aware that the psalms could be a window through which we can catch a glimpse of ancient worship, social relations, and more. But placing priority on these aspects would make the psalms arid, depriving them of the capacity to empower. In this sense, I accept McCann's approach, which is primarily concerned with the literary context rather than the historical context. McCann's identification of the psalmists with the oppressed victims of the unrighteous may be an overly simplified assumption. One might ask questions concerning the historical context, such as who the enemies were, with what evidence we could simply regard the victimized as righteous and the victimizer as wicked, and so forth. One might speculate about who the enemies were: (1) partisans who opposed the other groups, (2) pursuers who were after those who committed crimes against them and hid in the temple, (3) evildoers who caused misfortune or calamity upon others. Among these three hypotheses, the simplified righteous-unrighteous dualism would collapse.

To be sure, these hypothetical assumptions are certainly meaningful and legitimate, especially for the interpreters for whom the psalms are the object of their studies. However, for those who are reading these psalms in the most frustrated, threatened, and hopeless situations, and for those who are reading these psalms remembering their experiences of hopelessness, or remembering their family members, friends, or relatives who are in these situations, these academic assumptions may lose their significance. The fact that some of the imprecatory psalms, such as Psalms 83 and 109, were my empowering source during my imprisonment coincides with McCann's approach to these psalms. While reading these psalms in a prison cell, I never asked the academic questions above. They were extravagant questions in the situation, and I needed the power to survive. Rather, I read them in emotional solidarity with the victimized, the outcry-ers, or those who pray in suffering. Then the imprecatory psalms became a source of my empowerment.

I appreciate McCann's concept of God's biased love toward the victimized. His daring assertion that God stands with suffering victims is especially significant against an understanding of suffering as God's retribution (e.g., Deut. 28) that still works for many as a framework for understanding suffering. Understanding suffering as God's punishment undermines those who are suffering, that is, the victimized, in our discussion. The result is that the victimized are robbed of the chance to claim their legitimacy or even the power to defend themselves from false accusations. In my experience, during the very first sixty days while I was being detained in the basement of the national security agency, without any help from outside, before I had my first chance to defend myself in the court, I was already judged, shamed, and socially murdered by the public sentiment that was generated by the government-controlled public mass media. This manipulation of public sentiment was made possible by two erroneous beliefs: (1) that our social system, more specifically our judicial system, is reliable; (2) that suffering, especially incomprehensible suffering, is a result of God's retribution. Thus I was ostracized twice. In the eyes of others, socially I had become a criminal, and religiously I had become a sinner. From this experience I appreciate McCann's notion that God is with the victimized. This is right. When the social justice system collapses or turns evil, the only one in whom the victimized can put his or her hope of rectification is God. Indeed, even in the worst situation, the belief that "God is with me" sustains the victimized and empowers them to resist any attempt to tame them.

Praying to God implies abandonment of my own revenge. For me, this implication of the imprecatory psalms is the most significant point in relation to the topic of reconciliation. In his presentation, McCann does not clearly bring up the idea that vengeance belongs to God, not to humans. His conclusive statement, however, shows that he is clearly in line with the idea, although he chooses a different path to reach this conclusion: "More so than it may first appear, therefore, the book of Psalms invites readers and pray-ers toward a nonretaliatory, reconciliatory lifestyle, grounded in grace rather than revenge, in forgiving rather than finding fault." If we define "curse" as the words that release negative power or a spell that is effective upon others, the imprecatory psalms cannot be defined as curse. Neither are they verbal vengeance. Rather, they are prayers to God. The imprecatory psalms do not have a clear statement of this idea except for *layhwh hayĕšûʿāh* in Psalm 3:9 (3:8 NRSV). Of course, the translation of this clause is "Salvation (rather than vengeance) belongs to the LORD." But, considering that the Hebrew word *nāqām*, which used to be translated "vengeance" or "revenge," has basically the same sense as the Hebrew verb *yēšaʿ* (salvation), which appears in the clause above, the clause is worthy of mention. Outside the Psalter, however, this idea is dominant, as seen in "vengeance is mine" in Deuteronomy 32:35, "you shall not take vengeance" in Leviticus 19:18, and so forth.

Repeatedly for me, this implication is the most meaningful insight from the imprecatory psalms. On the basis of this insight, I form my ethical attitude toward those who put unbearable sufferings upon me in the past: I give up my own revenge, even in mind and thought. To be sure, this does not mean the abandonment of justice or ignorance of responsible actions for God's justice. Rather, this is the acknowledgment that at the very moment of abandonment of personal revenge my (imprecatory) prayers become yearning for God's justice.

Note

1. M. Dibelius and H. Conzelmann, *The Pastoral Epistles: A Commentary on the Pastoral Epistles*, Hermeneia (Philadelphia: Fortress, 1972), 147.

PART IV
POLITICAL FORMATION
AND PEACEMAKING

Chapter 12

Political Formation in the Letter to the Romans

NEIL ELLIOTT

He argue for etterical appropriate imperialism — i.e. of Roman elite or

What did Paul know about the house churches in Rome, and when did he know it?

Debate still swirls around important aspects of the occasion and purpose of the letter to the Romans.[1] Did the Edict of Claudius, which expelled at least some Jews from Rome in 49 CE, create a vacuum in the assemblies of Christ-believers that left non-Jews suddenly in the preponderance? After the death of Claudius, did the return of some Jews to these same house churches spark ethnic tensions between Jews and non-Jews? A growing number of interpreters give affirmative answers to both these questions.

But there is still no consensus about just how these answers help us to understand the argument of Romans. Is Paul primarily concerned to ameliorate these presumed "ethnic tensions" in the Roman churches? Or to defend himself against charges from the synagogue that he "negates the law," charges that have dogged him since he confronted a crisis in Galatia? Or to reassure the Roman churches that he is "kosher" enough to merit their support, as he prepares for an official visit to "unbelievers" in Jerusalem, or for a subsequent mission to Spain? Or is the letter written to accomplish some combination of all these goals at once?

On the reading of the letter that I find most convincing, although Paul clearly recognizes the presence in the Roman churches of some Jews (he greets them in Rom. 16; they are probably among the "weak," distinguished by their restricted diet, in Rom. 14:1–15:13), he just as clearly addresses the churches as included in his God-given commission to bring about "the faithful obedience of the nations" (1:5–7, 13–15; 15:15–18). Further, if, as many now recognize, the letter's rhetorical climax comes in chapters 9–11 and especially in the solemn, apocalyptically charged warning to the non-Jews not to boast over Israel (11:13–27), then the appropriate rhetorical-critical task is to determine how the argumentation of the preceding portions of the letter serve or contribute to that climax.[2] The heart of rhetorical criticism is to ask in what ways the actual argument of a speech or, by extension, of a text is appropriate to a presumed audience; though in approaching a collection of ancient documents such as the New Testament, we must also reverse that question, asking for what presumed audience the argument of the letter before us would have been appropriate.[3]

Although Paul greets members of the Roman churches by name (I take chapter 16 as an integral part of the letter), he also addresses them as a congregation about whose faith he has only heard (1:8), and says he must further postpone his long-desired travel to meet them (1:9–13; 15:22–23). That means that Paul must address them on the basis of his own sense—however well or ill informed—of who they are, what they know, and what their situation is.[4]

Who they are:

- small gatherings of Christ-believers, predominantly non-Jews, though with a significant minority of Jews in their midst

What they know:

- Israel's Scriptures, or at least the aura of authority those Scriptures held for Jews and non-Jewish adherents of the synagogue
- possibly, enough of a "Jesus tradition" to make Paul's probable allusions in chapter 12 meaningful[5]
- certainly enough of what Paul expects to be the common practice and belief of the early Christ movement that he can refer to the resurrection of Jesus Christ, to the power of the Holy Spirit, to a shared baptism, and to the ecstatic cry of "Abba" in worship as a common fund of symbols

What their situation is:

Though some interpreters still entertain lingering doubts that Paul knows, or is concerned to address, specific aspects of the situation in Rome, there is a growing consensus that Paul confronts "ethnic tensions" involving not just specific disagreements regarding dietary practices (chaps. 14–15), but also more global attitudes of superiority and disapproval between ethnic groups ("boasting," thinking themselves better than others, "judging," holding others in "contempt," attitudes addressed in chaps. 9–11 and 14–15 alike). The earlier chapters of the letter are increasingly read as Paul's attempt to "level the playing field" between Jew and non-Jew—that is, to demonstrate that neither is "ahead" or enjoys an advantage over the other—and to provide a new social identity "in Christ" that parties on both sides of the ethnic quarrel can embrace.[6]

Having reached this point, much scholarship on the occasion and purpose of Romans is satisfied. All that remains is to sketch out how Paul appeals to the common symbolic repertoire of the early Christ movement in such a way as to make his own claim on the acceptance, and even the adherence and support, of the Roman Christ-believers for himself and his mission. Though many interpreters recognize that the term *Christianoi* is premature for this stage, we may nevertheless expect that asking what sort of character formation is going on in the letter would elicit a straightforward answer: *Christian* formation. That is, Paul is forging a new social identity as people "in Christ" that includes (and thus relativizes) the conflicted "ethnic" identities of Jew and "Gentile."

Moving beyond the Issue of "Ethnic Tension"

I'm dissatisfied with the interpretive scheme I've just described, for several reasons.

First, this widely held interpretation still relies upon *unhistorical and prejudicial characterizations of Judaism* in order to explain how Paul's rhetoric in the early chapters of Romans serves to "level the playing field" between Jew and non-Jew. Happily, scholars increasingly recognize that identifying "works righteousness" as a characteristic aspect of Jewish religion is the unwarranted and pejorative projection onto first-century Judaism of all that Luther found wrong in sixteenth-century Roman Catholic Christianity. That characterization, however, has been replaced for many scholars by another characterization that has also been brought into serious question, namely, the characterization of Jewish "exclusivism" or "ethnocentrism," tied up with an interpretation of "works of law" (Rom. 3:20, 27–28) as "boundary markers" for Jewish identity. Was doing the works the law commanded considered an important expression of fidelity to the covenant God had made with Israel? Yes. Were some works of law markers of Jewish identity? Surely. But did Jews imagine that observing the works of law provided them the sort of impunity from accountability before God that Paul is at pains to refute in Romans 2–3? That possibility—a linchpin for the so-called new perspective on Paul—is not self-evident from contemporary Jewish literature. Or did Jews imagine that God willed the covenant to be restricted to those alone who bore the "boundary markers" of Jewish identity? Again, not so far as the preponderance of the evidence would indicate.[7]

Second, just here another problem arises for the emerging consensus view. Namely, if there is insufficient *historical* evidence that actual Jews held the views attributed to them by the new perspective, then understanding Romans as an effort, in part, to talk Jews out of assumptions that they did not in fact hold runs the risk of rendering the letter *rhetorically incoherent*. Paul seems to be attacking straw targets. To be sure, some scholars—most notably, E. P. Sanders and Heikki Räisänen—have drawn just that conclusion. This seems to me premature, however, in that it skips the crucial step of asking whether in fact Paul in the early chapters of Romans *meant* to "level the playing field" by undermining Jewish assumptions of impunity before God or of ethnic superiority over non-Jews.[8]

Third, my final objection to the consensus approach to Romans is that it fails to move beyond a construal of "ethnic" or cultural identity that has been soundly criticized in New Testament studies and in other areas of cultural and historical interpretation as well.

New Testament scholars routinely speak of "Gentiles" as if they were a distinct ethnic identity, like Syrians or Bithynians. The most authoritative recent Bible translations only reinforce that unfortunate impression when they render more and more occurrences of the Greek phrase *ta ethnē* with "Gentiles," a capitalized ethnic term equivalent, and opposite, to "Jews." But there was no such ethnic identity as "Gentile." When Paul speaks in Romans of *ta ethnē*, he explicitly cites what he reads as prophecies in Israel's Scripture that "the nations" will at last join with Israel in the worship of Israel's God.[9] That vision is at the core of his own sense of apostolic commission, and he clearly addresses the Roman assemblies as representative members of "the nations"—that is, as people holding a *variety* of "ethnic" identities—to which he is apostle.

The late Edward Said criticized the self-delusions nourished when "Western" interpreters perpetuate patterns of "Orientalist" thinking. Richard A. Horsley and Shawn Kelley have traced just such patterns through the influence Hegelian historiography exercised in shaping the dominant paradigms of modern New Testament interpretation.[10] Said argued that a more adequate interpretive agenda would attend to the dynamics of large-scale political power, specifically imperialist configurations of power, in shaping congenial cultural schemes and scripts. Similarly, in her essay on "decolonizing theory," Chandra Talpade Mohanty insists that any cultural criticism that "bypasses power as well as history," limiting itself to categories of ethnic diversity and pluralism, can suggest only "a harmonious, empty pluralism." The challenge of race and ethnicity, she writes, "resides in a fundamental reconceptualization of our categories of analysis so that differences can be historically specified and understood as part of larger political processes and systems."[11] If these patterns of interpretation stubbornly persist, perhaps it is because they are more congenial to the dominant configurations of power in our world. As Mahmoud Mamdani has pointed out, for example, the widespread perception today of a "clash of civilizations" between "the West" and "Islam," with its narrow focus on categories of ethnic, cultural, and religious difference, "masks a refusal to address our own failure to make a political analysis of our times."[12] From Chiapas, Subcomandante Marcos has sounded a similar protest against the perverse invention of racial categories to mask political and economic exploitation.[13]

These observations regarding *perspective* converge as we observe that there *was* a virulent "ethnic" script active in the social landscape of Paul and the Roman churches, and that it coincided perfectly with the reigning political ideology of the time. Much scholarship on Paul's letter has neglected this ethnic script, however. There were no "Gentiles" in the early part of the first century, but there was a clear, pervasive, and powerful ideology of "ethnic" supremacy abroad in the Roman Empire.

My purpose here is to explore possible echoes of that ideology of ethnic supremacy in the Letter to the Romans, and to ask how these echoes might reconfigure our understanding of the occasion and purpose of Paul's letter.

Aspects of Roman Imperial Ideology

The ideology of "ethnic" supremacy most prevalent in Paul's day was, of course, the Roman chauvinism that saturates elite sources from Cicero to Virgil, to Seneca, to the Neronian poets, and beyond. A brief rehearsal of key themes may be helpful:

• The Emperor Augustus himself, in the inscribed memorial of his beneficent achievements on behalf of the Roman people and indeed the world (*Res Gestae Divi Augusti*), describes his subjection of other peoples as bestowing upon them the "friendship" and fidelity of the Roman people. His defeat through warfare of his closest rivals in power and wealth is described as the miraculous achievement of worldwide peace, the Pax Romana.

• In the mythic perspective of contemporary poets, Augustus was empowered to achieve this miracle because of his own tremendous and meticulous piety, depicted in the Altar to Augustan Peace in the Forum (the *Ara Pacis*) by paired images of the pious Trojan hero Aeneas, offering sacrifices on the shore of Latium, and of the equally pious Augustus, offering sacrifice for the benefit of the Roman people.

• Augustus thus became the chosen instrument through which divine purposes, revealed in ancient prophecies regarding the glorious destiny of the Roman people, were brought to fulfillment. As Virgil tells it in Book I of the *Aeneid*, in the aftermath of the Trojan War Jove had assured the goddess Venus that her beloved hero Aeneas would survive to found a great city and to "beat down proud nations." His descendants would prosper, rising to "hold dominion over all sea and land"; named through Aeneas's descendant, Romulus, this people, the Romans, should "rule forever" as "masters of all the world."[14]

Recent scholarship has alerted us to the breadth and depth of this imperial mythology: to the saturation of the Roman world with a carefully managed repertoire of images depicting the piety and benevolent potency of the emperor, and of the routinized representations and celebrations of those virtues through a ubiquitous imperial cult.[15] We have also come to recognize that Rome did not have to impose this mythology, the repertoire of images, or the regimen of rituals upon the provinces. Rather, provincial elites were only too enthusiastic in developing their own symbolic representations, in imagery and ritual, of the new configuration of power in their cities, and in vying among themselves for preeminence in emulating Caesar's example of ritualized piety and benevolence to the extent that these values came to be identified with each other.[16]

It is important to understand the social construction of ethnicity within this imperial ideology. While bloodline—or its fictive equivalent, the delicate thread of ancestry through adoption—was the necessary fabric upon which the series of successions we call the Julio-Claudian dynasty was made to hang, non-Roman elites in the provinces could leverage their inherited status into a share of power and wealth in the new Roman imperial system through their enthusiastic participation in the imperial cult, and through ostentatious benevolence. They thus had the option, in the apt phrase of Gregory Woolf, of "becoming Roman, remaining Greek."[17] *Ethnicity* was not an absolute consideration. The imperial fantasy (which the magistrates labored, day by day, year by year, to translate into mundane reality) was of a world of diverse nations united in their glad servitude to Rome, massing to bring the "offerings of the nations" (*dona populorum*) to Caesar's feet (*Aeneid* 8.720–24).

To make much the same point from the converse side, recent scholars have argued that (except for a few spectacular examples, like Sejanus) Roman policy toward Jews did not generally spring from a focused *ethnic* prejudice or from the Jews offering any peculiarly characteristic irritant to Rome, but from the empire's interest in controlling an often restive urban population in general. Because of their distinctiveness as an ethnic group, and possibly because of their relative socioeconomic vulnerability (on Philo's account) as descendants of freed slaves, Jews in Rome and elsewhere simply offered a target of convenience when Rome sought to make a salutary example by rounding up troublemakers.[18] That is, in the case of the social mobility available to non-Roman "native" elites, and of the vulnerability of Judean communities in the imperial capital alike, *ethnicity* was a flexible category; its relevance and its value were determined by the prior imperial configuration of power relationships.

A Glimpse into an Alternative Transcript in Romans

If the earlier chapters of Romans, 1–8 or 1–11, are normally read as components of Paul's effort to "level the playing field" between Jews and "Gentiles" as ethnic groups in tension, the later parenetic chapters, 12–15, are usually read straightforwardly as moral exhortation. If the injunctions to sober self-assessment, mutual regard, and enthusiastic benevolence in chapter 12 are taken as having any connection to an actual situation in Romans (and not merely as generalized "parenesis"), their purpose is to encourage a general sentiment of mutual consideration that will find expression in Jews and non-Jews welcoming each other (14:1–15:13). Further, because the exhortations in Romans 12 resemble similar exhortations in Cynic and Stoic moral traditions, and because the injunction to "be subject to the ruling authorities" in 13:1–7 uses vocabulary similar to Hellenistic treatises on good kingship, some scholars have found it easy enough to assimilate Paul to those moral or philosophical traditions. Paul thus becomes a representative of Stoic conservatism regarding social convention or even "the ideological guardian of the processes and structures of imperial power."[19]

Heightened awareness of the Roman ideological context I've just described suggests a different reading of the letter, however. Decades ago Victor Furnish observed that the letter was structured around a fundamentally hortatory scheme. The exhortations in Romans 12 not to "be conformed to the scheme of this world," but to present one's body as a living sacrifice, holy and acceptable to God (12:1–2), inverts the spiral of depravity depicted in 1:18–32, in which rebellion against God and the worship of idols leads to increasing moral blindness and the abandonment of one's body to shameful and destructive practices. The inversion is possible, Furnish pointed out, because of baptism, which enables the baptized to resist and escape the lordly claims of sin and injustice upon their bodies (6:1–15). We may go further: their positive response to this exhortation would enable the recipients of the letter to guarantee the sanctity of the "offering of the nations" (15:16–32) that Paul says it is his responsibility to achieve, as apostle to the nations charged with securing their faithful obedience (1:6, 13–15).[20]

Note that this is not only the explicitly stated purpose of the letter; it also echoes key themes in Roman imperial ideology—the invitation to participate in an ethic of sacrifice by doing good (emulating Augustus himself), and thus to participate in the "offerings of the peoples" (brought, in Virgil's eschatological fantasy, to Rome; in Paul's, to Jerusalem). This comparison is not (so to speak) a *harmonic* convergence, however. The Roman ideological system offers a synergy of benefaction *in emulation of the Caesar, and in congruence with imperial policy,* and sacrifice *to the genius of the Caesar.* Paul is not simply playing with the same vocabulary; his appeal allows us to glimpse an alternative transcript in which the public transcript of Roman power is at least partly undermined.[21]

Recent scholarship offers a wealth of observations that tend to corroborate this picture of a partially hidden, alternative transcript in Romans. N. T. Wright has emphasized the full political connotations of Paul's use of the category "messiah" (*christos*) and of his usurpation of one of the Caesar's chief appelations, "lord" (*kyrios*).[22] Dieter Georgi has suggested, all too allusively, that Paul's emphatic announcement of a gospel concerning a Son of God from David's lineage, raised from the dead in power, by the "Spirit of holiness" (1:1–4), would have sounded provocative (to say the least!) set against the polite assent the senatorial class offered to the mythology and ritual of imperial apotheosis.[23] Elsewhere I have suggested that Paul's depiction of wholesale depravity in 1:18–32, which traces a descent from rebellion against God, through idolatry, to darkened understanding, to degrading and abusive sexual behaviors and ultimately a panoply of wickedness, would have evoked for contemporary Roman ears the vices of the imperial house.[24] I have also observed that the juxtaposition of God's righteousness and God's wrath—for so long a *crux interprum* in post-Reformation scholarship—neatly mirrors a rhetorical commonplace in Paul's day that concerned the specific judgment of God against spectacularly wicked and arrogant individuals.[25] And Mark Reasoner has placed the language of "weak" and "strong" clearly within the ideological vocabulary of the Roman elite, for whom "strength" or power was equated with honor and wealth, and "weakness" was identified especially with the shamefulness of the lower classes.[26]

It is tempting to pursue this line of questioning further throughout the letter, that is, to ask how other parts of the letter would have sounded echoes (or, better, counterechoes) in a chamber shaped by the themes of imperial ideology. What would Paul's insistence on judgment according to works (2:12–16), without regard to person or ethnicity, have meant in an ideological environment where the superiority of the Roman people was celebrated? What might the paradoxical insistence that being right with God was a matter of faithfulness (*pistis*), "apart from works" (*erga*), have meant in the context of Roman patronage, in which the "works" of benefactors were of supreme importance, and in which the gospel of the supreme benefactor, that is, Augustus, took the form of a proclamation of his own *Works*, the *Res Gestae*?[27] Again, what would it have meant for Paul to proclaim, for individuals from all the earth's peoples, an inheritance from a single primal ancestor, but to identify that ancestor as Abraham the "impious" (*asebēs*, Rom. 4:5), rather than Aeneas "the man of piety," or simply "pious Aeneas"?[28]

Those are provocative questions that I will not explore here—though I suggest they are as legitimate and as worthy of study as are the conventional questions that explore "intertextuality" in Paul against a single cultural repertoire, that of Roman-era Judaism.[29]

Ethnocentrism and Competing Political Formations

I will briefly explore one more aspect of Romans that, in my view, is best understood when set against the context of Roman imperial ideology. In separate studies, William S. Campbell and E. Elizabeth Johnson have shown that the thematic structure of key sections of the letter follows the scarlet thread of rhetorical questions, and that these have to do especially with the honor, faithfulness, trustworthiness, and justice of God, on the one hand, and with the apparent "stumbling" of Israel, on the other.[30] Only in the wake of the Second World War and the Nazi genocide against the Jews of Europe have Christian interpreters revisited what was once a common assumption, that Paul simply sought to defend God's integrity against the apparent challenge that most Jews in his day had failed to believe in Jesus. Recently scholars have gained enough distance from the Christian apologetic tradition to question *how* this "failure" to believe would have constituted Israel's *stumbling*, what Daniel Fraikin described as the "theological fact" that Paul apparently expected his readers in Rome to recognize.[31] The objection has been raised, most forcefully by Mark Nanos, that the "failure" of the Pauline mission would not itself have constituted the stumbling of Israel *as a people*.[32] The same objection should be raised against the suggestion, made first (I believe) by Hans Werner Bartsch, that the contempt in which non-Jews in the Roman churches were tempted to hold their Jewish neighbors was the direct result of the miserable estate of Jews returning to the city after being expelled by Claudius.[33] That is, on neither explanation is it clear why the particular situation of some Jews in Rome should issue in a generalization about the failure of Israel *as a peo-*

ple—unless, of course, the cultural environment already promoted the disposition to generalize about the inferiority of the people.

The wider cultural environment of Rome in the 50s did just that. The ideology of Roman supremacy involved the inferiority of other peoples who were destined to be subservient to the Romans; within this ideology, the Jews were on occasion singled out as a people "born to servitude." Close in time to the writing of Romans, Nero's advisor Seneca, observing the prevalence of Jewish practices in Rome, complained that "the vanquished have given laws to the victors" (*On Superstition*, as quoted by Augustine, *City of God* 6:10). Even if (on the view stated above) official actions like Claudius's edict were not primarily expressions of anti-Jewish prejudice, their effects could certainly be *interpreted* along stereotypical anti-Jewish lines. That suggestion has been made by others.[34] My point is to observe that although the resulting tension within the Roman churches may have presented itself along "ethnic" lines, it resulted not from fundamental ethnic or cultural differences between "Jews" and "Gentiles" as such (for the latter did not exist as an ethnic identity), but from a virulent imperial ideology that posed the Jews as only a particularly blatant example of the inferiority that fated the other peoples of the earth to serve the Romans.

Taking the ideology of Roman supremacy seriously means we can no longer simply assume that tensions in the Roman congregation may be attributed to any inherent weakness in Judaism itself, or that Paul confronted as a "theological fact" the "failure" of the people Israel to believe in Jesus as messiah. The *ideological* "fact" at work in the Roman churches was the presence of a contagion widespread outside the churches; *Roman* ethnocentrism—not Jewish—is the primary category necessary for understanding the argument of Paul's letter.[35]

Those conclusions require a different reading of the parenesis in Romans 12–15. Mark Reasoner has demonstrated that the wise self-assessment, mutual regard, and love for others urged in these chapters was in direct contradiction to the dominant ethos of honor (for the powerful) and dishonor (for the weak) in imperial Rome. The previous arguments require us to recognize that this contrast is not accidental. That is, the character formation at work in Romans 12 is not *coincidentally* at odds with dominant social mores; it is a direct confrontation with them. Resistance to "the scheme of this world" means refusing the alluring invitation to emulate the piety of the powerful—most conspicuously, Augustus—and siding instead with the lowly (12:16). Participating in the reign of justice into which baptism introduces believers (6:12–23) means refusing to participate in the reign of sin and repudiating the wickedness, depravity, and idolatry of those who claim to be wise, but have been shown at last to be under God's wrath (1:18–32)—as I would argue, members of the imperial house itself.

Romans is about *political* formation—the formation of a Christian identity in specific contrast to the reigning identity on offer in Roman imperial ideology. This formation involves the mutual recognition and acceptance of Jew and non-Jew, but this is not simply harmony between ethnic groups. It is participation in the prophesied chorus of the nations, who join with Israel in the worship of Israel's

Lord (15:1–13) and thus establish the sanctity of the "offering of the nations" for which Paul bears a priestly responsibility (15:16; 1:5–6). The confrontation with imperial ideology, according to which it is Augustus who acts as priest to gather the nations in pleasing worship before the gods, could hardly be clearer.

Notes

1. See the essays collected in Karl P. Donfried, ed., *The Romans Debate*, rev. ed. (Peabody, MA: Hendrickson, 1991); A. J. M. Wedderburn, *The Reasons for Romans* (Edinburgh: T.&T. Clark, 1991); David Hay and E. Elizabeth Johnson, eds., *Pauline Theology III: Romans* (Minneapolis: Fortress, 1995).
2. This is the task I took up in *The Rhetoric of Romans: Argumentative Constraint and Strategy "and Paul's Dialogue with Judaism"* (Sheffield: JSOT Press, 1990); similarly, Stanley K. Stowers, *A Rereading of Romans: Jews, Gentiles, Justice* (New Haven, CT: Yale University Press, 1994).
3. Stanley Porter, "The Theoretical Justification for Application of Rhetorical Categories to Pauline Epistolary Literature," in *Rhetoric in the New Testament: Essays from the 1992 Heidelberg Conference*, ed. S. E. Porter and T. Olbricht, JSNTSup 90 (Sheffield: Sheffield Academic Press, 1993), 100–122.
4. Rhetorical criticism is concerned with how an argument necessarily builds upon "previous stages of the conversation" (C. Perelman and L. Olbrechts-Tyteca, *The New Rhetoric: A Treatise on Argumentation* [Notre Dame, IN: University of Notre Dame Press, 1969]; Scott Consigny, "Rhetoric and Its Situations," *Philosophy and Rhetoric* 7 [1974]: 175–86).
5. Stephen Fowl, *The Story of Christ in the Ethics of Paul* (Ithaca, NY: Cornell University Press, 1990).
6. In different ways, Francis Watson, *Paul, Judaism, and the Gentiles* (Cambridge: Cambridge University Press, 1986); James C. Walters, *Ethnic Issues in the Letter to the Romans* (Valley Forge, PA: Trinity Press International, 1993), among others. Philip F. Esler has put this line of interpretation on a sounder methodological footing: *Conflict and Identity in the Letter to the Romans* (Minneapolis: Fortress, 2003).
7. E. P. Sanders (*Paul and Palestinian Judaism* [Philadelphia: Fortress, 1977]) is usually credited with the demolition of the "Lutheran reading" of Paul, though he repeatedly points to the valuable scholarship of many who came before him. The "New Perspective on Paul," so named by James D. G. Dunn in his now-famous article (*BJRL* 65 [1983]: 95–122), is the dominant paradigm in Pauline studies today, though it is also the focus of tremendous controversy. See *Justification and Variegated Nomism*, ed. D. A. Carson, Peter T. O'Brien, and Mark Seifrid, 2 vols. (Grand Rapids: Baker, 2004); Stephen Westerholm, *Perspectives Old and New on Paul: The "Lutheran" Paul and His Critics* (Grand Rapids: Eerdmans, 2003); Seyoon Kim, *Paul and the New Perspective: Second Thoughts on the Origins of Paul's Gospel* (Grand Rapids: Eerdmans, 2001); Andrew Das, *Paul, the Law, and the Covenant* (Peabody, MA: Hendrickson, 2001).
8. Sanders, *Paul and Palestinian Judaism*; Sanders, *Paul, the Law, and the Jewish People*; Räisänen, *Paul and the Law*. Other scholars have questioned whether the early chapters of Romans are aimed "against" presumed Jewish prerogatives, among them Stowers, *Rereading*; Lloyd Gaston, *Paul and the Torah* (Vancouver: University of British Columbia Press, 1987); John G. Gager, *The Origins of Antisemitism: Attitudes toward Judaism in Pagan and Christianity Antiquity* (Oxford: Oxford University Press, 1985); J. Gager, *Reinventing Paul* (Oxford: Oxford University Press, 2000).

9. Christopher D. Stanley, "'Neither Jew nor Greek': Ethnic Conflict in Graeco-Roman Society," *JSNT* 64 (1996): 101–24; James LaGrand, "Proliferation of the 'Gentile' in the NRSV," *Biblical Research* 41 (1996): 77–87; see now the extensive discussion of problems involved in the terms "Jew," "Gentile," and "Christian" by Esler, *Conflict and Identity* (who nevertheless continues to regard ethnic conflict as the salient issue in Romans).

10. Edward W. Said, *Orientalism* (New York: Vintage, 1978); E. Said, *Culture and Imperialism* (New York: Pantheon, 2000); Richard A. Horsley, "Submerged Biblical Histories," in *The Postcolonial Bible*, ed. R. S. Sugirtharajah (Sheffield: Sheffield Academic Press, 1998); Shawn Kelley, *Racializing Jesus: Race, Ideology, and the Formation of Modern Biblical Scholarship* (London: Routledge, 2002).

11. Chandra Talpade Mohanty, *Feminism without Borders: Decolonizing Theory, Practicing Solidarity* (Durham, NC: Duke University Press, 2003), 193.

12. Mahmood Mamdani, *Good Muslim, Bad Muslim: America, the Cold War, and the Roots of Terror* (New York: Pantheon, 2004).

13. *Our Word Is Our Weapon: Selected Writings of Subcomandante Insurgente Marcos,* ed. Juana Ponce de León (New York: Seven Stories Press, 2001), xx.

14. *Aeneid* 1:255–96; see P. A. Brunt, *Roman Imperial Themes* (Oxford: Clarendon, 1990); P. D. A. Garnsey and C. R. Whittaker, eds., *Imperialism in the Ancient World* (Cambridge: Cambridge University Press, 1978).

15. On the industrial proliferation of a specific repertoire of images of Augustus, see Paul Zanker, *The Power of Images in the Age of Augustus* (Ann Arbor: University of Michigan Press, 1988); on ritual, see S. R. F. Price, *Rituals and Power: The Roman Imperial Cult in Asia Minor* (Cambridge: Cambridge University Press, 1984).

16. Price, *Rituals;* Richard Gordon, "The Veil of Power: Emperors, Sacrificers, and Benefactors," in *Pagan Priests,* ed. Mary Beard and John North (Ithaca, NY: Cornell University Press, 1990), 199–232; on Greece, Susan E. Alcock, *Graecia Capta: The Landscapes of Roman Greece* (Cambridge: Cambridge University Press, 1993); Clifford Ando, *Imperial Ideology and Provincial Loyalty in the Roman Empire* (Berkeley: University of California Press, 2000).

17. Gregory Woolf, "Becoming Roman, Staying Greek: Culture, Identity, and the Civilizing Process in the Roman East," *Proceedings of the Cambridge Philological Society* 40 (1994): 116–43; idem, "Beyond Romans and Natives," *World Archaeology* 28:3 (1995): 339–50. On the prevalence of benefaction, Frederick W. Danker, *Benefactor: Epigraphic Study of a Greco-Roman and New Testament Semantic Field* (St. Louis: Clayton, 1982).

18. On this argument, see Leonard V. Rutgers, "Roman Policy toward the Jews," in *Judaism and Christianity in First-Century Rome,* eds. Karl P. Donfried and Peter Richardson (Grand Rapids: Eerdmans, 1998), 98–103; and H. Dixon Slingerland, *Claudian Policymaking and the Early Imperial Repression of Judaism at Rome* (Atlanta: Scholars Press, 1997).

19. See, for example, Troels Engberg-Pedersen, *Paul and the Stoics* (Louisville, KY: Westminster John Knox, 2000); F. Gerald Dowling, *Cynics, Paul, and the Pauline Churches* (London and New York: Routledge, 1998); Halvor Moxnes, "Honor, Shame, and the Outside World in Romans," in *The Social World of Formative Christianity and Judaism: Essays in Tribute to Howard Clark Kee,* ed. Jacob Neusner et al. (Philadelphia: Fortress, 1988), 207–19; H. Moxnes, "Honor and Righteousness in Romans," *JSNT* 32 (1988): 61–77. The last phrase comes from Bruno Blumenfeld, *The Political Paul: Justice, Democracy and Kingship in a Hellenistic Framework,* JSNTSup 210 (Sheffield: Sheffield Academic Press, 2001), 12–16.

20. V. P. Furnish, *Theology and Ethics in Paul* (Nashville: Abingdon, 1968), 101–6; Elliott, *Rhetoric of Romans,* 277–78.

21. The language of public and hidden transcript comes from James C. Scott, *Domination and the Arts of Resistance* (New Haven, CT: Yale University Press, 1990).
22. N. T. Wright, *The Climax of the Covenant: Christ and the Law in Pauline Theology* (Minneapolis: Fortress, 1991), chaps. 2, 3; N. T. Wright, "Paul's Gospel and Caesar's Empire," in *Paul and Politics: Ekklesia, Israel, Imperium, Interpretation; Essays in Honor of Krister Stendahl*, ed. R. Horsley (Harrisburg, PA: Trinity Press International), 166–67.
23. Dieter Georgi, *Theocracy in Paul's Praxis and Theology* (Minneapolis: Fortress, 1991), 85–86.
24. Elliott, *Liberating Paul*, 194–95.
25. Elliott, *Liberating Paul*, 190–95, 214–16.
26. Mark Reasoner, *The Strong and the Weak: Romans 14:1–15:13 in Context*, SNTSMS 103 (Cambridge: Cambridge University Press, 1999).
27. Danker, *Benefactor*, BDAG, s.v. *ergon* ("frequently used to describe people of exceptional merit, esp. benefactors"). The divine achievements or "works" of Augustus are set forth as his *praxeis* in the Greek translation of the *Res Gestae*.
28. *Pietate vir, Aenead* 1.10 and throughout; *pius Aeneas*, 1.305 and throughout.
29. I explore these questions further in *The Arrogance of Nations: Reading Romans in the Shadow of Empire*, forthcoming from Fortress Press.
30. E. Elizabeth Johnson, "Romans 9–11: The Faithfulness and Impartiality of God," in *Pauline Theology III: Romans*, ed. David Hay and E. Elizabeth Johnson (Minneapolis: Fortress, 1995), 211–39; William S. Campbell, *Paul's Gospel in an Intercultural Context: Jew and Gentile in the Letter to the Romans* (Frankfurt: Lang, 1991), 25–42.
31. Daniel Fraikin, "The Rhetorical Function of the Jews in Romans," in *Anti-Judaism in Early Christianity*, ed. Peter Richardson and D. Granskou (Waterloo, ON: Wilfrid Laurier, 1986), 91–106.
32. Nanos suggests that it was Paul's greater success at gaining converts that provoked "jealousy" in his non-Christ-believing fellow Jews, and that it was their opposition to his mission—not the relatively small number of Jews in the Christ communities per se—that Paul sought to address, indirectly, in this letter (*The Mystery of Romans: The Jewish Context of Paul's Letter* [Minneapolis: Fortress, 1994]).
33. Hans Werner Bartsch, "Die antisemitische Gegner des Paulus im Römerbrief," in *Antijudaismus im Neuen Testament? Exegetische und systematische Beiträge*, ed. W. Eckert et al. (Munich: Kaiser, 1967), 27–43, esp. 33–39.
34. In N. T. Wright's phrase, Rome presented a constant danger that "local anti-Jewish sentiment would lead Gentile Christians not only to isolate Jews within the Christian fellowship but also to marginalize a mission that included Jews" ("Romans and the Theology of Paul," in *Pauline Theology III: Romans*, 35). Similarly, W. S. Campbell speaks of "nascent anti-Judaism among the Roman Gentile Christians" ("The Rule of Faith," in *Pauline Theology III: Romans*, 260–61).
35. Mark Reasoner was the first to use the phrase, in *The Strong and the Weak*.

Chapter 13

Justification of Difference in Galatians

JAE WON LEE

[handwritten: I'm not sure that 2 follow the one]

Western Christianity taught us Asian Christians that there is neither "Western" *[handwritten: Amer.]* nor "Oriental" in Christ. But "in Christ" actually was equivalent to "in universal Christianity." By preaching that there is no Western-Oriental distinction, Western Christianity successfully persuaded us to believe that any ethnic specificity—whether it is Asian, African, or Latino/a—is irrelevant to the essence of the Christian faith. In order to accomplish its mission, Western Christianity tactfully deployed the Pauline discourse of "no distinction between Jews and Gentiles" as one of the main proof texts for the purposes of its own missionary and the inevitably attending imperial universalism. The discourse of "neither Jew nor *[handwritten: in Amer way?]* Gentile" was used by powerful Western Christianity to exercise hegemony under the guise of universal Christianity. Analogous to the Jewish identity/difference *[handwritten: T T]* that was deprived of its own ethnic specificity and historical memory in the later development of Gentile Christianity, the ethnic, historical, and cultural values of Korean identity/difference were suppressed by the universal discourse and imperialistic move of Western Christianity. *[handwritten: Lb Swedes a entity & de americanized]*

Western interpretations of Pauline universalism have had an enormous impact on the role of Korean Christianity in the history of Korea, as well as on Korean-American Christianity. Here I point out some negative effects that Western theological universalism imprinted on the predominant ethos of Korean Christianity. First, it contributed less to transforming and resisting the structural injustice of domination and oppression than to consolidating and maintaining the status quo of Korean society. The sociopolitical and communal dimensions of the embodiment of Christian faith were subsumed by an individualized, ahistorical (apart from specific contexts), and a-cultural faith (without being incarnated in local realities). Second, Korean Christian identity was assimilated into Western cultural universalism in such a way that the particularity of Korean identity/difference in its specific sociopolitical and cultural history became insignificant and inferior to universal "Christian" identity, which was actually nothing less than Western identity. Ironically, but not surprisingly, Christianity's assumed superiority over Judaism was translated into and identified with Christianity's superiority over other religions in Korea. In the Korean context, being "Christian" thus was not only identified with being conservative toward sociopolitical transformation but also with being uncritically exclusive toward the Korean traditional religious and cultural heritage.

Although the social conservatism and the characteristic exclusive stance of the predominant form of Korean Christianity toward other religions are complex issues requiring further consideration, the massive influence of the Western theological tradition cannot be underestimated. Especially, Western theological (mainly soteriological) readings of Paul, more precisely of the doctrine of justification by faith, have to a great extent shaped the conservative contour of Christianity in Korea. Even the most progressive Christians in Korea are not quite free of the traditional interpretation of Paul. This may explain why Korean *minjung* theology—like most of Latin American liberation theology—while achieving a significant political reinterpretation of the praxis of the historical Jesus, has not attempted a corresponding new understanding of Paul.[1]

As an effort to practice the ethics of interpretation against the dominant interpretation of Paul's universalism as difference-free Christian universalism, this essay revisits a familiar theme in Pauline scholarship, that is, the question of equality between Jews and Gentiles by bringing to the fore a distinct angle, namely, the problem of equality and difference. My interpretation focuses on a reading of Jew-Gentile difference in Galatians 1–2 and argues for an emancipatory meaning of justification of difference in Paul's politics of difference.

One of the arguments underlying this essay is that the problem of equality and difference between Jews and Gentiles cannot be treated simply in terms of abstract, theological principles, such as Pauline universalism and opposition to Judaism or Pauline universalism vs. Jewish particularism.[2] At the same time the issue cannot be understood merely as Paul's justification of the status of Gentile Christians,[3] or simply a matter of the diversity of first-century Judaism and early Christianity. There is a need, rather, for a *contextual* approach to the dynamic, relational meaning of equality and difference between Jews and Gentiles. This means paying particular attention to the *specific* situation of each *local* Christian community within the first-century Jewish and Greco-Roman context. This implies that both Jewishness and Gentileness need to be contextually related to the problem of equality and difference with reference to emerging hierarchical social relations between Jews and Gentiles in the early Christian movement. Who defines difference as inferior and improper, hence as otherness to be repressed and excluded? Who claims difference as equal-but-different and emancipatory, hence as identity to be reclaimed and included? Under what political, social, religious, and cultural conditions do these definitions and claims emerge? These questions crucial to the issue of equality (identity) and difference are not only relevant to the contemporary politics of difference[4] but also imperative for a fresh approach to the problem of equality and difference of Jews and Gentiles in early Christian communities.

The Issue of Equality between Jews and Gentiles

Indisputably an integral aspect of Paul's thought and practice was the inclusion of Gentiles and their full participation as equals to Jews in the nascent communities that were envisioning and anticipating the apocalyptic renewal of the kingdom of God within the Mediterranean basin of the first-century Greco-Roman world. Once having been engaged in the Pharisaic movement (Phil. 3:5–6; Acts 22:3–5), through a radical experience Paul became committed to the Jesus movement in the Diaspora, a renewal movement of Jewish apocalyptic hope in association with the person of Jesus, a Palestinian Jew who was crucified under the first-century imperial Pax Romana.

Of course, Paul was not the only person in his time who was engaged in the question of how Gentiles could enter and fully participate in the communal life with Jewish people, although he certainly became one of the most controversial of such figures. As some scholars characterize the question of Gentile inclusion as an "intra-Jewish" or "intramural" or "inter-Jewish and intra-Jewish" issue,[5] there was a wide spectrum of opinion and practice regarding the issue among various Jewish groups.[6] As early Christian groups in the Diaspora, particularly in Antioch, became more open toward the participation of Gentiles, and as the heterogeneous character of those communities became noticeable to the followers of Jesus in Jerusalem, conflicting views and strategies began to surface with respect to the nature, meaning, and extent of the inclusion and full membership of Gentile believers within the formative, yet complex, early Christian identity-making process. The problems involved in differences between Jews and Gentiles—and therefore questions of unity or equality between Jews and Gentiles within and among Christian groups—were raised particularly within *concrete* situations such as communal meal settings in which mutual interaction and integration among the members took place on a practical level.

This essay on contextual and dynamic differences between Jews and Gentiles at communal meals aims to problematize unquestioned assumptions current in contemporary discourse on Paul and the Jew-Gentile difference in early Christian communities. The conventional position has assumed that Paul advocates equality between Jews and Gentiles in the sense of the (categorical) abrogation

of difference among them,[7] or in the sense of the elimination of ritual distinction,[8] or in the sense of at least indifference to difference.[9] Even in the last case,
it is often argued that although *in theory* Paul valued "indifference" toward aspects
of Jewish law such as circumcision, the Sabbath, and food laws (neither forbid-
den nor required), *in practice* indifference did not work, and Paul actually
expected Christian Jews to give up such Jewish observances.[10]

One of the strongest expressions of the first position is given by Daniel
Boyarin—from a cultural-critical approach—when he interprets Paul and the
incident at Antioch:

> The crux of the matter . . . is the question of when (or indeed whether) Paul
> argued that circumcision and observance of such commandments as the
> laws of kashruth were abrogated *not only for ethnic gentiles but for ethnic Jews
> as well.* I suggest that for the logic of Paul's theology, which was complete in
> its entirety from the first moment of his revelation, there was *not the slight-
> est importance* to the observance of such rites for Jews or gentiles.[11]

According to Boyarin, Paul's passion for equality led him to equate equality with
sameness that "deprives difference of the right to be different, dissolving all others into a single essence in which matters of cultural practice are irrelevant and
only faith in Christ is significant."[12]

On the other hand, recently some scholars have challenged this position that
Paul's insistence on equality between Jews and Gentiles was motivated by and/or
resulted in the devaluation of the law and Jewish cultural practices.[13] They stress
that Paul's commitment to equality between Jewish and Gentile Christians entails
a tolerant attitude toward ethnic differences, in the sense that within the Christian community Jews remain Jews without giving up observance of Jewish law,
and Gentiles remain Gentiles without proselyte conversion. In the following, I
present my reading of Galatians 1–2 as an interpretation of Paul's politics of difference that justifies difference in light of solidarity with the weak.

One Gospel of Christ and the Problem of Difference (Gal. 1:6–9)

Remarkably Paul raises the question of difference right at the beginning of Galatians. In the opening address in 1:6–9 Paul explicitly states that he is shocked
because the Galatians[14] are turning into a different gospel: "I am astonished that
you are so quickly deserting the one who called you in the grace of Christ and
are turning to a different gospel (εἰς ἕτερον εὐαγγέλιον)" (1:6).

A proper interpretation depends on how the phrase immediately following in
1:7 is translated. The dominant interpretation, represented for instance by NRSV,
NIV, and the majority of commentaries, renders the relative clause ὃ οὐκ ἔστιν
ἄλλο as "there is no other one." This would mean that Paul starts Galatians with
the programmatic denial of difference. The Greek text, however, is literally "which
is not another one." In fact, this is how numerous other English translations render the passage.[15] This literal translation still could mean that Paul denies the exis-

tence of another gospel, if "gospel" is a term Paul wants to add after "another."[16]
As Paul, however, clearly talks about two different gospels in 2:7 ("the gospel of
foreskin [τῆς ἀκροβυστίας] and circumcision [τῆς περιτομῆς]"), as we will
see below, the puzzling contradiction between the two statements should not be
resolved too quickly. "You are turning to a different gospel" (1:6) and "the different gospel is not other" (1:7) is a juxtaposition that may indicate that Paul is handling the question of identity and difference in a much more dialectical and
challenging way than Western thought patterns have led us to believe.

Paul defines "the different gospel" simply as a gospel contrary to that which
Paul and his fellow missionaries preached to the Galatians. Again, the meaning of
this different gospel is emphasized as the gospel contrary to that which they
received and whose representatives are under a double curse (1:9). If my interpretation is correct, Paul wants to convince the Galatians not to turn to this different
gospel, whose existence is not denied—even if its "difference" is understood differently ("which is not other").[17] I propose understanding Paul's opening statement in 1:6–9 in the following way: Paul does not raise his tone to convince the
Gentiles of the Galatian churches that there is no other (different) gospel, except
the one that he preached to them. Rather he is angry, because the Gentiles of the
Galatian churches are taking over the different gospel assigned as the gospel of circumcision to the Jews at the Jerusalem conference in 2:7. Because they are Gentiles, the Galatians should stay with the gospel of foreskin (2:7) which initially they
received and to which they turned from their pagan gods (4:8–9). This means that
Paul tries to redefine the meaning of difference. The difference of the other gospel
is confirmed and denied at the same time. It is different, yet not other. But if the
gospel of circumcision to which the Galatians want to convert is "not another
one," why should they not take it over? This requires a further look at Paul's biographical account of the events leading to Antioch.

Paul's Call/Conversion: From One to Other (Gal. 1:11–16)

In the telling of his personal story, Paul strongly implies that the gospel he
preached in Galatia in itself is conceived to be "different" by a dominant (Jerusalem)
position of Jewish Christians. He takes pains to emphasize right from the beginning that his gospel was not "according to human beings," nor based on human
tradition, but was received through a revelation of Jesus Christ (1:11–12). Since
his life before his call was different from that of other apostles, Paul tries to explain
his call by stressing that only God changed the course of his own life and gave it
a new direction.

In Galatians 1:13–15 Paul describes his former life in Judaism as an example
of excellent accomplishment and distinguishable commitment with regard to the
traditions of his ancestors. He must have been very proud of it at that time. Paul
was standing, so to speak, at the top level in Judaism, and his extreme zeal was
oriented toward the law-adherent identity of Israel. Paul does not give exact reasons why he became a persecutor of the early Christian communities, but from

the context it is quite clear that his rigor as a Jew was closely linked to his violent opposition against the church of God.[18] As Paul states that he "advanced in Judaism beyond many of my people of the same age" (1:14), he must have held an extreme position that not only separated him from his peers in general, but was also irreconcilable with the theology of the post-Easter Jesus movement.

Even if many details remain unclear, three things appear obvious. (1) The whole conflict between Paul and the church of God takes place inside of Judaism, not between two different religions.[19] It is a struggle between a highly conservative stance[20] on the one hand and a position labeled as heretical/dissident "other" on the other hand. (2) The way Paul describes his conversion shows that he does not just take over the heretical position of "the church of God," but most likely goes far beyond it. His divine designation as an apostle of "the gospel for the Gentiles" now seems to have put him into a dissident position himself (1:16), more dissident than the former dissidents he persecuted. This becomes clear at the beginning of the Jerusalem account in 2:1–10, where Paul has to negotiate his different "gospel of foreskin" (2:7), which was looked at very suspiciously by the Jerusalem authorities (2:2). (3) Different from the account of Paul's conversion in Acts 9, Paul's own statement in Galatians does not give any details. Greater importance is attached to the elements he mentions: "But when he who had set me apart before I was born, and had called me, in order that I might preach him among the Gentiles . . . (1:15–16)." Like the prophets who were called (see Isa. 49:1), Paul is also called and sent to preach the gospel among Gentiles. That means that the structure of the argument in Galatians 1:13–16 is shaped by the polarity of Jew/Judaism (= Paul's previous position, 1:13) and Gentiles (= Paul's position after his call, 1:16). This suggests that a Jew-Gentile dichotomy underlies the debate on gospel and difference (1:6–9).

Equality with Difference:
The Jerusalem Conference (Gal. 2:1–10)

Paul's account of what New Testament scholarship has referred to as the Jerusalem conference or the Jerusalem council involves the role of Paul and that of the Jerusalem church, the nature of the leadership of the Jerusalem church, and the relationship between the Jerusalem church and the Antioch church during a most hidden period in the history of early Christianity.

Although there has been much debate regarding historical problems about the relation of the event described in 2:1–10 to Luke's account of the Jerusalem conference (Acts 15),[21] there is no scholarly consensus on the events surrounding the Jerusalem conference and related issues. Instead of trying to get into historical details in an attempt toward historical reconstruction, I will focus on the differences in status and hierarchical relations among major actors in the narratives in Galatians 2 and Acts 15 by considering the broad historical picture underlying the relationship between the community at Antioch and the community in Jerusalem.

Between Antioch and Jerusalem: Hierarchy Issues

Just before Paul mentions his second visit to Jerusalem with Barnabas (Gal. 2:1), he tells of his first encounter with Peter in Jerusalem (1:18–19) three years after his conversion. What motivated his visit and what conversation he had with Peter remain unknown. Likely at that time Peter was exercising the leading role in the community of the followers of Jesus in Jerusalem. Also it seems that the Jerusalem community was assuming the central role in the development of the Jesus movement in Judea after the death and resurrection of Jesus, especially because of the eschatological significance of that community.[22] Compared to Peter's position, Paul's position seems to be rather marginal. Peter and other apostles had been actually the followers of the historical Jesus since the beginning of Jesus' activities in Galilee, and they were, as Paul says, apostles before him (1:17), even though for apologetic and polemical reasons Paul is rhetorically so deliberate as to attribute his apostleship to divine authority.[23] Presumably his past activity of persecuting the church contributed to his marginal status immediately after his conversion (1:23; see 1 Cor. 15:9). Paul spent some time in Arabia, apparently without making direct contact with Judea or Jerusalem. He was unknown by sight to the churches of Christ in Judea even after his meeting with Peter.

Certainly at the time of his writing to the Galatians, Paul is claiming that his apostleship to the Gentiles depends on divine authority and thus is defending his independence from the Jerusalem authority. Yet it is possible to perceive Paul's marginality behind his rhetorical emphasis on his independence from the Jerusalem authorities and his mission to the Gentiles grounded upon the divine authority. In other words, Paul seems retrospectively to interpret his lack of authority in relation to the Jerusalem leadership at this early postconversion time as his independence. As we have seen already in our analysis of 1:11–16, Paul himself was, so to speak, a "difference." Moreover, the very language used in 2:1–10 indicates that Paul could not avoid recognizing the authority of the Jerusalem leadership around the time when he made his second visit to the Jerusalem leadership with Barnabas. Contrary to the conventional image of a dominant Paul, which has been partly created by the rhetorical dynamics of Galatians 1–2 itself, this same text rather clearly tells that in reality Paul was in a weak and marginalized position:[24]

- Paul has to go to Jerusalem and submit the gospel he preaches among the Gentiles.
- Without agreement or acceptance by the Jerusalem authorities, he feels that he will have run in vain.
- The practice in the Pauline congregations was subject to observation and inquiry from a superior position of some kind (spies, false brethren).
- Titus was not forced to be circumcised, but otherwise he could have been forced to do so.

- The Jerusalem authorities give Paul the right hand of the community, not vice versa.
- Paul insists that they did not impose an additional requirement,[25] which means that technically they were in a position to do so.

All this shows that Paul was not in a dominant position in the context of the Jerusalem conference. Even more important, Paul defends the freedom of Gentile believers (2:4) against a force exercised by dominant Jerusalem leaders (2:3). This means that Paul acts as an advocate of the "weak" against the "strong."

The Jerusalem Conference (Gal. 2:1–10)

When Paul presents Titus, an uncircumcised Greek, as a test case, the status of Gentiles as full members equal to Jews is the focus of discussion at the Jerusalem conference. Paul's version of the conference in 2:1–10 highlights the subtle hierarchical dynamics underlying the issues of equality and difference in the relationships between Paul (Antioch) and the Jerusalem church, and between Jews and Gentiles within the Christian communities.

Despite noticeable differences between Paul and Luke–Acts with regard to the Jerusalem conference, the accounts agree on one decisive point. The Jerusalem leadership agreed that Gentiles need not be circumcised (2:6; Acts 15:19). The decision was made essentially in favor of what the Antioch delegation sought. Yet, in recounting the decision at the conference Paul demonstrates the equality—in spite of difference and hierarchy—between himself and the leadership of the Jerusalem church. According to his argument, such equality with difference is grounded in God's impartiality (Gal. 2:6), and God's impartiality is understood not merely as indifference to difference, but as indifference to discriminatory distinction for the sake of equality with difference. This inclusive and nonhierarchical definition of difference is what Paul sees as the truth of the gospel (2:5) as it is practiced for instance at Antioch and affirmed by the Jerusalem leaders. And this is how the different gospel (1:6) can be understood as not "other."

On the basis of God's impartiality, which guarantees equality between Paul and the Jerusalem pillars, despite their differences, Paul interprets the decision of the conference as the unity of the gospel in terms of the gospel of both foreskin and circumcision (2:7). Moreover, notably Paul uses the passive πεπίστευμαι in order to define the gospel of both foreskin and circumcision as being derived from the oneness of God, who worked for the mission to the circumcised (through Peter) and to the Gentiles (through Paul).

Regarding the agreement at the Jerusalem conference, a number of scholars argue that missionary tasks were divided along ethnic lines.[26] Yet, given that the Antioch community was a mixed group of Jews and Gentiles and that Jews were dispersed throughout the eastern Roman Empire and beyond, a division along either racial lines or territorial areas seems untenable. Rather, the agreement more likely was that the gospel of circumcision, represented by James, Peter, and John, would be for Jews, and the gospel of foreskin, represented by Barnabas and Paul, would apply to Gentiles.

Difference Trouble: The Antioch Incident (Gal. 2:11–14)

According to Paul, Peter withdrew from table fellowship with the Gentile Christians in Antioch on account of some visitors from James (2:12),[27] and his example was followed by other Jewish Christians including Barnabas. Paul himself stood up against Peter. Although there are gaps to be filled for reconstructing the event, I aim to demonstrate that Paul's attitude toward the table fellowship with Gentiles in Antioch enables us to problematize and challenge the conventional universalizing interpretation of Paul's discourse and stance with regard to the Jew-Gentile difference.

Whereas the trouble at meals in Antioch was generated by the guests from Jerusalem, Paul's criticism was directed at Peter's change of behavior, not at those guests. Further, criticism of Peter's behavior focused on his withdrawal from mixed table fellowship. Paul attributes such a change to Peter's fear of the circumcision party. Galatians 2:12 shows that Paul is concerned about the unity of table fellowship between Jews and Gentiles—implying equality and mutuality—which was disturbed and discontinued. Paul described what happened at the mixed table fellowship by a change from the language of inclusion to that of exclusion. Moreover, the language that Paul uses has implications of power relations between Jews and Gentiles at the table fellowship.

Before some men came from James, eating together with the Gentiles in equality and mutuality went unquestioned among both Jewish and Gentile Christians. Before the mutual table fellowship with equality was disturbed, these guests were referred to as "some men" (unspecified)—albeit identified as "from James." But what happened with their presence was characterized by the language of exclusion and power relations. At the end of the verse these men from James are associated with "those of circumcision." Thus, the word "circumcision" stands out as marking a hierarchical difference between Jews and Gentiles that now rules the ethos of table fellowship in Antioch. It also represents tilting the balance in equal relationship between Jews and Gentiles in Antioch. This explains why, according to Paul, for fear of "those of circumcision," other Jews followed Peter.

Whether the Jewish Christians acted because of the force of Peter's example or not,[28] the persuasion and the hierarchal power relation were such that even Barnabas, who worked together with Paul in Jerusalem in order to ensure the equal standing of uncircumcised Gentiles, sided with the Jewish Christians of Antioch. Paul's use of language highlights the escalating weight of "Jewishness" or Jewish identity on the part of Jewish participants at table fellowship. Such a rhetorical move prepares for both Paul's rhetorical rebuke of Peter in 2:14 and his argument in defense of equality-with-difference—that is, the justification of difference—between Jews and Gentiles on the grounds of justification by faith in 2:15–21.

Despite the uncertainty, ambiguity, and contingency entailed in the interpretation of the Antioch incident, Paul makes at least three points explicit. These three points are crucial to understand Paul's position toward differences between Jews and Gentiles, as well as his understanding and articulation of the gospel in relation to the Jewish-Gentile difference. First, in Antioch, before the arrival of some men from James, the Jewish Christians in Antioch ate with the Gentile Christians. Clearly, the Antioch community not only accepted Gentiles as Gentiles, that is, as (for male Gentiles) uncircumcised Gentiles, but also practiced table fellowship with Gentiles (2:12). While there is evidence that some Jews could have social intercourse with Gentiles by dining with them,[29] the significance of the table fellowship that the Antioch community was practicing should not be underestimated. In one unified community of Jews and Gentiles, Jews were eating as Jews together with Gentiles, and Gentiles were eating as Gentiles together with Jews.[30]

Apparently Paul saw that such practice of eating together embodies the radical inclusivity of the gospel of Christ in which the differences of foreskin and circumcision remain ("the gospel of the foreskin [and] . . . of circumcision," 2:7). Through the practice of radical inclusivity, the differences of circumcision and foreskin are defined as mere differences and remain as such, not differences to be excluded and subordinated as "other."[31] Along with ethnoreligious and cultural differences that serve to demarcate and reinforce the boundary between Jews (us) and non-Jews (them), Jewish believers in Antioch, including Paul and Barnabas, regularly ate with Gentile believers. It is hardly questionable that they ate as Jews.[32] When Peter as a visiting missionary came to Antioch, he as a Jew willingly joined the practice of eating together with the Gentile believers.

Second, with the visit to Antioch by the men from James, the practice of Jewish Christians eating with the Gentile Christians was broken. The table fellowship turned out to be not the same as was practiced before, according to Paul, primarily because of Peter's change of practice. Peter stopped eating with the Gentile believers. Paul's language describing Peter's change of practice strongly suggests that the practice of radical inclusivity, recognizing differences as different (or equality with difference), was replaced by the practice of separation and exclusion, under the force of persuasion related to the power of circumcision as one of the foremost markers of Jewish self-identity.

What was problematic for Paul was the intensifying self-understanding of those of the circumcision and the underlying logic behind Peter's fear, which eventually led the practice of table fellowship embodying equality with difference into a different pattern, which can be construed as equality with sameness.[33] The oneness of table fellowship was shattered by the dominance of Jewish table practice, with the implication that Gentiles could not be included in table fellowship with Jews unless Gentiles became like Jews. Gentile difference would have to convert to sameness with Jews.

Third, Paul's criticism against Peter's change of behavior is concrete and explicit: Peter's refusal to eat with Gentiles was not faithful to the truth of the gospel. It is evident that by the truth of the gospel Paul means the gospel of foreskin and circumcision (2:7), on which Paul (Antioch) and Peter (Jerusalem) agreed. In other words, Peter's not eating with Gentiles, no matter what issues of Jewish food laws might be involved in such a change,[34] is not the right practice of the gospel that preaches oneness with egalitarian differences. On the other hand, Paul does *not* say that Peter's behavior is not the right practice toward the observance of the Jewish laws.[35]

Paul's criticism of Peter lies in that, influenced by the emerging privileging of Jewish identity/difference,[36] Peter's change of practice at table fellowship contributes to and promotes a nonegalitarian, hierarchical understanding of the Jewish-Gentile difference that relegates Gentile difference to an inferior position. The resulting consequence within the context of Antioch would mean, for Paul, that, unless Gentile Christians in Antioch become like Jews, they are unequal to the Jewish Christians and cannot remain as Gentiles in the community. Thus, Paul rebukes Peter: "If you, though a Jew, live like a Gentile and not like a Jew, how can you compel the Gentiles to live like Jews?" (2:14).

Paul's remarks here cannot be interpreted as an objection to the observance of Jewish laws or as the persuasion of Jews to give up Jewish cultural practices. His concern is with Jews who compel Gentiles to "live like a Jew." In his view, Peter's change of behavior contributes to establishing a dichotomy of "living like a Gentile" and "living like a Jew," with the latter privileged over the former. In such a case, Gentile difference becomes the opposite of Jewish identity/difference, and is relegated to difference to be denied and excluded. How can the difference of Gentile marginality be justified?

Justification by Faith and the Politics of Difference (Gal. 2:15–21)

Paul's account of the Antioch incident (2:11–14), as well as his articulation of justification by faith (2:15–21), reveals strong elements of literary coherence between the two passages.[37] The polarity between Jews and Gentiles clearly links 2:14 and 15. Moreover, Paul's reference to "us" as Jews at the beginning of 2:15 strongly suggests a continuity with the response of Paul, a Jew, toward the practice of Peter, a Jew, who is criticized in 2:14. Also, Paul's mentioning of "build[ing] up again the very things that I once tore down" most naturally refers to table fellowship and its subsequent collapse.

Thus, 2:15–21 fits well with the preceding Antioch narrative as the concluding argument recapitulating the significance of the equal standing of Gentiles with Jews at table fellowship. It further constitutes the climax of Galatians 1–2. Galatians 2:15–21 is not mere theological reflection on justification either by faith or by works of the law, separated from any concrete community context. Rhetorically and theologically it is tightly linked to the meal practice and the subsequent conflict at Antioch. Having encountered broken table fellowship and presumably a marginalized status of Gentile believers, including his own marginalized position, Paul must have felt a strong need to justify why his position is different from that of Peter and other Jewish believers, and why he defends and sides with Gentile believers at Antioch.

First, in criticizing Peter's withdrawal from table fellowship with Gentiles, Paul exposes and rejects a Jewish self-identity based on the polarity of (born) Jews/the righteous/pure/superior/the law versus Gentile/sinners/impure/inferior/ sin. Peter's position characterizes and represents an *essentialist* understanding of Jewish identity/difference; it defines the differences between Jews and Gentiles as two unchangeable essences and oppositional polarities that are inherently different. As a consequence, such a position assumes an exclusive, hierarchical understanding of differences by which not only are Jews and Gentiles different, but the latter is inferior to the former. Stemming from a Jewish insider, Paul's criticism of Peter's behavior challenges the emerging exclusive tendency of the politics of identity of "othering," which is contingent and not essential. This exclusive tendency functions to separate *us* Jews from *those* Gentile sinners.

Second, Paul sets up the beginning of his argument upon the common ground with which Paul thinks Peter would agree. The conviction that Paul and Peter share is stated in 2:16: "Yet (we Jews) knowing that a man is not justified by works of the law but through faith in/of Jesus Christ, even we have believed in Christ Jesus, in order to be justified by faith in/of Christ, and not by works of the law, because by works of the law all flesh will not be justified" (my trans.).

As we have seen, the self-identification we = Jews (2:15) indicates that the intra-Jewish dialogue regarding Gentiles within the community continues. Paul introduces the rhetoric of justification in order to problematize a logic of Jewish identity that excludes the full participation of Gentiles as Gentiles unless they become proselytes. In 2:15 he deconstructs the hierarchical framework of "us" Jews vs. "them" Gentiles and sinners.

Here it is important to distinguish points of agreement and disagreement between Paul and Peter. The point of agreement: Most Jews, Paul says, including Paul and Peter, would agree with the Jewish belief that a man is justified not by works of the law, but by faith.[38] Here the use of ἄνθρωπος ("man," "person") instead of ὑμεῖς ("we") is noteworthy, presumably because of Paul's intention to break the polarity of Jewish-Gentile difference. Furthermore, elaborating on this Jewish belief in justification, Paul emphasizes the common ground on which Paul and Peter are standing as Jews who believe in Jesus Christ. Then Paul reasserts the point of agreement saying that we (Jews) have believed in Christ Jesus, in order to be justified by faith in Christ and not by works of the law. In other words, the doctrine of *justification* is the point not of *disagreement,* but of *agreement.* It is an irony that in the history of interpretation Paul's justification by faith has been (mis)interpreted as marking the disagreement between Jewish and Gentile Christians, and thus the real impetus of the dichotomy of faith-works has been obscured.

Based upon this common ground, Paul clarifies justification by faith: "Because by works of the law *all flesh* will *not* be justified" (2:16, my trans.). This shows Paul's difference from Peter's view. Most translations prefer something like "no one will be justified by works of the law." However, considering Paul's rhetorical move and the flow of his argument, "all flesh will not be justified" makes better sense. "All flesh" here is an inclusive term for both Jews and Gentiles, which may carry overtones of the Jewish-Gentile difference in the "flesh" of circumcision. Paul here reiterates that neither Jews nor Gentiles are justified by works of the law. In other words, Gentiles cannot be justified according to the social and ritual functions of the law that legitimize the hierarchical dichotomy of us Jews vs. Gentile sinners and thus be excluded from the people of God. Hence, it should not be overlooked that the universalism intended in the use of "all flesh" cannot be characterized as the contemporary Hellenistic universalism framed in the dichotomy of spirit-flesh.[39] Rather, the universalism inclusive of both Jews and Gentiles is advocated on the basis of actual differences in the flesh but by deconstructing hierarchical relations between differences in the flesh.[40] If through faith in/of Jesus Christ both Jews and Gentiles are justified respectively as Jews and Gentiles with differences, the divisive "works of the law" no longer functions in the faith community of Jesus Christ. In a word, in Christ, Jews can no longer treat Gentiles as sinners per se.

In 2:17–18, Paul's argument moves to reconsider how the clash between Paul and Peter at the table fellowship in Antioch is related to the theological dimensions of justification by faith. In Paul's view, eating together with Gentiles in Antioch was done in conformity with the meaning of justification by faith: Jews as Jews were eating together with Gentiles as equals of Jews, not as sinners. Paul interprets this as an effort to build one egalitarian community of Jews and Gentiles: "endeavoring to be justified in Christ" (2:17). Paul does not concede that equal association with Gentiles is equivalent to associating with sinners. Otherwise, this would mean that Christ is a servant of sin.[41] It is not accidental that Paul uses the term διάκονος ("servant") in reference to Christ only in Galatians 2:17 and Romans 15:8, both of which are linked in context to table fellowship. I contend that Paul responded contextually to Jewish-Gentile difference in different local situations, which eventually shows that he approached his politics of difference from the perspective of solidarity with "the weak." Here in Galatians 2:17, by rejecting any possible charge against Gentiles in Christ, Paul sides with the minority Gentiles in Antioch, whereas his politics of difference leads him in Rome to side with Jews.

According to Paul's understanding of the apocalyptic significance of the Christ event, through his crucifixion Jesus Christ enabled Paul to deconstruct the power of sin of judging others as sinners ("what I destroyed," 2:18), in other words, making others inferior. To conclude, as a theological reflection on the practice of table fellowship between Jews and Gentiles, the primary concern of the doctrine of justification by faith is to support equal relations between Jews and Gentiles within the messianic community of faith.[42] Justification by faith for Paul justifies the differences between Jews and Gentiles in Christ and establishes a new relation of Jews and Gentiles in Christ.

Concluding Notes

In conclusion I would like to indicate briefly some implications that a liberative hermeneutics of inclusion in Paul's politics of difference discussed in this essay may have for Korean and Korean-American Christianity. In the vicissitudes of Korean history, the word *minjung* refers to people who were oppressed, powerless, marginalized, and invisible as "others" under multiple forms of economic, sociopolitical, religiocultural, patriarchal, and colonial injustice. As such, *minjung* stands for an individual subject as well as a collective subject. The thrust of Korean *minjung* theology's understanding of *minjung* lies in the subversive declaration that despite and in the very midst of the suffering, marginality, invisibility, and "otherness" of *minjung*, *minjung* has been the subject of the Korean history. Recognizing that the term calls to mind injustice and oppression, I suggest that *minjung* encloses the plurality of differences in itself. *Minjung* is the notion that most appropriately embraces the second terms relegated to the inferior position in the construct of binary dichotomy, such as women, slaves, the poor, the weak, blacks, Asians, Jews, non-Christians, the colonized, and others. In a word, *minjung* embraces difference.

In appropriating a postcolonial perspective on difference, I want to reflect on a further implication of refocusing *minjung* as difference. Because the *minjung* constitute the majority of Korean people, the meaning of *minjung* cannot be separated from that of the Korean nation (*minjok*). From the beginning of the last century, the Korean nation went through Japanese colonization for thirty-six years. After her independence from the Japanese rule, the nation was divided into North Korea and South Korea by foreign powers, especially by U.S. imperial hegemonic interests and strategies. For more than a half century since then, the Korean nation and people have been suffering from the division of land, history, family, and national identity. At the very heart of the oppression and sufferings of the Korean *minjung* lies the tragic reality of the divided nation. Any discourse on difference within the Korean context cannot avoid the issue of Korean difference as a divided identity.

The most violent repression and denial of Korean identity, including Korean Christian identity, is enforced by the imperial means of dividing the Korean nation and people into two oppositional differences. During the last half century, both the North Korean and South Korean people have been compelled to see each other in terms of oppositional difference, that is, as the other whose difference should be denied, suppressed, and ultimately eliminated. A dominant form of Korean Christianity has functioned as an ideological machine to maintain and reinforce such an exclusive politics of identity. Korean Christians have rendered their Korean identity to Western universal Christian identity under the logic of faith.

A new way of considering differences between North Korea and South Korea has finally emerged in the minds and hearts of South Korean and North Korean *minjung* at the turn of this century. There is a growing awareness that the unity of the Korean people and nation cannot be accomplished by the logic of an absorptive reunification that means unity with sameness, but a new pattern of confederative reunification, which is equivalent to unity with difference. This radical inclusivity of difference is to be grounded on the power of sharing differences and the persistent praxis of solidarity with/among the "weak." Furthermore, this paradigm shift may suggest a new avenue toward globalization with difference (subject), which challenges the present mode of globalization with sameness and its logic of domination.

Notes

1. A notable exception is Elsa Tamez, *The Amnesty of Grace: Justification by Faith from a Latin American Perspective* (Nashville: Abingdon, 1993). In the North American context, some scholars have begun to pay attention to Paul's encounter with the Roman Empire: Neil Elliott, *Liberating Paul: The Justice of God and the Politics of the Apostle* (Maryknoll, NY: Orbis, 1994); Dieter Georgi, *Theocracy in Paul's Praxis and Theology* (Minneapolis: Fortress, 1991); Richard A. Horsley, ed., *Paul and Empire* (Harrisburg, PA: Trinity Press International, 1997); Richard Horsley, ed., *Paul and Politics* (Harrisburg, PA: Trinity Press International, 2000).

2. Neil Elliott sharply criticizes the "new perspective on Paul," James Dunn's expression for the contribution of E. P. Sanders's *Paul and Palestinian Judaism* and its further development, including Dunn's work. For Elliott, it replicates "Bauer's old dialectic of 'Pauline universalism' versus 'Jewish particularism' in sociological terms" (*Liberating Paul*, 70). For a challenge to interpreting early Christian universalism as all-inclusive at the expense of Judaism, see Denise Buell and Caroline Johnson Hodge, "The Politics of Interpretation: The Rhetoric of Race and Ethnicity in Paul," *JBL* 123 (2004): 235–51.

3. Esp. John Gager (*The Origins of Anti-Semitism: Attitudes toward Judaism in Pagan and Christian Antiquity* [New York: Oxford University Press, 1983]) and Lloyd Gaston (*Paul and the Torah* [Vancouver: University of British Columbia Press, 1987]) overemphasize this one-sided interpretation of the relation between Jews and Gentiles.

4. For my theoretical and hermeneutical framework on Paul's politics of difference, I have critically engaged postmodern discourse on difference, feminist discourse on difference, and postcolonial discourse on difference in critical dialogue with Korean *minjung* theology's discourse on *minjung*, both as the socially oppressed and marginalized, and yet as the subjects of history. For the phrase "politics of difference" and the distinction between "an ideal of assimilation" and "the emancipatory politics of difference" I am indebted to Iris Young's *Justice and the Politics of Difference* (Princeton, NJ: Princeton University Press, 1990): "The assimilationist ideal assumes that equal social status for all persons requires treating everyone according to the same principles, rules, and standards. A politics of difference argues, on the other hand, that equality as the participation and inclusion of all groups sometimes requires different treatment for oppressed or disadvantaged groups" (158).

5. Traditionally Paul's attitude toward Judaism was understood as a debate between Christianity and Judaism as separate religions. Present scholarship recognizes that the debate was under way among different Jewish groups before the Jesus movement, that Christian groups were not separated from Judaism before 70 CE, and that the debate involved the status of Gentile members within these early Christian groups. James Dunn uses "intra-Jewish" for all these ("Echoes of Intra-Jewish Polemic in Paul's Letter to the Galatians," *JBL* 112 [1993]: 459–77). Paula Fredriksen treats the inclusion of Gentiles in a rather restrictive way as "an intramural controversy, a question of concern and interest only to those already within these groups" (*From Jesus to Christ: The Origins of the New Testament Images of Jesus* [New Haven and London: Yale University Press, 1988],

152–53). Arguing that "the Galatians . . . are members of Christ-believing sub-groups within larger Jewish communities," Mark Nanos uses both "inter-Jewish" and "intra-Jewish" ("The Inter- and Intra-Jewish Political Context of Galatians," in Richard Horsley, ed., *Paul and Politics: Ekklesia, Israel, Imperium, Interpretation*, Essays in Honor of Krister Stendahl [Harrisburg, PA: Trinity Press International, 2000], 146–59).

6. See Shaye Cohen, "Crossing the Boundary and Becoming a Jew," *HTR* 82/1 (1989): 13–33; S. Cohen, "Respect for Judaism by Gentiles according to Josephus," *HTR* 80/4 (1987): 409–30; Paula Fredriksen, "Judaism, The Circumcision of Gentiles, and Apocalyptic Hope: Another Look at Galatians 1 and 2," *JTS* 42/2 (1991): 532–64. Recently Buell and Johnson Hodge challenge the totalizing use of the dichotomy of Jewishness versus Gentileness and call for a dynamic understanding of these notions in terms of the flexibility and complexity of ethnic identity in Paul's "ethnic reasoning" (Buell and Johnson Hodge, "Politics of Interpretation," 235–52).

7. E.g., Daniel Boyarin, *A Radical Jew: Paul and the Politics of Identity* (Berkeley: University of California Press, 1994).

8. E.g., Alan Segal, *Paul the Convert: The Apostolate and Apostasy of Saul the Pharisee* (New Haven and London: Yale University Press, 1990).

9. E. P. Sanders, *Paul, the Law, and the Jewish People* (Philadelphia: Fortress, 1985).

10. Sanders, *Paul, the Law*, 143–62. See also H. Räisänen, "Galatians 2:16 and Paul's Break with Judaism," *NTS* 31 (1985): 543–53.

11. Boyarin, *Radical Jew*, 111 (my emphasis).

12. Boyarin, *Radical Jew*, 9.

13. See esp. Mark Nanos, *The Mystery of Romans: The Jewish Context of Paul's Letter* (Minneapolis: Fortress, 1996); Peter Tomson, *Paul and the Jewish Law: Halakha in the Letters of the Apostle to the Gentiles* (Assen: Van Gorcum, 1990); John Barclay, "'Neither Jew nor Greek': Multiculturalism and the New Perspective on Paul," in Mark Brett, ed., *Ethnicity and the Bible* (Leiden: Brill, 1996); Terence Donaldson, *Paul and the Gentile: Remapping the Apostle's Convictional World* (Minneapolis: Fortress, 1997).

14. I consider the main audience of Galatians to be Gentiles or, in Mark Nanos's terms, Christ-believing Gentiles considering conversion to proselyte status (*The Irony of Galatians: Paul's Letter in First-Century Context* [Minneapolis: Fortress, 2002], 75–85).

15. Brigitte Kahl makes this observation. My following reflections on "one and other" are indebted to her article "Gender Trouble in Galatia? Paul and the Rethinking of Difference," in D. Sawyer & D. Collier, eds., *Is There a Future for Feminist Theology?* (Sheffield: Sheffield Academic Press, 1999), 57–73. Nanos is also faithful to the Greek in his interpretation of irony in Galatians. He understand Paul's use of "which is not another (gospel)" as irony that affirms a different gospel but denies it the status of gospel. Though provocative, Nanos interprets this different gospel not as good news of Christ, as in the conventional interpretation, but as good news according to those who are influencing the Galatian addressees for incorporating Gentiles into the people of God through circumcision (*Irony*, esp., 201–321).

16. E.g., J. Dunn, *The Theology of Paul's Letter to the Galatians* (Cambridge: Cambridge University Press, 1993), 20, 26–28; Hans D. Betz, *Galatians: A Commentary on Paul's Letter to the Churches in Galatia* (Philadelphia: Fortress, 1979), 49; Sam K. Williams, *Galatians* (Nashville: Abingdon, 1977), 39; Nanos, *Irony*, 284–316.

17. If while denying the existence of another gospel in 1:6 (if translated "there is no other gospel"), Paul himself mentions another gospel of circumcision in 2:7, he

creates a striking contradiction between 1:6–7 and 2:7. This is noted by Betz (*Galatians*, 58, 96) and Dunn (*Theology of Paul's Letter to the Galatians*, 27). Dunn's solution is confusing: "And yet Paul denounces the one circumcision gospel (1.6–9) while seeming content to recognize the other (2.7–9). The answer must be that . . . there was a lack of mutual recognition and acceptance: the other missionaries had criticized Paul's gospel as inadequate, and Paul denounced their gospel as no gospel." Nanos reaches a similar conclusion with a slightly different tone: "Paul actually denies that this other 'good news' should rightfully be considered 'another'" (*Irony*, 287).

18. On the sociopolitical dimension of Paul's persecution activity, see Fredriksen, "Judaism, the Circumcision of Gentiles," 541–42; Elliott, *Liberating Paul*, 140–80.

19. This view constitutes a major contribution of Krister Stendahl, "Paul among Jews and Gentiles," in *Paul among Jews and Gentiles* (Philadelphia: Fortress, 1976), 1–77.

20. I do not mean this exclusively in reference to the rigorous observance of the Jewish laws, but rather in reference to a much broader politically realistic stance that Paul as a Pharisaic Jew might have taken before his conversion. See Elliott's political interpretation of Paul's conversion in *Liberating Paul*, 140–80.

21. See Craig Hill, *Hellenists and Hebrews* (Minneapolis: Fortress, 1992), 103–47; Richard Bauckham, "James and the Jerusalem Church," in R. Bauckham, ed., *The Book of Acts in Its Palestinian Setting* (Grand Rapids: Eerdmans, 1995), 415–80, esp. 467–75; Betz, *Galatians*, 81–83; Segal, *Paul the Convert*, 187–94.

22. J. Dunn, "The Relationship between Paul and Jerusalem according to Galatians 1 and 2," in *Jesus, Paul and the Law: Studies in Mark and Galatians* (Louisville, KY: Westminster/John Knox, 1990), 108–28. Richard Bauckham, "James and the Jerusalem Church," in R. Bauckham, ed., *The Book of Acts in Its Palestinian Setting* (Grand Rapids: Eerdmans, 1995), 415–80, esp. 467–75.

23. Dunn, "Relationship between Paul and Jerusalem," 108–28; Nicholas Taylor, *Paul, Antioch and Jerusalem: A Study in Relationships and Authority in Earliest Christianity* (Sheffield: Sheffield Academic Press, 1992), 88–122; Betz, *Galatians*, 58–62; R. E. Brown and J. P. Meier, *Antioch and Rome: New Testament Cradles of Catholic Christianity* (New York: Paulist, 1983), 28.

24. For a similar explanation, see Segal, *Paul the Convert*, 189–91.

25. On this point the account of Galatians differs from that in Acts 15.

26. E.g., Betz, *Galatians*, 100; H. Conzelmann, *History of Primitive Christianity* (Nashville: Abingdon, 1973), 86; S. G. Wilson, *The Gentiles and the Gentile Mission in Luke–Acts* (Cambridge: Cambridge University Press, 1973), 185; G. Lüdemann, *Paul: Apostles to the Gentiles* (London: SCM Press, 1984), 72.

27. On problems involved in such a visit, see Mark Nanos, "What Was at Stake in Peter's 'Eating with Gentiles' at Antioch?" in M. Nanos, ed., *The Galatians Debate* (Peabody, MA: Hendrickson Publishers, 2002), 282–318.

28. See Taylor, *Paul, Antioch and Jerusalem*, 132; B. Holmberg, *Paul and Power: The Structure of Power in the Primitive Church as Reflected in the Pauline Epistles* (Philadelphia: Fortress, 1980), 34.

29. See E. P. Sanders, "Jewish Association with Gentiles and Galatians 2:11–14," in Robert T. Fortna and Beverly R. Gaventa, eds., *The Conversation Continues: Studies in Paul and John in Honor of J. Louis Martyn* (Nashville: Abingdon, 1990), 17–88; Tomson, *Paul and the Jewish Law*, 230–36; Nanos, "What Was at Stake?" 282–318.

30. Segal sees this as a consequence of Paul's conversion and one of the issues that put Paul in trouble with Jewish Christians: "From a legal perspective Paul did not startle the Jewish Christian community by saying that circumcision was

unnecessary for gentile salvation per se. His claim that the saved Jews and gentiles could form a single new community and freely interact was more innovative. The issue was not how the gentiles could be saved but how to eat with them and marry them" (*Paul the Convert*, 194).

31. I suggest that in this regard Paul's rhetoric and practice prefigures what Iris Young proposes for emancipatory politics of difference (*Justice and the Politics*, 156–91).

32. See esp. Nanos, "What Was at Stake?" 282–318.

33. Characterizing the practice with μετὰ τῶν ἐθνῶν συνήσθιεν in Gal. 2:12, Paul used the prefix συν- as a reference to togetherness to integrate Gentiles into table fellowship without rendering difference into sameness. By contrast, in 2:13 the prefix συν- is linked to the actions of Jewish believers (συνυπεκρίθησαν, συναπήχθη).

34. For a detailed discussion of the issue, see J. Dunn, "The Incident at Antioch (Gal 2:11–18)," in *Jesus, Paul, and the Law: Studies in Mark and Galatians* (Louisville, KY: Westminster/John Knox, 1990), esp. 129–36.

35. For a similar conclusion, see Nanos, "What Was at Stake?" 292–300.

36. For the possible historical situation, see Dunn, "Incident at Antioch," 129–74.

37. New Testament scholarship is divided on whether Gal. 2:15–21 is a summary of the episode at Antioch or a separate elaboration on justification by faith. For a review of the scholarship, see Dunn, "Incident at Antioch," 172n117; Betz, *Galatians*, 114.

38. See Segal, *Paul, the Convert*, 128: "No other Jews in the first century distinguish faith and law in the way Paul does. For a Jew, faith fundamentally precedes anything as well, but there is no need to distinguish between it and law. Jews perform the commandments because they are commanded by God, not because they guarantee justification." When Betz considers justification by faith in 2:16 as "part of Jewish Christian theology," he misinterprets it as "the denial of the orthodox Jewish (Pharisaic) doctrine of salvation," which claims that "justification by doing and thus fulfilling the ordinances of the Torah" (Betz, *Galatians*, 115–16).

39. Against Boyarin, *Radical Jew*, 57–85, esp., 65–69.

40. It is noteworthy that in dealing with the relationship between Jews and Gentiles Paul uses the term σάρξ in reference to his Jewish people in Rom. 9:8 and 11:14.

41. See Rom. 15:8: "For I tell you that Christ became a servant (διάκονον) to the circumcised to show God's faithfulness, in order to confirm the promises given to the patriarchs" (my trans.).

42. I find Robert Brawley's approach similar to my argument for equality with difference when he emphasizes unity in Christ as "complementarity of the law and Christ" in his intertextual treatment of the relationships of the two covenants (Mosaic and Abrahamic) in Galatians, especially in reference to the relationship between Jews (law) and Gentiles (promise) in Christ. See "Contextuality, Intertextuality, and the Hendiadic Relationship of Promise and Law in Galatians," *ZNW* 93 (2002): 99–119, citation 103.

Chapter 14

"If Any Want to Become My Followers"

Character and Political Formations via the Gospel of Mark

C. DREW SMITH

Theology and Politics in Mark

We are often told that religion and politics should never be mixed and that one's religion should never influence one's politics.[1] Yet the reality of our current democracy offers a different point of view, as we have witnessed many elections where the focal point of concern has been of a religious nature.[2] While post-Enlightenment thinking might try to hold to the ideal of separation of religion from politics, in the real world most folks consider their religion to be a vital part of who they are and a vital framework within which to think and act politically. In other words, religion, whether we are honest about it or not, does form our political ideas and actions.[3]

But this is not something that is exactly new to the world, of course. Historians agree that the Roman Empire itself was very religious and that religion played a key role in the political power of Rome.[4] Indeed, when Augustus claims the title of *pontifex maximus* around 12 BCE, he solidifies his role as both religious and political leader of the empire, establishing the imperial cult of Rome and using religion as a powerful force to maintain his rule.

It is also within the religious-political context of the empire that the Gospel of Mark is penned.[5] Scant scholarly work has been written on Mark that sees the narrative within this political context. Most works on Mark have concentrated on other concerns, for example, theology, audience, literary criticism. But the narrative itself details conflicts at various levels that offer a clue to understanding its political nature. This does not mean that the conflicts in Mark are solely political; they are also theological. Yet the religious conflicts that take place, particularly between Jesus and the religious leaders, must also have political dimensions. It is well known that the religious leaders of Jerusalem were the political leaders and puppets of the Roman Empire. Their seeming cooperation with Rome kept them in power in Jerusalem. Thus the conflicts with Jesus were as much political as theological. The Gospel is penned within this hotbed of politics.

In a refreshing approach to Mark, Richard Horsley reminds us that Mark's story was highly political and focused on God's covenant renewal of Israel in the face of Roman imperial power and oppression. He views Mark's story of Jesus as one of a prophet in the line of Moses and Elijah, who sets about starting a movement among the villages and countryside of Galilee in an attempt to bring about a politically and economically egalitarian covenantal community. We owe much to Horsley's work in this area, which sheds great light on the politics of Rome and the political message of Jesus and Mark's Gospel, but space precludes a through discussion of his book.[6]

Yet Horsley's otherwise thought-provoking work on Mark has two serious flaws. First, Horsley takes Christology out of the equation, even denying that the narrative is about Christology. This is of course a radical move away from the historical interpretation of Mark and ignores a major, if not the major, impetus of the narrative. Second, Horsley suggests that the Gospel is not about individual discipleship, as most other Markan scholarship has argued. While I would agree with him that Western society does tend to read the narrative from an individualistic perspective, to deny the narrative's impact on individual discipleship is again to deny the history of the interpretation of Mark and indeed how Mark may have been first understood within the first century. My question concerning Horsley's arguments is, Do we need to take Christology and discipleship out of the discussion in order to see the political component of the Gospel of Mark? Or is it possible to view the narrative of Mark as utilizing Christology to speak both to individuals about their discipleship and to the political environment in which a community of individual disciples would live? In other words, should we not see the story that Mark tells as a christological story that involves both shaping character ethics in individuals, namely, discipleship, and also group political formation?

In this essay I will argue that we can view Mark's narrative as a story of character and political formation addressed to communities of followers of Jesus, who were challenged in their allegiance to Jesus by the continual existence of the power of Rome via the imperial cult. The paper focuses on the central section of Mark, often called the discipleship section, to demonstrate that the narrative works in two ways. First, the narrative forms character in community by spelling out the ethics of the kingdom of God as expressed through Jesus' example and teachings. Second, this community of character, to borrow a phrase from Hauerwas, must be seen as a political community that, though powerless in the face of imperial Rome, finds power in its understanding of God's coming rule, its character and political formation as a group, and its resistance to the politics of Rome through its beliefs and actions as an alternative political community.

This chapter is based on a number of assumptions about Mark's narrative that cannot be thoroughly argued here. First, the Gospel of Mark must be seen as a narrative whole, as Horsley argues. While redaction criticism can offer much insight into the traditions passed on about the historical Jesus, a concern for the narrative whole must be prominent in one's understanding of what the narrative is doing in the life of the community.[7] Second, the structure of Mark suggests that the narrative may well have served in some way as a manual of discipleship. Unlike Horsley, I see the structure of Mark as a christological structure intended to lead to faithful discipleship. The movement of the Markan Jesus from baptism to temptation to preaching the gospel of God to crucifixion and then to resurrection may very well have reflected the life and hope of Jesus' faithful followers, particularly as they challenged the political authority of the imperial government through their confession, their baptism, and their practices. Third, these two assumptions lead to one other understanding of the function of the narrative of Mark. If, as most would agree, Mark's presentation would have been in an oral setting, the narrative, as it progresses in the hearing of the audience, works to form a symbolic existence, an escape, for a community threatened by the power of Rome.[8] This symbolic world can serve as a political alternative to the political power of Rome, even though the threat of power of the latter was more real for earliest Christians.

Given these assumptions, we might see more clearly the intention of the narrative to use Christology to speak to the situation of the Gospel's audience and to offer them internal ethics regarding how they ought to live in community.

Social Identity and Character Formation
via the Gospel of Mark

There have been many and various contributions made to the study of New Testament ethics. Some scholars have been concerned with identifying a Markan ethic.[9] Most of these deal with the ethical teachings found in Mark, a very helpful start to understanding the ethics of the Gospel. However, more light might possibly be shed on the ethics of Mark if we concentrate more on how character is formed through the hearing of the narrative itself.

In order to accomplish this task, I have found somewhat helpful the methodology from social sciences known as social identity theory.[10] Originally developed in the early seventies, this theory focuses on group identity and how individuals who join a group are quickly socialized into the norms of that particular group. The individual who joins a group finds a new identity shaped and formed by the norms of the group. Through these norms particular groups view the world and form their attitudes toward the world and their own existence in the world. Sociologist Rupert Brown has defined norms as "a scale of values which defines a range of acceptable (and unacceptable) attitudes and behaviors for members of a social unit."[11] He goes on to say that norms "specify, more or less precisely, certain rules for how group members should behave and thus are the basis for mutual expectations among group members.[12] Norms, then, are not rules but can embody rules or ethics. Norms are ways of expressing the virtues of particular groups and function to keep the group's sense of its own identity, particularly in opposition to other groups or the outside world in general.

Before applying this methodology to Mark 8:27–10:52 and to how this section of the narrative functions to form character in individual disciples, we need to have some general understanding of the Christology of Mark's narrative, something Horsley sees as problematic. While space prevents a thorough discussion of this, two things can be said about the Markan Christology with a great degree of certainty.[13] First, Jesus' actions in Mark function as actions of/for God. Jesus speaks and acts for God as the inaugurator of God's coming rule. This indeed pushes the political struggle between Jesus and the religious leaders as they clash over who speaks and acts for God.[14] But at the same time we can also see that Jesus' teachings and miracles function as apocalyptic signs of God's invasion into the world, an invasion that spells defeat for the enemies of God, including the empire of Rome.

Coinciding with the presentation of Jesus as apocalyptic actor for God is the presentation of Jesus as a paradigm for faithful discipleship.[15] His submission to baptism, his facing temptations, his proclamation of the gospel of God and the coming kingdom of God in word and action, his persecution and death, and his vindication are the model of true faithfulness for believers in the Markan community.

This is further highlighted when we understand Jesus' use of the enigmatic title "Son of Man." While much debate has taken place concerning the use of this title by the historical Jesus, it seems reasonable to hold to the idea that his consistent use of "Son of Man" is in reference to himself and signifies, at least in part, that he is the paradigmatic human being who is bringing into existence a new community of individuals whose character is formed by his example.[16] Jesus, then, is both the authority and the norm of social/political identity.

This is of particular interest for our investigation of the so-called passion predictions of Jesus and the pericopes tied to them. We might view these sayings, in which Jesus specifically predicts his death at the hands of others, as paradigmatic possibilities, or norms, for disciples. While Jesus does not explicitly state that each follower will incur the wrath of Rome, the political possibility and probability of such an end is ever more increased when the disciples choose to model their lives after him, that is, when character is formed via the norms of Jesus. Certainly Jesus defines his own death differently from those of his followers (see 10:45), but he nonetheless calls them to take up the cross and follow him.

In this way, Jesus becomes the norm for social/political identity in the Markan community. His invitation to follow him is directly linked to taking up the cross of death, and thus his sacrificial death, as he defines it in Mark 10:45, becomes the norm that forms social identity for disciples.[17]

Thus community is formed as each disciple enters the community of the risen Jesus through the initiation of baptism and their identity is formed by the norms of that community, norms represented by the character of Jesus. And from this identity formation develops character formation, which associates the new follower more with the community of Jesus and less with the larger outside religious and political culture. Outsiders become insiders and are continually formed by the group's identity. This, of course, creates cohesion with other insiders and discord with outsiders.

The text of Mark 8:27–10:52 has been the focus of much scholarly discussion; most scholars agree that these verses form a literary unit. Scholars have always noticed the particular repetitive pattern of 8:31–38; 9:30–50; and 10:32–45. Each of these contains a form of Jesus' prediction of his impending arrest, trial, death, and resurrection, the characterization of the disciples as miscomprehending these predictions, and some sort of corrective teaching by Jesus in which he calls them to understand his mission and their role in his mission. It is in these teachings that we find social identity formation and character formation to be the strongest.[18] Before moving to discuss the specifics of this character formation, we need to view this pericope within the framework of the narrative's portrayal of crucifixion as political resistance.

The exchange between Jesus and Peter in Mark 8:27–33 sets the tone for that which follows. After rebuking Peter for his misunderstanding the role of the messiah, Jesus also makes clear to the crowd and the disciples that following him brings tremendous costs. His invitation to follow him is coupled with the dominant symbol of discipleship in Mark: taking up the cross and following Jesus. There are no other options for followers but to take up the cross of death and follow Jesus. While modern Christians "spiritualize" the text to mean any form of suffering, the hearers of Mark's narrative would have taken this statement very literally. Mark's Jesus is set to go to Jerusalem to challenge the authorities, and in doing so, he is giving himself up for death by Roman execution.

Through this narrative, the Gospel communicates to the audience that crucifixion, not acquiescence to the political norms of the Roman Empire, becomes the norm of faithful existence and a form of internal cohesion and resistance against the politics of Rome. The cross, a symbol of Roman tyranny, becomes the internal symbol of community life and faithfulness for the community of Mark. In sociological terms, the cross is the norm of the community of Mark and of character and political formation. The cross is a reminder of Jesus' intentional movement toward Jerusalem and his challenge to the Jewish and Roman authorities—in other words, a political challenge. The result of this challenge is his death by crucifixion, which comes to serve as a form of resistance to the political power of Rome. The practice of crucifixion was the supreme form of deterrence against rebellion and insurrection against the state, but in the narrative of Mark, it becomes the symbol of normality, character formation, and political resistance and formation. By this symbol allegiance to Jesus and his message is tested.

The intentional casting of the cross as a positive metaphor of faithful discipleship certainly has strong political meaning as a form of both criticism of and resistance to the Roman Empire. Most historians agree that, of all the groups under Roman authority, the Jews in particular had options in choosing how they would relate to the power of Rome, particularly the imperial cult. First, there was the option of full cooperation, which can be seen in the Herodians. Second was the option of acquiescence, which some Pharisees took and which allowed them to continue to practice their ethical and religious teachings. The third option, seeking to overthrow Rome through violent revolution, was chosen by the Zealots. A fourth option, withdrawal, was illustrated by the Essene community.

These options may have also been available to early followers of Jesus, but Mark implicitly denies any of these choices as faithful to the norms of Jesus. Indeed, the only choice for the community of Jesus is to confront the politics of Rome—not to consent to their authority—through submission to the cross as a symbol of the power, not of Rome, but of God. In this way, the believers are formed by the character of the community to embrace the cross as a symbol of God's coming kingdom.

The cross as the norm of the community, moreover, is symbolic of the internal ethic of the community. In his own death on the cross, the Markan Jesus gives his life for many (10:45). Thus his crucifixion is not simply a political statement. It is also an ethical action that forms the norms of character formation in the community of faith. This character formation is spelled out in 8:27–10:52.

Obviously we cannot perform a detailed exegesis of this central pericope of Mark, and so I offer here a categorizing of virtues expressed through this passage that become the norms for insiders. These character traits form a political community who view themselves in opposition to that which is present in the outside world and culture of the Roman Empire.

Service, not political domination, is the norm of collective relationships in the community of character. Mark's Jesus again serves as the paradigm of character formation as he claims to give his life for others (10:45). In doing so, he sets forth the norm of character formation in the Markan community. This ethic of service also calls for a subversive reversal of status within the new covenantal community. The invasion of God in the coming of Jesus into the narrative world of Mark brings challenge to the rule of power, particularly that of Roman power.

The social identity of Mark's community is, therefore, to be a community in which imperial ideas of authority are cast out and replaced by a new ethic of service. The political symbol of Roman power and domination, the cross, now becomes the symbol of service in the community (8:34),[19] and the pattern of lordship practices among the ἔθνη are to be replaced by the service demonstrated by the Son of Man, who gives his life as a ransom for the many (10:32–45). One who seeks to be great in the present rule of God, then, must become a servant (διάκονος) of all (9:35; 10:43) and a slave (δοῦλος) of all (10:44). Service in the present rule of God, then, is viewed as true greatness.

This ethic is in direct opposition to the ubiquitous patronage system of the Roman Empire, in which actions by a client are done so that a patron will act in return for the benefit of the client.[20] Jesus' statement that the norms of his community are in direct opposition to those of the ἔθνη, who "lord" over one another, subverts the dominant social system of the empire, replacing it with humility and service. In this way, the norms of the Markan narrative serve as subversive socialization for the initiated who have become accustomed to the norms of the empire.

Inclusive welcoming, not exclusion based on status, is the norm of community formation. The discussion of who was the greatest among the Twelve prompts Jesus to take unto himself a child and declare that faithfulness to Jesus and to his God is found in the actions of welcoming a child, perhaps representing those seen as weak or of lowly status. The language fits the idea of social welcoming and hospitality in the first century, which would have been extended to friends and family.[21] The child, possibly representing the fellow believer,[22] is to be welcomed by other followers of Jesus.

Jesus further attacks the exclusive actions of his own disciples in 9:38–41. John, in what may be taken as self-seeking praise, reports to Jesus his action of preventing someone from exorcising demons "because he was not following us" (9:38). Jesus refuses this exclusion and commands John not to stop him. John seems to fail on two counts. First, John puts himself in the place of authority that only the appointed Son, Jesus, is recognized as taking. Second, he assumes that doers of the will of God must be those who follow him. Jesus' rebuke of him gives way to character formation in the community, calling for welcoming, not exclusion.

Roman society, both in the republic and then in the imperial period, was built on a distinct class structure. Of course, wealth was an important factor in determining the class in which one found oneself. This strict system helped to maintain the practice of patronage, through which clients were held down. Moreover, this class structure prevented social mobility, which meant that the classes maintained a degree of pedigree and segregation, preventing social interaction between the classes, except when necessary.

Jesus rebuffs this standard of exclusion by declaring that the weakest of a society must find inclusion in the community of Jesus. The practice of such inclusion may have been shocking to new members, who may very well have struggled with letting go of their status over another within the new community. Yet the norm of the community was one of inclusion, the welcoming of all. This is illustrated in the life of Jesus himself as he welcomes the marginalized and as he institutes the community meal. Meals would certainly have served as symbols of exclusion, as the menu of the wealthy was more elaborate and indulgent than that of the poor.

Humility, not imperial power, is the norm for making and keeping peace. The notorious Pax Romana ultimately could be maintained only through the military power of the emperor to exhort his legions upon the subjugated peoples of the empire. Greatness was classified by this power, and weakness and suffering were viewed as detriments to the honor, peace, and unity of the Roman Empire.

In rejecting this, the Markan Jesus calls his followers to "be at peace with one another" (9:50). Yet such peace is not achieved through one being dominant over another. Rather, in rejection of dominance, the community of Mark is formed by the norms of humility. This may be of particular importance if the poison of exclusion had entered into the Markan community. Perhaps like the disciples themselves, some had not remained loyal to the message of Jesus and thus had stumbled in their faith. Others within the community may have considered themselves as greater than these, thus creating a "spiritual" class system in which they "argued with one another who was the greatest" (9:34). Jesus' admonition of the Twelve's prideful and exclusivist attitudes speaks to the community about the norms of living in peace, a peace sustained by humility and welcoming, not by force and exclusion.

Simplicity and communal sharing of possessions, not indulgence, are the economic norms of the community. Jesus' encounter with the rich man who seeks eternal life (10:17–22) serves the audience of Mark as instruction on the use and possession of worldly goods in the community of Jesus. The man desires eternal life and, upon hearing Jesus state the commandments, which he claims to have kept, the man assumes that all is well. Yet Jesus calls him to live out his faith by selling his many possessions and giving the money to the poor—a choice he cannot make.

The story does not reveal how this man came about his wealth. We do not even know he is wealthy until he walks away (10:22). So why does Jesus pick this man to issue this demand? Perhaps this man has gained his possessions through some form of oppression of others. More certainly we can assume that he has neglected caring for others by hoarding his wealth, since he cannot give up what he has on earth to gain eternal life.

How might this exchange be heard by the audience of Mark? At one level, the narrative calls those with possessions to use these to provide for the needs of those poor in the community. Those in the community of Jesus who have wealth must relinquish their control over their own wealth and give it to the community to be used to care for those in need. Yet there also may be something said here concerning the issue of status in the community.

Wealth in the Roman Empire was normally viewed as the ticket to power, particularly political power. The wealthy classes, senatorial and equestrian, used their wealth to gain and keep their political power. Moreover, because of their wealth, they viewed themselves as superior to the lower classes in intelligence and ethical conduct.[23] The joining of the Jesus movement demanded a renunciation of one's wealth as a tool of power and called for one to use those possessions for the good of the community.

Jesus again serves as the norm, but we also see the disciples themselves expressing the norm of character formation in the community. Peter's declaration that they have left all to follow Jesus triggers Jesus to respond with the assurance of reward for his sacrifice (10:28–31). In this way, the Markan Jesus offers to the audience an assurance of provisions in the kingdom of God.

The virtues that the narrative of Mark communicates to the audience under Roman authority are modeled by Jesus in the narrative and become the norms for forming a community of discipleship. Christology becomes the force through which character is formed as each person joins the community and is quickly socialized by the norms of Jesus. Within the political framework of the Roman Empire, the virtues of service, inclusion, humility, and economic simplicity become the norms that set Mark's community apart from the Roman culture, which places value on status, domination, power, and wealth. Through the narration of the Jesus story, then, the Gospel of Mark forms a social movement of character that counters the politics of the empire.

Social Movement Theory and Political Formation via the Gospel of Mark

Western Christianity, since the Reformation and then the Enlightenment, has privatized religion. In the case of the Reformation, Luther and others were looking for a more inward religion, one in which the individual found meaning in his relationship to God. With the Enlightenment thinkers, religion needed to be marginalized to the private world of the individual, among other reasons, to prevent religion from becoming a cause for bloodshed.

This privatization of Christianity seems to be in direct opposition to the original call of Jesus, who, although calling *individuals* to follow him, called them to a social community in which they were formed by his character and in which they found meaning and identity. This is seen in Mark primarily in the calling of disciples and in Jesus' declaration that those who do the will of God are part of his family. In this way, the Christian community carried forth a socialization of individuals to form their lives by the norms of Jesus and his followers. This process of socialization created a social movement that was an alternative to the society outside the group.

"Social movements," as one sociologist has put it, "are products of the interaction of people mutually influencing each other."[24] Within these movements, individuals are formed by the norms of the group to share activities and beliefs about the group and the society in which the group exists. The movement will have "perceptions of what is wrong with the society, the culture, or the institution, and what can and should be done about it."[25] In response, the movement will develop "collective action," which implies "discontent with an existent situation and some desire to create a new one."[26]

Even a cursory reading of Mark will convince us that the community formed by the Markan Jesus fits the ideas of social movement and collective action. Certainly we cannot see such collective action in modern terms, but the creation of an alternative community, whose norms are counter to the empire, is a form of collective action in and of itself. Moreover, seeing the community of Jesus as a social movement does not negate the theological impetus of Mark, nor does it reduce the movement of Jesus simply to a social movement apart from its apocalyptic thrust. Indeed, we must remember that the social and political situation of Rome was such that religion permeated society and politics. Thus religion might be seen as the power force behind the social and political movement narrated in the Gospel of Mark, but certainly not separate from it. Whatever conclusions we reach concerning this apparent dichotomy, it should be plain to all that Mark's portrayal of Jesus forming a community of followers fits the definition of a social movement.

In this regard, the invitation to discipleship offers an alternative social and political existence to those who choose to take up the cross and follow Jesus. This does not mean that this group exists as an equal or challenging power over against the political powers of the Roman Empire, but it does exist in opposition to Rome because of its beliefs, activities, and norms. The narrative understands the power of Rome, power to put to death the founder of the movement and power to put to death those who follow. But the character formation communicated through Mark offers a form of protest against the political power of Rome, a protest empowered by the divine presence. In this way, the radical norms of Jesus become powerful collective actions that offer an alternative view of politics to the politically disinherited.

Translating Mark's Character and Political Formation into the Twenty-first-Century American Political Context

Since the time of Constantine and the rising dominance of Christianity in the West, the "established church" has not experienced much confrontation from political authorities.[27] For Constantine, the sacred symbol of Christ, the XP, became the symbol of earthly power and might. In essence, this meant that a shift took place from viewing the cross as a symbol of God's power through selfless discipleship to seeing the cross as a power by which to conquer through violence and oppression. Christianity then moves from the marginalized alternative community of character and political formation to the dominant symbol of power in the West.[28] This power existed throughout the medieval period as religion and politics were wedded together to keep order in society.

During the Enlightenment, religion and politics began an acrimonious separation. Indeed, democracy in the United States, influenced by Enlightenment principles, adopted the ideal of the separation of church and state. Deistic founders of this country ensured that though religion was important, one religion ought not to be favored over another. Indeed, as is well known, the Constitution never mentions God and there is certainly no reference to Jesus. The founding fathers most certainly intended to establish the politics of this nation in separation from any one religion.

While this is true, the current political context in the United States has given Christians pride of place. Despite some on the Christian Right claiming one form

of persecution or another, and despite claims that the American culture has
become less Christian, whether the media, leftist politicians, or liberal judges are
at fault, Christian ideas still pervade our culture and particularly our politics. This
is not bad in and of itself, but for the most part the production and publication
of these ideas are monopolized by the so-called Christian Right. This has caused
our alleged Christian culture to see Christianity as a religion of power, wealth,
and violence instead as one of humility, generosity, and nonviolent peace building. In a very real sense, power has become the religion of our culture, a culture
some often claim to be Christian.

So how are we to translate the message Mark, originally addressed to a marginalized Christian community oppressed by the empire, to a Christian community that has pride of place in the American republic? Can the first-century
political message speak to the political formation of twenty-first-century American Christians? I think it can.

Mark is well known for portraying humanity within two separate spheres of
existence: insiders and outsiders. The irony of the story is that often those who
might be insiders very much resemble outsiders. In other words, while some
think they are insiders, the text will often expose them as outsiders. This is particularly true with the disciples.[29] While debates continue over the literary purpose of Mark's characterization of the Twelve, a reasonable reading of the text
demonstrates that they often, very often, do not understand Jesus or his mission.
In fact, their motives and actions suggest that they are working in opposition to
Jesus, declaring that he will not be put to death, believing that they will be powerful in the coming kingdom, and taking up the sword in the face of Jesus' nonviolent actions. They are very often portrayed as working against Jesus' character
and political formation, even though they are privy to inside information.

This rhetorical device serves the audience in two ways. First, it continually
reminds them that Jesus, rather than Jesus' disciples, is the paradigm of character and political formation. Second, the presentation of the disciples as insiders
who act like outsiders serves as a continual challenge to the audience of the narrative, in all times and places, not to assume that they are insiders. If those closest to Jesus fail in their understanding and in their actions, then others may fail
as well. The audience of Mark's story, then, cannot subdue the narrative for its
own benefit or support for its own political agenda. Rather, the narrative of Jesus
works to subdue the audience, even rebuke the audience, reminding them that
the character and politics of Jesus, service, inclusion, humility, and simplicity are
the norms. Just when an audience thinks they have the text understood, the narrative Jesus gives correction to their misunderstanding.

How does this speak to the current political situation of the American democratic process, in which Christianity is often used as a tool of power? In other
words, how do we face the onslaught of a political world in which an American
form of Christianity dominates the political landscape, in particular, one that
seems to claim truth to the exclusion of other religious perspectives, including others who practice various forms of Christianity? Does Mark's narrative offer help?

First, Mark's story is a continual reminder that insiders can be outsiders and that the problem is in not understanding when you are in and when you are out.[30] Those who claim to be Christian and yet are formed by contradictory character and social norms are not formed by the politics of the Markan Jesus, but by the politics of power and empire. This challenges Christians of various sides of the political debates not to assume they are privileged with knowing the truth or with having the last word on moral values, for such may not be the case. Insiders might very well be outsiders, and the only way to know one's place is in measuring one's character against the social norms of the Jesus community.

Second, for those who claim to be insiders because they claim to know the will of God, the ending of Mark's narrative points them back to the beginning.[31] From a literary perspective, the disciples in Mark never do reach the point of understanding the mission and message of Jesus and must continually return to hear the story again and be shaped by it. This is really the purpose of Mark's narrative, to be an echoing call to faithfulness. In this sense, Christian character must still be shaped and reshaped by this story. Through this reshaping, the story forms a community that is more in line with the character of Jesus than with the wider culture.

Third—this follows the other two and is in fact a determining factor in completing the other two—we must see ourselves as the blind man in Mark 10, who in juxtaposition with James and John, who ask for seats of authority and power, simply asks to see. At this point James and John are far from the kingdom of God, and the blind man is close to it. Their blindness to the service, humility, simplicity, and inclusion practiced by Jesus causes them to be the true epitome of those who claim to be insiders, but are truly outsiders. The blind man serves as the stock character of what it means to seek in the community of faith a continual recognition of our blindness and to cry for Jesus to heal us.

Religion will always influence politics, and there is nothing inherently evil about this reality. Indeed, removing religion from politics might be impossible. As Jefferson is often quoted as saying, "No nation has ever yet existed or been governed without religion." But those of us who claim Christianity as our religion must take great care to have our eyes continually open to the character ethics that are the norms of God's kingdom. Allegiance to Jesus and his politics, and not allegiance to the politics of the state, is primary. The church must find its identity as an alternative political community in which individuals are formed not by power, greed, exclusion, and self-interests, but by the norms of Jesus.

Notes

1. A recent book by former U.S. president Jimmy Carter, *Our Endangered Values: America's Moral Crisis* (New York: Simon & Schuster, 2005), argues this very point.
2. A good resource on the current debate about the role of religion in America politics is the collection of essays in E. J. Dionne Jr. et al., *One Electorate under God? A Dialogue on Religion and Politics* (Washington: Brookings Institution, 2004).
3. It often seems to be ignored, particularly by the media, that Martin Luther King's nonviolent civil rights movement was based on his religion. His speeches and

writings, containing many biblical references and allusions, support his under-standing that his political and social movement needed a religious basis.

4. See for example S. R. F. Price, *Rituals and Power: The Roman Imperial Cult in Asia Minor* (Cambridge: Cambridge University Press, 1984).

5. Biblical scholars are well aware of the debates over the dating of Mark. Without offering justification here, I hold to the view that the Gospel was written some-time between 68 and 71 CE. There is also some debate as to the province of Mark's intended audience. Brian J. Incigneri, *The Gospel to the Romans: The Set-ting and Rhetoric of Mark's Gospel* (Leiden: Brill, 2003), argues that Mark was written in 71 to Christians in Rome who were facing threats of persecutions after Titus, the son of Emperor Vespasian, returned from his destruction of Jerusalem and the temple.

6. R. A. Horsley, *Hearing the Whole Story: The Politics of Plot in Mark's Gospel* (Louisville, KY: Westminster John Knox, 2001). For a serious critique of Hors-ley's work, see R. H. Gundry, "Richard A. Horsley's *Hearing the Whole Story*: A Critical Review of Its Postcolonial Slant," *JSNT* 26.2 (2003): 131–49.

7. Obviously I do not desire at this point to enter into the debates about the his-torical Jesus. While such discussions are necessary for understanding how the writer of Mark interprets the traditions, I am more concerned with the world in and in front of the narrative.

8. Some debate has taken place concerning the situation of the Markan audience. Most scholars tend to see that audience as a persecuted community and rely on the narrative itself to supply this evidence. I am of the opinion that this was the case for the Markan community. See the arguments in J. Marcus, *Mark 1–8*, AB 27 (New York: Doubleday, 1999), 28–29.

9. See, for example, D. O. Via, *The Ethics of Mark's Gospel: In the Middle of Time* (Philadelphia: Fortress, 1985).

10. See Henri Tajfel, *Differentiation between Social Groups: Studies in the Social Psy-chology of Intergroup Relations* (London: Academic Press, 1978); H. Tajfel, *Human Groups and Social Categories: Studies in Social Psychology* (Cambridge: Cambridge University Press, 1981); J. C. Turner et al., *Rediscovering the Social Group: A Self-Categorization Theory* (Oxford: Basil Blackwell Press, 1987).

11. Rupert Brown, *Group Processes: Dynamics within and between Groups*, 2nd ed. (Oxford: Blackwell, 2000), 56.

12. Brown, *Group Processes*, 56.

13. Significant works on Mark's Christology include the following: William Wrede, *Das Messiasgeheimnis in den Evangelien* (Göttingen: Vandenhoeck & Ruprecht, 1963 [ET: *The Messianic Secret*, trans., J. C. G. Greig; {London: James Clarke, 1971}]); Johannes Schreiber, "Die Christologie des Markusevangeliums: Beobachtungen zur Theologie und Komposition des zweiten Evangeliums," *ZTK* 58 (1961): 154–83; Leander E. Keck, "Mark 3:7–12 and Mark's Christol-ogy," *JBL* 84 (1965): 341–58; Vernon K. Robbins, "The Christology of Mark" (PhD diss., University of Chicago, 1970); Theodore J. Weeden, *Traditions in Conflict* (Philadelphia: Fortress, 1971); Eduard Lohse, "Apokalyptik und Chris-tologie," *ZNW* 62 (1971): 48–67; Norman Perrin, "The Christology of Mark: A Study in Methodology," *JR* 51 (1971): 173–87 (reprinted in Norman Perrin, *A Modern Pilgrimage in New Testament Christology* [Philadelphia: Fortress, 1974], 104–21); Otto Betz, "The Concept of the So-Called 'Divine Man' in Mark's Christology," in *Studies in New Testament and Early Christian Literature: Essays in Honour of Allen Wikgren*, ed. D. Aune (Leiden: Brill, 1972); Etienne Trocmé, "Is there a Markan Christology?" in *Christ and Spirit in the New Tes-tament: In Honour of C. F. D. Moule*, ed. B. Lindars and S. Smalley (Cambridge: Cambridge University Press, 1973), 3–13; Robert Tannehill, "The Gospel of

Mark as Narrative Christology," *Semeia* 16 (1979): 57–95; Philip G. Davis, "'Truly This Man Was the Son of God': The Christological Focus of the Markan Redaction" (PhD diss., McMaster University, 1979); Jack Dean Kingsbury, *The Christology of Mark's Gospel* (Philadelphia: Fortress, 1983); M. Eugene Boring, *Truly Human/Truly Divine: Christological Language and the Gospel Form* (St. Louis: CBP Press, 1984).

14. On this see C. D. Smith, "'This Is My Beloved Son: Listen to Him': Theology and Christology in the Gospel of Mark," *HBT* 24:2 (2002): 53–86.

15. On this, see P. Davis, "Christology, Discipleship, and Self-Understanding in the Gospel of Mark," in *Self-Definition and Self-Discovery in Early Christianity*, ed. D. Hawkin and T. Robinson (Lewiston, NY: Mellen, 1990), 101–19.

16. Horsley sees the "Son of Man" title as either only a self-reference by Jesus or as a figure who will come in the future. Yet it seems better to see the phrase as titular and as a reference to Jesus, both in his humanity and in his state of future vindication. In Mark, Jesus is the human one who will be vindicated by God.

17. R. B. Hays, *The Moral Vision of the New Testament* (San Francisco: Harper-Collins, 1996), makes similar arguments.

18. This does not mean that other teaching passages are less important. But what seems to be going on in Mark 8–10, particularly in the specific passages mention above, is a clarifying of the basis for discipleship actions.

19. Hays is right to argue that in Mark the cross is the norm of discipleship (*Moral Vision*, 84). Certainly it is symbolic of the servant community and indeed the possible suffering and persecution that may be upon Mark's audience.

20. On patronage in the ancient world, see Andrew Wallace-Hadrill, ed., *Patronage in Ancient Society* (New York: Routledge, 1989), and Richard P. Saller, *Personal Patronage under the Early Empire* (New York: Cambridge University Press, 1982).

21. Bruce J. Malina and Richard L. Rohrbaugh, *Social Science Commentary on the Synoptic Gospels* (Minneapolis: Fortress, 1992), 237; Craig A. Evans, *Mark 8:27–16:20* (Dallas: Word, 2001), 62.

22. On this see Larry W. Hurtado (*Mark* [Peabody, MA: Hendrickson, 1983], 153), who suggests that "in my name" implies the child to whom Jesus refers is the fellow servant. Evans (*Mark 8:27–16:20*), 62, sees this saying in a context of mission, and the terminology of welcoming in the name of Jesus supports this.

23. J. A. Shelton, *As the Romans Did: A Sourcebook in Roman Social History* (New York: Oxford University Press, 1988), 10.

24. J. R. Gusfield, *Protest, Reform, and Revolt: A Reader in Social Movements* (New York: John Wiley & Sons, 1970), 2. Gusfield's definition of the social movement is "socially shared activities and beliefs directed toward the demand for change in some aspect of the social order" (2).

25. Gusfield, *Protest*, 2–3.

26. Gusfield, *Protest*, 3.

27. This is not to say that there was a complete absence of confrontation, for we know that during the medieval period and during the Reformation, political leaders often stood in opposition to some form of the church's authority.

28. I am not making a judgment on the church's decision to accept the favored status offered by Constantine and then by Theodosius. While some would argue that this decision was one of great negative significance, I am not sure that any Christian living at the time of Diocletian's persecutions would have turned down the offer of Constantine.

29. Even Jesus' own family are portrayed as "outside" in Mark 3:31–35.

30. Frank Kermode, *Genesis of Secrecy: On the Interpretation of Narrative* (Cambridge, MA: Harvard University Press, 1979), remarks that readers of Mark ought always to see themselves as outsiders. In this way their interpretations are not governed by self-interest or political powers.

31. On this see M. D. Hooker, *Endings: Invitations to Discipleship* (Peabody, MA: Hendrickson, 2003), 25–28.

Chapter 15

Peacemaking Pillars
of Character Formation
in the New Testament

WILLARD M. SWARTLEY

This chapter focuses on NT texts on peace and peacemaking that contribute to moral formation. I locate my methodology within two analytic contributions. The first is that of Johannes A. van der Ven, in his *Formation of the Moral Self*. Van der Ven helpfully identifies alternative paradigms used to conceptualize how formation of the self occurs. The five paradigms are individualism, communitarianism, institutionalism, pluralism, and multiculturalism. The five are not mutually exclusive. For example, communitarianism and multiculturism could be combined, but each brings with it "baggage" from underlying assumptions that determines methodology. Van der Ven analyzes the strengths and weaknesses in each of these educational paradigms, and proposes yet another: *interactionism*, an approach that seeks to combine the "pole of the individual" with the "pole of the community and society."[1]

Further, van der Ven devotes his massive study to six modes of informal and formal education. The informal are discipline and socialization while the formal

This essay, presented at the Society of Biblical Literature in 2003, is an adapted version of chapter 15 in my recent book *Covenant of Peace: The Missing Peace in New Testament Theology and Ethics* (Grand Rapids: Eerdmans, 2006), 399–414. Used with permission. All Scripture quotations are from the NRSV, unless designated otherwise.

are transmission, cognitive development, clarification, and emotional formation.[2] Finally all these converge in a culminating chapter on education for character. His section on "A Narrative Account of Character"[3] is most helpful, for it
joins his contribution to the wider discussion on the interplay between narrative
and character formation and between the practice of virtues and character formation (MacIntyre, Hauerwas). This emphasis underlies my assumptions and
approach in this paper. However, I am interested in the formation not only of
the moral self, but also of the moral ecclesial community.

The second "locating" signal for my essay is the combination of contributions
from Charles Wood's *Formation of Christian Understanding* and Stephen E. Fowl
and L. Gregory Jones's *Reading in Communion*.[4] First, a key point from Fowl and
Jones: "the importance of moral rules is not *independent* of the formation of character in socially-embodied traditions."[5] Second, "The aim of Scriptural interpretation is to shape our common life in the situation in which we find ourselves
according to the characters, convictions, and practices related in Scripture."[6]
They hold that Scripture interpretation "is not only bound up with particular
social contexts, but it is also related to the character of the interpreter."[7]

The canonical shape of Scripture is determinative for my use of Scripture in
this essay. I will not address the historical development of precanonical tradition
or even the significant influences from Jewish and Hellenistic sources.[8] I focus
rather on the NT canon's abundant testimony to peace/peacemaking emphases,
with the conviction expressed by Charles Wood, "The principal aim of Christian
understanding is the knowledge of God. The canon serves chiefly as the criterion
of that knowledge: Whatever we know, or think we know, of God is to be assayed
in the fire of that self-disclosure of God to which scripture as canon attests."[9]

Within this context of methodological approaches and theological convictions for utilizing Scripture for the moral life, I now focus on peace texts in the
NT that are formational of character. The number of occurrences of the noun
peace (*eirēnē*) and the verb *to make peace* (*eirēneuete*) is about 100. Other texts,
while not using the word "peace," are inherently related to peace/peacemaking.[10]

To organize the vast diversity of witness, I utilize the four modes of hermeneutic appeal to Scripture for moral formation proposed by Richard Hays: commands or rules, principles, paradigms, and symbolic world.[11] I shift his order,
however, and begin with the symbolic world. Then I consider three basic paradigms and join principles to the paradigms, since I believe principles are embedded in or develop from paradigms or are derived from the symbolic world. Then
I list "rules or commands," which may be considered principles also when viewed
as normative moral guidelines.

Symbolic World Peace Perspectives

Here I consider five NT textual contributions as most significant: (1) Jesus' seventh beatitude: "Blessed are the peacemakers"; (2) Paul's unique title for God as
"God of peace"; (3) the NT imitation and discipleship texts; (4) Paul's bold claim

that "Christ is our peace"; (5) and the Lamb's war in Revelation. Perhaps we should consider also a sixth: the shape and structure of the Synoptic Gospels' narrative portrait of Jesus' life, death, and resurrection. Hauerwas rightly contends that this "master narrative forms identity for the early Christians:[12] Jesus is the story that forms the church."[13]

(1.) I classify the beatitude, "Blessed are the peacemakers, for they shall be called children of God," as an aspect of the symbolic world of the NT's contribution to Christian moral formation, because I regard it not as a command, but as a blessing to those who are peacemakers. The Beatitudes assume an ecclesial-eschatological context, and as such expound the character of the kingdom of God. They announce a reality that is *present* through the proclamation, life, death, and resurrection of Jesus Messiah. They describe and validate the new gospel reality.

The beatitude is thus an identity-forming declaration. It assumes the gift of the gospel's grace, and it also calls forth *blessedness* for those who receive the gospel of the kingdom. Becoming and being a peacemaker draw on God's gift of grace. Within this context *peacemaking* is also a virtue for God's kingdom people, a value believers cultivate and practice.[14] This beatitude is conceptually linked to the love of enemy command that occurs later in 5:48 and thus connects with the "rule, command" form of moral instruction.

(2. I include in symbolic world the Pauline (plus Hebrews's) frequently used "God of peace" title because it connotes depth in symbolic world. The phrase occurs seven times in Paul, once in Hebrews, and only once outside the NT, in *T. Dan.* 5:2.[15] Five occurrences, including the one in Hebrews, are benedictions:

> 1 Thessalonians 5:23: May the God of peace himself sanctify you entirely; and may your spirit and soul and body be kept sound and blameless at the coming of our Lord Jesus Christ.

> 2 Thessalonians 3:16: Now may the Lord of peace himself give you peace at all times in all ways. The Lord be with all of you.

> Romans 15:33: The God of peace be with all of you. Amen.

> Philippians 4:9: Keep on doing the things that you have learned and received and heard and seen in me, and the God of peace will be with you.

> Hebrews 13:20–21: Now may the God of peace, who brought back from the dead our Lord Jesus, the great shepherd of the sheep, by the blood of the eternal covenant, make you complete in everything good so that you may do his will, working among us that which is pleasing in his sight, through Jesus Christ, to whom be the glory forever and ever, Amen.

Two more are in assurances or promises:

> Romans 16:20: The God of peace will shortly crush Satan under your feet. The grace of our Lord Jesus Christ be with you.

2 Corinthians 13:11: Finally, brothers and sisters, farewell. Put things in order, listen to my appeal, agree with one another, live in peace; and the God of love and peace will be with you.

One is in a moral sanction for order in congregational prophecy:

1 Corinthians 14:33: for God is not a God of disorder, but of peace.

It is indeed significant that Paul so frequently uses this title for God. By comparison, "God of hope" occurs only once (Rom. 15:13) and "God of love" only once—in conjunction with "God of peace" (2 Cor. 13:11). Other similar phrases accentuating divine attributes are absent in Paul but occur in Jewish literature: "the God of wisdom" (*1 Enoch* 63:2; Josephus, *Ant.* XI.64) and "the God of righteousness" (1QM 18:8; *Tobit* 13:7).[16] Mauser rightly notes that Paul's choice of this term likely reflects the Jewish *shalom* benediction.[17] Other attributes of God are not so privileged. Nowhere does "God of wrath" or "God of judgment" occur.[18] In light of the role that "God as warrior" carries in the OT (Exod. 15:3), it is striking that no such appellation for God is found in Paul or any other NT writer.

The favored status of "God of peace" is a key to Paul's larger theology, to his central doctrinal emphases that are intertwined with peacemaking.[19] Insofar as these occurrences, especially the benedictions, are liturgical, they evidence the symbolic world of Paul and early believers. Liturgy fundamentally forms moral consciousness; it is thus one of the most powerful influences upon character formation. Granted, not any one given community of early Christians that received Paul's writings heard more than one or two of these blessing/benedictions, but for the churches a generation later that regarded the Pauline corpus as Scripture, these benedictions entered the life of the community and formed strong moral perception of God identity.

3. The NT texts on *imitation* together with the pervasive emphasis on discipleship form another stream in the symbolic world of the NT that authorizes peacemaking.[20] A discipleship and imitation pattern lies at the heart of the NT. *Imitation* and *discipleship*, grounded in *imitatio Christi* and *Dei* (Eph. 5:2), are the means of forming moral character, which in turn shapes moral identity. In light of point 2 above, that identity includes becoming people of peace, since God is a God of peace. Indeed:

A mimesis pattern lies at the heart of NT thought. . . . Just as world culture generally manifests energy via mimetic desire, so life in the kingdom of God, the new creation, is animated and empowered also by a mimetic model. The key difference is that the lead Model is the new Adam precisely because he was tempted with the acquisitive mimeses in all ways such as we are but did not yield to that mimetic pattern that generates rivalry and violence. Jesus as faithful Servant of the Lord has opened up for us a new world of hope and potential; we are saved by his transforming of our desire. Then we seek to follow in his steps and be conformed to his image.[21]

Commitment to pattern one's life after this model leads to moral and spiritual *practices of formation in daily life*. Such practices shape a person's character into the new creation mimesis, in exchange for the mimesis that leads to rivalry and violence. Participation in a community that seeks faithfulness in discipleship and new creation imitation of Jesus Christ further strengthens the Christian formation of believers committed to this pattern and practice of spiritual discipline.

4. "Christ is our peace" (Eph. 2:14). The dominant contribution of Paul's mission and theology is the actualized eschatological vision of uniting formerly alienated peoples into one body in Jesus Christ. Though Ephesians may be post-Pauline, it sums up well the core of Paul's contribution forged in his life mission and theology, evident especially in Romans 14–15 and 2 Corinthians 8–9, texts in which the relief gift is the material embodiment of the symbolic world that Jew and Gentile are one in Jesus Christ.

Erich Dinkler describes well the central role of Christ in Paul's peacemaking manifesto, in his comment on Ephesians 2:14–18:

> This passage . . . , which posits enmity and peace to be antithetical, marks the crucifixion of Christ as a turning point. It declares Christ to be the bringer of peace, the one providing access to God as well as creating a new unity for those once separated in this world and living as enemies, objectively speaking. The *dual element* of the passage is:
>
> (1) Peace and reconciliation are tied to Jesus Christ in such a way that the cause for peace is anchored in the blood of Christ, in his crucifixion. Peace is constituted through the cross, and at the same time the crucifixion with its offensive character as *skandalon*[22] is interpreted as peace.
>
> (2) Peace as the abolition of enmity carries two dimensions of meaning, though with no clear separation between them: the reconciliation affects the *God-human* relationship, giving the reconciled person free access to God; and it leads to the *unity in the church* of those separated, thus tearing down the walls of enmity. This joining together of peace as gift of God in Jesus Christ to the believers, which grants them access to God, with peace as humanity's unity of racially separated peoples in the body of Christ, is constitutive, that is, foundational to the understanding of *eirene*.[23]

Reconciliation is the outcome of God's peacemaking event through Jesus Christ, incarnating God's love for enemies. "All this is from God, who reconciled us to himself through Christ, and has given us the ministry of reconciliation: that is, in Christ God was reconciling the world to himself, not counting their trespasses against them" (2 Cor 5:18–19). Although this text does not use the word "peace," it contributes to the moral vision of peace because of the firm connection between peace and reconciliation in three other important texts (Rom. 5:1–11; Col. 1:15–22; Eph. 2:14–18). The enactment of this vision becomes the ecclesial moral embodiment that shaped early Christian moral self-understanding. The union of believing Jews and Gentiles in one body in Christ was the formative narrative of the symbolic world that formed Christian self-identity, corporately and personally. As Paul puts it, "And let the *peace of Christ* rule in your hearts, to which indeed you were *called in one body*. And be thankful" (Col. 3:15, emphasis added).

K. Haacker's thesis that Romans is best understood as a "Friedensmemorandum" is sterling perception. Haacker places Paul's peace teaching in a dual setting, the general political ferment that occasioned Romans 13:1–7 (the Claudius Edict of 49 CE expelling Jews—and Jewish Christians—from Rome), and the tensions between Jews and non-Jews, especially as they surfaced in the Christian churches.[24] Given this political context, the Pauline effort to unite Jewish and Gentile Christians into one bond and body in fellowship and love was no small undertaking. Indeed, it was a miracle, empowered by Christ and the Holy Spirit. God's peacemaking, anchored fully in the cross of Jesus Christ, disarmed the powers (Col. 2:15), forgave sins (Col. 1:13–14; Eph. 1:7), and united formerly alienated parties, Jews and Gentiles, in common access to God. Paul's "God of peace" benedictions thus symbolized a concrete ecclesial and moral reality: Christ is our peace, who has made us both one.

The *cosmic* goal of God's peacemaking salvation in Jesus Christ was and is to reconcile all things to God's self "by making peace through the blood of his cross" (Col. 1:20). Paul speaks of being redeemed from under the law and being freed from "the elemental spirits (*stoicheia*) of the universe" (Gal. 4:5, 8–9; see also Col. 2:8, 18–23).[25] The peacemaking victory of the cross has consequence also for the principalities and powers. Believers are freed from their domination. In some texts Christ's victory is portrayed as "destroying [or better, 'rendering powerless'] every rule and authority" (1 Cor. 15:24–28; see 2 Thess. 2:3–11), but other texts speak of a reconciliation of the powers to God's purpose (Col. 1:19–20; Eph. 1:9–10). What is clear in both emphases is Jesus' lordship over the powers.[26]

(5.) A fifth powerful shaping metaphor for early Christians in their moral formation as peacemakers is the imagery from Revelation, commonly referred to as the Lamb's war. Revelation raises several crucial issues for peacemakers. The word *eirēnē* occurs only twice: in the liturgical introit in 1:4, "Grace to you and peace from the one who is and who was and who is to come." Its second use occurs in the dismaying declaration concerning the red horse: "its rider was permitted to take peace from the earth" (6:4). Further, words used relatively seldom elsewhere in the New Testament appear here quite frequently: twice the Lamb makes war in 2:16 and in 19:11, where the warfare is linked with judging "in righteousness."[27]

In what way then does the Lamb's war contribute to the believers' moral formation as peacemakers? What is the role of the Lamb, and how is this related to the warrior on the white horse of 19:11–16? What Revelation contributes to an understanding of peace is that when peace is taken away from the earth, the lives of Jesus' followers confess with heart, soul, and strength that God is sovereign, is alone the One to be worshiped, knowing that through faithful endurance God's victory will shine forth like the sun (see Ps. 37:6), after the present chaos ends and mighty "Babylon" falls. As Elizabeth Schüssler Fiorenza puts it, "The central question of these chapters [4–5] as well as of the whole book is: Who is the true Lord of this world?" And the answer: "The author insists that the 'Lord' of the world is not the emperor but Jesus Christ who has created an alternative reign and community to that of the Roman empire."[28] Revelation forces a choice between loyalty to the "Herrschaft Gottes" or the "Herrschaft Roms" and the only Christian possibility for the Revelator is a decision against the political-religious power of his time.[29]

What role do the saints play in the war and the victory? George B. Caird rightly understands the victory of the Lamb, that is, of Jesus Christ, as prototypical for his followers. In the Lamb's war God triumphs through the slain Lamb; the battle against evil and Rome's tyranny is won by no other weapons than the Lamb slain on the cross and the testimony (*martyria*) of his followers. Commenting on the Song of Moses in 15:2–4, Caird says, "Because [God's] triumph has [now] been won by no other weapons than the Cross of Christ and the martyr testimony of his followers, this song [of the saints] is also the song of the Lamb." As for the warrior on the white horse, it is clear that the name "Word of God" refers to the "sharp sword" tradition of the power of the prophetic word (Isa. 49:2; Heb. 4:12; and Eph. 6:17). Caird thus says that "the only weapon the Rider needs, if he is to break the opposition of his enemies, and establish God's reign of justice and peace, is the proclamation of the gospel."[30]

Revelation also makes clear that when evil spiritual powers control and inspire the actions of earthly rulers, the role of believers is to persevere in trust and worship of God. The believers' refusal to comply with Rome's demands, but rather to commit themselves to suffer persecution and death, is their passive resistance.[31] Their proclamation of God's sovereignty through praise and worship and their identification with the Lamb's war are their means of active resistance. The Lamb is paradigmatic and normative for believers, a model in which one gives one's own life rather than taking another's. The power of the word, cross, and song of praise assures the fall of mighty Babylon, symbol for all deified political power.[32]

Paradigms (and Principles)

Numerous portions of NT Scripture could be cited as "peacemaking pillars" contributing to character formation. I describe three basic paradigms.

1. The gospel narrative as a whole presents Jesus as a paradigm for peacemaking. The manner of his birth, with the angelic proclamation, "Peace on earth" (Luke 2:14), and Jesus' pattern of behavior before the authorities in his passion are the bookends of this peaceable Messiah. This depiction of Jesus is later echoed in the famous *kenosis* hymn in Philippians 2:6–11; in the exhortation to "follow in his steps" (1 Pet. 2:21–23); and again in Hebrews, esp. 2:9; 5:5–10; and 12:2. Jesus exemplifies the paradigm of faithful perseverance in suffering without retaliation. Foundational to the gospel pattern, this emphasis is the core motif in the symbolic world of the gospel.

Within this master paradigm are subparadigms. One is Jesus' sustained teaching of his disciples on *cross, humility,* and *servanthood* in Mark 8:27–10:52, a classic narrative exemplar. In this carefully crafted structure, Mark develops three interrelated themes: Jesus' messianic identity with focus on the Son of humanity who must suffer; the recurring passion-resurrection predictions; and the subsequent recurring teaching on discipleship (8:31–38; 9:31–50; 10:32–45).

Jesus instructs his disciples how they must live if they follow him on this way. The focal images for character formation are taking up the cross, valorizing a child, and living as a servant, in contrast to seeking power, prestige, and position. Concluding his teaching in Mark 9, Jesus commands "to make peace with one another." Drawing on the imagery of well-prepared salted sacrifices (Lev. 2:13), Jesus calls for the self to be purified of evil and ambitious desires and for his followers to live peaceably with one another (*eirēneuete en allēlois,* Mark 9:50d). To live peaceably with one another contrasts to the segment's initial portrait of the disciples disputing with one another over who is the greatest. To walk Jesus' way means giving up rivalry, seeking not to offend "the little one," and striving to live peaceably with one another.[33]

While it is possible to extract principles from Mark's *hodos* ("way") teaching as well as from the paradigm stories of the Good Samaritan and Jesus and the Samaritan woman, they are all better viewed as paradigms, set firmly within the gospel as narrative. This assures that moral principles won't be abstracted to bolster natural wisdom (generic moral values that do not conform to the cruciform gospel narrative). For the *hodos* teachings are embedded in the particular story and identity of Jesus in the Gospels. This roots the moral life christologically. It is inextricably tied to knowledge of God revealed in Jesus Christ.

(2.) The second master paradigm in the NT canon is that of Paul's extensive participation and correspondence parenesis for becoming Christian in character and conduct. Paul uses numerous images to describe the believer's copositioning with Christ. The coidentity with Jesus Christ and fellow believers enables us to learn a new mimetic pattern, one that leads not to rivalry and violence, but to building others up, avoiding scandal, preferring one another, empowering the other, and nonretaliation against evil, in order that as members of the community of the new creation we break the spiral of violence and become the strands of yarn that by God's Spirit are knitted into the display of love, justice, and shalom.[34]

Jim Fodor's critique of Girard's theory speaks specifically to the issue of consequences for the moral life and character formation. Fodor regards Girard's theory of mimesis and generation of violence as too abstract and formal, not sufficiently consequential for understanding the role of mimesis in Christian formation. As he puts it:

> [Girard] does not take the care to elaborate in any great detail the positive, alternative practices, ways of life, or patterns of behavior enjoined by the gospel. But what is finally compelling, I would contend . . . is not the mere idea of nonacquisitive mimesis but how it is that one might become initiated in and apprenticed to a particular way of life that actually manifests non-acquisitive, nonviolent mimesis. In other words, unless and until nonacquisitive desire expresses itself in particular habits of attention, practices,

patterns of behavior, and forms of worship and praise, it is hard for anyone to understand its character, let alone experience its power, be persuaded of its virtues, assess its merits, or gauge its veracity.[35]

Fodor contends rightly that discipleship, peacemaking, participating in Christ, *kenosis,* and mimesis of God's love, for neighbor and enemy, must come to terms with the need for God's empowerment. The matter of *agent* is important. The human will, of one's own efforts, is not able to perform it:

> [A]ny model that separates the will from prayer, contemplation, and dispossession is woefully inadequate. . . . the disciple is not first and foremost one who constructs herself or himself in the process of performance; if that were the case, the meaning of our actions would unavoidably and exclusively terminate in the will's success. Not only that, but given what Girard rightly describes as the competitive, Hobbesian-like character of unregenerate human life, any attempt to extricate ourselves from unredeemed human structures of desire would inevitably fail. We would remain trapped in a never-ending, downward spiral of animosity, conflict, rivalry, and violence.
>
> Discipleship, however, is grounded in God, not in our own will or desire. External autonomous achievement does not secure our status as Jesus' disciples. On the contrary, the disciple's adequacy or excellence or attunement to God lies, in its most determinative sense, outside the agent's control. Our actions, in the final analysis, are grounded in God rather than in our own desires. In that respect human acts of faithfulness always show more than the life of the agent: they show the character of the Creator.[36]

Fodor grounds discipleship in the Trinitarian model of *perichoresis,* the model of God's own peaceable life as the basis of our peacemaking. The atonement in this context is the salvific grounding of our moral life. Echoing themes in this chapter, Fodor says,

> Christian teaching on atonement, discipleship and imitation are inextricably linked with God's work of redemption in Christ. Without being bound to Jesus as the ransomed are bound to their ransomer, without becoming friends of God in Christ, without actually taking up, participating in, being conformed to, and living out an atoning way of life, the whole point of the incarnation is thwarted. In other words, the incarnation is more than just the communication of the *idea* of reconciliation. The incarnation includes actual training and participation in particular peaceable relations and reconciling patterns of existence. It means learning a whole new *idiom,* a completely different set of skills and practices and language games.[37]

(3.c) A third peace paradigm emerges in the gospel's attitude toward government powers. While there are in the NT diverse portraits of the church's stance toward government powers, as Walter Pilgrim has shown,[38] from the stance of the Gospels as an "ethic of critical distancing" to the more "subordinationist ethic" of Paul, it is clear that the Gospels and Paul creatively forge a vision of an alternative socioeconomic-political community. Jesus fulfills Isaiah 52:7, a text quoted or alluded to more than a half dozen times in NT writings. Thus the phrase announcing good news of peace (*euangelizomenos shalom/eirēnē*) influences NT writers more than usually noted. Isaiah 52:7 and Isaiah 61:1–2, quoted by Luke (4:18–19) for Jesus' platform address in the Nazareth synagogue, are strategic to the Gospels' overall theological and ethical emphases.[39] Healings, announcing the gospel, and the downfall of Satan are part and parcel of the gospel of peace. In Acts, Luke sums up the ministry of Jesus: "preaching the gospel of peace through Jesus Christ" (10:36, *euangelizomenos eirēnē dia Iēsous Christou*).[40]

As the book of Acts further demonstrates, the community of Christ testifies to the kingdom of God spreading like strawberry runners, in diverse political, cultural, and economic settings. It breaks barriers that alienate and forms community that the Pax Romana was never able to achieve. As the church lived through numerous faces of persecution, it nonetheless testified to God's peace as an enduring gift for shaping moral life and forming the corporate character of peacemakers. Acts testifies that by God's grace the kingdom of God takes root in diverse settings, even in the empire's capital city.

Thus the new creation, God's people of peace, has its own kingdom mission and agenda. It neither courts nor condemns Rome and the contemporary nations of this world. Nor does it give its main energies to aid or block the imperialistic pacification programs, of which the Pax Romana was a grand model. Rather, the new humanity of Christ's body welcomes people to become "children of peace," freed from the tyranny of the powers in whatever personal, national, socio-economic, political, or ideological guise they manifest themselves.[41] This new humanity, in contrast to the dominant cultural power structures, expends its primary energies building communities of faith, hope, love, and peace.

Further, Luke–Acts shows us a Savior who weeps in lament: if only you would know those things that make for peace (Luke 19:42). It also presents a model of how to witness boldly to the powers. As Cassidy has argued, in Acts Luke's purpose is to encourage believers in their allegiance to Jesus to witness boldly before kings and governors.[42]

Indeed, the history of the faith of God's people, in both the older and younger covenants, witnesses to the survival and flourishing of God's people even amid the collapse of the nation. None of the Caesars of this world, monarchs, or presidents even of democracies is worthy to receive the honor, power, and glory that belong to the Lord God alone. We can be subject to the nation's leaders, because our Liberator, whom we acclaim as mighty Lord, is the Lord of hosts, Lord of the powers.[43]

Rules/Command Derived from the Symbolic World or Embedded in Principles

1. "Love your enemy." Jesus' *command* to love enemies (5:44–45) identifies this moral behavior with identity, namely, being "children of God." This command correlates with the seventh beatitude, which promises "peacemakers" that "they shall be called children of God." *Being* peacemakers and loving enemies are thus

intrinsically linked to God's moral character. Being children of God depends upon Jesus' disciples becoming and being peacemakers who love their enemies. Peacemaking marks those who follow Jesus and are children of God, *his* and *our* heavenly Father.[44]

To love enemies is beyond our human capacity, for our natural response is to retaliate against an enemy act. Rarely does one think of responding in a manner that might convert enmity into friendship! But this is the gospel of Jesus. The Sermon on the Mount stands as the frontispiece of Jesus' proclamation of the kingdom in Matthew. Since the love of enemy command is linked to God's moral character, the teaching is essential to the character formation of Jesus' followers. It is not superfluous to the gospel, but lies at the heart of the gospel.

2. Correlative to Jesus' love of enemy command is the command "not to resist the evil one" and not to "repay evil" for evil." Jesus' teaching appears also in Paul, who likewise unites commands to love the enemy and not to retaliate. The key text is Romans 12:14–21 (with similarity to 1 Pet. 2:18–3:18). The command not to retaliate occurs also in 1 Thessalonians 5:13b, 15: "Be at peace among yourselves. . . . See that none of you repays evil for evil, but always seek to do good to one another and to all."[45]

Gordon Zerbe cites more than thirty texts that witness to some form of non-retaliation, including not cursing, not litigating, forbearing, enduring, and being at peace.[46] Several times, in discussing dual loyalty, with Christ above Caesar,[47] Luise Schottroff rightly perceives that refusal to retaliate and love of enemy are two sides of the same coin:

> Matthew 5:38–41 . . . commands the refusal to retaliate [and thereby announces] as well prophetic judgment of violent persons. . . . As imitators of God, Christians are supposed to confront the enemies of God with his mercies. . . . Loving one's enemy is the attempt to change the violent person into a child of God through a confrontation with the love of God. That is, love of one's enemy can be concretely presented as the prophetic proclamation of the approaching sovereignty of God.[48]

3. Paul exhorts believers to fulfill the command to love the neighbor and to pursue peace. Believers are admonished to be at peace with one another and to seek/pursue peace: Romans 12:18 quoting Psalms 34:19; 1 Thessalonians 5:13; 2 Corinthians 13:11; 2 Timothy 2:22; 1 Peter 3:11; Romans 14:19; see Hebrews 12:14. William Klassen has summarized the "pursuit of peace" and "peace commands and exhortations" texts in Paul, grouping them by categories into diagram form.[49]

The six blocks are separated, three blocks in each, into God's/Christ's peace in the first set, with the various ethical admonitions in the derived second ethical set: have peace with God, with each other, and with all ("Be at peace with God, with fellow believers, with all people, even with outsiders"). By stating that the nature of both God and Christ is peace and peacemaking, the ethical mandates are anchored theologically and christologically.[50] The commands to make or pursue peace (2 Tim. 2:22; 1 Pet. 3:11; Heb. 12:14; Rom. 14:19), recurring throughout the NT, draw upon the symbolic world that describes God's own character and action. Peaceful relationships are desirable and possible because of what God has done for us. God loved us even when we were enemies, and acted in Jesus Christ to make peace with us his enemies (Rom. 5:10). Hence, the command stands not as a law beating us on the head, but as a privilege possible because we are children of God whose work in Jesus Christ is a paradigm for just this pattern of moral response. This is the character of the new person described in many and diverse ways in NT parenesis.

These repeated commands "to make peace" and "to pursue peace" also draw upon the symbolic world that describes God's own character and action. Peaceful relationships are desirable and possible because of what God has done: God loved us even when we were enemies, and acted in Jesus Christ to make peace with enemies (Rom. 5:10). As Ronald Sider has put it: "One fundamental aspect of the holiness and perfection of God is that He loves His enemies. Those who by His grace seek to reflect His holiness will likewise love their enemies—even when it involves a cross."[51] This love of enemy command stands thus not as coercion, but as a privilege possible because we are children of God whose work in Jesus Christ is a paradigm for just this pattern of moral response. This is the new person character described in many and diverse ways in NT parenesis.

Indeed, believers are called to peace (1 Cor. 7:15); to "pursue what makes for peace and mutual upbuilding" (Rom. 14:19); as members of one body they are to make "every effort to maintain the unity of the Spirit in the bond of peace" (Eph. 4:3–6). Further, the peace of God is power that "guards your hearts and your minds in Christ Jesus" (Phil. 4:7; see 1 Thess. 5:23).

Another emphasis to consider is that of Christian virtues. Admonition in Paul to cultivate virtue (often in language of "put on") occurs frequently. Glen Stassen provides us with two table summaries on NT virtues. First, he presents a basic correlation between Jesus and Paul:

Paul's Virtues Parallel the Beatitudes[52]

Jesus' Beatitudes	Paul's Virtues
humility and meekness	humility and gentleness
righteousness	righteousness
mercy	kindness, compassion, love, forgiveness
purity of heart	purity or goodness
peacemaking	peace, tolerance, unity, patience
suffering persecution for justice's and Jesus' sake	endurance
(blessed are you)	joy

The similarity of emphasis is striking. Further, the emphases I listed above under commands or rules may also be considered virtues, for they are actions that flow from formation of character rooted in discipleship and imitation. These are loving enemies, not retaliating, blessing those who curse us, praying for those who persecute us, seeking to overcome evil with good, not avenging ourselves against one who does wrong but deferring to God's judgment, and reconciling with or forgiving one another when wrong is done. Most of these occur more than once in both the Gospels (Jesus) and Paul. Adding these seven to the seven above describes Christian character. Together they form a profile of Christian values and practices.

The profile is even richer in Paul's letters, in his admonition and encouragement. Stassen and Gushee present a listing of virtues that Paul exhorts believers in the churches to emulate. The base list is from Colossians 3:12–17:

Virtues in Paul's Lists[53]

Col. 3:12–17	Phil. 2:2–3	Eph. 4:2–3, 32	Gal. 5:22–23	Rom. 14:17; 15:4–5	2 Cor. 6:4–10
love	love	love	love		
compassion		compassion			
kindness		kindness	kindness		
humility	humility	humility			
gentleness		gentleness	gentleness		
patience		patience	patience		
tolerance		tolerance			
forgiveness		forgiveness			
	unity	unity	unity		
gratitude	like-mindedness				
wisdom					
peace		peace	peace	peace	
				righteousness	righteousness
			joy	joy in the Holy Spirit	joy
				endurance	endurance
				hope	
			goodness		purity
			faithfulness		understanding
			self-control		kindness
					patience

unless IT P's "leader") virtues

As Stassen and Gushee indicate, other NT texts from the Pastorals and Peter's writings both concur with the list above, but also add a few:

> First Timothy 4:12; 6:11; 2 Timothy 2:22; 3:10: 1 Peter 3:8; and 2 Peter 1:5–7 advocate basically the same virtues that we have seen already: love five times, faith three times, righteousness twice, godliness twice, purity and purity of heart, endurance, perseverance, gentleness, peace, harmony, sympathy, compassion, kindness, humility, goodness, knowledge, and self-control. They would add faith to our list of those mentioned twice or more.[54]

This contribution by Stassen and Gushee, together with my analysis of "correspondence" and "imitation" language in regard to John H. Yoder's work in *Politics of Jesus*, profiles Christian character, formation, and living. One significant list overlooked by Stassen and Gushee, and Yoder as well, is in Philippians 4:8, which puts "truth" first, a new entry to the lists above. This virtue is evident also in Ephesians 4:15, where Paul enjoins believers to be "truthing in love" (literal trans.). *Truth* is a significant addition (see also Eph. 4:21, 25) and contrasts with "the lies" at the end of the vice lists.[55] Granted, Paul's phrasing of the virtues in the Philippians text is a bit different, since he sets the virtues in goal-type form: "Whatever is true, whatever is honorable, whatever is just, whatever is pure, whatever is pleasing, whatever is commendable, if there is any excellence and if there is anything worthy of praise, think about these things." Nevertheless, they are generally regarded as virtues by commentators, and as a list resembling Greek virtue lists. Paul, however, connects them directly to Christ and God. The list is prefaced by "the peace of God, which passes all understanding, will keep your hearts and minds in Christ Jesus" (4:7). It is followed by "the God of peace will be with you all" (4:9b). God as "God of peace" frames the virtue list. This feature itself is a stellar expression of my central thesis that God's children seek to be peacemakers because God is the "God of peace," whose love even for enemies transforms people through Jesus Christ into children of peace. This is the foremost truth that the NT invites us to believe and live.

Epilogue

The permeation of the NT with *peace*, including the distinctive appellation "God of peace," signifies a major emphasis in moral formation. Correlated with the love of God and neighbor commands, it is foundational to Christian moral formation. It appears also in the latest written canonical Gospel. The Gospel of John promises to Jesus' disciples peace such as the world cannot give (14:27; 16:33). In John 20 Jesus greets his disciples three times, "Peace be with you" (20:19 end, 21, 26 end). The first two uses preface John's commissioning of his disciples to go forth to "forgive and retain" people's sins. The third use prefaces Thomas's existential encounter with Jesus as "My Lord and my God!"[56]

Indeed, the peace greeting in the epistles is not simply a cultural form[57] but is laden with the long-hoped-for shalom of the messianic age. These greetings in the Gospels culminate a narrative that proclaims fulfillment of the peace of the messianic shalom. Jesus brings that peace and promises his followers, "Peace I leave with you." It remains with us as a gift of grace and task for our vocation (*Gabe und Aufgabe*).

The connection between peace/peacemaking and the formation of virtue may be demonstrated in relation to each person of the Trinity, the *God of peace* in Philippians 4:7–9, the *Christ of peace* in Colossians 3:12–15, and the *Spirit of peace* in Galatians 5:22. These texts make clear the vital connection between the pervasive NT emphasis on peace and character formation, in the cultivation of the virtues that permeate NT writings, whether in the Beatitudes, Pauline exhortation, or the moral instruction of Jesus in the Gospels, such as in Mark 8:27–10:52. The connection is intrinsic to what formation in Christ (2 Cor. 3:18) and "Christ being formed in you" (Gal. 4:19) mean for our lives today. This formation is not limited to the personal sphere of life but consists of the fostering of *shalom* in its iridescent dimensions—personal and corporate in all dimensions of life: material (economics), political, and indeed spiritual.

As Revelation and the "God of peace" benedictions have reminded us, worship consisting of prayer and blessing to God is a cardinal means of orienting our lives to ever increasing moral formation. Quite rightly, Nicholas Wolterstorff addresses the need to renew the authenticity of our worship and liturgy in his excellent contribution to spurring us toward the embrace of justice and peace.[58] A daily commitment to praying the Lord's Prayer—and meaning it—is a helpful beginning to put the quest for peace and justice into divine sovereign perspective. The "Our Father" prayer forms the chiastic center of the Sermon on the Mount, reminding us that empowerment through such communion with God is strategic to living the *gospel peace* of God's reign. For the heavenly Father grants the *blessing* to be formed as and bear the mark of *peacemakers*.

Notes

1. Johannes A. van der Ven, *Formation of the Moral Self* (Grand Rapids: Eerdmans, 1998), 21–31.
2. Van der Ven, *Formation*, 40–337.
3. Van der Ven, *Formation*, 358–60ff.
4. Charles Wood, *The Formation of Christian Understanding: Theological Hermeneutics* (Valley Forge, PA: Trinity Press, 1993); S. Fowl and L. Jones, *Reading in Communion: Scripture and Ethics in Christian Life* (Grand Rapids: Eerdmans, 1991). Both these works are influenced by the contribution of Stanley Hauerwas, especially his *Character and the Christian Life: A Study in Theological Ethics* (San Antonio: Trinity University Press, 1975); *A Community of Character: Toward a Constructive Christian Social Ethic* (Notre Dame, IN: University of Notre Dame Press, 1981); *The Peaceable Kingdom* (Notre Dame, IN: University of Notre Dame Press, 1983).
5. Fowl and Jones, *Reading in Communion,* 10.
6. Fowl and Jones, *Reading in Communion,* 20.
7. Fowl and Jones, *Reading in Communion,* 103.
8. Willard M. Swartley, *Israel's Scripture Traditions and the Synoptic Gospels: Story Shaping Story* (Peabody, MA: Hendrickson, 1994).
9. Charles Wood, *Formation,* 112.

10. For usage and related emphases, see Willard M. Swartley, *Covenant of Peace: The Missing Peace in New Testament Theology and Ethics* (Grand Rapids: Eerdmans, 2006), 42, 191–92.

11. *The Moral Vision of the New Testament: A Contemporary Introduction to New Testament Ethics* (San Francisco: HarperSanFrancisco, 1996), 208–9. See also his discussion of the same in *New Testament Ethics: The Story Retold* (Winnipeg, MB: CMBC Publications, 1998), 32–33.

12. Hauerwas, *Peaceable Kingdom*, 24–30; esp. chap. 5, "Jesus: The Presence of the Peaceable Kingdom," 72–95, and *Community of Character*, chap. 2, "Jesus: The Story of the Kingdom," 36–52.

13. Hauerwas, *Community of Character*, 50. I treat portion of this story under "paradigms."

14. See here Glen Stassen's "Virtues of God's People," chap. 2 in Glen H. Stassen and David P. Gushee, *Kingdom Ethics: Following Jesus in Contemporary Context* (Downers Grove, IL: InterVarsity Press, 2003), 32–54. Alasdair MacIntyre and Stanley Hauerwas are well-known advocates for virtue ethics. Joseph J. Kotva Jr. in *The Christian Case for Virtue Ethics* (Washington, DC: Georgetown University Press, 1996) provides a good explication of just why virtues ethics has returned in ethical discourse. He addresses matters of definition and need, theological links and biblical connections, and finally an appeal for ethicists and Christian believers to commit to virtue ethics.

15. The text here reads:

> Each of you speak truth clearly to his neighbor,
>   and you will not fall into wrath and troublemaking,
> but be at peace, holding to the God of peace.
>   Thus no conflict will overwhelm you.

16. Ulrich Mauser identified these in his manuscript on "God of Peace," later published in a different version as *The Gospel of Peace: A Scriptural Message for Today's World* (Louisville, KY: Westminster/John Knox, 1992). The printed version does not contain these attributes of God. Robert D. Rowe, in *God's Kingdom and God's Son: The Background to Mark's Christology from Concepts of Kingship in the Psalms* (Leiden: Brill, 2002), lists numerous titles for God as king, such as "King of goodness" and phrases such as "glory/spendour of the King" in several Qumran documents (*Songs of the Sabbath Sacrifice, 4QBlessings, Community Rule,* and *Damascus Document*), but "King of peace" does not occur (100–103)! Gideon's naming the altar "Yahweh-*shalom*" (Judg. 6:24) and the messianic title "Prince of Peace" in Isa. 9:6 are the chief precursors to the indeed rare "God of peace" title.

17. Note also Paul's frequent use of grace (*charein*) in salutations (see Mauser, "God of Peace," 107–8).

18. Mauser, "God of Peace," 106.

19. For fuller discussion, see Swartley, *Covenant of Peace*, 208–13.

20. Swartley, *Covenant of Peace*, chap. 13: "Discipleship and Imitation of Jesus Suffering Servant: The Mimesis of New Creation," treats this topic more fully. The article earlier appeared in *Violence Renounced: René Girard, Biblical Studies and Peacemaking*, ed. Willard M. Swartley (Telford, PA: Pandora Press U.S. [now Cascadia Publishing House], 2000), 218–45.

21. Swartley, *Covenant of Peace*, 375–76.

22. Repeatedly in the beginnings of Christian theology, according to Dinkler, the concern is to take away from the death of Christ on the cross its element of offense and to see it as salvation. That is the intent of Eph. 2; Col. 1:20; 1 Cor.

1:18ff; 2 Cor. 5:14ff; Rom. 5:1–11. The theme is the cross, whereas *peace* is an interpretation of the cross of Christ.

23. Erich Dinkler, "*Eirene*—The Early Christian Concept of Peace," in *The Meaning of Peace*, ed. Perry B. Yoder and Willard M. Swartley, 2nd ed. (Elkhart, IN: Institute of Mennonite Studies, 2001), 95–96. For further explication see Swartley, *Covenant of Peace*, 198–206.

24. Klaus Haacker, "Der Römerbrief als Friedensmemorandum," *NTS* 36 (1990): 25–41.

25. Ulrich Mauser's analysis of "the rudimentary elements of the world" (*stoicheia*) in Colossians is pertinent here. He contends that these likely refer to the four primary elements, held by the Greek philosopher Epimenides to be fire, water, air, earth (*The Gospel of Peace* [Louisville, KY: Westminster/John Knox, 1992]), 143–44. In order not to offend these powers, the Colossian Christians performed various ascetic and ritual practices. By honoring these powers as gods, they undermined the all-sufficiency and supremacy of Jesus Christ.

26. For elaboration on Christ's victory over the "Powers," see Swartley, *Covenant of Peace*, 228–36; "War and Peace in the New Testament," *ANRW* II. 26.3, ed. W. Haase and H. Temporini (Tübingen: W. de Gruyter, 1996): 2350–54.

27. Two words for wrath, *thymos* and *orgē*, are used ten and six times respectively, far more often than elsewhere in the New Testament, except in Romans for *orgē*. The Greek *thymos* occurs a total of eighteen times and *orgē* thirty-six times, with twelve in Romans.

28. *Justice and Judgment, Invitation to the Book of Revelation* (Garden City, NJ: Doubleday, 1981), 72.

29. Elisabeth Schüssler Fiorenza, "Religion und Politik in der Offenbarung des Johannes," *Biblische Randbemerkungen*, ed. H. Merklein and J. Lange (Würzburg: Echter, 1974), 269–70.

30. *The Revelation of St. John the Divine* (London: A. & C. Black, 1966), 198, 245.

31. For an analysis of various forms of resistance in Judaism and those forms advocated by Revelation, see Adela Yarbro Collins, "The Political Perspective of the Revelation to John," *JBL* 96 (1977): 245–56. See also my critique in *Covenant of Peace*, 329–30.

32. On this, see Jacques Ellul's perceptive contribution, *Apocalypse: The Book of Revelation*, trans. G. W. Schreiner (New York: Seabury, 1977), 92–98.

33. Elsewhere I have written extensively on this section: *Mark: The Way for All Nations* (Eugene, OR: Cascade Books [Wipf & Stock], 1999), chaps. 7–8; *Israel's Scripture Tradition*, 98–102, 111–15; "Discipleship and Imitation" in *Violence Renounced*, 230–34: *Covenant of Peace*, 100–112.

34. Swartley, "Discipleship and Imitation," 237–39; *Covenant of Peace*, 371–75.

35. Jim Fodor, "Christian Discipleship as Participative Imitation: Theological Reflections on Girardian Themes," in Swartley, ed., *Violence Renounced*, 249–50.

36. Fodor, 256. The same sentiment is expressed by Marlin E. Miller in "Girardian Perspectives and Christian Atonement," in Swartley, ed., *Violence Renounced*, 45:

> A Girardian perspective highlights the God revealed in and through Jesus Christ as the God whose love is perfect, to use the word from Matthew 5. God's love is without violence and without limits. God calls human beings to a nonviolent mimesis: to accept God's forgiveness, to love one another, and to follow Jesus in life and in death. Jesus calls his disciples to follow him not only by his words but by his whole existence. Since his own desires and ambitions were focused on the will of the Father, he assigns the same goal to his disciples.

37. Fodor, "Christian Discipleship," 264.
38. Walter Pilgrim, *Uneasy Neighbors: Church and State in the New Testament* (Minneapolis: Fortress, 1999).
39. See Swartley, *Covenant of Peace*, 15–22, 93–95, 121–28, 135–40, 152–53, 161–63 for explication.
40. The phrase in LXX form also occurs in Eph. 6:15 to describe the Christian armor, "feet shod with the preparation of the gospel of peace," to thwart the wiles of the devil in the struggle against the principalities and powers and specifically, the spiritual powers in heavenly places (referring to the demonic spirits that incite the powers). In some manuscripts, the full LXX phrase, "preaching the gospel of peace," occurs also in Rom. 10:15 to describe the proclamation of the gospel messenger.
41. See Swartley, *Covenant of Peace*, chaps. 5–6.
42. Richard J. Cassidy, *Society and Politics in the Acts of the Apostles* (Maryknoll, NY: Orbis, 1987), 144, 156–79.
43. It would be appropriate to address here the form that the church's witness to the powers might take in a North American context. But this is a topic for another paper. The church's witness to government is rooted first and foremost in the sovereignty of God. Years ago John Howard Yoder carefully considered various models of the church's witness to government on issues of peace and justice. Written in the era when J. H. Oldham's and John C. Bennett's concept of "middle axioms" was in the air, Yoder used this concept as a bridge for the witness of the church to the state (*The Christian Witness to the State*, IMS Series No. 3 [Newton, KS: Faith and Life Press, 1964; 2nd ed., Scottdale, PA: Herald Press, 2002]). By use of the "middle axiom" Yoder proposed a model by means of which the *agapē* norm connects to the statesman through a "spring tension" that exerts the ideal of love and justice upon moral political values (1964, pp. 34, 72). Yoder was careful to maintain an ecclesial identity in the witness, and not to allow so-called political realism to accommodate moral principles held by the church into political quagmires that eviscerate the church of its moral distinctiveness.
44. Hauerwas rightly regards this moral vision of being perfect, as God is perfect, as a command (Matt. 5:48; 1 Pet. 1:17) for Jesus' followers to accept and perform, since the formation of the self has duration in time that enables growth and "practice" to become what God intends us to be (*Character and Christian Life*, 178–79).
45. I treat both the love of enemy and do not resist commands extensively in *Covenant of Peace*, 57–72.
46. Gordon Zerbe, "Paul's Ethic of Nonretaliation and Peace," in *The Love of Enemy and Nonretaliation in the New Testament*, ed. Willard M. Swartley (Louisville, KY: Westminster/John Knox, 1992), 179–80. See Swartley, *Covenant of Peace*, 213–16, for fuller exposition.
47. Luise Schottroff, "'Give to Caesar What Belongs to Caesar and to God What Belongs to God': A Theological Response of the Early Christian Church to Its Social and Political Environment," in Swartley, ed., *Love of Enemy and Nonretaliation*, 223–57.
48. Schottroff, "Give to Caesar," 232.
49. William Klassen, "Pursue Peace: A Concrete Ethical Mandate (Romans 12:18–21)," in *Ja und Nein: Christliche Theologie im Angesicht Israels*, FS Wolfgang Schrage; ed. Klaus Wengst and Gerhard Saß (Neukirchen-Vluyn: Neukirchner Verlag, 1998), 195–207, diagram on p. 197 and in Swartley, *Covenant of Peace*, 212–13.
50. Klassen, "Pursue Peace," 197–98.

51. Ronald J. Sider, *Christ and Violence* (Scottdale, PA: Herald Press, 1979), 26.

52. Glen H. Stassen and David P. Gushee, *Kingdom Ethics: Following Jesus in Contemporary Context* (Downers Grove, IL: InterVarsity, 2003), 48.

53. Stassen and Gushee, *Kingdom Ethics*, 50.

54. Stassen and Gushee, *Kingdom Ethics*, 48–49. Stassen and Gushee compare this list to Benjamin W. Farley's in *In Praise of Virtue: An Exploration of the Biblical Virtues in a Christian Context* (Grand Rapids: Eerdmans, 1995). They comment that "Farley does not note the extensive biblical theme of *peacemaking*" (Stassen and Gushee, 49).

55. A table of vice lists is in Swartley, *Covenant of Peace*, 373–74; *Violence Renounced*, 236.

56. Luke has the same greeting (24:36) as preface to the meal at which the risen Jesus discloses himself to his disciples gathered in response to the report of the Emmaus road encounter. Though some manuscripts omit it, I believe it should be included as original.

57. Mauser, *Gospel of Peace*, 29, 107–9.

58. Nicholas Wolterstorff, "Justice and Worship: The Tragedy of Liturgy in Protestantism," in *Until Justice and Peace Embrace* (Grand Rapids: Eerdmans, 1983), 146–61.

To WDB to cap
from your friend U
Beechtule

Chapter 16

The Beatitudes as Eschatological Peacemaking Virtues

GLEN STASSEN

Which virtues should Christians nurture? Virtue ethicists are often strangely ambivalent or indefinite. I turn to the Beatitudes for guidance.

But what narrative sets the meaning context for the Beatitudes? Not the narrative of human striving for self-perfection in order to achieve the human good. Nor the narrative of idealism: "If only people would act according to these ideals, then good things would happen." Nor the narrative of entrance requirements for the kingdom of God: If we are virtuous, pure in heart, and peacemakers, then we can enter the kingdom of God.

We know from long historical experience that this "high ideals" interpretation creates serious problems:

1. It focuses attention on our own good works, rather than on God's grace. It makes the gospel into works righteousness.

2. It causes feelings of guilt and resistance. So the more we emphasize these teachings as ideals to live up to, the guiltier we feel. Therefore, we ignore or evade

Jesus' teachings. No wonder the Beatitudes and the Sermon on the Mount are so seldom taught, preached, or lived.

3. Or if we think we do live up to these ideals, we fall into self-righteousness. We thank God that we are not like other people, who are not as virtuous as we are. Our moralistic arrogance makes us hard to live with.

4. We understand them as a set of ideals floating above our heads, imposing an ethic on us from above us that does not fit our real struggles. They are foreign to our nature, like a suit of armor that doesn't fit our body, or a job that doesn't fit our gifts and interests. We try to make our reality fit the ideals, but it simply does not fit. This is a *heteronomous ethic*, imposed on us by an outside authority, and not fitting our nature or our real situation in history. If virtue ethics is an ethics of high ideals, then virtue ethics is unrealistic. This criticism is a major theme of Dietrich Bonhoeffer's *Ethics*.[1]

5. This "high ideals" interpretation does not fit what Jesus in fact teaches. It imposes a foreign philosophy of idealism on the real Jewish Jesus, who identifies with the realistic tradition of the Hebrew prophets, not the tradition of Greek idealism.

A Grace-Based Prophetic Interpretation

The narrative that is the context for the Beatitudes is prophetic and eschatological; it is about the coming of the reign of God, God's action to deliver (rescue, free, release) us from mourning into rejoicing. "Congratulations to those who mourn, *because God is gracious and God is acting to deliver us* from our sorrows." So the virtues in the Beatitudes are first of all *God's* virtues as merciful deliverer, bringer of the reign of God. Only secondarily are they our virtues.

The tradition of ideals or wisdom (1) speaks to people who are not what the ideals urge, and (2) promises them that if they will live by the ideals they will get the rewards of well-being and success. The Beatitudes are not like that. (1) They speak to disciples who already are being made participants in the presence of the Holy Spirit through Jesus Christ—we already know at least a taste of the experience of mourning, mercy, peacemaking, and so forth. And (2) they do not promise distant well-being and success; they congratulate disciples because God is already acting to deliver us. They are based not on the perfection of the disciples, but on the coming of God's grace, already experienced in Jesus, at least in mustard-seed size (Matt. 13:31; 17:20; Mark 4:31; Luke 13:19).

Robert Guelich pioneered in showing that the Beatitudes echo the prophetic passage of deliverance, Isaiah 61—the passage that Jesus read when he gave his inaugural sermon in Luke 4:18–19.

Dead Sea Scroll 4Q521 shows nicely that Isaiah 61 was understood in Jesus' time as a prophetic and messianic passage of deliverance by God's Spirit:

> 1 [for the heav]ens and the earth will listen to his Messiah, 2 [and all] that is in them will not turn away from the holy precepts. . . . 5 For the Lord will observe the devout, and call the just by name, 6 and upon the poor he will

Isaiah 61	Matthew 5
61:1 The Spirit of the Lord is upon me, because the Lord has anointed me to preach good news to the poor. (The connection is all the surer since, in the Synoptic tradition, "to preach good news" is so closely bound to the reign of God.)	5:3 Blessed are the poor in spirit, for theirs is the kingdom of heaven.
61:2 To comfort all who mourn.	5:4 Blessed are those who mourn, for they shall be comforted.
61:1 To preach good news to the humble; 61:7 they will inherit the earth.	5:5 Blessed are the humble, for they shall inherit the earth.
61:3, 8, and 11 all speak of "righteousness."	5:6 Blessed are those who hunger and thirst for righteousness. . . .
61:1 To heal the brokenhearted.	5:8 Blessed are the pure in heart, for they will see God.
61:3, 8, and 11 speak of righteousness. 61:1 to preach good news: (the good news is the news of the kingdom of heaven.)	5:10 Blessed are those who have been persecuted for . . . righteousness, for theirs is the kingdom of heaven.
61:10–11 Let my soul be glad in the Lord.	5:11–12 Blessed are you when people revile you. . . . Rejoice and be joyful, for your reward is great in heaven; for so persecuted people the prophets.[2]

place his Spirit, and the faithful he will renew with his strength. 7 For he will honour the devout upon the throne of eternal royalty, 8 freeing prisoners, giving sight to the blind, straightening out the twisted. . . . 11 and the Lord will perform marvelous acts such as have not existed, just as he sa[id], 12 for he will heal the badly wounded and will make the dead live, he will proclaim good news to the meek [or poor], 13 give lavishly [to the need]y, lead the exiled and enrich the hungry.

Similarly, the Beatitudes concerning the merciful, the pure in heart, and the peacemakers (Matt. 5:7–9) echo psalms that praise God's works of deliverance.

In the Beatitudes, Jesus is saying we are blessed because we are experiencing God's reign in our midst and will experience it yet more in the future reign. Each beatitude begins with the joy, happiness, blessedness, of the good news of participation in God's gracious deliverance. And each concludes by pointing to the reality of God's coming reign: in God's kingdom, those who mourn will be comforted, the humble will inherit the earth, those who hunger for righteousness will be filled, mercy will be shown, people will see God, peacemakers will be called children of God, and the faithful will be members of the kingdom of God. An ethics of virtue must be our way of participating in God's grace and deliverance, justice and righteousness, peace, and presence. The first step in peacemaking is grace that undermines self-righteousness and calls us to humility.

Which Virtues?

Once we see the virtues Jesus names as discipleship that participates in the larger drama of the reign of God, we can see their unity more clearly. Let us examine the Beatitudes, one by one, seeking precision and accuracy in understanding and giving special attention to Jesus' references to the Old Testament. I agree with Richard Hays: ethical positions should be "argued on the basis of deep exegetical engagement with the New Testament documents," rather than reading casually or superficially.[3] I have sought to follow this standard and mine deeply, but cannot show all that in this context.

1. Matthew 5:3. "Blessed are the poor in spirit." Luke 6:20. "Blessed are you who are poor."

These are translations of Jesus' quotation from Isaiah 61:1. The Hebrew combines both meanings—economically poor and spiritually humble. Brown, Driver, and Briggs give the following meanings: poor, oppressed by the rich and powerful, powerless, needy, lowly, humble, pious.[4]

The focus of the poor in spirit is not on their humility, but on God's grace; not on pointing to themselves as somehow virtuous, but pointing to God's compassion and to their own need for God. God says: "I live . . . with the one who is contrite and lowly in spirit, to revive the spirit of the lowly and to revive the heart of the contrite." "This is the one I esteem: he who is humble and contrite in spirit, and trembles at my word" (Isa. 57:15; 66:2).[5] Nor is humility always calling attention to how lowly I am, but giving myself over to God, surrendering myself to God.

In the Bible, the poor rely more on God. Yet the poor are blessed, not because their virtue is perfect, but because God especially does want to rescue the poor. God knows that people who have power often use that power to guard their own privileges and to seek more power. The poor get pushed aside and dominated.

> The reliance upon God results from the consistent Old Testament portrait of God as being the protector and vindicator of the poor (2 Sam 22:28; Ps 72:2, 4, 12; Isa 26:6; 49:13; 66:2; Zeph 3:12). His concern for the plight of the poor is also reflected in the Law (Exod 22:25–27; 23:10–11; Lev 19:9–10; 23:22; Deut 15:7–11) and his vindication of the poor means that justice will be done and judgment will be the lot of the rich and powerful who abuse the poor by misuse of the Law (e.g., Pss 7; 10; 35:10; 37:14–15). . . . The prophets echo the theme of vindication and judgment. They charge the rich and powerful of the nation with abusing the poor and helpless and announce God's coming judgment accordingly (Amos 8:4; Isa 3:14, 15; 10:2; 32:7; Ezek 16:49; 18:12; 22:29; see Jer 22:16; Zech 7:10).[6]

Jesus fulfilled Isaiah 61:1–2, bringing good news to the poor (Luke 4:16–21; Matt. 5:3ff.; 11:5; Luke 7:22). He embraced the social and religious outcasts. His presence to them, his inviting them into community, sharing food with them, was grace-based deliverance. Because God is actively delivering the humble and the poor, Jesus' followers can rejoice—because as a community we participate in this deliverance. Shalom making requires humility, and it requires economic justice.

In a nutshell, *blessed are the humble before God, who cares for the poor and the humble.*

2. Matthew 5:4. "Blessed are those who mourn, for they shall be comforted."

Mourning, too, like *poor in spirit*, has a double meaning. It means the grief, the sadness, of those who have lost someone or something they care about deeply. But it also means *repentance*: sinners mourn for their own sins and the sin of their community and truly want to end their sinning and serve God. The prophet Amos pronounces God's judgment on those who do not mourn. They oppress the poor and crush the needy, and then say to their husbands, "Bring wine, that we may drink!" They sin and then bring sacrifices to the temple, thinking their sacrifices cover their sins, when they continue to practice injustice. God pronounces woe on those who do not mourn; "Woe to those who are at ease in Zion. . . . Woe to those who lie upon beds of ivory, . . . who sing idle songs to the sound of the harp, . . . but are not grieved over the ruin of Joseph! . . . 'Surely I will never forget any of their deeds. Shall not the land tremble on this account, and everyone mourn who dwells in it? . . . I will turn your feasts into mourning'" (Amos 4:1–5; 5:6, 14; 6:1–7; 8:7–10; 9:5). Both meanings come together, once we see that the focus is on God, who will wipe away the tears from every face, and death and mourning will end (Isa. 25:8; Rev. 21:4).

In a nutshell, *blessed are those who mourn what is wrong and unjust with sincere repentance toward God, who comforts those who suffer and those who truly repent.*

3. Matthew 5:5. "Blessed are the humble, for they shall inherit the earth."

Here Jesus is quoting Psalm 37:11 (see below), which uses the same Hebrew word for *humble* that we saw in Isaiah 61:1, quoted in the first beatitude. So this beatitude has basically the same meaning: *"humble" in the sense of surrendered to God.* And *socially and economically poor or powerless.* Donald Hagner concludes: "In view are not persons who are submissive, mild, and unassertive, but those who are *humble* in the sense of being oppressed (hence 'have been humbled'), bent over by the injustice of the ungodly, but who are soon" to be delivered.[7] Clarence Jordan says it would be better to translate the word "tamed," rather than "meek," in the sense that their wills have been tamed by God's will:

> It is used in particular to describe two persons—Moses (Numbers 12:3) and Jesus (Matthew 11:29). One of them defied the might of Egypt and the other couldn't be cowed by a powerful Roman official. . . . People may be called [tamed] to the extent that they have surrendered their wills to God and learned to do his bidding. . . . They surrender their will to God so completely that God's will becomes their will. . . . They become God's "workhorses" on earth.[8]

The word has another connotation as well. The Greek (*praüs*) in the NT regularly points to peacefulness or peacemaking. Matthew 21:5 is a quote from Zechariah 9:9, where the entrance of the *nonviolent or peacemaking* messianic king is described:

> Your king is coming to you,
> his cause won, his victory gained,
> *humble* and mounted on an ass,
> on a foal, the young of a she-ass.
> He shall banish chariots from Ephraim
> and war-horses from Jerusalem;
> the warrior's bow shall be banished.
> He shall speak peaceably to every nation,
> and his reign shall extend from sea to sea,
> from the River to the ends of the earth.

The peacemaking theme is clear also in Psalm 37:

> 8 Cease from anger, and forsake wrath; . . .
> Those who wait for the Lord, they will inherit the land. . . .
> 11 *The humble will inherit the land. . . .*
> 14 The wicked have drawn the sword and bent their bow,
> To cast down the oppressed and the needy,
> To slay those who walk uprightly. . . .
> 35 I have seen a violent, wicked man. . . .
> 37 The man of *peace* will have posterity. . . .

Hans Weder concludes: "The blessing . . . stands historically in the context of the Zealot temptation. It is no accident that Christ in Matthew twice is designated as meek. Therein rightly lies the heart of his differentiation from the Zealots, from the violence-using battlers for the reign of God. Blessed the nonviolent. They will inherit the world."[9]

Once again the several nuances of meaning come together into a unity when we see that the focus is on surrendering ourselves *to God*. The God to whom we surrender is "the God of peace" (Rom. 15:33). God is the God who gives rain and sunshine to enemy as well as friend, and calls us to love our enemies (Matt. 5:43ff.). Martin Luther King Jr. said, "Jesus understood the difficulty inherent in the act of loving one's enemy. . . . He realized that every genuine expression of love grows out of a consistent and total surrender to God."[10] Jesus does not just teach this, but brings God's love to disciples, and leads disciples to have the experience of welcoming tax collectors, Gentiles, and outcasts into the fellowship.

In a nutshell, *blessed are those who are surrendered to God, who is the God of peace.*

4. Matthew 5:6. "Blessed are those who hunger and thirst for righteousness, for they shall be satisfied."

The key here is to understand the meaning of the word "righteousness." New Testament scholars generally agree that righteousness and the kingdom are two central themes of the Sermon on the Mount—probably the two central themes. The question they usually ask is whether righteousness is something God gives us or something we do. But the often overlooked question is, What does righteousness mean? What is its shape, its content?

The question is especially important because the word in English communicates a false meaning. Because our culture is *individualistic* and *possessive*, people think of it as an individual possession. But that is *self-righteousness*.

The Greek word here, *dikaiosyne*, and its root, *dike*, have the connotation of *justice*. Furthermore, Jesus is quoting Isaiah 61, which rejoices four times that God is bringing righteousness or justice (vv. 3, 8, 10, and 11). The word there is the Hebrew, *tsedaqah*. So we need to ask what *tsedaqah* means in Isaiah and elsewhere in the Law and Prophets. It means *delivering justice* (a justice that rescues and releases the oppressed) and *community-restoring justice* (a justice that restores the powerless and the outcasts to their rightful place in covenant community). Or in simpler words, *restorative justice*. That is why the hungry and thirsty hunger and thirst for righteousness; they yearn bodily for the kind of justice that delivers them from their hunger and thirst and restores them to community where they can eat and drink.

It is no accident that in the Sermon on the Mount Jesus emphasizes giving to the one who begs, and to the one who wants to borrow; giving alms as service to God rather than for show; and not hoarding money for ourselves but giving it to God's kingdom and righteousness (Matt. 5:42; 6:2–4; 6:19–34). Luke, in his parallel version of these teachings (Luke 6:20–26), and writing for Greek-speaking readers who would not have understood the Hebrew behind the word, does not use the word *righteousness* but emphasizes even more strongly coming to the aid of the poor rather than hoarding money for ourselves. The prophets of Israel and contemporary political science are clear that injustice and relative deprivation are major causes of war and terrorism.[11]

So, in a nutshell, *blessed are those who hunger and thirst for a justice that delivers and restores to covenant community, for God is a God who brings such justice.*

5. Matthew 5:7. "Blessed are the merciful, for they will be shown mercy."

The Greek word for mercy here, *eleeō*, means being *generous in doing deeds of deliverance*. Mercy is about an action, that is, a generous action that delivers someone from need or bondage. It echoes Proverbs 14:21 and 17:5.[12] Mercy in the Gospels can mean forgiveness that delivers from the bondage of guilt, or (more often) an action of deliverance in the sense of healing or giving. When Jesus walks down the road and a blind or crippled person calls out, "Have mercy on me," he does not mean, "Let me off easy," but "Heal me, deliver me from my affliction." That is why in Matthew 6:2, doing mercy, *eleemosynen*, means giving alms for the poor.

In a nutshell, *blessed are those who practice compassion in action, covenant faithfulness toward those in need.*

6. *Matthew 5:8. "Blessed are the pure in heart, for they will see God."*
Contrary to a Neoplatonic split between outward action and inner heart, the biblical understanding is holistic: there is one whole self in relation to one God, the Lord of all. The heart is the relational organ. When God speaks to me, or I act angrily, my heart beats faster. The real split is not between inner and outer, but between God-serving and idol-serving. It is between giving aid to the poor in order to be noticed and respected by others, and giving as service to God. It is between serving my desire for wealth and serving God's reign and justice.

"Purity of heart must involve integrity, a correspondence between outward action and inward thought (cf. 15:8), a lack of duplicity, singleness of intention . . . , and the desire to please God above all else. More succinctly: purity of heart is to will one thing, God's will, with all of one's being [and doing]."[13]

So the sixth beatitude means, in a nutshell, *blessed are those who give their whole self over to God, who is the only One worthy of the heart's full devotion.*

7. *Matthew 5:9. "Blessed are 'the peacemakers,*
for they will be called children of God."

"'Peacemaker' . . . is the right translation . . . , for a positive action, reconciliation, is envisioned: the 'peacemakers' *seek to bring about peace.* . . . Since the previous beatitudes concern social relations, surely the meaning here is social, not simply peace between individuals and God," as is frequently claimed. "For Jesus as the bringer of peace, see Luke 2:14; 19:38; Acts 10:36; Rom 5:1; Eph 2:14–18; Col 1:2; Heb 7:2 (see Isa 9:5–6; Zech 9:10). In being peacemakers, disciples are imitating their Father in heaven, 'the God of peace' (Rom 16:20; cf. Rom 15:33; Phil 4:9; 1 Thess 5:23; 2 Thess 3:16; Heb 13:20)."[14]

Because it is about positive action, and not simply not doing violence, Christian ethics needs to focus on peacemaking initiatives, or what I have called transforming initiatives of peacemaking, and just peacemaking theory—not only debates about nonviolence vs. just war theory. We are called to peace*making*, not only war avoidance, and certainly not only war *debatance.*

Donald Hagner writes: "In the context of the beatitudes, the point would seem to be directed against the . . . Jewish revolutionaries who hoped through violence to bring the kingdom of God. Such means would have been a continual temptation for the downtrodden and oppressed who longed for the kingdom. . . . But Jesus announces . . . it is the peacemakers who will be called the 'children of God.' . . . This stress on peace becomes a common motif in the New Testament (cf. Rom 14:19; Heb 12:14; Jas 3:18; 1 Pet 3:11)."[15] Richard Horsley and others have suggested that the historical Jesus was concerned only with peacemaking within the villages, and not with Romans, although he has discovered Jesus' interest in the Roman Empire in his more recent *Jesus and Empire.*[16] N. T. Wright answers: "It was precisely in her tendency to violent nationalism that Jesus saw the true depth of Israel's present exile."[17]

Being a peacemaker is part of being surrendered to God, for God brings peace. We abandon the effort to get our needs met through the destruction of enemies. God comes to us in Christ to make peace with us; [and] we participate in God's grace as we go to our enemies to make peace. This is why the peacemakers "will be called sons of God."

In a nutshell, *blessed are those who make peace with their enemies, as God shows love to God's enemies.*

8: Matthew 5:10. "Blessed are those who are persecuted for righteousness' sake, for theirs is the kingdom of heaven."

9: Matthew 5:11–12. "Blessed are you when people revile you and persecute you and utter all kinds of evil against you falsely on my account. Rejoice and be glad, for your reward is great in heaven, for in the same way they persecuted the prophets who were before you."

These two beatitudes summarize and climax the nine beatitudes. They are about persecution for righteousness and for Jesus—as the prophets were persecuted. The beatitudes should be interpreted in the context of the prophets with their emphasis on God's reign and God's call for righteousness/justice, and the suffering that they bore for calling Israel to covenant fidelity in their own day.

In a nutshell, *blessed are those who suffer because of their practices of loyalty to Jesus and to justice.*

Virtues Elsewhere in the Biblical Drama

When I asked in the introduction above what narrative sets the meaning context for the Beatitudes, I argued it is clearly the narrative of the coming of the kingdom, the reign of God. That suggests another significant connection. Jesus taught about the kingdom with parables, many of which are called "parables of the kingdom." The logical question follows: Is there a connection between the virtues in the Beatitudes of the kingdom and the parables of the kingdom? Can the virtues suggested by the Beatitudes be illustrated by Jesus' parables? I believe looking for the answer discovers an interesting and intriguing affirmation. The space to develop that does not exist here, but I have sought to suggest the connection in my book *Living the Sermon on the Mount.*[18]

A further question: How do these virtues compare with the virtues taught in different places in the Pauline letters? The lists of virtues in those letters differ; clearly they do not imply that there is one exact set of seven or eight Christian virtues, no more and no less. Nevertheless, when we compare these lists, they correlate remarkably nicely with the above interpretation of the Beatitudes. Willard Swartley presents a summary in chapter 15 of this book.

The virtues emphasized at least twice in the Pauline letters are love, compassion, kindness, humility, gentleness, patience, tolerance, unity, peace, joy, righteousness, forgiveness, and endurance. These match the virtues that Jesus teaches in the Beatitudes so closely that hardly any need discussion: Paul's virtues of tolerance, unity, and patience, which he especially emphasized as needed for peacemaking in the churches, match the virtue of peacemaking in the Beatitudes. If goodness in Galatians 5 is like purity in 2 Corinthians 6, then we have a match for purity of heart in the Beatitudes. That leaves only Jesus' teaching, "Blessed are they who mourn," which we saw implies repentance. Surely Paul calls for repentance often enough throughout his letters, even though he does not call it a virtue! Of course, Paul gave these virtues a slightly different meaning in his historical context, as he was writing to churches two decades after Jesus, and before Matthew. Nevertheless, the match is remarkably close (see Swartley's chapter).

How Shall We Relate Gospel Virtues to Traditional Virtues?

The literature of Christian virtue ethicists values tradition, and so it tends to affirm the four traditional Greek virtues, supplemented by Paul's emphasis on faith, hope, and love. But the authors seem uncertain or ambivalent. They do not argue persuasively for these particular virtues. So Stanley Hauerwas points out: "From the point of view of modern philosophical ethics, one of the things that must make attention to the virtues so unappealing is the lack of consensus about which virtues are morally central; and perhaps even more frustrating is the absence of any principle or method to determine what the primary virtues are or how they might be interrelated. . . . Certainly, no agreement exists about which virtues should be considered central."[19]

And Jonathan Wilson observes: "The tradition of virtue ethics comes from the Greek philosopher Aristotle's *Nichomachean Ethics*, but as many have pointed out, Aristotle's account is incompatible with Christianity. For instance, Aristotle has no place for the virtue of humility, and his account of friendship precludes the possibility of friendship between God and humanity."[20] Furthermore, Aristotle says we can have friendship only with people like us, and equal to us. But Jesus' teaching emphasizes friendship with outcasts and the powerless. Aristotle also advocated other virtues, including generosity, magnificence, high-mindedness, gentleness, truthfulness, wittiness, friendship, and a proper amount of ambition but not too much. He chose these virtues by observing admired males in a hierarchical and warlike society that defended slavery and male superiority and did not believe in the God of Israel.

Hence Hauerwas and Pinches reinterpret Aristotle's virtues to make them accord more with the Christian story. They point out that Aquinas reinterpreted the four cardinal virtues so they would be guided more by love, but that his reinterpretation still retained some of Aristotle's patriarchalism. They conclude: "What Aristotle and Christians mean by being happy is quite different. . . . Aristotle suggests we can be happy only if we achieve a self-sufficiency that guards us against outrageous fortune. Christians claim, on the other hand, that we are happy only to the extent that our lives are formed in reference to Jesus of Nazareth." Furthermore, Aristotle's account is empty at the core; it begs for a Christ-centered narrative that will fill the emptiness.[21]

Aristotle's cardinal virtue of courage glorifies courage in warfare. So Aquinas transformed Aristotle's understanding of courage into the courage of the martyr and not the soldier, with the weapons of patience and faith. He redefined courage as "persevering in doing what is just"—with justice defined by compassion for the underdog.[22] This resembles Jesus' commendation of willingness to be persecuted for his sake and the sake of justice.

Virtues are character traits that enable us to contribute to community—to the particular society in which we live. Peter Paris makes this clear: "The virtues of African and African American ethics are . . . determined by the goal of preserving and promoting community" or "the community's well-being."[23] Here Paris is studying African spirituality, whose orientation toward community is closer to biblical understanding than American disconnected individualism. Character ethics intends to correct disconnected individualism, emphasizing virtues that contribute to the common good of the community. Similarly, John Milbank shows that the great African saint, Augustine, sees God's forgiveness, peace, and justice as the order of reality that is normative for society. So his virtue ethics is a corrective for the good of society.[24] In biblical character ethics, the good we serve is the reign of God, and the reign of God is oriented toward community with God (God's presence and salvation) and community with our fellow human beings (peace and justice). The biblical virtues are keys to community well-being: peacemaking, hungering for justice, doing mercy, integrity, humility, and caring for the poor and the mourning. And they are the way of participation in community with God.

Different kinds of society need different kinds of virtues.[25] The question for us, then, is which society, which politics, we live in. Jesus said we are blessed because we are living in the society of the mustard seeds. We are living where God is bringing the deliverance of God's presence, salvation, justice, and peace. The biblical virtues fit that reign. All of us are also participants in one or more other societies: our hometown, our educational community, our church, our nation, the rapidly growing global community. We need to learn some virtues for making our contributions to those communities also (Jer. 29:7). Those virtues differ. But our central virtues, by which the others are judged, are the virtues of the reign of God.

Today one may affirm the virtues of mutual respect, antidomination, and participation in community that Michael Walzer advocates.[26] These seem especially appropriate for a biblical Christian, and they do make coalition with a leading philosophy of our time that speaks to the needs and realities of a democratic, pluralistic, historically conscious, economically driven, postmodern society. One could include James McClendon's insightful and persuasive advocacy of the virtue of *presence*.[27] Peter Paris develops and advocates six virtues that reclaim African American roots in African culture's God-centeredness and community-centeredness, with a strong emphasis that "a person becomes morally virtuous in order to make a substantial contribution to the preservation and promotion of the community."[28] Four of his virtues—beneficence, forbearance, forgiveness, and justice—are very close to the virtues we have seen in Jesus, Paul, and biblical tradition. Because of its emphasis on holistic community, reconciliation, forgiveness, and God, African tradition produces virtues significantly closer to biblical virtues than Plato and Aristotle do.

But I ask, Why start with Aristotle? Why not start with Jesus? Don't we need a clear virtue ethics of peacemaking more than an ethics of warmaking, halfway modified?

Notes

1. Dietrich Bonhoeffer, *Ethics*, vol. 6, *Dietrich Bonhoeffer Works* (Minneapolis: Fortress, 2005), 47–53; See *Ethics* (New York: Touchstone, 1995), 186–93.
2. The chart is adapted from W. D. Davies and Dale Allison, *The Gospel according to St. Matthew*, vol. 1 (Edinburgh: T. & T. Clark, 1988), 436–40. Robert Guelich developed this insight in articles he published and then in his book *The Sermon on the Mount* (Dallas: Word, 1982).
3. Richard Hays, *The Moral Vision of the New Testament* (New York: HarperCollins, 1996), 291; see chaps. 11–13.
4. Francis Brown, S. R. Driver, and Charles A. Briggs, *The New Brown, Driver, Briggs, Gesenius Hebrew and English Lexicon* (Peabody, MA: Hendrickson, 1979), 776.
5. See Donald Hagner, *Matthew 1–13* (Dallas: Word, 1993), 92.
6. Guelich, *Sermon*, 68–69.
7. Hagner, *Matthew*, 92–93; see Guelich, *Sermon*, 81–82.
8. Clarence Jordan, *Sermon on the Mount* (Valley Forge, PA: Judson, 1974), 24–25.
9. Hans Weder, *Die "Rede der Reden": Eine Auslegung der Bergpredigt Heute* (Zurich: Theologischer Verlag, 1987), 62 (my trans.).
10. Martin Luther King Jr., *Strength to Love* (Minneapolis: Fortress, 1981), 48.
11. Glen Stassen, *Just Peacemaking: Ten Practices* (Cleveland: Pilgrim, 1998/2004), chaps. 1, 5, and 6.
12. Hagner, *Matthew*, 93.
13. Davies and Allison, *Matthew*, 456.
14. Davies and Allison, *Matthew*, 457–58.
15. Hagner, *Matthew*, 94.
16. Richard Horsley, *Jesus and Empire: The Kingdom of God and the New World Disorder* (Minneapolis: Fortress, 2003).
17. N. T. Wright, *Jesus and the Victory of God* (Minneapolis: Fortress, 1996), 253ff.; also 286, 290ff., 317, 322–36, 348–59, 385, 390, 447ff., 462.
18. Glen Stassen, *Living the Sermon on the Mount* (San Francisco: Jossey Bass, 2006).
19. Stanley Hauerwas, *Community of Character* (Notre Dame, IN: University of Notre Dame, 1981), 121. See also the parallel criticism of MacIntyre's lack of specifying shared virtues in Jean Porter, *Recovery of Virtue: The Relevance of Aquinas for Christian Ethics* (Louisville, KY: Westminster/John Knox, 1990), 83.
20. Jonathan Wilson, *Gospel Virtues* (Downers Grove, IL: InterVarsity, 1998), 18–19.
21. Stanley Hauerwas and Charles Pinches, *Christians among the Virtues* (Notre Dame, IN: University of Notre Dame, 1997), 16, 29.
22. Hauerwas and Pinches, 151, 159–164.

23. Peter Paris, *The Spirituality of African American Peoples: The Search for a Common Moral Discourse* (Minneapolis: Fortress, 1985), 130–31, 134.
24. John Milbank, *Theology and Social Theory* (Cambridge, MA: Blackwell, 1995), 409ff.
25. Wilson, *Gospel Virtues*, 122.
26. Glen Stassen, "Michael Walzer's Situated Justice," *JRE* 22 (1994): 382–87.
27. J. McClendon, *Ethics*, rev. ed. (Nashville: Abingdon, 2002), 115–18.
28. Paris, *Spirituality*, 134ff.

Index of Ancient Sources

Index of Names

205 Justificat' "th answers afear" "moral formation"

93 missive : letter

sermon - "guided
with authority"

class

211 213 217
many involved : & church

212 VC as th' middle year "" X/mas

235 on VC leading (summ' us
245 & Beatified

245 Beatitude
! th' "visitor"

188 class title fr section"
Paul

211 march - "a manual
discipleship"

"" sermon - it not about us
'49 "u

152 man - "image-bearers"
"god us od" (I) /god

7

33 Locke "reason is the candle of the Lord
(esse gift of light)

" some authors "turn from the text of C S the author holds
the text, to the reader in front of the text, meaning for
them is not in the text, but is created by the reader of the
text"

33 & Ille "To try to dress like St Francis (or Jesus) does
not make you a Franciscan or a Christian.

149 " bow the knee" of PS. (Idel)

149 Philo gave "lip service" to Rome but not his worship
(is that our role in USA)

175 If all suffering is due to a prior sin, then the V is
persecuted" for righteousness' sake are doing wrong. To be
biblical, it disproves the MG unhap.

204 Korean "minjung

220 N Carter "our endangered values" (his time USA)

221 he lives "in the middle of time" - between Xmas & Easter

234 "none home of the Caesars of the world, monarchy, or
presidents, even democracies is worthy to receive the
honor, power, glory that belongs to the Lord God alone

240 " " the cross not as offence but is always" in NT writer

241 on Col "the rudimentary elements"
- 2:18-23

66 intercalation inter...
73 deontology = moral obligation
39 "reactor - response 226
"disc on
86 discursive universe" =

class character formation
class
VVIII
...doing another
...Rom
IX - Aristotle

Ch 8 another class 14
problem. This one is
political hints & ...
136 134, 127
172
Rom 12:5 ?
184
187

2) 9 ethos, ethos
...new creation - orientation
disorientation, reorientation

183 ...Augustus Caesar
219 worshipped ... in ...
it's a language by ... etc.
O "Chr" political ethos
...titled "a polite...
world..."

238
133
on the new ... wisdom
28 on the Beatitudes
ch 5 Rom. (Paul)... I do...

184
148
p 248 7
29
80
78
81
Ch4 - a few contents
...studying Mark...
X Ch 6 on the Beatitudes
p7 M...

Ch 7 - Galatians
...alba 116
107-8

55 LL ... the largury
43-8 ... the woman
Lk 7:36-50

Ch 4 on Mt X
5:22
5: 25-34

146
A 9 b Rom 2:20
Ch 8 Titus X
3:8
185
194 Gal 1:6
44-8 Rom 2:24

220 Mk 10
185